Top right: Oscar Deutsch in the late 1930s. Above: Odeon Weston-super-Mare a few weeks after opening, in early July 1935. Note the publicity given to the organist over the entrance doors. (Courtesy of Bruce Peter.) Right: the page boy at the Odeon Wrexham is the late John (Jack) Lloyd. (Courtesy of Mrs. L. Lloyd and Hugh Sykes.)

ODEON CINEMAS

1: Oscar Deutsch Entertains Our Nation

Odeon Leicester Square in 1937. Right: Odeon Kingstanding in 1935. Two photographs by John Maltby.

ODEON CINEMAS

1: Oscar Deutsch Entertains Our Nation

ALLEN EYLES

CINEMA THEATRE ASSOCIATION
DISTRIBUTED BY BFI PUBLISHING

 Publishing

First published
in 2002 by the
Cinema Theatre Association
34 Pelham Road
London N22 6LN

Distributed by
bfi Publishing
British Film Institute
21 Stephen Street
London W1T 1LN

The CINEMA THEATRE ASSOCIATION
was formed in 1967 to promote serious
interest in all aspects of cinema buildings.
It publishes a newsletter and the journal
Picture House, maintains an Archive, and
organises visits and lectures.

For further details, contact
Membership Secretary – CTA
Flat One, 128 Gloucester Terrace
London W2 6HP
or visit: www.cinema-theatre.org.uk

The BRITISH FILM INSTITUTE exists
to promote greater understanding and
appreciation of, and access to, film
and moving-image culture in the UK.

For details of *bfi* services and current
activities, please call the 24-hour *bfi*
events line: 0870 240 40 50 (national
call rate) or visit: www.bfi.org.uk

ISBN 0 85170 8137

Design consultant
Malcolm Johnson

Printed in Great Britain by
Biddles Limited
Guildford and King's Lynn

CONTENTS

Odeon Canning Town.
(Courtesy of the late Keith P. Roberts.)

ACKNOWLEDGEMENTS

I particularly regret that Robert Bullivant did not live long enough to see this history, to which his contribution will be self-evident, while during its writing I have been pleasantly reminded of the many conversations and letters in which the late Dickie Dewes patiently expounded on the minutiae of Odeon history. I dedicate this book to the memory of both these gentlemen.

For reading and making valuable comments on much of the text, I am most grateful to John Fernee, Richard Gray (Chairman of the Cinema Theatre Association), Elain Harwood and Bruce Peter. Bruce was also most helpful in supplying the perfect cover image and some other key illustrations while Elain additionally saved me from a picture research trip to Swindon. Giles Woodforde kindly read the final page proofs and handled the printing arrangements.

Members of the CTA Committee were very supportive with information and other assistance: Louis Barfe, Jeremy Buck, David Eve, Oliver Horsbrugh, Tim McCullen, Sally McGrath, Brian Oakaby (CTA Archive), David Simpson and Adam Unger. As CTA Sales Officer, Jeremy Buck has also shouldered the considerable and essential task of distributing this book to members.

I am indebted to the Cinema Theatre Association for funding the basic cost of a research trip to Birmingham, to The Weedon Partnership (Shirley Joseph, Melanie Whild) for allowing me to examine at length their remaining records, and to my sister, Barbara Newman, for piloting me around the Birmingham suburbs for another look at the Perry Barr, Kingstanding and Sutton Coldfield Odeons.

Spencer P. Hobbs generously shared his meticulous research into the cinemas of Bromley while John Gibson submitted his record of programming at the Paramount Newcastle. Gillian Grute provided me with a copy of her seminar paper on Odeon with its useful leads. I have also drawn on the 1985 research into the planned Cambridge Odeon by Les Lutner and Clifford S. Manning, while other information on T. Cecil Howitt came via Richard Gray and from Ernie Scoffham. Marysia Lachowicz kindly showed me her correspondence with Robert Bullivant.

John Billington ably researched most of the inside cover advertisements on my behalf. Brian Gauntlett also contributed to these and ensured that I knew everything I wanted to know about Odeon in the Portsmouth area.

CTA members who kindly provided assistance during the writing of this book include James Bettley, Peter Clark, Clive Garner, Brian Hall, Carl Chesworth, Ken George, Frank Snart, Stan Thompson, Tom Wade, Norman Walley and Philip Yaxley.

After asking for information about the current use of certain Odeon sites in the *CTA Bulletin,* I am grateful to the members who took the trouble to reply, often at some length: Gordon Barr, David Bennett, John Benzing, John Brierley, Peter Brummell, James Byrne, Ian D. Carter-Chapman, Carl Chesworth, Michael Crowle, Linton Culver, Robin Dakin, David G. Daykin, Gary Dickinson, Ben Doman, David A. Ellis, Dave Fleming, Tim Hatcher, Janice Headland, Roy E. Heaven, Brian Heedy, Brian Hemingway, John Hickey, Graham Hornsey, Peter Lawley, Martin Lightfoot, George Lockyer, Peter Luxton, John Makins, Thomas Maxwell, John J. McKillop, Peter Morgan, Charles Morris, Peter Nash, J. A. Parkinson, John Platford, John M. Pritchard, Andrew Roberts, Gil Robottom, David Roddis, K. Saunders, David Sharp, Clifford Shaw, Stan Smith, Stuart Smith, Derek Swaffer, Hugh Sykes, Martin Tapsell, A. Thompson, Bernard Tonks, Sebastian Weber, Gerry Williams, Ned Williams, Trevor Williams, Mike Wood and John Yallop.

The RIBA Drawings Collection and BFI Special Collections (Janet Moat) provided access to other source material.

I owe a great debt to Chris Moore who, as Information Services Controller of Rank Organisation's leisure division, opened the doors for me to visit so many Odeons and Top Rank Clubs in the 1970s.

As with the preceding Granada history, Malcolm Johnson diligently processed the text and assembled the pages to make the book look better than it was in my mind's eye, spotting the odd inconsistency and pausing only to offer the comment "heartbreaking" in the margin alongside the history of the Odeon at Streatham which we both remember from its Astoria days...

For their practical help with the illustrations (which has directly enabled so many to be reproduced), the Cinema Theatre Association is extremely grateful to: the BFI National Library (David Sharp); Brighton & Hove Council, Libraries and Museums (Stephanie Green); National Museum of Photography, Film & Television, Bradford (Colin Harding); The National Monuments Record of English Heritage (Anne Woodward); The Record Office for Leicestershire, Leicester and Rutland (Clive Chandler); and Wandsworth Local History Service.

INTRODUCTIO[N]

The story of how Oscar Deutsch and his associates created the Odeon cinema circuit provides one of the most remarkable episodes in the history of the British film industry. Of all the numerous exhibition chains that were created in the 1930s, only Odeon rose to rival the big two, Gaumont and ABC – becoming not just a third national circuit but arguably the pre-eminent one, leaner and fitter with its greater stock of recently-built cinemas and its stronger hold on the public consciousness through its progressive architectural style and distinctive logo as well as the prominence of its "governing director", Oscar Deutsch. Unlike Gaumont and ABC, which built upon an amalgamation of existing circuits, Odeon started from scratch, opening 136 new cinemas from 1933 to 1939, almost as many as the other two combined over the entire decade. The decisive years were from 1931, when the first sites were selected, to 1936/7 when Deutsch committed Odeon to become a fully national circuit by acquiring sites in London's West End and almost all of the key cities as well as setting virtually all the other locations where Odeons would open before World War Two. After that, Deutsch had his eye on expansion overseas while in Britain he came close to controlling Gaumont as well as Odeon. But the outbreak of war stopped progress on either front and his continually precarious health failed, bringing about his death at the age of 48 in 1941.

Although Oscar Deutsch clearly recognised the growth opportunities in film exhibition at the start of the 1930s, he had no goal of building a third national circuit from the start and his early group of mostly small town or suburban ventures of modest size and cost rang no alarm bells in the executive suites at ABC or Gaumont. Many other entrepreneurs set about establishing small circuits in the gaps left by the two majors. Oscar Deutsch was unusual in that he initially created a chain of entirely new cinemas – but, to speed up expansion, he soon added many existing halls. He had many rivals, including Granada under Sidney Bernstein, County under Charles J. Donada, Union under Fred Bernhard, London & Southern Super Cinemas under Arthur Cohen, H. D. Moorhouse in Manchester, and Shipman and King. Many established local companies for each new cinema in the way that Deutsch did (to attract local partners and isolate the

damage if [...] rivalled or [...] Deutsch d[...] find, even [...] cost and [...] direct opp[...] had their [...] attraction[...] not represented. Deutsch made Odeon large enough to set up its own weekly release, depriving his rivals of many films they would have liked to show.

Odeon was able to exploit three advantages: one (shared with County) was a tie-up with a major film distributor that ensured a supply of quality British and American films; another (that gave it an edge over ABC and Gaumont when becoming a public company) was its lack of involvement in the financially hazardous area of film production (it also had no interest in film distribution); and the third was Oscar Deutsch's own charismatic personality and an ambition given urgency by his poor prospects of longevity.

Despite his unprepossessing appearance, Deutsch had a good voice for public speaking and he put himself in the limelight as much as possible – being accessible to the press and ready to express a forthright opinion on any film industry matter, thereby boosting shareholder confidence and reinforcing the impression that Odeon was setting the pace in British film exhibition with new initiatives, opening more modern cinemas with better design than anyone else, and giving the most consideration to the comfort of patrons and the quality of their entertainment.

But, although Deutsch became the public face of Odeon, he was not a lone operator. He was a skilful delegator, a considerate employer who inspired others to do their best for him but was sometimes blind to their failings. He was almost undone by the sheer complexity of the business organisation he masterminded – until a young accountant called John Davis saved the day.

In initially researching Odeon for a magazine article in 1974/5, I was fortunate to be able to interview one of Oscar Deutsch's key executives, Sidney Swingler. After the article's publication, I had extensive conversations and received carefully written memoranda from another key figure, R. H. (Dickie) Dewes. This book includes lengthy comments from both, especially Dewes, that have not been published before to give inside detail of the Odeon organisation.

The design factor

This book is not just the history of a successful commercial undertaking. It is as much an account of how Oscar Deutsch sponsored some of the most progressive and distinctive design work of the decade. While investigating Odeon in 1974/5, I made contact with Robert Bullivant, Keith P. Roberts and Frederick Adkins, all of whom were key figures in the design of Odeons. In writing this book, I resumed contact with Robert Bullivant and he provided much new information in response to specific queries before his death in January 2001.

Much of Odeon's design success was due to the friendship and trust that developed between Oscar Deutsch and an equally charismatic figure, the Birmingham architect Harry Weedon. But just as it grossly distorts the truth to portray Deutsch as a solitary genius, so it is wrong to give Weedon all the credit for what is known as "the Odeon style". Like Deutsch, he headed a team (that included J. Cecil Clavering and Robert Bullivant), and it was they who created a series of landmark buildings. But there were other architectural practices that created memorable Odeons, even before Weedon appeared on the scene. Equally, for a number of reasons, there were many mediocre Odeons: Deutsch was expanding too fast to ensure uniformly high standards, he took over existing schemes that were not re-designed in the circuit style (to avoid both delay and extra cost) and he acquired cinemas that were already under construction and beyond radical change, while in some instances planning authorities drastically interfered with schemes that would have been more in the house style.

When Odeon started, the design of British cinemas was at a crossroads. The predominant influence on the large cinemas of the late 1920s and early 1930s was American, as seen in the 'atmospheric' and classical interiors of the period – at the Empire and Plaza in London's West End, the Paramount Manchester, the Trocadero Elephant and Castle, and the Astorias of Finsbury Park and Brixton. Established cinema architects and proprietors acknowledged visiting America to study the latest developments.

But the Depression and a widespread excess of seats brought North American movie theatre construction to a virtual halt by 1933. If this left any indication of the future path of cinema design, it was in the success of the Radio City Music Hall in New York, one of the very few large entertainment buildings to embrace the modern movement and art deco.

In Britain, cinema construction became one of the few boom industries for entrepreneurs and builders. Architects were aware of the remarkable work being done in Germany, which had developed its own distinctively clean, striking and unfussy style of cinema design from as early as 1912. Photographs and descriptions of Berlin cinemas such as the 1927 Titania-Palast by Schöffler, Schloenbach and Jacobi and the 1928 Universum by Erich Mendel-sohn were published in film and architectural journals and the buildings were there to be visited.

Naturally, their appeal was more to young architects and new entrepreneurs than to established designers and cinema proprietors. It took the progressive head of Provincial Cinematograph Theatres, Will Evans, to gamble on the Germanic designs for the New Victoria at Victoria, London, that were put forward by the untried thirty-year-old E. Wamsley Lewis. Opened in 1930, the New Victoria was hugely controversial, especially for its streamlined exterior. Lewis has referred to the strong influence of the Universum and, for the interior, the Grosses Schauspielhaus (1919) by Hans Poelzig. Evans was soon ousted from office and Lewis never built another cinema.

Oscar Deutsch had no great vision of how his cinemas should look. In fact, the first ventures in which he was involved were very routine in appearance. A cinema at Perry Barr, Birmingham, was actually called Odeon and introduced the distinctive style of lettering, but Deutsch did not see right away the potential of the name or the way it was designed and almost called his new circuit Picture Houses instead of Odeons. But, from the reaction to cinemas like the Odeon Worthing, he came to realise that an ultra-modern or avant-garde look was the best way of attracting attention and distinguishing his cinemas from existing ones. Whether he actually liked innovative design or merely appreciated its usefulness is ultimately immaterial. What is important is that he encouraged a house style of exteriors that were aggressively modern in sharp contrast to their surroundings.

And what is remarkable about so many of the new Odeons is that they were at the "cutting edge" of design in the 1930s and yet they seem to have been enthusiastically accepted by the public in every type of district. It offers a rare instance of a time when imagination in design was in step with public taste (contrast this with the multiplex era and its play safe mentality). Of course, it was not just Odeon that benefited from the public's embrace: ocean liners, railway stations (especially those of the London Underground) and airport terminals, department stores, garages, lidos, blocks of flats and hotels successfully adopted the modern look that made the 1930s such a distinctive decade in architecture. (Indeed, in some places, such as Southgate and Surbiton, the stations were more notable than the Odeons.)

And Odeon was demonstrably keen to test new ideas: from

discussed in kalomirakis

influenced

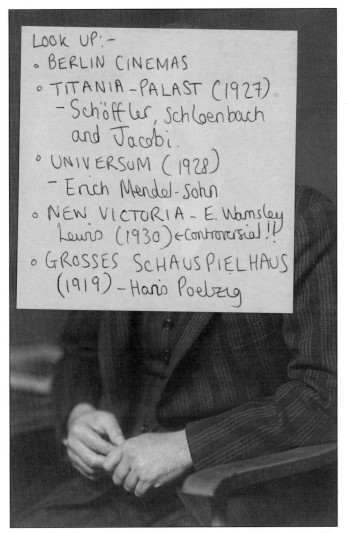

LOOK UP :-
- BERLIN CINEMAS
- TITANIA - PALAST (1927)
  - Schöffler, Schloenbach and Jacobi.
- UNIVERSUM (1928)
  - Erich Mendel-Sohn
- NEW VICTORIA - E. Wamsley Lewis (1930) ← Controversial !!
- GROSSES SCHAUSPIELHAUS (1919) - Hans Poelzig

Oscar Deutsch.

travelling neon signs to better springs in the seats to the plastic padding of stair rails.

The Odeon style

What, precisely, was so distinctive about Odeon?

The logo, soon registered as a trademark, has already been mentioned. Its bright red lettering, usually with yellow-gold edging (bevelled on larger signs) was one of the most effective instances of branding in the 1930s and its positioning made it a vital element in the composition of front elevations. (Remove it from its position at Harrogate, as shown on the front cover, and the right-angled recess would lose its point.)

Another feature particularly associated with Odeon is the use of faience or glazed terracotta as a facing material in a colour variously described as cream, biscuit, buff or light yellow. There was nothing new about faience cladding. Many shops, public houses and cinemas had used it – but most often in a colder white or ivory colour, and not adapted to a modern style. It was the use of vast expanses of smooth faience, often contrasted with areas of brick and broken up by narrow stripes of red or green, that made so many Odeons stand out, along with their rounded corners, fin or slab towers, and generally streamlined appearance.

In addition, faience provided Deutsch with exteriors that would remain bright and attractive in Britain's smoke-laden Victorian towns and cities. Smoke abatement was not yet practised and urban sites were very hard to keep clean. Faience was popular because it created an impression of cleanliness and was easily washed down.

Then there was the disciplined use of neon to emphasise the main lines of the buildings after dark rather than to overlay additional, unrelated shapes. Odeons by night (barely illustrated in this book for lack of space) were far more striking than rival cinemas.

In its foyers, Odeon placed furniture and fittings in a style created for the circuit: rounded settees with tubular chrome frames; silver metallic ashstands with the Odeon name, painted red, vertically supporting the bowl; and carpet (usually green, occasionally red or orange) with an overlapping fan-shaped pattern that extended into the auditorium.

Oscar Deutsch sought a pleasant, relaxing atmosphere in an Odeon auditorium. These were generally on the plain side, with stepped down ceilings that helped focus attention on the screen, reduce heating costs and create a more modern look, though dados were often panelled with expensive Empire timbers and all the seats had padded arm rests, not just the most expensive ones. Changing lighting effects on curtains and side walls were achieved with three colours of concealed bulbs: this was still something of a novelty when many patrons still relied on gas lighting or even oil lamps at home, but it was seen at most new cinemas. Odeon's chief felt that it was pointless to spend large amounts of money on the interior when the lights were up for perhaps three minutes during a performance.

Nevertheless, there was considerable care taken to harmonise the decorative scheme within a particular auditorium. The colours varied considerably and were determined by Deutsch's wife, Lily, based on what she deemed appropriate for each location. As the original decorative schemes, carpeting, lighting and curtains were not renewed but crudely replaced by the early 1960s at the majority of Odeons, and as no colour interior photographs exist from the 1930s of these buildings in pristine condition, it is easy to overlook the more subtle qualities that an Odeon interior originally possessed.

Odeons had two sets of side-opening curtains (or tabs): the outer ones were comparatively plain but the circuit introduced vividly coloured and highly stylised inner "screen tabs". These were usually on display during intervals and they added a dramatic splash of colour as well as focussing audience attention at the right place. The curtains generally depicted outdoor themes and appeared in some thirty different designs, used until wide screens arrived in 1953 and 1954. It was the practice to close both sets of curtains before the start of the main feature, then open the outer set followed by the colourful screen tabs which disappeared behind "side legs" (dark green, like the masking of the screen) to avoid any risk of catching light reflected off the screen. No other circuit made such a feature of screen tabs.

Although Odeons were called "Theatres", few had any real provision for stage shows other than a couple of dressing rooms and a minimal stage for guest appearances and announcements. Oscar Deutsch saved construction costs by committing his cinemas to film use only, making no provision for fallback live show use.

About this book

This volume covers the period to Oscar Deutsch's death at the end of 1941. Every purpose-built Odeon is included, with reference to the competitive situation it faced and with comments on its original design. All the photographs within this book were taken in Oscar Deutsch's lifetime, except for one of Ayr, so close that it sneaked in. (The front cover is a recent image confined to 1930s features.) Exterior and auditorium shots of every cinema that opened as an Odeon are included, except for an exterior view of Dalston and interior views of Hamilton, Middlesbrough and Newport (Monmouthshire, now Gwent) for which no pre-

1942 images have been located. (Later photographs filling these gaps will be included in the second half of the Odeon story, along with illustrations of many of the cinemas taken over by Odeon for which there was no room in this present study.)

Commenting on every Odeon one by one risks turning the book into a repetitive catalogue; but many readers will be looking for specific buildings and would be disappointed if there was no coverage of the Odeons that particularly interest them. Inevitably, some Odeons gain more text and have more illustrations than others, not just because of their intrinsic interest but because more background information and photographs have come to light. At the same time, those cinemas which are the most interesting architecturally were not always the most successful commercially and would not justify so much attention in a purely business history.

I have not mentioned the present status of individual Odeons in the main text. This is to approach each cinema equally without dwelling on those that have been fortunate enough to survive, and to concentrate on the period under review and the original look of the buildings, leaving later, often radical, changes to the next volume. (To preserve the period feeling, I have also located cinemas in the counties they occupied during the 1930s.)

However, the subsequent history of each building is summarised in the Chronology at the back of the book and, as the follow-up volume that deals with the later changes will not be immediately available, here is a summary of the best remaining examples of original Odeons, beginning with the cinemas opened by the circuit and still operating (in July 2001) that have been listed for their architectural or historical interest (grade II unless otherwise indicated):

Odeon Barnet (1934)
Odeon Weston-super-Mare (1935)
Odeon Chester (1936)
Odeon Faversham (1936)
 (now independently run as the Royal)
Odeon Sutton Coldfield (1936)
Odeon Harrogate (1936)
Odeon Muswell Hill (1936) (grade II★)
Odeon York (1937)

In addition, the Odeons at Leeds and Newcastle are also listed grade II: these were Paramounts taken over in the 1930s and are still operating at the time of writing. (The Odeon Richmond is also listed, but was taken over after 1941.)

And these are the former Odeon cinemas in other uses or disused that are listed:

Odeon Kingstanding, Birmingham (1935) (bingo hall)
Odeon Scarborough (1936) (live theatres)
Odeon Well Hall, Eltham (1936) (disused)
Odeon Dudley (1937) (church)
Odeon Wolverhampton (1937) (bingo hall)
Odeon Woolwich (1937) (church)
Odeon Newport (Gwent) (1938) (disused)
Odeon Leicester (1938) (disused)
Odeon Luton (1938) (church)
Odeon Blackpool (1939) (disused)

In addition, the Astoria Brixton (grade II★), Picture House Chesterfield, Avenue Ealing (grade II★), Astoria Finsbury Park (grade II★) and Grosvenor Rayners Lane (grade II★) were taken over in the 1930s, renamed Odeon, and are in other uses at the time of writing.

At first sight, this would seem to represent a substantial selection of buildings, but it does not take into account the alterations that had often taken place by the time they were listed and the "reversible" changes that have been permitted since listing.

Externally, the Odeons at Harrogate, Muswell Hill, Sutton Coldfield and Weston-super-Mare, all of which retain their buff faience cladding, remain splendid to behold. The brick faces of the Odeons at Chester and York also survive well.

Harrogate and Sutton Coldfield are almost identical examples of the Odeon style at its zenith. Both have lost the large name sign placed horizontally on the faience-clad side wall, although at Sutton Coldfield it now appears vertically on the back of the projecting slab tower. These cinemas, in the summer of 2001, have become the last to display original signage in its original position on the faience-clad wall on the corner. The neon-reinforced red letters with yellow edges retain their eye-catching impact more than sixty years on. (The Odeon sign at Muswell Hill is of simplified design, its more compact letters in red only, and has been relocated. The Odeon sign on the tower at Weston-super-Mare is a modern variant on the original.) Sutton Coldfield has lost the top of the slab tower on which the word CINEMA appeared. At Harrogate, the CINEMA sign remains (as shown on the front cover) but an obtrusive safety rail has been added very recently just below it. Both cinemas have modern readographs mounted on the rounded faience above the entrance doors but this is a minor intrusion on these classic exteriors.

The neon that outlined these frontages was not replaced after World War Two but it has been restored elsewhere: to another outstanding Odeon exterior at Scarborough as part of the building's conversion to live theatres under a different name, and on the modernised coal-black exterior of the flagship Odeon at Leicester Square. In both cases, it shows how dramatically effective neon must have been in its widespread use in the 1930s.

Foyers were not the strongest point of Odeon schemes but Muswell Hill still has a superb entrance hall discernible through altered circulation and the removal of a central paybox while its inner foyers are essentially intact with their original art deco light fittings. The imposing foyer at Sutton Coldfield has disappeared behind concession stands and a false ceiling, while the mural at the bottom of the stairs has vanished and the opening on the upper landing blocked in.

No undivided auditorium survives in Odeon film use except for the flagship, Leicester Square, which has been partially restored to its original splendour and partially modernised with some skill. Every other auditorium has been subdivided. Only one original cinema survives with the view from the balcony intact: the Odeon Muswell Hill. Here the auditorium design is keyed to a dramatic linear light fitting extending down the ceiling that would be spoilt if a new screen was erected immediately in front of the balcony as elsewhere.

Odeons in other uses or standing disused have inevitably lost their original signage. This is particularly regrettable at Kingstanding where the fin exclaiming CINEMA has been somewhat crudely and incompletely covered over with the word BINGO; but the building had long been a bingo hall when it was listed and the auditorium remains essentially intact with original cinema seating in the small balcony. However, higher lighting levels, brighter decoration, levelled stalls floor and opening up of the stage all erode the original ambience here as elsewhere. Church use is kinder, as at Dudley, but higher lighting levels are still needed to read hymn books.

Some cinemas named Odeon may seem to be missing from this book. These are the ones taken over after 1941 or opened postwar – or Gaumont cinemas renamed Odeon after the two chains merged (the latter are already detailed in the companion book, *Gaumont British Cinemas*). These additions will be covered in the second volume, provisionally titled *Odeon Cinemas 2: J. Arthur Rank And After*, which will extend the history of the circuit up to its sale by the Rank Group in 2000. This will include a list of all Odeon cinemas alphabetically by location as in the volumes on ABC, Gaumont and Granada in contrast to the chronological listing in this book.

OSCAR DEUTSCH ENTERS FILM EXHIBITION

Oscar Deutsch was born on 12 August 1893 at Balsall Heath, Birmingham. His father was a Jewish scrap metal merchant, Leopold Deutsch, who had emigrated to this country from Betzho, Hungary, and died in a domestic accident in 1904. Oscar's mother, Leah (née Cohen), was also a Jewish immigrant, from Poland.

Young Oscar attended the King Edward VI Grammar School, Birmingham, until 1910. At the age of seventeen, he joined his late father's business, Deutsch and Brenner, which was run by the surviving partner, Adolf Brenner, a close family relative. In 1918, Oscar married Lily Tanchan. Their first child, Ronald Leopold, was born in 1920. Two other sons followed: David, born in 1926, and the younger Gerald (birthdate not known).

Although Oscar was made a director of Deutsch and Brenner when he was twenty-one and remained on the board, his prospects within the company were limited as Adolf had two sons, both older than Oscar, who would take precedence (Oscar's son Ronald seems to have joined the family firm in due course).

In 1920 Oscar became chairman of Victory Motion Pictures Ltd., a regional film distribution company he formed with two cinema enthusiasts, Michael Balcon and Victor Saville.* Victory acted as the Midlands agents for the W&F distribution company in London. In 1923, Deutsch was one of the investors when Balcon and Saville, having moved to London, made their first film, *Woman To Woman*, for W&F release.

"Deutsch was a financier of modest range," his close associate R. H. "Dickie" Dewes has noted. "In this regard, he did not specialise, but was prepared to consider any commercial proposition on its merits. As a provider of capital for speculative ventures, Deutsch was extremely skilful and astute, but in the early days the time taken in the process was sometimes extremely long. It was this uncanny ability, however, which was the foundation of his success. He could be very charming, with great persuasive power, and was strong in debate. On one occasion he stopped an extremely vitriolic attack stone dead by saying his feelings had been terribly hurt by a man he had always regarded as a good friend. He then buried his face in his hands. There was a dead silence. When the debate restarted, the attacker said he had not meant his remarks to be taken quite at their face value, and the heat had gone from the dispute."

In Birmingham, Oscar Deutsch entered the exhibition side of the film world as the result of a business opportunity brought to his attention by Finn Balcon, the brother of Michael Balcon and manager of W&F's Birmingham office. A small circuit, Midlands Entertainment Ltd., had collapsed, owing film rental fees to W&F among others. The Receiver had contacted Balcon who put him in touch with Oscar Deutsch.

Deutsch formed a partnership with Reginald Noakes, also from the metal trade, to buy the three cinemas belonging to the company.* One of the three – the Scala Wolverhampton – was then sold to Associated Provincial Picture Houses by Deutsch and Noakes before the takeover date of 1 June 1925 and so was never operated by them. But, on that same date, the other two cinemas – the Crown and the Globe at Coventry – became the first ones to be run by Oscar Deutsch.

Among the staff that Deutsch and his partner inherited were R. H. Dewes, manager of the Globe; Sidney Swingler, the Globe's chief projectionist, electrician and deputy manager; and W. J. [William Joseph] Taylor, office manager for the company which had previously operated the small circuit. These three men were to become some of Deutsch's most trusted lieutenants in the years ahead, although they did not work together in harmony.

According to Dewes: "Deutsch first employed Taylor as an

---

* Oscar Deutsch was not at the same school as Michael Balcon, as has sometimes been stated. Balcon attended the George Dixon Grammar School. And Victor Saville, similarly linked to Deutsch and Balcon, went to the King Edward's Grammar School at Camp Hill whereas the King Edward's Grammar School attended by Deutsch was the one in New Street, later moved to Edgbaston after the New Street site made way for the Paramount cinema. (Information supplied by Jeffrey Richards, letter to the author, 2 December 1980.)

* For a full history of the previous owners, Midlands Entertainments, see "A Midland Tale – Cinemagoing in Silent Days" by R. H. Dewes in *Picture House* no. 3, Spring 1983.

assistant dealing with accounts and various matters, and eventually gave him the title of general manager. With due respect to Taylor, he was never a general manager in the accepted sense of the word, for he tended to avoid accepting responsibility. This was unfortunate, for when the building rush [of Odeons] commenced there was no halfway stage between Deutsch and the departments. So a lot of matters went to Deutsch via Taylor which didn't merit that treatment at all, and in consequence much time was wasted and decisions seriously delayed.

"His work appeared chiefly to be the delivery of instructions from Deutsch, and ensuring that any policies laid down were implemented. Taylor was married to a very determined lady who had inherited a substantial amount of money, and who influenced her husband in various directions which were distinctly detrimental to his best interests and his commercial career."

Dewes recalled Sidney Swingler as follows:

"Swingler was a youth of an extremely individual kind. He was fanatically keen on engineering and technical matters – electricity, cinematograph projection, later talking pictures – and the mechanical side of motor cars and motor cycles. His driving was expert and extremely fast. In appearance he was either covered in oil and grease or was dressed in an ultra immaculate fashion. The staff of the Globe Theatre informed me that at about the age of fourteen before leaving school he had become fascinated by the cinema and took to frequenting the building whenever he could find the least justification. Helping without pay in the projection suite followed, and then he joined the projection team as a junior. When I was first appointed manager of the Globe Theatre on 22 July 1922 I found Swingler acting as electrician, chief of the projection staff, and deputy in charge of the cinema when the manager was absent. He was aged 18 years and nine months at that date.

"During his first few years at the Globe Theatre, he was an ideal assistant – hardworking, very enthusiastic and extremely capable. He turned his hand with great keenness to the various film exploitation tableaux which we ran from time to time, and the theatre won a good deal of prize money in the competitions run by the *Kinematograph Weekly*. I formed a high opinion of his work as an electrical engineer, and this remained the position for several years. Then Swingler's views and characteristics gradually altered. He developed various strong and unusual – indeed unorthodox – views on cinematograph questions, and was involved in a number of bitter and prolonged disputes. I no longer saw eye to eye with him on some of his policy opinions – quite the opposite – but retained my opinion of him as an electrical engineer of high ability."

Dewes himself was born at Tipton in the Black Country in 1893, the same year as Oscar Deutsch, and, like Swingler, he

had become hooked on cinemas. He was seeking a job in the Birmingham film world at the time the First World War broke out. While training with a battalion in the Home Counties, Dewes and two friends visited the cinemas in small agricultural towns, where they were the only form of night life, and rated them for such features as seat comfort, leg room, heating, projection, auditorium rake, decoration, draught protection and risk of flooding, faulting most of the buildings on more than half of the headings they devised.

After the war, Dewes was taken on by the Scala Wolver-hampton and trained to become an assistant manager. In his spare time he tried and failed to promote a cinema scheme in Nottingham.* He became a cinema manager, noted for his lively campaigns promoting the films he was showing.

It was as the manager of the Globe Coventry that Dewes first met Oscar Deutsch in 1925, and he has provided a vivid and extraordinary account of his new boss's state of health at that time. Dewes received a phone call from W. J. Taylor informing him that Deutsch and Noakes would be visiting the cinema during their first week of ownership.

"Taylor told me: 'As you probably already know, Mr. Deutsch is in very poor health. He had a most serious operation last year, and certain portions of his stomach were removed. When he makes his visit to you he will be accompanied by a nurse. Provide her with a seat in the theatre during your interview with them in the office. During the entire time Mr. Deustch is at the theatre, a room for him to rest if necessary and full toilet facilities are to be reserved exclusively for his personal use.'

"I quote this statement because it gives a clearer picture than could any words of mine of the state of Mr. Deutsch's health at that exact time. When talking officially, we never mentioned the word 'cancer' but, of course, we all knew the truth."

Reviewing the years that followed, Dewes added:

"The health of Mr. Deutsch did improve from that point onwards for a period, and the constant attendance of the nurse became unnecessary, but after a time the improvement faded out. There were constant ups and downs in his physical condition – good months and bad, good weeks and bad, days which changed before night, business conferences in his bedroom, family meetings to decide upon the next step, periods in hospital, further operations.

"This went on and on until his death sixteen-and-a-half years later. Naturally, after some of the operations there were longer periods of relief from pain, and of course some of the shorter periods of relief enabled him to act normally while they lasted. I

* See "My Nottingham Venture" by R. H. Dewes in *Focus On Film* no. 32, April 1979.

can remember him sometimes at openings or functions joking and laughing as though he had not a single care in the world. At such times he appeared to be perfectly fit and happy. It is hard to believe, however, that when the gay mood of the moment passed, and before the period of relief actually ended, he was not again conscious of the grim fact that he was a slowly dying man. He used to lie awake at night for hours on end – thinking about his plans – and usually had various items for discussion in the morning. Actually, he could carry on with very little sleep.

"To be fair, one must have full realisation of this vivid picture, and view everything he did or didn't do, and everything he said or didn't say, against that overwhelming background. One could not in common justice apply the normal rules to him."

Oscar's initiation into the film business was not a smooth one, for Dickie Dewes has recorded:

"When Deutsch and Noakes took possession of the Globe Theatre it was anticipated by all concerned that a renovation scheme would be carried out immediately. The building was in a deplorable condition. Oscar Deutsch joined in the discussions on a complete overhaul, but he said nothing definite. I enquired if I could continue with exploitation displays, but was asked to leave it for the time being. This, of course, left me with no elasticity in management whatsoever.

"Compared with the previous year, the take in the next thirteen weeks was £700 down. Deutsch was extremely concerned. I reported to his house each evening with a continuing tale of woe. Faced with the statement that only a substantial scheme for improving the auditorium would arrest the fall, Deutsch said when he bought a business he was content to use all profits made for a time for the purposes of renovation but he didn't expect to be called upon to provide additional capital.

"During the next quarter, receipts fell by a further £300 and the theatre was making hardly any profit at all. At the commencement of the third quarter, the receipts ceased to fall and they ran level with the previous year until the end of the current one. The reason for the £1,000 fall and the sudden reversion to the old take has never been explained.

"The improvement in the take, however, naturally provided some profits for the last two quarters of the financial year and on 25 July 1926 the theatre closed for a complete renovation. The take went up by £2,000 in the next financial year and by a further £1,000 in the year after that. The ship was sailing in smooth waters again. I resumed film exploitation."

Without that earlier box-office recovery, it seems very likely that Deutsch might have been deterred from continuing in film exhibition. Another business venture – as a director of Radiovisor Foreign & Colonial – had no such happy outcome. Here again, Dickie Dewes is the source of the inside story:

"About a year after he came into the exhibition field, Oscar Deutsch began to talk about a company of which he had become a director, and I think, the chairman. I got the impression that Deutsch had put in a substantial amount of capital, and later happenings confirmed this.

"The company owned the United Kingdom rights in a burglar alarm which operated with a special ray and raised the alarm whenever any object entered its path. The patent rights for the UK had been purchased by the company from the holder of the world rights. Deutsch was very keen and appeared very confident. Gradually his confidence waned. The ray was an unqualified success when it worked, but more than half the time it didn't work and the engineers couldn't establish the cause. Commercially, the rights became worthless.

"A dispute then arose, the Deutsch company contending that the parent company had guaranteed the workability of the ray. This the parent company denied, saying that the Deutsch company had purchased the ray after tests by its own engineers and that no false representation had been made during the negotiations. The case went to law and up to the Lords. Every decision was against the Deutsch company. When the rejection of the appeal by the Lords reached Deutsch by a telephone message, Taylor and I were with him. He showed distinct signs of shock and distress and my impression, that the amount of his investment had been pretty substantial, was confirmed."

The story illustrates Deutsch's keen interest in technological developments which would later lead him to invest in sound equipment for cinemas, sophisticated accounting machinery for Odeon, and big screen television.

In the early years of working for Oscar Deutsch, Dickie still retained aspirations of succeeding on his own account even though he lacked any substantial financial resources. He had suffered a temporary career setback while working for Deutsch. When attendances again dropped at the Globe Coventry, Oscar consulted Michael Balcon who recommended a new showman manager he knew was available; and so Dewes was transferred to the smaller and less important Crown, feeling frustrated and humiliated. Fortunately for Dickie, the replacement at the Globe disgraced himself both socially and business-wise (details are lacking) and Deutsch appointed Dewes manager of both cinemas, giving him an assistant.

Dewes really won back favour with Deutsch after overhearing his boss dictate a letter in which he had misunderstood company law. Dewes intervened: "I'm sorry, Mr. Deutsch, but you can't say that." "Who says I can't?" barked Deutsch. Dewes explained and Deutsch's only response, according to Dewes, was to tell his secretary the letter was cancelled and he would re-dictate it later. "He never mentioned the subject to me again, but two days later he came into my office with a fairly large wad of papers and said, 'I want your opinion on this, and I want it first thing in the morning. Bring the papers into my office yourself.'"

Dewes caused a temporary upset in their relationship when he organised the sale of the Crown cinema to a Coventry businessman, Hubert F. Allen. The details are of no significance but the story is worth quoting because it supports the suggestion that Deutsch was primarily a businessman and would sell anything if it was worth his while. It also shows Deutsch as less decisive than might be imagined, and as a man who could doubt a decision he had made.

"Allen was a friend of mine and he was very ambitious", Dewes recalled. "He was a young estate agent and the local agent for the Abbey Building Society. I, of course, was still desirous of getting an interest in a cinema. I asked him if he had the capital and he said no – but he was certain he could raise it. I then asked Deutsch if he wanted to sell the Crown. He said he would sell – but with great reluctance. The price would have to be £21,000. Allen and I then decided to find out how much financial support we could get locally – chiefly from Allen's clients and friends. At the end of a month, people were actively interested to the extent of £10,000 – £8,500 of this was firm. Allen had put in £1,000 himself and his father had done likewise. I put my name down for a few hundred. It appeared safe to go ahead and, of course, it would not be necessary to raise the entire amount in the form of share capital – the balance could be by a loan or bank overdraft.

"The time seemed to have arrived for face to face negotiations and we met at ten o'clock at night at Deutsch's house in Edgbaston. Deutsch had got a collection of liqueurs and we had a drink and then started. Things looked hopeful but Allen seemed to be afraid that he would pledge the position before he was sure he could find the difference between the financial support we already had and the cost price.

"At this stage it was understood that, if the deal came off, Deutsch and Noakes would book for the new company as they were booking for the Globe, and they would permit me to act as advisor to it for a nominal fee. The new company would let me have a certain number of shares. In the meantime, Deutsch had offered to assist the new company by having a certain amount of the purchase price on loan, but the actual price had not been stipulated.

"After two-and-a-half hours of haggling, the purchase price was fixed at £20,000, which was obviously the figure Deutsch had in mind from the start. The second question was the money to be left on loan. Allen was showing signs of nervousness and what I wanted to avoid at any cost was a postponement. I knew

Allen had thought the loan should be £7,500; Deutsch would agree to £5,000, but would much prefer it to be £3,000 – and it would be for five years. I took the risk of finishing the issue and said something on the following lines: 'Gentlemen, we do want to settle this matter tonight but the hour is getting very late and I think this is a proposal to which everybody will agree – the price is to be £20,000 and the loan, if required, is to be £7,500 for five years. Does either party dissent from this?' The higher sum for the loan had evidently calmed Allen's fears and he agreed. Deutsch, looking extremely pained (as he always did under such circumstances), said, 'Yes, I suppose I do, too.'

"I immediately volunteered to prepare the Memorandum of Agreement. I was scared to death that somebody would suggest leaving it to the next day – which is always fatal in negotiations of this kind. Both parties signed it, and Allen handed over a cheque for £1,000. The deal was done. Then we left.

"Cheques can be stopped, of course, and I slid back into the house and asked Deutsch for the cheque which I said I would pay into the bank first thing on the following morning. He readily agreed and Allen and I started back for Coventry. The time was three o'clock.

"The precautions I had taken were wise. Both Deutsch and Allen woke the following morning with the feeling that throughout the negotiations I had been working in the interests of the other side. Allen went straight to his solicitor and said, 'I have signed this Memorandum of Agreement. Get me out of it.' The solicitor said, 'You cannot do that.' Allen was not convinced but he took no decisive action that day which meant that the cheque was cleared."

Deutsch now owned only one cinema, the Globe Coventry, but his company booked the Crown and another Coventry cinema, the Prince of Wales, when Hubert F. Allen took over the lease. After Allen passed both cinemas on to one B. G. Britton in 1932, Deutsch's Cinema Service continued booking them until circa 1934.

THE FIRST ODEON AND OTHER EARLY DEUTSCH BUILDING VENTURES

After a couple of years of running the Globe Coventry in partnership with Alfred Noakes, Oscar Deutsch became involved in building some new cinemas, always as part of a consortium or syndicate.

His first venture was the Picture House on the Laurels Estate at Brierley Hill, near Dudley, in Staffordshire. In February 1928, he formed a company with M. and M. G. Mindelsohn (the two brothers who were behind Wrenson's, the grocery chain in Birmingham), local solicitor Alfred L. Hawkins and others to build an unremarkable, modest-sized hall in the "Assyrian style", seating under one thousand. The architect, Stanley A. Griffiths, came from nearby Stourbridge and the Picture House opened on 1 October 1928.*

Two months later, a group that included Oscar Deutsch was represented by an estate agent called Jack Cotton when provisional approval was sought for a new cinema on a site that Cotton had found at Perry Barr, Birmingham.** The application came before the Birmingham Public Entertainments Committee on 17 December 1928. The only immediate opposition was the

* The *Kinematograph Weekly* (20 December 1928) reported a "cinema being built in Brasshouse Lane, Smethwick, for Mr. Deutsch". The only cinema that fits this brief note is the Beacon, which opened on 30 September 1929 without any involvement on Deutsch's part. The chronicler of Black Country cinemas, Ned Williams, names Percy Dyche as the promoter. Perhaps Deutsch sold him the scheme, but more likely the trade paper had its facts wrong. Similarly, *The Bioscope* (13 November 1929) reported that Deutsch and Noakes had just bought the Grand Foleshill, Coventry, and Broadway Coventry, but entries for these cinemas in the *Kine Year Book* do not reflect this. Perhaps the deal fell through or they were bought and quickly sold again.

** Owing to a quirk in the law, a cinematograph licence could not be granted until a cinema was actually in existence. A licensing authority would examine plans and might give an opinion, not legally binding, that, if the building was erected as shown, it knew of no reason why a licence would not be granted. Sometimes, there would be successful opposition to the plans and this "promise" of a licence would not be forthcoming. However, when this so-called "provisional" licence was offered, it invariably led to an actual licence being granted after the completed building was inspected and any required modifications made.

early Birchfield Picture House, less than half a mile away, which, according to Sidney Swingler, was thought unlikely to survive. The owners of the Birchfield Picture House naturally objected to the scheme but a petition in favour, organised by the promoters, had been signed by 5,730 residents of the district. Dickie Dewes remembered that Jack Cotton made an excellent impression appearing as a witness to argue that there was sufficient density of population to justify the proposed cinema. Approval was granted. "Deutsch and Cotton were close friends then, and remained so for a time afterwards. The two families were very friendly. The men co-operated in several business ventures, but they tended to disagree in the commercial field, and the business association ended. The two men were alike in some respects. Both could display exceptional charm of manner. I only worked with Cotton for a short time – in connection with the Birmingham court hearing – but he was a very pleasant person to co-operate with."

In January 1929, Deutsch and W. G. Elcock formed Picture House (Worcester) Ltd. to take over the existing Silver Cinema. This seems to have been the first business partnership between Deutsch and the man who would become his key financial adviser and fellow director in developing the Odeon circuit. William George Elcock was, and remained, a partner in a Birmingham firm of chartered accountants which had done work for Deutsch previously. (Elcock was later involved in local politics as a councillor, representing the Small Heath ward from 1933 for several years.)

In March 1929, Picture House (Perry Barr) Ltd. was formed to build the cinema on the site which had been acquired through Jack Cotton. Deutsch was again in partnership with the Mindelsohns and other businessmen. This was to be a large cinema, seating over 1,600, designed by Stanley A. Griffiths in collaboration with another local architect, Horace G. Bradley.

It was the widespread adoption of talking pictures that first enabled Oscar Deutsch to achieve national prominence in the film trade. Although the big American concerns which had pioneered sound – Western Electric and RCA – fitted out the most important cinemas, including those of the big Gaumont and ABC circuits, several less expensive British-made alternatives

Picture House Brierley Hill in 1935.

were offered to smaller halls and independents. Deutsch announced his intention to enter this highly competitive field in October 1929 and formed Sound Equipment Ltd. in December 1929 with F. A. Enders to market the British Thomson-Houston Company's sound system. Whereas Western Electric and RCA's Photophone cost a minimum of £1,710 and £1,950 respectively, BT-H asked £1,250 for an auditorium seating up to 2,000. There were twenty sound systems on offer and British Talking Pictures was initially the most successful domestic company. However, British Acoustic and BT-H were soon making substantial sales. Through Sound Equipment, the BT-H system was first installed in Deutsch's Globe Coventry and, with later refinements, went into every cinema that Oscar built. It was certainly installed in many other Birmingham cinemas, including the five halls of the Hewitson company in Smethwick. However, in the long run it was only Deutsch's continuing support of a British-made sound system that kept BT-H a significant supplier.

When building started on the Perry Barr scheme, a problem arose. Despite the company name, the new cinema could not be called Picture House as this would lead to confusion with its rival at Birchfield. After two months of deliberation, Mel Mindelsohn came up with a suggestion during one of the partners' site visits.

"Odeon" was Mindelsohn's proposal, suggested by a recent trip he, his brother and their families had made to Tunis. This is how Dickie Dewes remembered Mindelsohn explaining it to him: "We saw the word 'Odeon' being used as the name of a building in everyday use, and it struck me that as a title the word had possibilities. It was short, dignified, unusual, but without being bizarre. Use of the word as a title for a cinema or other hall in the British Isles would possibly be original. What did rather grip our imagination, however, was the fact that the first letter of the word was the initial of Oscar Deutsch, and the next two letters were the first two letters of his surname. I discussed the matter fully with my brother, and we agreed that 'Odeon' would make a good title for the cinema, and would, at the same time, be a very nice compliment to Oscar. We made the proposal to him accordingly and after a discussion he agreed. We were pleased."

And so the Perry Barr cinema opened as the Odeon on 4 August 1930. Dickie Dewes emphasised: "The choosing of the name 'Odeon' was a decision regarding that building only. No one was then conscious of any wider implications."

Oscar's wife, Lily, later suggested that the "on" part was also appropriate because her husband was so very much "on", brimming with energy and ambition. Odeon would eventually be interpreted as an acronym of Oscar Deutsch Entertains Our Nation.

In later years, the Odeon name would be linked with the

Odeon Perry Barr. Night exterior from 1930.
Day exterior and auditorium in 1935.
The name sign is in thinner lettering than later on.
The cinema had two car parks.

Odeions or amphitheatres of ancient Greece as continuing a tradition of presenting the finest in entertainment. The Odeon Perry Barr was the first time that any cinema in Britain had taken the name but it was well established elsewhere by 1930. The Odeon in Milan, for example, was the town's leading cinema by that time, and there was another prominent Odeon in Marseilles. And, of course, the word "odeon" was familiar as part of "nickelodeon", used for early American cinemas charging five cents for admission. One such hall closed with the name Odeon Theatre in Birmingham, Alabama, and was demolished around 1929. Odeon was also used in other fields, being the name of a prominent café in Zurich in the 1920s.

It was not only the name that first appeared at Perry Barr. At the moment it was being decided upon, a young man named Harold Pearce called, seeking a contract for his family's company to supply the sign (Pearce Signs claimed to have been going since 1791). According to Sidney Swingler, on hearing the name "Odeon", Pearce sketched out the letters in a distinctive, straight-edged, somewhat classical style in red with gold edging while they were still talking. This was adopted and installed at Perry Barr and other early Odeons as a "halo sign" which was lit up from behind (neon came later) and, of course, the design survives with modifications to this day as one of the most recognisable of all logos. The design was registered as a trademark, which did not prevent other businesses using the Odeon name although no other British cinema ever did (names like Avion and Orion were suspiciously close, sometimes combined with an imitation of the Odeon style of lettering).

The Perry Barr cinema was entirely in the fashionable Moorish style with a dazzling white exterior. It occupied a rectangular site between two roads but the auditorium was somewhat unorthodox in that it widened in the front stalls area. An orchestra provided musical interludes but was dismissed after a few weeks. The ushers and usherettes were fitted out in trousers, anklets, veils and turbans – a very novel idea, at least for that area. However, Moorish scenes on the auditorium walls were added when the cinema was closed in early 1931 for the walls to be treated with a material called Cellotex to improve the acoustics.

Ross projectors were installed and a side-expanding screen fitted so that the picture could be enlarged from a normal width of 28ft. 9ins. to 40ft. wide to cater for a shortlived interest in wide screen.

There were festoon curtains of silk brocade that could be looped in forty different ways and floodlit with dozens of colour changes. Former projectionist Bernie Weavers still remembers the warm smell of the gas secondary lighting and how the balcony was badly designed because the heads of patrons could easily get in the way of the projection beam.

Royal Alfreton in 1935.

Although it introduced the Odeon name, the Perry Barr cinema has nothing whatever to do with the formation of the Odeon circuit. It only became part of that circuit in 1935, along with other early properties in which Deutsch was involved. By the late 1930s, it functioned as the circuit's test site or, as an Odeon trainee of the period, Dennis Williams, labels it, "the Meccano set". Williams recalls: "Perry Barr was Odeon's experimental theatre – so anything new in the way of uniforms, sets, carpets, barrier ropes, any bits of new equipment that came on the market, were tested out at Perry Barr. There would be various manufacturers' reps going round with clipboards taking notes. The projection room was permanently haywire. It broke all regulations. There was flex and wire hanging down all over the place. They would change screens about three or four times a year. BT-H were always carrying out tests to amplifiers, [carbon projector] arcs. It was also one of Odeon's training schools, training managers."

In 1931, Deutsch was one of the directors behind the new Royal cinema at Alfreton, Derbyshire, built to the plans of Harry Clayton with a mock Tudor frontage and seating 1,450. He also teamed up with Alfred Noakes, the Mindelsohns and Alfred L. Hawkins to form a company to take over the Grosvenor at Bloxwich, Staffordshire, towards the end of the year.

Around 1930, Deutsch had formed Cinema Service Ltd., which booked the films at the various cinemas in which he had an interest and also for outside cinemas. Circa 1932 it leased the Empire Seaford, Sussex, and did the booking for the Rialto Southampton; the Cosy at Heanor, Derbyshire; and the Palladium Bournemouth. Cinema Services may have provided other assistance as it did in later years, making bulk purchases of such supplies as light bulbs.

Deutsch also improved his standing in the exhibition field by serving as chairman of the Birmingham and Midlands branch of the principal trade body, the Cinematograph Exhibitors' Association, after a period as vice-chairman. He was elected chairman on 30 January 1931 and served in that post for two years. While in office, he was faced with a bid from the leaders of the Film Industries Co-Operative Society Ltd. to recruit members in his area. The Co-Op's executive directors included Will Evans, former joint managing director of Gaumont-British, Sir Gordon Craig, Major A. J. Gale and, locally, councillor G. F. McDonald. The company was anxious to enlist the many Midlands independent exhibitors in its plan to form a powerful booking unit to fight the two major chains, ABC and Gaumont, for a better share of product. Deutsch was fiercely opposed to the idea, either because it threatened Cinema Service and his own expansion plans or because he feared it would become a third behemoth that would make life even more difficult for anyone that did not join it – or for both reasons. With characteristic shrewdness, he decided not to quash the Co-Op directors' arrangement through McDonald to address the CEA branch meeting at the Chamber of Commerce on 27 November 1931 because McDonald could easily fix a separate meeting for local exhibitors. Instead, Oscar invited the Co-Op directors to lunch before the meeting to put them off guard while he urgently sought the advice of his old friend, Michael Balcon, on good speakers to oppose the scheme. It seems, from Deutsch's subsequent report to Balcon (preserved in the Balcon papers in the BFI National Library's Special Collections), that the scheme came under heavy fire at the meeting. At any rate, it was soon dead.

More publicly, Deutsch led the CEA's campaign to open Birmingham's cinemas on Sundays and was one of a deputation who met eighteen local Members of Parliament to press the case for a reduction in Entertainments Tax. He gained a listing in the *Kine Year Book*, appearing in the section on "Who's What in the Trade" from the 1932 edition onwards. In his private life, he held another important office, being elected president of the Birmingham Hebrew Congregation in 1932.

1933: BIRTH OF THE ODEON CIRCUIT

The Odeon circuit came into existence in 1933 with the opening, in successive months from June onwards, of five cinemas in the south of England.

Why Deutsch, who came from the Midlands and whose previous connections with the film business had been there, should have set about establishing a circuit in the south is not known. It seems likely that he felt this part of the country was weathering the Depression better and offered the richest returns.

Odeon cinemas – in common with most other building projects – often took a long time to come to fruition. Even when work started on a site, it could take a year to complete construction and open to the public, and often plans would have been first submitted to the local authority a year or more before that. The Odeon circuit was particularly slow in getting under way and Deutsch must have felt extremely frustrated at times. Financial arrangements for the first two cinemas at Kingston-on-Thames, Surrey, and at Weymouth, Dorset, were discussed in 1931, but it took ages for these to be settled and no actual building work commenced during that year.

In 1932, Deutsch and his associates began working on further schemes for: Canterbury, Kent; Worcester Park, Surrey; Worthing, Sussex; Raynes Park, Surrey; South Harrow, Middlesex; and Tolworth, Surrey. During this same year or early in 1933, detailed planning work began on cinemas at Wallington and Weybridge in Surrey, and at Wimbledon in south London. Separate companies were formed for each project. By May 1933, five cinemas were under construction.

Dickie Dewes is the source of much inside detail on the problems attending the first two Odeons. "The Odeon Kingston was the theatre with by far the longest run up to opening date. The story of its erection is a list of frustrations. Weymouth was another proposition which, for different reasons, had a long run up to opening date."

The Odeon **Weymouth,** which opened first, was originally to be called the Picture House, like the earlier cinema that Deutsch had built and opened at Brierley Hill. Dewes continued: "Letters from the directors to me and from my department to the outside world were headed: 're The Picture House – Weymouth'.

The owning company was duly registered as Picture House (Weymouth) Ltd. in May 1932.

"Then Mr. W. J. Taylor, the general manager, gave me a verbal message from Oscar Deutsch. He said it had been decided that all theatres opening in future would be named Odeon unless there was a governing reason for using another title. There had been certain somewhat casual discussions on the subject from time to time, but the sudden and decisive ruling was rather a surprise to me. Taylor was not in a position to supply much additional information, but I gleaned that the decision followed telephone exchanges between Deutsch and the other directors, and that steps were being taken to ensure that a resolution was minuted by all the companies concerned covering the point." Dewes dated this decision as being made sometime between the beginning of June and the end of October 1932. (The first companies to use the Odeon name were registered for the Canterbury, Worcester Park and Worthing schemes in November 1932.)

The Weymouth cinema was an adaptation of a former Georgian stables which had become the Gloucester Garage, a base for vehicles from the fleet of Rambler Motor Coaches, a company owned by George K. Spivey who lived locally. He contributed the building and became a director of Picture House (Weymouth) Ltd. along with Deutsch and George Elcock. The architect for the conversion, which cost just under £6,000, was Harry Clayton, who was based in Chesterfield and received a fee of £114.10s.0d. (Clayton had designed the Royal at Alfreton for Deutsch.) The scheme was first announced in the trade press in June 1932. At Spivey's suggestion, it was he who lodged the original application for a cinematograph license on behalf of the local company to take advantage of his position as a leading Weymouth businessman. The full council considered the scheme on 21 July 1932.

Although Dewes did not directly provide any details of the difficulties of retaining Mr. Spivey as a partner, a carbon copy survives of a memorandum he sent to Oscar Deutsch on 3 January 1933: "I took Mr. Spivey out to lunch yesterday, after he had had an interview with Mr. Elcock. He was quite affable, but he gave me the definite impression that he is not prepared to wait

Odeon Weymouth. On the exterior, seen in mid-1935, note the generally old-fashioned appearance and the elaborate stained glass windows on the first floor with a sunburst pattern on the lower panes. A further sunburst design appears on the front doors. Inside, the decoration on the screen tabs continues the semi-atmospheric scheme. The lower walls have been painted to represent stonework, an effect spoilt by the radiators in the recesses. Three fibrous plaster features in the ceiling cover up ventilation outlets. The before-opening view at lower right includes part of the back wall with its window-like openings for the projection ports.

very much longer. He says he has an offer to rent the Gloucester Garage for one year..." It seems that there was a misunderstanding over the value of the property: Spivey thought it was worth far more than the Deutsch side. "He says that, if the deal is off, it will be very easy to show, in the open market, that the property was not over valued. Of course, it would not have been tactful on my part to have entered into an argument with Mr. Spivey, so I simply let him talk... We parted very affably, but he stressed that he expected to hear from Mr. Elcock by the end of the week." *

The Odeon Weymouth eventually opened on 2 June 1933. External evidence of the building's past features remained in a bricked-up door and disused lunette window on a side wall. There was no indication of these in the long, narrow, single-floor auditorium. From each side of the foyer, patrons went up steps and a slope to reach gangways that ran down each side of the auditorium in the direction of the screen, leaving most of the seating in one central block. An exit halfway down the left-hand side intruded into the auditorium and the gangway cut into several rows of seats to get round it.

A cross aisle, connecting the points of entry to the auditorium, divided off a rear section, which contained the most expensive seats, from the main block of seating. This had a central gangway to the back – with an increased rake rather than steps – splitting the seating into two blocks.

The face of the clock (to the right of the screen) was used to reinforce the cinema name, replacing the twelve numerals with the letters of ODEON and THEATRE.

The "semi-atmospheric" decorative scheme of the auditorium attempted to give the audience an impression of sitting outdoors. It was the work of artists from a Birmingham firm, Allied Guilds, led by John Jackson.

CTA member Peter Clark declares: "As a youngster, I remember the original decorative scheme from attending the Mickey Mouse Club on Saturday mornings in the 1930s. The building was a stadium type with 541 seats. Each of the side walls was divided into panels by seven fluted columns topped with inverted cones to provide indirect house lights.

"Originally in each of these panels were painted rural scenes likened to the Dorset countryside. On each side, the two panels nearest the screen had acoustic padding about six inches deep covering approximately the lower two-thirds of the area and painted as hillsides. On the back wall the rural scene continued

* Spivey was later connnected with a provisional scheme for a cinema in King Street, Weymouth. Announced in January 1938, this was to seat 1,500, with bomb-proof basement accommodation for the same number, and be designed by E. Wamsley Lewis, the architect of the London New Victoria, who was now living in Weymouth.

by picturing an oak-framed cottage with the projection ports incorporated to look like windows. There were four ports: two for the projectors, one for observation, and one for a slide projector (showing advertisements) which was occasionally adapted for a spotlight.

"The original decorations remained intact until the cinema was redecorated to a design scheme by the wife of Oscar Deutsch, Lily, just before the war. The new design was predominantly green and cream (the then house colours) and the murals disappeared under the new colour wash. Even the elegant screen tabs [curtains] were replaced by new tabs made up of three-foot vertical green and cream striped panels. In later years, the outline of the hills on the panels nearest the screen could still be discerned due to the dust which settled on the ridges."

The observation port mentioned was in the non-sync room (where interval music was played on a turntable). The projection room had a door at one end which opened out onto the street at first-floor level, with a rope ladder for use in an emergency.

The Odeon Weymouth gave the circuit a thoroughly inauspicious start. It competed with two Gaumont halls, the larger Regent and diminutive Belle Vue.

The Odeon **Kingston-on-Thames** opened a month later. Dickie Dewes noted: "It was the Kingston proposition which brought F. S. (Benny) Bates into the Deutsch circle. Bates had some of his own money in the scheme and progress was deadlocked. Deutsch agreed to try and do the financing, and Bates was associated with him in one way or another from that time on."

Born in 1899, and therefore six years younger than Deutsch, Frederick Stanley Bates was educated at Marlborough College and Jesus College, Cambridge. A keen sportsman, he had played cricket for Hampshire and also enjoyed golf. His first ten years in the business world were with the Anglo-American Oil Company. According to Alan Wood (in his biography of J. Arthur Rank), Bates acquired a number of sites while involved financially with the oil company on which it was originally planned to build petrol stations. Kingston was certainly one of these – and just as suitable for building a cinema.

Surviving plans dated December 1931 by architect Col. James E. Adamson in collaboration with Marshall and Tweedy show that the cinema was originally (or at least provisionally) called the Riverside, appropriate to its location (the plans display a different frontage to that actually built). Built on the southern edge of the town centre, it backed on to the River Thames which would frequently flood the lower end of the auditorium.

Dewes' memories of Kingston continue: "Deutsch and Bates came into contact with a speculator named [Peter] Olsen. He offered to supply certain credit cushions and to build a theatre

Odeon Kingston in the summer of 1935. There is a café and dance hall on the first floor. The lofty auditorium was, according to one oral reminiscence collected by the local museum, always cold. The screen initially had the variable masking fashionable at the period that could be opened up to provide a larger image during a spectacular sequence, using a magnifying lens on one projector at a reel changeover. The aisle carpet is a jazzy precursor of the later standard pattern.

to the specification for a fixed sum, using a qualified builder of his own choice. The deal was finalised. The building work started, and went merrily on. Then a creditor of Olsen made him bankrupt.

"The complications which followed, and the efforts made to untangle the financial mess, are beyond description. There were, of course, three parties to the dispute – Deutsch, the Olsen estate, and the builder. Month after month slipped past but matters were straightened out in the end and I do not think Deutsch suffered any great loss – except, of course, in the matter of time."

Another cause of delay at Kingston was a dispute over a right of light which took several months to settle during which building operations were suspended.

The Odeon Kingston had a front elevation of cream-coloured faience relieved by wide bands of green across the top and narrower bands edging the slight recesses in which tall windows were set. The use of buff or cream faience with relieving colour bands was already well established – as at the Astoria Finsbury Park, north London, opened in September 1930 – but it did not give Kingston the appearance of being in the "Odeon style" as the frontage lacked the essential streamlining and rounded corners.

The auditorium at Kingston similarly lacked the features that were most characteristic of later Odeons. It was tall and narrow with much use of concealed lighting and with attractive fountain uplights along the side walls of the stalls floor. The carpet was not in the later circuit style (although quite similar with its blade-like shapes). But one aspect of Deutsch's Odeon philosophy was clearly established: all the seats were the same, with padded arm rests (not found on the cheap seats at many cinemas).

The Odeon Kingston entered a highly competitive local market: the huge Regal had already opened on the other side of town while the smaller Elite (co-designed by Adamson) and the Kinema were more centrally placed. It had a Compton organ of three manuals, seven ranks ("all in one chamber with a narrow sound opening into the cinema!" Ivor Buckingham has noted), illuminated console and lift. The organ was included to compete with those at the Regal and Elite. Similarly, all three cinemas had cafés.

The third Odeon was at **Canterbury**, in The Friars. Dickie Dewes recalled: "By a most astounding coincidence, a small dance hall was already operating in Canterbury with the title 'Odeon'. We offered compensation and expenses if they would change their name, but the negotiations came to nothing. In view of the location of the theatre 'The Friars' was absolutely perfect for a second choice, and so The Friars the cinema became. It will be noted that The Picture House no longer ranked as second choice." (The prior use of the Odeon name serves to confirm that it was already considered an appropriate one in England, as well as abroad, for a leisure attraction.)

The Friars was a rather undistinguished cinema, typical of its period, designed by local architects Alfred and Vincent Burr – whose later Empire at Sandwich, Kent, proved a delightful cinema with art deco trimmings. Canterbury was ripe for a new cinema, being served only by two small picture houses: a point taken by another ambitious company of the time, County Cinemas, which developed its own scheme in a less central location. Oscar Deutsch found himself in a race with County to open first. It ended in a dead heat, with County opening its larger, more modern-looking Regal on the same day as the Friars – a unique occurrence. The date, 5 August, was particularly attractive, being at the beginning of Cricket Week with the town full of visitors, and both cinemas should have made a good start.

Quickly on the heels of Canterbury came the cinema that first established a distinctive Odeon image, at **South Harrow,** Middlesex. It was designed by the Harrow-based A. P. Starkey whose practice delivered several more Odeons in a very similar style, mainly in the Harrow area.

Not a great deal is known about Arthur Percival Starkey. He completed his articles with a Coventry architect before enlisting in the Boer War, after which he stayed in South Africa for several years working for various architects in Johannesburg. Returning to England in 1905, he joined Baillie Scott's office in Bedford, then worked for the Lancashire County Architect's office at Preston. During the First World War he worked in the Admiralty Air Department. He set up his own practice as an architect in Harrow around 1919 and was mainly involved in housing. The Odeon South Harrow was his first cinema.

"Harrow came to us as a scheme for a full-stage 2,200 seater, the most elaborate thing you've ever seen," recalled Sidney Swingler. "So we cut it down, cut the price down to one of the cheapest we built. Starkey was very co-operative because he realised there would be more work to come. We were not interested in the most elaborate forms of decor, which we felt were relics of the ancient music hall - the Marc Henri and Laverdet schemes, the Komisarjevsky schemes. They typified full-stage theatres which we were not interested in. The same with organs – there were only a few theatres which we built as Odeons which had organs installed. We also kept down the cubic capacity. We brought the ceiling lower for economic reasons and because it was the cheapest form of producing good acoustics."

The Odeon South Harrow was an astonishing building externally, quite unlike any cinema built before it, and A. P. Starkey has not received the credit and recognition he deserves, both for the intrinsic quality and originality of his practice's Odeon work

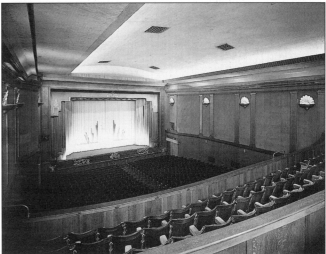

Friars Canterbury in the summer of 1935. Note the huge forecourt which provided access to a car park behind the cinema.
The large name sign is in the Odeon style but with fatter letters than previously. Signs hanging from the canopy mark the doors for the cheapest seats on the left and for higher prices on the right.

Odeon South Harrow, with the circuit's first great exterior by A. P. Starkey, seen in the summer of 1935. It made a totally modern statement, in sharp contrast with its surroundings, particularly the church seen in the distance. The two drainpipes on the back wall of the recess provide the only incongruous touch. The horizontal strips of neon tubing directly alongside the canopy were a later addition, as may have been the further Odeon signs mounted vertically on each of the wings. The Odeon Radio shop just beyond the canopy matches the Odeon Café in style of signage, and could have been another Deutsch enterprise.

Odeon South Harrow. The auditorium in mid-1935.

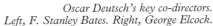

Oscar Deutsch's key co-directors.
Left, F. Stanley Bates. Right, George Elcock.

and for establishing the characteristically modern Odeon look. The long, low frontage clad in buff faience must have been quite startling in its suburban setting: if it had not been handled so effectively, it would have been a real eyesore. (In contrast, almost opposite is a contemporary parade of shops incorporating a Woolworth's that is a dull, safe exercise in brick with stone dressings.)

The most arresting feature of the Odeon's design was the huge central recess, taking out two floors of space which might have been used for other purposes, such as a café or more offices or flats (in fact, a café was situated in two of the ground-floor shopping units). This deep recess had its greatest impact at night when it was floodlit with the Odeon sign on the back wall standing out in silhouette from lighting behind the individual letters. On the canopy, the front and side edges were lit from within so that the titles of the current attractions stood out, an unusual device that may have originated here.

The vast expanse of faience-tiled surface was punctuated by narrow openings in the built-out back corners of the recess, each carrying a vertical line of small round windows. Wider tall windows appeared above the shops in the three-storey wings of the development. There were no bands of colour in the faience, but the upper rows of tiles carried vertical fluting. However, as a contrast, the entrance recess was tiled in black.

The auditorium, seating 997, extended parallel to the frontage. There was only a modest foyer as patrons went immediately from the paybox into the stalls on one side or ascended some stairs to come in at the back of the raised rear section.

The simple interior was nowhere near as striking as the exterior but nevertheless it offered a well-proportioned and comfortable space with excellent sightlines. The principal illumination came from a laylight in the ceiling and from concealed lighting of the proscenium arch. There was little or no wasted space, with the upper side walls sloping inwards and the inner doors of the front side exits intruding into the auditorium. The proscenium arch took up virtually the entire end wall – its stepped corners, neatly integrated with the stepped ceiling, were echoed in the corners of the laylight. The clock was rather awkwardly mounted on the left side exit and, like that at Weymouth, had the words ODEON THEATRE in place of the numerals.[*]

Starkey's achievement is all the more impressive when it is appreciated that, as Sidney Swingler indicated, the Odeon at South Harrow was particularly inexpensive, costing about £10 a seat – half the figure for Kingston, considerably less than Canterbury. It is to Oscar Deutsch's great credit that he accepted

[*] Kingston and Canterbury had ordinary clocks, but every Odeon from South Harrow onwards displayed a lettered clockface. However, the octagonal frame, matching the shape of the letter O in the Odeon design of lettering, had yet to arrive.

Odeon Lancing in the summer of 1935. The corrugated roof of the auditorium can just be seen in the background on the right. The two small Odeon signs on the sides of the canopy are connected by a line of neon. In the auditorium, the aisle is curiously off-centre.

the ultra-modern look of the scheme, but one wonders whether he was impressed more by the low cost than by the look of Starkey's building. Still, it is evident that he did not object to its appearance as Starkey continued to devise Odeon exteriors in the same style.

According to Frederick Adkins, who joined Starkey's practice just after South Harrow opened: "Mr. Deutsch's co-director, F. Stanley Bates, was in touch with Mr. Starkey. As a matter of interest, a small group of businessmen in the Harrow area got together to finance these early Odeons, and Oscar Deutsch had only a small interest in each – I believe they were leased to the Odeon circuit for the first few years before being taken over as the circuit gained strength. Every effort was made to build these early Odeons at a very economical figure. The first few Odeons that Starkey and I did had about one thousand seats and were built on the 'stadium' principle, with a raised tier for the circle rather than an overhanging balcony, which gave economy in construction."

All the sites were extremely wide, incorporating shops and flats that generated useful income to offset the cost of the cinema. The stadium type of auditorium reduced the number of seats as well as the construction costs. This carried an aesthetic advantage externally in lowering the bulk of the building and making it easy to hide the pitched roof from the front. Strictly speaking, most of the Starkey auditoria were "semi-stadium" with a raised and quite separate rear section rather than a stepped-up continuation of the main floor. This enabled the rear section to be called the circle and clearly separated patrons in the most expensive seats from those in the cheaper rows below but they were further away from the screen than they would have been in the front section of an overhanging balcony.

One of the quirks of cinema development was that architecturally outstanding buildings sometimes arose in close proximity to each other, perhaps due to a spirit of competition (as could be the case with the Odeon and Granada at Woolwich). The Odeon South Harrow was somewhat eclipsed in 1936 by the arrival a short distance away of F. E. Bromige's flamboyant Grosvenor at Rayners Lane, which soon fell under Odeon control.

The next Odeon at **Lancing**, Sussex, did not feature in the list of cinemas that Oscar Deutsch was developing in 1931 and 1932. Clearly, it was a late addition. Quite why Deutsch and his associates, Elcock and Bates, took up this scheme is a mystery, as they already had a much better cinema going up in the area at Worthing. They joined R. A. Gates as directors of the venture: Gates held the mortgage of £7,500 and was probably the local partner who brought the scheme to Odeon. Although Lancing lacked a cinema and its population was increasing, the location was extraordinarily poor, outside the centre down a side road that was mainly residential. Whereas specific architects are associated with other Odeons, company records indicated in the case of Lancing that the architect was "arranged by builder". On top of £7,500 spent on building the cinema, £2,000 was spent on furnishing and equipment with £100 of additional expenses, making a total of £9,600 – less than a quarter of what would be spent on the Worthing Odeon. The company expected to pay £520 per annum in mortgage interest and £300 per annum to redeem the mortgage over twenty years.

This Odeon had a two-storey front section with shops to each side of its entrance and the main Odeon sign at roof level (two small Odeon signs were later mounted on each side of the canopy). Despite its location, it opened with a café on the first floor. The auditorium was built some way behind, on fields that had previously been used as a nursery, and extended past the back gardens of the row of houses adjacent to the cinema.

The decorative style of the auditorium was "atmospheric", as in the Weymouth Odeon. The side wall dado was painted to look as if it was made of stone while above there were images of blossoming bushes, cypress trees and distant hills and valleys to suggest a sunny southern European landscape. In a true atmospheric cinema this would have been carried out in relief while the ceiling would have been curved to represent the sky, descending behind the side walls. Here the flat ceiling was left plain but decorative ventilation grilles interrupted any suggestion of open air while modern radiators in the "stone" walls provided another jarring note. The side exits were worked into the decorative scheme, representing entrances with red tiled roofs to the gardens depicted on the side walls while small balconies had shutters and similarly tiled roofs on each side of the proscenium arch.

A few further touches were at odds with the general decor. The curtains were decorated in a modern style rather than continuing the outdoors theme as at Weymouth. An Odeon clock was mounted on one of the balconies. And for the first time, what would become the standard design of Odeon carpet is seen.

The opening report on the cinema in the *Kinematograph Weekly* is seemingly the first to credit Mrs. Oscar Deutsch with the decorative scheme. Whether she attended the opening is unclear, but her husband certainly did.

This Odeon became an embarrassment to the circuit – old-fashioned in contrast to the nearby Worthing cinema which opened five months later, and barely if at all profitable. It seemed such a let-down to the circuit image that it was renamed Regal in 1936, which enabled the Worthing Odeon to advertise in the area without causing confusion. When another, better sited cinema was being built in Lancing in 1939, Deutsch leased his cinema to the owner, making it the first new Odeon to leave the circuit (although it eventually came back).

Cinema Service

On 5 August 1933, the 803-seat Corinth at Hayes, Middlesex, designed by J. M. Wilson and T. Elsom Hardy, was opened by F. J. Partner & Co. Ltd. Oscar Deutsch was a director of the company and it was booked from opening for a year or so by Cinema Service but it had no other link with Odeon, did not look like an Odeon, and was never controlled by Deutsch.*

Besides its previously mentioned links with the Rialto Southampton, Cosy Heanor and Palladium Bournemouth, Deutsch's booking and management company also added the Kings Exmouth, Devon, to its roster of clients for a year or so.

All these booking agreements seem to have been terminated by 1935 as Deutsch concentrated on building up his own circuit which now had sufficient booking power of its own.

Non-starters

During these early years, there were several announcements of Odeons that never materialised.

In February 1932, a scheme designed by Col. James E. Adamson for East Street, Farnham, Surrey, surfaced in a trade report. Negotiations were pending over the setting back of the building line. This scheme passed to the rival County circuit and resulted in the opening of the Regal in March 1933 (which eventually become an Odeon).

Reigate Picture House Ltd. was registered on 26 February 1932 to build a cinema in London Road. The directors were Deutsch, Bates, M. Tanchan, and a local figure, G. A. Hodgkins. Plans prepared by Col. James E. Adamson in association with Marshall and Tweedy were passed in April 1932. Perhaps a rival proposal for a second cinema by the owner of the town's Hippodrome scuppered the idea – that led to the opening of the Majestic in 1935.

There was one indication of Oscar Deutsch being involved in a scheme in the Midlands. The *Kinematograph Weekly* (14 April 1932) notes that Deutsch, George Parker and W. W. Turner (the head of a cinema seating company named after him) had teamed up on a cinema scheme at the junction of Kings Road and Kettlehouse Road in Kingstanding, Birmingham. This collapsed... but Deutsch would become involved in a later proposition for the same site.

In August 1933, Deutsch withdrew from a cinema scheme at Tewkesbury, Gloucestershire, designed by Satchwell and Roberts, which had been announced in the trade press a month earlier,

* In November 1933, the *Kinematograph Weekly* reported that a site in Cobham, Surrey, adjacent to the White Lion Hotel, had been acquired for an Odeon. This seems to have evolved into another enterprise of F. J. Partner and associates, but without Deutsch: the Savoy, which opened there in July 1936, had no connection with the Odeon circuit.

linking him with another ambitious entrepreneur, S. W. Clift (later head of the Clifton circuit). This seems to have been abandoned.

Deutsch's deepest involvement in an unrealised scheme at this time concerns the proposed Odeon for Raynes Park, Surrey, near Wimbledon. In December 1932, Odeon (Raynes Park) Ltd. was registered. The 1,000-seater in Coombe Lane was designed by Yates, Cook and Darbyshire. Raynes Park already had a cinema and it is possible that Deutsch's interest simply shifted to a site on Worple Road, Wimbledon, where he opened an Odeon using the same architects. Another abandoned project linked to the same architects was for an Odeon in East Barnet at the junction of Cat Hill and Brookhill Road: this was active in August 1933, and has no connection with the later Barnet Odeon.

In late 1932/early 1933, there was trade mention of an Odeon for Northolt, Middlesex, with no indication of the architect. (This might be a confused reference to the Odeon South Harrow which was in Northolt Road.)

Another early scheme concerned an Odeon at Seaford, Sussex. As in many other instances, this was to be built on a large site outside the commercial centre of the town – here, the former pound for stray cattle – that had been optioned at a low price because it seemed to have little commercial potential. The threat of competition alarmed the owner of the town's small Empire, Victor Bravery, and the current operator, Mrs. Isobel Merriman Langdon, who with her late husband had acquired the lease from Oscar Deutsch's Cinema Service only months before. In an article for *Picture House* ("Ritz Seaford", no. 9, Winter 1986), John Fernee noted: "At a meeting between Mr. Bravery and Mrs. Langdon, it was suggested that she should see Oscar Deutsch to discuss the matter. Victor Bravery promised that if Mrs. Langdon could persuade Deutsch not to proceed with his Odeon Seaford scheme, he would purchase the site and build a brand new cinema for her to lease. [...] Mrs. Langdon visited Oscar Deutsch in London, and pointed out that it was hardly fair trading, in her opinion, to sell the lease of one cinema, the Empire, to her late husband and herself, and then build a brand new cinema in direct opposition! Surprisingly, Deutsch agreed, and explained that with his programme of new Odeons gaining momentum, his agents were exercising options on sites all over the country, and that he had overlooked the position at Seaford. Under the circumstances he was quite prepared not to proceed with the proposed Odeon at Seaford." Bravery built the Ritz on the site instead.

Cinema Equipment

In April 1933, Sound Equipment, the company which Oscar Deutsch had co-founded to market the BT-H sound system, became Sound and Cinema Equipment to market not only the sound apparatus but a full range of projection room and other cinema requisites now being made by BT-H including projectors, spotlights and earphones for the hard of hearing. Early Deutsch properties had been fitted with Kalee projectors but only BT-H equipment was installed at Odeons as soon as it became available.*

---

* Dennis Williams, who worked for Odeon as a relief manager and took a keen interest in technical matters, describes the BT-H projectors and soundheads as "marvellous" but recalls that the amplifiers were "inadequate" so that Odeons had inferior sound compared to cinemas with Western Electric and RCA installations. In his experience, the problem was worst in the biggest Odeons with the larger BT-H amplifiers which were underpowered so that the volume had to be turned up to the maximum, leading to distortion and clipping on loud passages.

1934: SEVENTEEN NEW ODEONS

In January 1934, the *Kinematograph Weekly* reported that Oscar Deutsch planned to open twenty-five cinemas during the year. He managed seventeen. These were mostly in Surrey and Sussex, but later in the year Odeons appeared in the Midlands and north of England. Many of the seventeen were modest developments, seating around one thousand, built in suburban areas of rapidly increasing population, although Worthing and the later cinemas of the year were appreciably larger in capacity.

With the exception of Worthing, none of the cinemas were in highly competitive situations. Even in Worthing, the existing halls were run by a local independent.

Deutsch was still a small player, feeling his way, concentrating on inexpensive sites, not yet ready to enter into direct confrontation with the big two, ABC and Gaumont, in major centres. Typically, in the Brighton area, he opened a cinema at Kemp Town in an outlying district and another in the nearby town of Lewes but did not tackle the city centre. His Odeon in Wallington, near Sutton, Surrey, was very much the poor relation of the huge Plaza which opened three months later in the centre of Sutton itself. That was bought by an expanding chain just before opening: but the chain was Granada, not Odeon. Deutsch was not yet playing in that league.

The New Odeons

At **Worcester Park** and **Tolworth** in Surrey, where no cinemas existed, Yates, Cook and Darbyshire provided well-appointed but uninnovative designs for two Odeons.
The Worcester Park frontage seems to have been one of the first on which long runs of neon (in this case, red) were used to highlight the building at night, although the main sign was still of the halo type.

Tolworth was on a greenfield site that aroused much ridicule. Sidney Swingler recalled a trade paper depicting Oscar Deutsch with double-barrelled shotgun shooting rabbits with only a half-finished Odeon in sight.

This cartoon was in the same spirit as a "poem" by the editor of the *Daily Film Renter,* recollected by Dickie Dewes, which ran:

There's an old mill by the stream, Nellie Dean
Where we used to sit and dream, Nellie Dean
Where once we'd bill and coo, there's a concrete mixing crew
Deutsch is going to build there too, Nellie Dean

Dewes noted that new building estates were provided with Odeons before the houses were finished, presumably to head off competition.

W. "Bill" Cartlidge, in his autobiography, *Golden Hill To Golden Square,* recalled: "Odeon were... opening cinemas in the most remote places. It used to be a standard joke in the industry for someone to say 'I was travelling in the countryside around Birmingham the other day, and what d'you think I saw?' and the inevitable reply was 'An Odeon'. Some of them had quite a struggle to survive until the war came along, after which all the cinemas which seemed originally to be in the wrong locations were then exactly where everyone wanted them to be."

In September 1936, Bruce Allan, the London correspondent of the American trade paper, *Motion Picture Herald,* wrote: "A trade joke current these past two years is that Deutsch builds theatres in rural districts where the population cannot be expected to reach cinema density for a very long time, but, in fact, in making his Odeons features of development schemes in new residential areas, Deutsch has not only reduced his construction costs, but in frequent instances has proved that he can draw paying audiences from the beginning, at the expense of adjacent heavily populated areas linked by road or rail to his sites."

Another modest Odeon appeared in Surrey at **Wallington,** where Yates, Cook and Darbyshire provided a low frontage of Portland stone with a corner entrance. This was reinforced by two lines of horizontal neon that enclosed the main halo name sign and extended to almost the far end of the auditorium wall on the side road. Wallington also had what was originally (to judge by the photographic evidence) an attractive single-floor auditorium. But this relied heavily on superficial effects: the flat side walls were painted to suggest shallow vertical fluting while the sides of the proscenium opening had lively and colourful decoration. It is highly unlikely that any of this survived the first

Odeon Worcester Park in mid-1935. As if there isn't enough advertising already, a crude poster largely obscures the windows above the canopy.

Odeon Tolworth in mid-1935. Just visible is the top edge of a poster frame mounted on the wall of the auditorium block. The semi-stadium arrangement allows for a low frontage with inner foyer under the raised rear seating.

Odeon Wallington. Exterior in mid-1935.
As at several other Odeons from this period, the canopy edge
lit up from within at night, silhouetting the slotted lettering.
The inner foyer view, looking back to corner entrance, and
auditorium both date from mid-1934.
Note the cross aisle in the raised rear section of the auditorium,
separating the front five rows of highest-priced seats from the rest.

Odeon Kemp Town, seen in mid-1935. The Odeon Cinema sign on the corner was a later addition with neon (lacking on the main sign), placed there to be visible from the sea front some distance away. In the auditorium, note the angular rather than curving line of the rows of seats in the raised rear section and the flower display in the space above the right side exit, also the curious absence of any central lighting feature.

redecoration. The orchestra barrier was solid and completely plain while the ventilation openings on the side wall had straight bands across rather than decorative grillework. Minor as this Odeon may have been, it still finished off the existing Gaiety cinema in Wallington.

Andrew Mather began his lengthy association with Odeon as one of its three principal architects on two cinemas in Sussex: an adaptation of stables at **Kemp Town** (or Kemptown, as it was sometimes advertised), and a purpose-built Odeon at **Lewes,** Sussex. Mather had made his name as the architect of the Capitol Haymarket, in London's West End, opened in 1925. He was also responsible for the Leicester Square Theatre in 1930.

Kemp Town already had a tiny independent, the Kingscliff, while Lewes had the more substantial and centrally located Cinema De Luxe which split the new films with the Odeon, which was on the fringe of the shopping area. Both these new Odeons had stadium-style seating. Sidney Swingler recalled that Mather brought to Deutsch "cut-and-dried schemes with all the facts and figures" that were cheap to construct.

Odeon was not yet fully committed to the style of lettering devised by Pearce for its main name sign. The architect's sketch of the exterior in the opening programme for Lewes shows the main Odeon sign in a blobby or inflated design although the Pearce one was actually used. CTA member John Fernee has noted another, thinner design of lettering for the Odeon name on the side walls of the entrance (the O was in the shape of an equilateral triangle with rounded corners, the other letters treated similarly) and this style was regularly used on Odeon still cases of the period.★ (Fernee also notes another variant, on the rubber flooring of the foyer, in which a round O enclosed the remaining four letters of the name.) Certainly, Odeon used a variety of styles in press advertisements until the Pearce design became standard from the autumn of 1935 and was noted, in small print, as being a registered trademark.

Another of the main Odeon architects, George Coles, began his association with Deutsch on an oddity – the Rothbury at **Portslade,** Sussex. This was a 550-seat adaptation of a partly-built assembly hall which competed for local custom with the much smaller, independently-run Picturedrome. Although Oscar Deutsch attended the opening and definitely claimed it as part of the Odeon circuit, it did not long remain so. It was far too small to suit the circuit he was establishing and the absence of the Odeon name is significant. John Fernee has noted: "The original directors were Oscar Deutsch (chairman), F. S. Bates

★ The Lewes cinema is fully explored by John Fernee as "a superb place to watch films, and very generously appointed" in the article "The Odeon Lewes" in *Picture House* no. 2, Autumn 1982.

Odeon Lewes in mid-1935. The frontage was crudely built up to dominate the far end of a picturesque street too narrow to allow a real canopy. The café was in a long arcade before the foyer was reached. The auditorium extends straight back. The false door frame by the front of the balcony matches a real opening on the righthand side. Odeon seemed to favour wide proscenium openings – this one is 55ft. across – but it was a way of maximising the number of seats.

and A. L. Middleton, who was the local builder of the theatre... The name 'Rothbury' was chosen by Mr. Middleton, as his birthplace was Rothbury, Northumberland. Deutsch and Bates withdrew from the Rothbury early on for unspecified reasons, leaving A. L. Middleton to run the theatre. He knew nothing about the operation of cinemas and quickly got into considerable difficulties. He appealed to Mrs. I. Merriman Langdon of the Ritz cinema, Seaford, to help him and in 1938 she signed a 21-year lease to operate the cinema. Her daughter is positive that Deutsch had completely withdrawn before her mother came anywhere near the Rothbury."

George Coles' first actual Odeon was at **Welling** in Kent.

Born in 1884 at Dalston, north London, Coles studied architecture at the Regent Street Polytechnic, then worked as an assistant to architect Percy Adams, and became a member of the Society of Architects in 1909.

By 1912, Coles had become Adams' partner and the practice worked on many cinemas, its first major achievement being the huge Rivoli at Whitechapel, east London, which opened in 1921. Practising on his own from 1922, Coles turned an old tramshed at Stratford, north-east London, into the vast Broadway Super cinema. Also in London, between 1928 and 1930, he designed the Carlton Upton Park and the Carlton Islington with their Egyptian-style frontages, and the Palace Southall with Chinese-style frontage. Coles demonstrated a flair for interior design with the classical treatment of the huge auditorium of the Elephant and Castle Trocadero in south London, opened in 1930. The Trocadero was followed by the Troxy, Stepney, in 1933.

Coles became the doyen of independent cinema designers in the 1930s, working on tight budgets and even tighter deadlines for many of the promoters and syndicates of the period. He was also highly influential in the film trade as architectural editor from 1932 of *The Ideal Kinema*, a supplement to the *Kinematograph Weekly*. His continuing work for Oscar Deutsch, among others, is testimony to his skill in satisfying clients.

The Odeon Welling was a somewhat heavy-handed scheme compared to his later work for Deutsch, with rather old-fashioned, ornately decorated bands and other dated touches in the auditorium – although it did feature an early example of one of his favourite devices, linear lighting down the centre of the ceiling. This was the first cinema in Welling, a rapidly expanding dormitory suburb of London, but in nearby Bexleyheath (which already had its independent Broadway and Palace cinemas) the very large Regal with an ultra-modern auditorium design had opened a few weeks earlier. By the end of the 1930s, Granada would add a cinema on the main road through Welling in a superior position to that of the Odeon.

A. P. Starkey departed from his Harrow patch to design the

Odeon Welling in mid-1935. There are three vertical bands of neon to each side of the projecting pilasters and further neon to each side of the ornately decorated capitals but no neon on the name sign. On the front edge of the canopy, "IN", "THE" and "OF" have been condensed and angled to help fit a long film title.

Odeon Weybridge in mid-1935. The slit windows of Starkey Odeons contained circular leaded panes that can be seen here where sections have been left open. The still cases at ground level are well positioned. The auditorium extends back with a brick wall exposed along the side road.

Odeon at **Weybridge,** Surrey, a logical outcome of his close association with Deutsch's co-director, F. Stanley Bates, who lived there. Far away from the town centre and its old-fashioned King George's cinema, the Weybridge Odeon was more conventional externally than Starkey's other work of the period, squarely massed without any deep central recess. But it was consistent with South Harrow in being tiled without any colour banding and using fluted tiles for variation across the top. The entrance was flanked by tall slit window openings while an unattractive horizontal vent above the canopy was covered by plain grillework. A parade of seven shops and flats extended to one side with a pitched roof. There was no neon added to the frontage, which was floodlit from the canopy, and advertising was discreet. The overall impression was dignified but dull, as though to avoid causing Bates the slightest possibility of embarrassment.

The auditorium at Weybridge was very similar to that of South Harrow but had a small fully fledged balcony. The decoration was slightly more elaborate with concealed lighting in side wall recesses and grille-covered openings to each side of the proscenium arch above side exit doors (the auditorium seems to have been wider than South Harrow).

The cinema as a whole was slightly more expensive, at £18 per seat, than other work by Starkey at this period which cost around £14. This could have been because of a higher finish to suit Bates or because it was erected in just twenty-five weeks. This speed was possible because the builder was one of the directors of the local company formed for the scheme.

The Kingsbury and Wealdstone Odeons brought A. P. Starkey back to the Harrow area. **Kingsbury** had been open countryside until the Metropolitan Line extension to Stanmore created a station here in 1932. A wide, gently curving high street, built up piecemeal around the station, included the Odeon at the western end as its most distinctive and only distinguished building, almost opposite the station entrance. The site was much narrower than at South Harrow but Starkey repeated the idea of the wide, low frontage with central recess, although here it was more infilled, and there was space for only one shop on each side. Like South Harrow and Weybridge, the facade featured tall windows and a single buff shade of tilework with contrasted fluted and plain surfaces. The auditorium extended straight back rather than across the site, and was slightly plainer than its two predecessors.

The Odeon at **Wealdstone,** to the north of Harrow, was more impressive but had a curious layout. By this time, Starkey had recruited Frederick Adkins as his senior assistant. Adkins has declared that he was responsible for designing Wealdstone and all the subsequent Odeons handled by Starkey after some involvement in Weybridge and Kingsbury. Previously contributing

Odeon Kingsbury in mid-1935. A single line of horizontal neon seems to have been added in line with the front edge of the recess. The building immediately adjacent to the left (not visible) made a startling contrast in mock Tudor. The auditorium side walls are plain except for the horizontal ventilation openings.

to the design of several cinemas in the practice of J. Stanley Beard and Clare (including the Forum Ealing, Morden Cinema and Luxor Twickenham), Adkins had most recently assisted W. E. Trent and W. Sydney Trent on the Gaumont Palace Derby.

The corner site at Wealdstone was almost square in shape and very oddly used. Externally, the Odeon had a long, low, buff-tiled exterior that swept around the corner and down a side street without any recess. It was simpler than previous Starkey exteriors with fluted tiles here linking the line of windows, behind which lay the large café which added £4,000 to the cost of the building and included a grand piano. The kitchen and servery were at the far end. Below the café, a circular entrance hall led to a long inner foyer, after which a flight of steps led to an octagonal shaped upper foyer. The café had an entrance from the inner foyer as well as one on the side road.

The auditorium, with a semi-stadium seating arrangement, did not extend at right angles to the line of the foyers and café but ran parallel – with, most unusually, the screen end at the front of the site. In fact, the short tower feature sticking out over the pavement with vertical Odeon signs on each side enclosed the chamber for the speaker behind the screen!

Adkins introduced a much softer, more streamlined auditorium than those of earlier Starkey Odeons. Ceiling ribs and horizontal bands in the side walls guided the eye towards the wide proscenium. Here, for the first time in an Odeon, there were clocks on each side of the auditorium over the side exits, rather than just one on one side, and this became standard. Although the seating totalled a fairly modest 1,222, this was one of the few Odeons provided with an organ. The British-made Compton had two manuals, five ranks, and an illuminated "jelly mould" console that changed colours on a lift in the centre. Quite why this moderately sized Odeon, in an outlying district of Harrow, had an organ (as well as such a substantial café) is a mystery. Its *Kine Year Book* entry refers to "occasional variety" and a 14ft. deep stage but merely the customary two dressing rooms. The only immediate competition was the small independent Coronet but perhaps it had an intimation of the competition to come from the Granada in Harrow.

The **Surbiton** Odeon was a striking addition to the circuit, less than a mile away from the Odeon at Kingston. Surbiton already had a small, old-fashioned cinema, the Coronation, around the corner. Despite its exterior expanse of buff-coloured terracotta, this Odeon must have been a scheme taken over late in the day as it was unlike any other and came with a 12ft.-deep stage, several dressing rooms, band room and lift in the orchestra pit – facilities far in excess of the Odeon norm. The architect here was Joseph Hill, not an Odeon regular, and the striking design of foyers and auditorium was by Mollo and

Odeon Wealdstone in the summer of 1935. It is surprising that no additional name sign appeared on the corner over the entrance. Notice the contrast between the Odeon's stark, gleaming modernity and the row of houses down the side street.
The auditorium features a more elaborate screen curtain than before, a precursor of those to follow. By this time, the standard fan-shaped pattern of Odeon carpet was being regularly installed. This seems normally to have been in shades of green.

Odeon Surbiton. Exterior in the summer of 1935.
Above left, the foyer, seen at the time of its opening, has a streamlined paybox with chrome bands. The rubber composition flooring is in tones of grey, red, purple and peach. The decoration on the walls is unmistakably the work of Eugene Mollo. No other Odeon foyer looked like this.

Auditorium views date from 1934. A curved proscenium frame corresponds to the curved corners of the screen

Egan, who had no other connection with Odeon at this time.

The entrance was set back within a parade of shops and flats towards the far right end of the development where there was space for a large auditorium to extend back behind. Light tiles contrasted with the brickwork of the adjoining flats. The two tall corner windows marked exit staircases from the rear of the balcony – rather pointlessly, huge raised letters in the tilework above the doors to the street identify each as an EXIT (it must have encouraged kids to dart in any time a door was left open). Thin black bands in the tilework linked the bottom corner of the glazing to the exits. The novel Odeon sign on the canopy had distinctive letters in art deco style that were 9ft. high in Staybright steel, perhaps contributed by Mollo or Egan. The standard Odeon halo sign appeared higher up, in odd contrast, but the original proposal had been for another variation by which the circular vent, just below where the sign did appear, was to carry a large O with the letters DEON inside. Instead, the opening was covered by strips, leaving brickwork visible behind. The base of the flagpole had to be raised to make room for the standard sign.

The distinctive, highly dramatic auditorium with its tongues of concealed light and rows of circular lights on the side walls bear the signature of Mollo and Egan. There were clear echoes of the team's decorative scheme for the foyer and auditorium of the Plaza Worthing in 1933, from the curved corners of the architraves and design of the internal doors down to the narrow-ribbed plasterwork around the front side exits (which is also reminiscent of their contribution to many Robert Cromie cinemas).

Highly unconventional was the treatment of the proscenium opening with its ribbed edge curving inwards at the bottom corners only to be terminated instead of continuing across to complete the surround. Instead it gave way to concealed three-colour footlights.

At Surbiton, patrons could buy tickets to the cheapest front stalls seats at a paybox down the side of the theatre and enter the auditorium through the right hand doors by the screen. This was a widespread feature at ABC cinemas and at many others built in the 1930s but seems to have been a rarity at Odeons.

Only two of the year's Odeons were heavy hitters in terms of box-office takings. One of these was the Odeon at **Worthing**, Sussex, opened in March 1934. It was by far Oscar Deutsch's biggest and boldest venture to date. The architects were Whinney, Son and Austen Hall.

This Odeon illustrated the extra risk, problems and costs involved in building in a big town centre. Worthing already had three cinemas but was ripe for a modern addition. As a result, three rival schemes were announced in late 1932. This led to the Plaza opening with just over 2,000 seats in December 1933, followed by the Odeon in March 1934. The third project was abandoned, although a fourth scheme, to convert a live theatre, was started and then dropped.*

The Odeon Worthing cost more than twice as much to build as the smaller Odeons of this period, although half as much as it was claimed the Plaza had cost. Making commanding use of an awkward island site, it was the first Odeon to contrast brick and faience and to balance rounded and rectangular elements. In contrast to the strong horizontal emphasis of South Harrow, this Odeon introduced a tower feature with name sign and clock to draw people's attention. The clock face with 8ft. diameter spelled out the words ODEON THEATRE (it is surprising that such a good advertising feature was not used elsewhere). The 67ft.-high flat-topped tower was partly a response to the location, which was slightly off the main shopping street and well back from the sea front, and so the Odeon needed to advertise its presence. The top of the tower was illuminated from within at night. This was the first cinema in Britain (and perhaps anywhere else) to have had such a tower in a modern style.** The low, streamlined forward extension containing the café made clever use of the site's difficult shape and linked up with the lower rounded cinema entrance. The treatment of the brick facade above the entrance seemed rather dull.

This second landmark Odeon exterior was highly influential in the development of a circuit style as well as on British cinema design generally, being widely illustrated in the film and architectural press. The Odeon was, in fact, a key building in the evolution of British cinema architecture.

The canopy extending around the entrance and the café extension was used to floodlight the exterior. The café was strongly advertised both on the tower and curving front in Odeon-style lettering: most Odeons of this period offered some light refreshment facilities but this was the circuit's most prominent venture into catering. The café proved a popular attraction in a seaside town full of visitors in the holiday season and was no

* The Plaza Worthing had been opened at the end of 1933 by the entrepreneur Lou Morris who made a habit of selling off his cinemas and moving on to new schemes (the Plaza Sutton was another instance). In 1934, he agreed to sell the Worthing cinema to the owner of the town's three older cinemas, C. A. Seebold. This would have given Seebold a huge advantage with film distributors and Oscar Deutsch quickly stepped in to acquire the Plaza for Odeon. (Seebold successfully sued Lou Morris for breach of contract.) However, Odeon had no real need for a second large cinema and in 1936 the Plaza was leased to the major ABC chain which played its own weekly fixed release there.

** The later Palace Chatham had a very similar tower, but entirely in brick, with modern clock faces on two sides. The inspiration for Worthing's clock tower may have been the one on Willem Dudok's Hilversum Town Hall (1931) but the two were not very alike.

Odeon Worthing, seen in the summer of 1935. The Odeon sign on the tower just below the flat roof was the first in the extended lettering that eventually became standard. Two narrow, horizontal projecting bands in jade green mark the line of café windows.

Odeon Worthing. The wide auditorium in 1935.

doubt prompted by the need to match the one at the recently opened Plaza.

In the entrance hall, the Odeon name was set in mosaic across the floor in front of the paybox – a striking decorative feature which reinforced the corporate image. (Many other Odeons had their name set in rubber flooring, as previously mentioned at Lewes.) From the foyer a curving staircase at the corner of the building led up to the circle (the curve might have been expressed on the outside to link up with the other rounded features).

The auditorium, with a little over 1,500 seats, was particularly wide because of the shape of the site. The side walls and ceiling were linked by wide plain bands closing in on the proscenium arch which was lit by concealed lighting and superficially decorated with a wavy pattern. Decorative interest was added directly above the front side exits by abstract bas-relief plaques which contrasted awkwardly with illuminated grillework in a repetitive, fountain-like pattern above. However, the auditorium was dominated by a circular, layered lighting fixture in the centre of the ceiling with a ring of stars in its base.

As both the Plaza and the older Rivoli had organs, the Odeon was provided with one. The organ was, as usual, a British-made Compton, of three manuals, six ranks plus solo cello, with a specially designed illuminated "jelly mould" surround to the console which was on a centrally placed lift in front of the proscenium arch. The sides of the console as well as the back of the illuminated seat featured the Odeon name, although not in the style of the main signs.

Whinney, Son and Austen Hall were also responsible for designing another south coast Odeon but the one at **Bognor Regis** was nowhere near as striking as Worthing.

The exterior featured a tall central recess faced in buff-coloured faience tiles, at the back of which the Odeon sign seemed to rest on four black piers which were crossed by narrow jade green bands. The height emphasised the cinema entrance over the long wings of shops with flats above to each side. These wings were in brick with a horizontal emphasis in the lines of windows. Two circular decorative features were placed above the windows, showing Pan on a donkey against a jade green background.

The Odeon had a splendidly streamlined foyer with trough lighting, leading to a semi-stadium style of auditorium which extended at right angles to the entrance and had all the charm of an aircraft hanger, improved marginally by the concealed lighting in the ceiling and bold curves on the stage curtain.

The second major addition to the circuit in 1934 was the Odeon at **Haverstock Hill,** which brought Deutsch into the inner London suburbs, in the plush Hampstead/Swiss Cottage area on land leased from the Eyre Estate. This was the only large cinema designed in the 1930s by T. P. Bennett and Son

Odeon Bognor Regis. This was one of several Odeons which opened before adjacent flats and shops were finished. Oscar Deutsch is seen enjoying a good laugh at the first night, with (from left) seating manufacturer W. W. Turner (sometimes an Odeon co-director), S. W. Clift (another occasional director, who later headed his own Clifton chain), W. J. Taylor, Odeon's general manager, and the local manager, Harry Yorke, holding souvenir programme. The view of the completed exterior and auditorium date from mid-1935. The aisle carpet is not in the circuit design.

(although the practice was responsible for the Saville Theatre in London's West End in 1931 and the small Royal cinema, Edgware Road, London, in 1938).

When the project was first announced, the London correspondent of the American trade paper *Variety* commented (31 October 1933): "There is not a picture house within a mile of the location, the nearest of any consequence being Golders Green on the north, Camden Town on the east, and Kilburn on the west. Many attempts have been made to secure property in the Swiss Cottage district but the price has always been regarded as prohibitive. Considerable mystery surrounds the new lessee. It is understood, however, that the scheme is sponsored by Oscar Deutsch..."

This was by a slight margin the most expensive Odeon of the year on a cost-per-seat basis, but it was money well spent and Haverstock Hill was an outstanding cinema well suited to serve as the flagship of the circuit until Leicester Square opened. Its prices of admission were significantly higher than other Odeons, ranging from one shilling to three shillings and sixpence (Worthing ranged from ninepence to two shillings and sixpence).

Built into the centre of a row of flats, the Odeon's entrance block was an incisive arrangement of stepped and curved facets which enclosed a condensed version of the standard Odeon sign – seemingly the first to add neon shaped to the individual letters. This was mounted above a tall, rectangular light box on which the current programme details were slotted in two sizes of lettering. At night the lettering was backlit and thereby silhouetted – very striking indeed, and perhaps the first time the idea had been used with such prominence (the letters on the front and sides of the canopy were also backlit, as at some earlier Odeons). The frontage was covered in biscuit-coloured terracotta with green bands, and with green neon outlining the salient features of the elevation.

Inside, Haverstock Hill had a superb fan-shaped auditorium on semi-stadium lines seating a substantial 1,544.★ Five lines of stepped trough lighting framed the proscenium opening: these could be arranged to go off in sequence from the outer row inwards before the curtains parted – a spectacular lead-in to the film and an idea further explored at the Odeon Leicester Square.

★ The fan-shaped auditorium was a good shape acoustically and aesthetically but comparatively rarely seen because sites most often lent themselves to long parallel walls which were only narrowed at the screen end to enclose exits, toilets, etc. and reduce the proscenium width. Besides Haverstock Hill, other notable fan-shaped auditoria included the Gaumont Palace/Odeon Lewisham, south London, and – much later - the main screen of the National Film Theatre on the South Bank in London. The Regal Hackney, north London, was a rare ABC hall that adopted the shape to make the best use of an extremely awkward site.

Odeon Haverstock Hill, circa April 1935. Besides the condensed lettering of the name sign and the unusual backlit advertising panel (with badly arranged lettering), note the unusual feature for this period of a paybox open to the street. The stills display case is perhaps the first to be headed by the Odeon name in the classic extended style. There is no call for a window over the entrance as the stadium plan eliminates the usual circle foyer. The vertical neon tubes on the projecting edges are in green.

Odeon Haverstock Hill. Interior view from early 1935. The Odeon clocks are set just outside the bands of trough lighting. As was usually the case, the raised rear section is separated from the front area.

Odeon Blackheath in early 1935. Another cinema in semi-stadium style with a wide frontage.

Odeon Cleveleys, seen here in mid-1935, was a takeover scheme but the exterior in faience with green bands had elements of the circuit style.

Additional lighting came from a large central fitting further back within the stepped edges of the ceiling. Lily Deutsch later declared she had taken a hand in the interior decoration and described it as one of her best achievements.

The cinema's flagship status called for another of Odeon's rare Compton organs – with three manuals, six ranks and solo cello. In 1976, Ivor Buckingham noted: "The illuminated console surround was reputed to be equipped with a light/sound device similar in principle to devices in use in discos today. If this is true, it is the only known instance of such a thing being used and was probably not successful."

Deutsch's first Odeon in the north of England was taken over halfway to completion – a very modest affair at **Cleveleys,** a coastal town near Blackpool. This was one of many cinemas designed by area specialist George E. Tonge who was one of the four directors of the local company formed to acquire it, the others being Oscar Deutsch, George Elcock and one T. Livesey. This incorporated a parade of five large shops to the left and had a large café.

During this year, Deutsch returned to home ground in the West Midlands, opening Odeons at Blackheath and Warley.

The Odeon **Blackheath** – designed by Stanley A. Griffiths, who had collaborated on the Odeon Perry Barr – had a low, light tiled frontage with dark copings in the form of a jazzy frieze higher up. According to Sidney Swingler, the auditorium was re-designed to resemble that of South Harrow. It bears some resemblance but is still rather more fussy.

Three days before Christmas 1934 came the opening of the **Warley** Cinema at West Warley, which was just over the Birmingham city boundary. This was originally announced in tandem with a Shirley Cinema, the Birmingham practice of cinema specialists Roland Satchwell and Ernest S. Roberts draw-ing up plans for both that were approved in November 1933.

Jack Cotton had put the Warley site together and the original promoters included Captain S. W. Clift and W. H. Onions. They had difficulties arranging the finance and Oscar Deutsch came on board, taking the post of chairman, with W. G. Elcock becoming one of the directors. Both Clift and Onions remained as directors, along with J. B. Whitehouse and J. H. Lyndon. The cinema retained the Warley name although the signage used the Odeon style of lettering and the building was advertised as the Warley Odeon within a couple of years of opening.

Deutsch was particularly sensitive about how the Warley cinema would look, as it was local to his home in Edgbaston, and it seems that he was dissatisfied with Satchwell and Roberts' efforts. The exterior was redesigned by the Nottingham-based T. Cecil Howitt, a rising architect who made a small but continuing and extremely significant contribution to the Odeon style.

T. Cecil Howitt's original scheme for the exterior of the Warley Cinema and a night view of the completed cinema.

The Warley, West Warley, as built. Among the many unusual features of this striking building was the flower bed in a black trough in front of the entrance steps. The word ODEON was soon added below WARLEY on the tower. The foyer was particularly wide and shallow with steps up to both stalls and balcony. The auditorium clocks had the letters WARLEY CINEMA replacing the numerals.

Born in Hucknall, near Nottingham, in 1889, Thomas Cecil Howitt worked in London from 1907 to 1909 before returning to Nottingham. After serving in World War One, he joined the Nottingham City Engineer's Department in 1920 and designed houses as well as the Council House (completed in 1929). After his scheme for the Birmingham Municipal Bank won a competition in 1930 (being completed in 1933), Howitt set up his own private practice.

The Warley Cinema was his first involvement in cinema work and a complete break from the classical style of his earlier public buildings. Howitt confined his cinema work to Odeon, evidently respecting Oscar Deutsch as a client, until 1939 when he provided one unrealised scheme for the Danilo circuit. His handful of Odeons were interspersed with major civic and commercial projects which brought him the greatest renown, and there is some evidence that he did not regard his cinemas as highly as his other work.★

As a newcomer to cinema design, Howitt must have referred to earlier Odeons for an indication of what was required and it is clear that he adopted the tower feature of Worthing for Warley – and considerably refined it. He initially came up with a spectacular scheme boasting a much taller tower than Worthing, clad only in faience, with a similar flat top (but on rounded piers) and another Odeon clock on its face. To reduce costs, the tower was substantially shortened and the clock eliminated.

Curved corners softened the vast areas of buff faience on the front elevation, the individual rectangular tiles being arranged in a basketweave pattern (in pairs at right angles to adjacent pairs) with the squares each pair made being emphasised by thicker joints. This became a standard feature of Howitt's Odeons and was adopted at times by other architects. The buff tiles were relieved by horizontal bands in jade green reinforced by neon across the top.★★ Further neon outlined the projecting edge of the top of the tower and the letters of the name sign. A huge recessed window appeared above an unusual curved canopy (with no provision for lettering). This was one of the simplest and most imposing cinema frontages of the 1930s.

★ Cinemas were generally handled by specialist architects who were looked down upon by the rest of the profession. One reason was the speculative nature of such schemes and the sometimes dubious characters of their promoters. The architect Julian Leathart told a group of colleagues in November 1933: "Of all the possible jobs you can get, cinemas are the worst – if you are able to build one out of every twenty cinemas you prepare, that is a good average."

★★ These narrow green bands would become a regular feature of Odeons. They were sometimes recessed and usually reinforced by neon tubes which were hidden by the green during the day. Presumably, white neon was used which would appear green at night.

Harry Weedon (top) began his long association with Odeon when his practice undertook the design of the Warley auditorium.

It is evident that Oscar Deutsch didn't care for Satchwell and Roberts' interior design either. He brought in an architect of his acquaintance, Harry W. Weedon, who had designed the rebuilding of enlarged premises for the family concern, Deutsch and Brenner, in Barr Street, Hockley, Birmingham. (Roland Satchwell retained credit for administering Howitt's scheme locally. His partnership with Ernest S. Roberts had been dissolved on 29 September 1934 and Roberts gained no mention.)

Weedon would become the key figure in Odeon design, even more significant than Howitt. Born Harold William Weedon in Birmingham in 1887 or 1888, he was educated, like Deutsch, at King Edward's Grammar School. He began studying architecture in Birmingham in 1904 and was articled to Robert Atkinson (architect of the highly regarded Regent Brighton) before being admitted as an associate of the RIBA in 1912, aged twenty-four. He went into partnership with Harold S. Scott and in 1912 designed at least one cinema, the Picture House at Birchfield, which opened on 1 April 1913. (This was the cinema competing with the Odeon Perry Barr.)

When World War One started, work dried up and the practice ceased by 1915. (Scott went on to become a prolific if uninspired architect of 1930s cinemas in his own right.) Weedon, who had recently married, volunteered for the Royal Flying Corps (precursor of the RAF). He was musically talented and had played the organ in his local church at Handsworth in Birmingham. When not in the air, he organised concerts and played the piano.

After demobilisation in 1917, he set about building up an architectural practice again. The war had transformed his personality and he was no longer happy with his wife, who had remained as she was. An affair with the young wife of an elderly neighbour resulted in a double divorce and a scandal that ruined his business reputation. Weedon moved to Leamington to work for a friend and became the successful manager of a catering firm there.

A few years later, Weedon was in Birmingham on business and ran into a member of his old Masonic Lodge whose friendly greeting made him realise that he would be welcomed back, and so he set up in practice again as an architect. He gained work in the housing, commercial and industrial fields and in 1932 first met Oscar Deutsch, six years his junior, on the assignment for Deutsch and Brenner. They hit it off immediately and a casual reference to his work on the Birchfield cinema led Deutsch to invite his ideas for the interior of the Warley cinema.

Weedon immediately looked for an assistant with cinema experience to join his office, which then numbered a mere half-a-dozen people. It seems that he never directly designed any of the cinemas that subsequently came from his practice but relied on a team of young assistants. (His role might therefore be likened to that of an executive producer like Michael Balcon at Ealing Studios who did not actually make films but closely supervised the work to ensure that his high standards were met.)

To handle the Warley interior, Weedon took on twenty-three year-old J. Cecil Clavering, who has described his background: "I trained at Armstrong College, [at Newcastle, then part of] Durham University, under Professor R. A. Cordingley and up to my third year I was steeped in Italian Renaissance. About that time I did some work on the Palladium, Harton, near South Shields, Co. Durham, for R. H. Morton and found that the application of 'classical' motifs not only looked ridiculous when reproduced in faience or terracotta – the only materials that could be afforded – but were difficult to design because of allowances for shrinkage and also late delivery slowed down building to a considerable extent. The answer appeared to be the new architecture advocated by Corbusier and the Germans." Clavering also opposed the use of classical architecture as being too grand for the poverty-striken north east of England. He was the draughtsman for three cinemas with classical motifs and designed one cinema more or less on his own, the Regent at Westoe, South Shields, which opened in October 1935 with classical touches dictated by the client.

The Warley auditorium bears some resemblance to that of Worthing, being dominated by a large circular fitting with concealed lighting in concentric circles. However, there was a hint of German design in the strong horizontal banding on the side walls. Rather unusually for an Odeon of medium size (1,530 seats), there were slips from the balcony leading to side exits in the splay walls.

Clavering devised the colour scheme in green, silver and black for the approval of Lily Deutsch. It is undoubtedly true that Oscar's wife chose the interior decorative schemes for Odeons, but it is less clear whether she ever originated any of them. At the very least, she can be credited with excellent taste.*

Other schemes

Perhaps the biggest scheme of the year to which Deutsch's name was attached, although only for a while, was one that would have replaced his old school and playground in the centre

---

* There was a precedent for her role, of which she was perhaps aware: Eve Fox, née Leo, the wife of American film magnate William Fox, took a keen interest in her husband's Fox theatres. She was a devoted if penny-pinching overseer of the furniture and decorations that appeared in her husband's vast movie theatres. She travelled to Europe and North Africa to buy works of art and furnishings to put on display at the San Francisco and Atlanta Fox Theaters, among others, and influenced the interior design of the Fox Theaters in St. Louis and Detroit.

of Birmingham. The site was acquired for a new cinema for £400,000, enabling the King Edward Grammar School to move to Bristol Road at Edgbaston. The proposal for a 3,000 seat cinema, designed by Frank Verity and Samuel Beverley and costing £1 million in all with shops and offices on the New Street frontage, was linked to Deutsch and Odeon in December 1934 but it was too large for him to handle at this time and by April 1935 Paramount had taken over the project (although it would not be until September 1937 that the last of the American company's provincial chain opened there – with 2,424 seats, and a small but striking frontage on New Street).

An insight into the way cinema schemes developed was provided by a case that came to court in July 1936. A Solihull builder, Alfred Ford, unsuccessfully sued Oscar Deutsch at the Birmingham Assizes for breach of contract. In January 1934, a Birmingham estate agent had suggested a good site to Deutsch for an Odeon at Banbury, Oxfordshire. Ford claimed that he was encouraged to buy the site and that Deutsch had agreed to lease it on 6 July of that year. It was alleged that Deutsch then attempted to alter the agreement but Ford would not accept the changes. Deutsch returned the lease, unsigned, in February 1935 and did not reply to a letter sent by Ford two months later. Ford's counsel suggested that the owners of an existing cinema in Banbury had persuaded Deutsch not to proceed. The Union circuit ran the Palace there and it could have been part of a shortlived reciprocal agreement between Union's Fred Bernhard and Deutsch not to build on each other's toes. On the other hand, Union may have caused Deutsch to lose interest by threatening to put up a new Ritz there: it claimed to have a site in November 1935 (possibly the one that Ford owned) and even listed the Ritz as a *fait accompli* in the 1937 *Kine Year Book* although it had not been built. Deutsch denied having made any agreement with Ford and won the case with costs.

Any agreement that had existed between Union and Odeon went spectacularly sour, according to W. "Bill" Cartlidge in *Golden Hill To Golden Square*: "Fred Bernhard, for some reason best known to himself, seemed to be waging a personal war against Oscar Deutsch. We all had strict instructions to report on any activity which could conceivably involve Odeon. If there was the slightest rumour that Odeon were going to build in a certain town, then Joe Kean, Fred Bernhard's site finder, was tied down to the area until he could come up with something to oppose Odeon. Whether or not Oscar Deutsch used similar tactics I know not."

By the end of the year, with his stream of openings and announcements of acquired sites, Deutsch had stirred up opposition within the film trade. The Cinematograph Exhibitors' Association launched its "limitation policy" to curb expansion, by which it actively helped exhibitors oppose the granting of provisional licences to new cinema schemes. It seems that the CEA may have funded (or helped to fund) appearances by a specialist lawyer, E. T. Rhymer, who put forward the argument of "surfeit" or "redundancy" or "over-seating" that was only occasionally successful.

1935: THIRTEEN OPENED AND FIRST TAKEOVERS

Odeon opened thirteen new cinemas during the first ten months of the year. There was then a dry spell of more than three months before the next Odeon appeared at the end of January 1936. Perhaps it just happened that no site was ready. There was certainly other activity: several existing cinemas were taken over during the hiatus. And, after all, the year's earlier openings were unevenly spaced, with none occurring in February, June or August. But the gap might be linked to Oscar Deutsch's medical problems during this period, which attracted trade attention. Although he was at the opening of the Odeon Finchley on 14 October, seated on stage in a Lloyd Loom chair with the other VIPs, he was unable to make his usual speech. *Kinematograph Weekly* of 17 October 1935 commented: "His health has occasioned considerable anxiety recently." A month later, the *Kine* reported that Deutsch was "not yet in full harness [but] making good progress" (21 November 1935). This was only a year after Deutsch had entered a nursing home for a "slight operation" (*Kine*, 29 November 1934).

The new cinemas notably included four more of A. P. Starkey's distinctive contributions. But the year was most significant for the opening of the first Odeons from T. Cecil Howitt and Harry Weedon after their work on separate aspects of the Warley Cinema. Their buildings at Kingstanding and Weston-super-Mare set new standards in contemporary cinema design.

But Oscar expanded his circuit even more than in 1934 by other means. His earlier properties – the Royal Alfreton, Grosvenor Bloxwich, Picture House Brierley Hill, Odeon Perry Barr and Silver Worcester – had been grouped as The Picture Houses (Midlands) Ltd., with M. G. Mindelsohn as managing director, and managed by Cinema Services. Now they were taken into the Odeon circuit and the first three renamed Odeon.

Deutsch seems to have been frustrated at the rate of expansion, given the confidence he had gained in running cinemas. He was certainly not short of sites to develop and had seemed initially intent on building up a circuit of entirely new Odeons. His growth was now fuelled in part by taking over schemes from other promoters and even cinemas that were half-constructed, not always in the modern style which he now preferred. He had

acquired a few small, early picture houses but only to provide the core of new Odeon sites, their demolition usefully reducing competition at the same time.

In 1935 he began taking over important existing cinemas for continued operation as part of the Odeon circuit, branding them with the Odeon name. In fact, during the year more cinemas were purchased than opened. This had the effect of diluting the Odeon image as some of the takeovers were old and second-rate properties, but Deutsch must have made a decision that this was a necessary step to speed up growth and make full use of the financial resources at his disposal. The success of some of the less satisfactory properties in places like Bath and Croydon proved that having the right film and the right location mattered more than anything else, but these cinemas would always be a letdown in terms of what Odeon represented. Others, however, were more recently opened cinemas of fully acceptable standard if not in the circuit style. (See the takeovers section at the end of this chapter for a fuller survey.)

It was also during 1935 that the Odeon name signs in red with gold edging became regularly reinforced by red neon shaped to the letters in place of the backlighting and halo effect. However, at some Odeons with more than one sign, smaller ones more visible from afar carried neon while the main signs did not: this applied to Starkey Odeons with their deep recesses and to Southgate.

And in this same year a young photographer, John Maltby (1910-80), was commissioned to photograph each new Odeon at opening for publicity purposes. He was also paid to record the earlier Odeons and the cinemas that were taken over. His negatives (now held by the National Monuments Record) are the basis of an invaluable pictorial record to which this book is greatly indebted.

For much of the year there were continuing negotiations with United Artists over the American distributor's acquisition of an interest in Odeon in exchange for guaranteeing access to its major British releases and Hollywood fare. Deutsch was anxious to secure a steady supply of quality domestic pictures because of his patriotic desire to show British pictures and his need to meet

Odeon Weston-super-Mare. The exterior postcard view, taken shortly after the cinema opened, contrasts it with the much older buildings opposite. (Courtesy of Philip Yaxley.) In the auditorium view looking forward, the lighting on the fluted columns at the sides of the proscenium opening makes it hard to distinguish them from the curtains.

In the view to the rear, note the padded arm rests even in the front row, the dull design of seat standards, and the straight edge of the orchestra front with the organ console partly visible behind. The balcony front is more curved than it appears.

quota obligations without alienating audiences with quota quickies. He also required major Hollywood films if he was to build successful Odeons in the larger towns, including a new theatre in the heart of London's West End. United Artists desired to improve its receipts from the British market and shrewdly recognised Deutsch as a good bet to achieve this.

New Odeons

This year's Odeons were almost all in London and the outlying suburbs. There were two additions in the Birmingham area and one in the West Country. The average size of the cinemas was rising.

T. Cecil Howitt's superb Odeon at **Weston-super-Mare,** Somerset, opened in May. This was the first instance of a small cinema being demolished to provide part of a site.

The architect made spectacular use of a prominent corner location. The frontage was dominated by a square tower like the one he had introduced at Warley, its flat slab top with rounded corners carried on twelve short rounded columns. The tower was lit up at night from within and flower boxes were at one time placed between the columns. The tower and other rectangular elements were tied together by the canopy sweeping around the corner. As at Warley, the biscuit-coloured faience tiles were arranged in pairs to form squares with a subtle basketweave pattern. The mass of faience was again relieved by a large recessed win-dow which allowed light into the balcony foyer, as well as by four parallel green bands – reinforced by neon tube lighting, at the top edge of the facade, bypassing the tower – and by the red and yellow Odeon sign mounted on one side of the tower. The recessed window incorporated some decorative work in stained glass.

Below the canopy was a curving entrance with side walls tiled in the light faience and raised flower beds in front. The front of the flower beds, the flanking walls and the surrounds to the rows of shops to either side were faced in black vitrolite. A similar use of black had occurred at the entrance of the South Harrow Odeon.

Howitt's first Odeon interior had a clean, geometrically precise and (for the period) simple design. The main foyer gave slight but proper emphasis to the broad flight of stairs at the far end, leading to the balcony, with the stalls entrance doors to the right. The staircase divided at the half landing and doubled back on each side to the lounge overhead and the entrance doors to the balcony.

This was a wide auditorium with the largest capacity (1,807 seats) of any of the year's new Odeons. Howitt seems again to have modelled his approach on Worthing but pared down the treatment (no ornamental grillework, no central light fitting).

There was a close similarity in the way the walls and ceiling narrowed only slightly towards the screen in flat, plain steps but, whereas Worthing introduced curves, Howitt was more rigorous and used straight lines. He added concealed lighting to the edge of the bands across the ceiling, as well as within the proscenium as at Worthing. The proscenium arch seemed to rest on the wooden architraves of the side exits which incorporated the very first Odeon clock faces to be enclosed by an octagonal frame echoing the shape of the letter O in the trademark sign (this clock shape became standard in following Odeons). The one seemingly unnecessary feature at odds with the rest of the design was the fluted columns at each side of the proscenium opening.

Concealed trough lighting illuminated the rear stalls while the rim lighting of a large recess in the ceiling provided illumination for the balcony. Horizontal panels of decorative grillework with cylindrical light fittings at each end made a small contribution to relieving the severity of the side walls. More than other Odeons, much use was made of combing the plaster to break up the surfaces in varied perpendicular bands. Doubtless, Howitt would have preferred a straight balcony front with straight rows of seats, as found in many early cinemas – but these were in the now customary gentle curve that improved sightlines.

Because this cinema was in a resort, a three manual, six rank Compton organ with solo cello was provided with a "jelly-mould" illuminated console.

The Harry Weedon practice was commissioned to design a cinema for the Birmingham area of **Kingstanding** by B. G. Vale, formerly known as Beniamino Giuseppe Domenico Valsecchi, a naturalised Briton who described himself as a film renter making his first venture into cinema building. The cinema was to be called the Beacon.

Kingstanding was a rapidly expanding new council suburb with 5,167 houses within a mile of the site, and 4,000 more imminent. The potential for a cinema on this location, where six roads converged on a large roundabout, had been obvious for some time. As mentioned earlier, in April 1932 a partnership of Oscar Deutsch, George Parker and W. W. Turner had been granted an option on the site by the Birmingham Estates Committee. Two years later, long after the option had expired, B. G. Vale gained a lease at a lower price than that which had been offered Deutsch and applied successfully for a provisional licence in April 1934. After the cinema had been designed, Vale teamed with W. H. Onions (another promoter who was sensitive about his name: he liked it pronounced O'Nions), and the pair then sold the scheme to Picture House (Kingstanding) Ltd., a new company formed by Deutsch, with Vale becoming a director who would also manage the new house. Under Deutsch, building

Odeon Kingstanding. The round brick corners with faience base and narrow doorway enclose the separate projectionists' staircases.

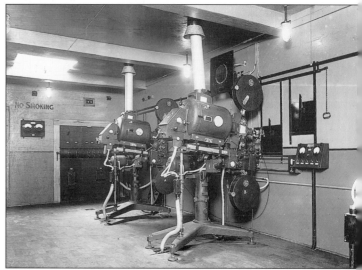

Odeon Kingstanding. The neon does not outline the building at night as thoroughly as later installations. In the projection box, the projectors are British Thomson-Houston. Note the handle on the front wall at right, for dropping shutters in case of fire.

work started in September 1934 with a mid-April 1935 completion publicly announced by Weedon.★

Harry Weedon had given J. Cecil Clavering the job of designing the Beacon after his work on the Warley Cinema. Clavering came up with the striking scheme that was built, omitting only his idea of a searchlight mounted on the central fin to comb the sky (probably suggested by the beams of light emanating from Rudolf Fränkel's Lichtburg in Berlin, opened in 1930). By April 1935, when it was three-quarters built, the cinema was set to be part of the Odeon chain. It opened under the Odeon name towards the end of July.

In 1972, Clavering recalled: "About the time I joined Harry Weedon, Leathart and Granger had just finished Dreamland at Margate with its fin-like vertical feature and this motif seems to me the ideal emblem for a cinema. It provided the height necessary for displaying the Odeon by day and particularly by night to a wide area and the vertical line took the eye down to the programme displayed on the canopy over the main entrance. I [later] worked with Julian Leathart during the War and he used to pull my leg unmercifully for lifting his Dreamland idea for the glorification of Oscar Deutsch.

"I was asked to prepare an interior perspective and I remember doing a simple German type interior in green, black and silver which pleased Mrs. Deutsch very much, especially as it was cheap to carry out compared with the atmospheric Greek, Roman, Egyptian and Moorish interiors of the time. So here again another standard symbol came about.

"There then followed quite a number of cinemas on the same design basis – they included Sutton Coldfield, Colwyn Bay and Scarborough, and they were all done in one week and submitted on the same day for planning approval.

"Why were we so far ahead of the Twenties? Well, I think the answer was the need for speed in design and construction which required a simple approach and standard design themes which could be applied to any situation, and this was not possible with any historic forms.

★ This optimistic date may have been given to deter a rival scheme. The nearest cinema to Kingstanding was the Mayfair on College Road at Perry Common, opened in 1931. The Mayfair's directors made strenuous efforts to gain approval for a new 1,500-seater designed by Hurley Robinson for a site 600 yards away from the roundabout, on the Kingstanding Road near Oscott Hill. Permission was refused in April 1934 when Vale's scheme was approved, refused again on 16 July but granted on a third application on 15 October. Vale had successfully played the "little man against the big operator" card, only to have it turned against him when he went into partnership with Deutsch and other "big names". However, by this time Vale had such a lead that the Mayfair scheme was abandoned.

"Harry Weedon never interfered with the design. He used to come in with a site plan and say, 'Deutsch would like X number of seats and when can I show him a scheme?' The scheme was supported by one of my rather wooden perspectives. I think most schemes took about a week and a perspective perhaps two days. I don't remember any criticism by either Harry Weedon or Deutsch and they appear to have accepted thankfully whatever was offered."

Although the Odeon Kingstanding was only a modest-sized suburban development that would never be a top money-maker for the circuit, it was externally one of the most spectacular and brilliantly designed of all 1930s cinemas, its impact reinforced by a spacious site that allowed the facade to be set well back from the road and the building to have plenty of space all round, including a large car park at the back. It would have been possible to put a cinema with twice the seating capacity on the site.

The exterior at Kingstanding included all the elements that were to provide the essence of the Odeon style, brought together with a perfection that would not be surpassed. There was the skilful use of high-quality facing brick to contrast with the faience tiles; the rounding of corners for a softening, stream-lining effect; the minimal introduction of windows; and the prominent placing of a vertical feature (here fins, elsewhere sometimes a tower) to advertise the position of the cinema from a distance. By night, there was the use of neon to dramatise the shape of the building and provide continuity with its daytime appearance.

This cinema partially introduced one of the nicest aspects of Weedon Odeons (not emulated by most of the circuit's other architects): that the ugly auditorium roof should be concealed from view as far as possible. Here, Clavering increased the stepping-up of the brickwork towards the fins as a last-minute measure to hide the pitch of the roof (the original plans show a single step, evidently insufficient). The back wall was also built up by several feet to conceal the roof from patrons using the car park. While the roof could be seen from the side, this was not the case in later Weedon Odeons.

The Odeon sign at Kingstanding was enormous while the announcement of the current attraction was modestly confined to the canopy edge and small posters rather awkwardly positioned at each side. The sides of the fin carried the word CINEMA rather than ODEON indicating that the latter word had some way to go before it became a household name.

The auditorium behind this show frontage was in one respect weakly designed, perhaps to cut construction costs. The front and rear exits from the stalls, the rear stalls toilets, and the staircase exits from the balcony were built out from the auditorium walls rather than fitted inside the basic shape. This did at least avoid extending the exits into the auditorium. Front stalls toilets were placed to each side of the stage but the splay walls were so minimal that the space behind them was only sufficient for storage whereas in larger cinemas there was room for exit passages and toilets. The result was a number of awkward extensions to the main auditorium shape but they were well finished in quality facing brick.

Internally, the cinema was a bit of an anti-climax: comparatively plain and unexciting, but in accordance with what would become the circuit ideal of an eye-catching exterior and a comfortable but unostentatious and therefore more relaxing interior.

The auditorium was particularly economical in design, virtually stadium-style with no overhang of the small and rather remote balcony and a low, constant-height ceiling. The balcony seating, in nine curved rows of thirty-six seats, was unusually well spaced, providing plenty of leg room. Square art deco suspended lighting troughs were the main source of illumination, along with concealed lighting around the proscenium. Fountain-style decorative grilles by the side exits were very similar to those at Worthing.

The cinema's frontage made a huge impression, especially in architectural circles. It was prominently featured in the *Architects' Journal*'s immensely popular Special Cinemas Number (7 November 1936, reprinted as a booklet), where it led the pictorial section on recently completed cinemas with day and night exteriors, simplified plans and small interior view.

The warm response must have elated both Oscar Deutsch and Harry Weedon, cementing their professional and personal relationship and encouraging them to adopt elements of its design as the Odeon house style.

Sidney Swingler recalled, "Though [its design] wasn't copied, it did make Oscar Deutsch change his mind about neon because those vertical strips of neon certainly made the architectural features stand out much more than they would have done with floodlighting."

W. H. Onions had commissioned the Weedon practice to handle a cinema scheme he was promoting at West Bromwich, and this too was designed by J. Cecil Clavering. Oscar Deutsch was expected to join the venture but he did not like its location outside the town centre at Carters Green and ruled out any participation in January 1935, four months before construction commenced. By this time, the original plans for a 1,560 seater had been revised to bring the capacity up to almost 2,000, increasing the cost to £55,000. Called the Tower, it opened as part of a small circuit headed by C. O. Brettell in December 1935 with 1,922 seats, café and a Compton organ – it had no tower feature, but was named after a well-known clock tower at a nearby tramway junction.

The building had a streamlined exterior above a black plinth

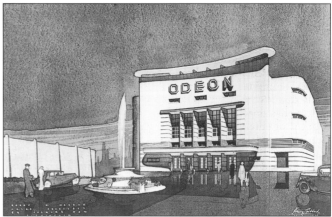

Top: Tower West Bromwich in 1936. This Weedon design had no connection with the Odeon circuit but looked like an Odeon and is shown here to demonstrate how it provided a model for later Odeons such as Loughborough.
Above: a 1936 sketch of the unbuilt Odeon that the Weedon office designed for West Bromwich. (RIBA Library Photographs Collection.)

in biscuit-coloured faience relieved by three bands of green across the top with superimposed neon strips. Although the Tower never had any connection with the Odeon circuit (and within a year became part of the rival ABC chain), its design did provide a model for later Odeons at Boston and Loughborough. The circle foyer and wide auditorium were not in the later Odeon style, although the design of grilles seen in the ceiling above the balcony at Kingstanding was repeated here.

The Tower would seem to be the cinema in the following story related by Robert Bullivant (who joined the Weedon practice and worked with Clavering under circumstances to be described later): "It's hard to believe but on one of the very earliest ones – fortunately not for Oscar, it was for another firm – we put in the balcony and, if you have a gangway running across it from side to side half way up the balcony, then you change the rake because otherwise people sitting in the back half of the balcony can't see over the heads of the people in the front half. I remember going with Weedon to see the client on the site and having to admit that we'd made a cock-up of the whole thing – it was sheer ignorance on our part. We made several changes and paid for it ourselves. We had to learn as we were going along."

Deutsch found a location he did like in West Bromwich during 1935 and engaged Harry Weedon to design an Odeon for it. The site was that of Hudson's Dry Soap Factory at Queen Street and Pitt Street. Plans were submitted in January 1936 but the local Watch Committee turned the scheme down, the unofficial reason being that it considered saturation point had been reached with six cinemas operating in the town. Deutsch had misjudged his chances of entering West Bromwich. He would not have done badly making the Tower part of his Odeon chain as it had a good run under ABC, only closing in 1968 to become a bingo hall.*

A. P. Starkey's four Odeons of 1935 were the last with deep central recesses on wide frontages and all were outside the Harrow area. Designed for (or with) Starkey by Frederick Adkins, they were less severe externally, introducing decorative touches and colour highlights. The Odeon at Colindale opened in January and the other three opened in quick succession in September

* An unexplained Weedon scheme of this period is for a cinema in Alcester Road, Moseley, Birmingham, at no. 82 and adjoining Lonsdale House, opposite the junction of Alcester Road and Park Road. Weedon applied for a licence in February 1935 but the name of the promoter for whom he was acting is not indicated and the cinema was never built. No Odeon link has been established. After the Tower, C. O. Brettell engaged Weedon to design his Regal at Darlaston but the final scheme for the cinema, as opened in September 1938, was by Ernest S. Roberts. Otherwise, all Weedon's subsequent cinema work until 1939 was for Oscar Deutsch.

Odeon Colindale, circa April 1935. The shops were leased by a tobacconist, confectioner and estate agent and for a piano showroom. See overleaf for auditorium view.

Odeon Colindale, circa April 1935. (This was the first cinema that John Maltby photographed for Odeon, three months after opening.)

Odeon Sudbury Town in September 1935. The vertical Odeon signs carry neon but not the one on the back wall. Neon outlines the edge of the recess and adjacent parade. The faience cladding continues along the shopping parade at ground level, but gives way to brick and a pitched roof at the upper levels further along to the right. The dark panels between the narrow windows on the wings recall Colindale. Sudbury is one of two auditoria where the seat standards display the Odeon name.

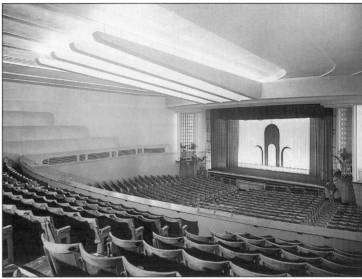

Odeon Finchley. Night view courtesy of Philip Yaxley. The attached retail space was large enough to accommodate a showroom to the right for Hall's Car Sales — a very long term occupant. In the auditorium, the "orchestra rail" provides an opportunity for art deco embellishment and all the Starkey Odeons took advantage of this. Photographer John Maltby seems to have been particularly impressed by this example as he did not normally record them in close-up (reproduced by permission of English Heritage.NMR.)

and October at Sudbury, Finchley and Sidcup. All were in the semi-stadium style. Starkey and Adkins also handled one later Odeon at Reading but this was more in the Weedon manner.

The Odeon **Colindale** was on the main Edgware Road between Hendon and Edgware in north London, close to Burnt Oak. It seemed to have a rather remote location although the eye-catching exterior would have registered with the busy flow of drivers, there was a substantial car park, and the surrounding flats and houses offered an immediate potential audience.

This development was comparatively expensive, according to Dickie Dewes, because the sloping site was extremely difficult to build on and added to the cost of the car park, while require-ments by Middlesex County Council (not specified) were a further complication.

In this instance, the entire back wall of the recess rose above the two wings and the buff-yellow tiles gave way to four or five bands in orange across the higher area which enclosed the Odeon sign. Placed above four shiny black piers (an idea possibly borrowed from Bognor Regis), the name sign was underlined by a narrow band of light green. The upper edge of the recess and of the low, box-like back corner extensions was picked out in the same shade of green, also used to highlight token keystones above the windows of the flats to each side. Further cladding in dull black emphasised the narrow entrances to the flats and formed a panel between the first and second floor windows on each wing.

The semi-stadium auditorium at Colindale was even plainer than those of the early Starkey cinemas (could it have been designed ahead of the more streamlined treatment of Wealdstone but delayed?). It made a rather ponderous impression with side walls sloping inwards the entire length of the auditorium (slightly claustrophobic but money-saving) while front side exits intruded into the auditorium. The only decorative interest along each side was a strip of grillework illuminated at intervals by cylindrical light fittings. The main source of illumination was a large laylight in the ceiling, which ran towards the screen, plus the concealed lighting around the proscenium.

The Odeon at **Sudbury Town**, near Greenford, west London, occupied one side of a large triangular development in the midst of new housing in the area called Sudbury Heights where Allen-dale Road and Sudbury Heights Avenue converged. The rest of the site was used for a V-shaped Odeon Parade of four-teen shops with flats above which included the apex of the site where the two roads converged. The cinema was less conspicuous with its entrance at the far end of the Allendale Road side. The auditorium was set behind at an angle to extend straight to Sudbury Heights Avenue where the back wall was exposed to view with exits at each side and a door to the stage in the centre.

There was no road extending along the third side of the triangle. Housing came right up to the site and had the useful effect of largely concealing the auditorium from view on that side. The right side was hidden by the shops and flats, although most of the brickwork was on view in the open service core of the development. There was a very small car park near the cinema entrance, just outside the triangle.

More than any other, this Odeon gave the impression of being a very local amenity, serving a small neighbourhood as part of a shopping centre, and is known not to have been very successful. It was close to Sudbury Town Underground station (but out of sight of Charles Holden's 1931 landmark and off any main road).

The cinema entrance was much narrower than at Colindale and other Starkey sites. The recess above the ground floor entrance here curved back with a horizontal green band near the top interrupted by the Odeon sign and forming the base for a line of short vertical green stripes all the way round. In contrast to the four black columns at Colindale in the centre of the recess, a black fluted column was placed across each corner where the cinema met the shops and flats.

The entrance hall was semi-circular in shape, reflecting the recess above. As in many other instances, the word ODEON was set in the rubber flooring, here extending from near the central entrance doors to the paybox set into the back wall.

The auditorium was livelier than the one at Colindale, with a strong horizontal emphasis towards the screen, especially from the long lighting troughs in the ceiling. The side walls were parallel and only the front exits, angled to face across the audi-torium, and the stepped ceiling above reduced the width of the proscenium opening.

The Odeon at **Finchley,** north London, had the most severe exterior to come from Starkey and Adkins. The frontage in North Finchley extended 270 feet along the High Street between two side roads and had the usual two wings of shops and flats with a particularly wide central recess marking the cinema. This featured rounded projections like turrets in the corners with narrow windows and floodlights on top (you half expected to hear the 20th Century-Fox fanfare). At night the edges of the front-tage were picked out by green neon, supplemented by flood-lighting, but by day there were no bands of green tiles and no black piers beneath the main Odeon sign on the back wall to relieve the mass of smooth biscuit-coloured faience. The recesses on Starkey's frontages offered promotional space for managers with a taste for showmanship and none more than Finchley's which boasted many attention-grabbing displays related to the films on offer.

Finchley was somewhat larger than most of Starkey's earlier

schemes, seating 1,296. The auditorium was taller, with four fins carrying concealed lighting in the main ceiling and guiding the eye towards the proscenium. The higher seating capacity was probably a response to plans for a rival cinema on the larger and more conspicuous Tally Ho Corner site almost opposite, announced in the summer of 1934. This would certainly explain why provision was made for an organ even though none was ever installed, as the Gaumont which eventually opened across the road had one. The extra seating reduced the space for car parking, which was in two separate small areas.

However, the Odeon at **Sidcup,** Kent, was the largest of Starkey's schemes of this period and, apart from Weybridge, the furthest away from his Harrow base. Although near the railway station, its location was not as good as that of the older Regal in the High Street, which was taken over by the Union circuit around this time.

This Odeon's frontage was in the familiar style but somewhat modified and softened. The space in the recess was reduced by a central extension over the entrance hall which brought the name sign forward while strip windows broke up the mass of buff faience.

The auditorium had bands in the ceiling with concealed lighting extending toward the screen while the side walls here curved inwards towards the proscenium with horizontal bands that also led the eye forward and that had varied patterns or textures imposed on the plaster.

What ended Starkey's run of Odeons? According to Frederick Adkins in a 1974 letter to this writer: "Mr. Starkey had the opportunity of dealing with the bulk of the Odeons as the circuit gained financial strength, but declined to cut fees, so Weedon and Mather were brought in, although Starkey did one or two more." Adkins went into further detail at my request: "The normal architects' fee of six per cent then applied (as it still does). Regrettably, hard-headed businessmen applied pressure to architects to work for reduced fees with the prospect of a flow of work, and this is what happened with Starkey and the Odeon work and this went elsewhere."*

In the spring of 1935, Oscar Deutsch made a further addition in the Harrow area by opening an Odeon at **Kenton,** less than a mile to the east of the town centre at the far end of a shopping area on the Kenton Road. Designed by the George Coles practice, this was very dull compared to Starkey's work in the same area – perhaps it was an existing scheme taken over. Coles set the tall entrance block, faced in cream terracotta, at one end with a two-storey parade of shops in contrasting brick. The large auditorium with overhanging balcony (which raised the seating capacity to 1,396) seemed rather old-fashioned, with delicately moulded fountain features on the splay walls lit from below, although the plain vertical ribbing above the front side exits, extended across the ceiling, was a more modern touch. The foyer, although seemingly rather bare, featured an art deco oval paybox.

Opened nine days later, the Odeon at **Isleworth,** an outer district of Hounslow, also came from Coles and was more notable. In a similar fashion to Kenton, the entrance was flanked on one side by a row of shops (only single-storey high) while the auditorium extended parallel some distance behind. Coles devised an oval outer entrance hall that was particularly striking, both in daytime and lit up at night. The main Odeon sign was mounted vertically with the letters condensed as they had been at Haverstock Hill (although a set of standard-width Odeon letters was widely spaced out over the bays in the brickwork on the side wall of the auditorium visible from the main road). The auditorium had a modern treatment of the splay walls, incorporating one of Coles' linear lighting features which rose vertically and extended over the ceiling, flanked by unusually plain bands of ribbed plaster like grating. The ceiling was stepped up around a central light fitting rather than descending towards the proscenium.

Opening in May, the Odeon at **Guildford,** Surrey, was perhaps the most important new build of the year in terms of location and business potential. This large town already had three small-ish cinemas and the Odeon would be the only major addition of the period. Andrew Mather shared credit with J. Raworth Hill for the design of the scheme, financed by Prudential Assurance after it bought the site in Upper High Street. Earlier plans for a cinema on the same street, and presumably the same location, had been put forward in January 1934 by architect Edward A. Stone: these were for an Astoria to follow the one just opened in Brighton for the same promoter, E. E. Lyons, but the scheme foundered because of "insufficient space" and then Lyons' death in August 1934.

---

* After I quoted these comments to Weedon architect Robert Bullivant, he responded (in a letter dated 23 May 1975): "By saying that Mr. Starkey declined to work for reduced fees, some people might receive the impression that Harry Weedon and others did work for fees lower than those set out in the RIBA Conditions of Engagement. Harry Weedon always upheld the ethics of his profession and would only agree to such fee adjustments as were permitted under the Conditions of Engagement." Bullivant later noted that Weedon took part of his payment in Odeon shares. Sidney Swingler told me that Odeon were entitled to pay lower fees because of the help the company gave: its architects' instruction book ran to over 100 pages and included information on the best positions for publicity material; for payboxes to ensure economical staffing; stage and projection room layouts including stage platforms; floor and wall finishes, and standard seating plans and the rakes for stalls and circle/raised tier, the latter kept low to ensure a low projection rake and reduced keystone effect on the picture. See Bullivant's description of the collaboration between Odeon and architect in the chapter "A Romance of Finance".

Odeon Kenton.

Odeon Sidcup. The horizontal strips to each side of the Odeon sign
are in black. The rounded columns by the entrance doors are in dark
green tiles. The strip neon was apparently in blue. The two lock-up
shops were originally rented for £100 per year.

Odeon Isleworth. The last letter of an Odeon name sign can just be seen on the side wall of the auditorium behind the parade of shops. The entrance was dramatically lit at niught. The striking screen tabs on display in the auditorium herald the more fanciful designs that would follow.

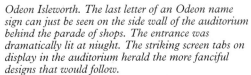

Below, George Coles, the architect of Isleworth and many other Odeons.

The Odeon occupied a difficult sloping site, and its entrance was set at the higher far end of the main frontage, most of which was occupied by a large four-storey development of shops with offices above, called the Prudential Buildings and partly occupied by the insurance company. The cinema space was leased to Odeon by Prudential.

Capped by a name sign, the Odeon's facade towered above the line of shops and offices to each side. The cinema was required to blend in with the rest of the development and it used brick and stone dressings rather than faience. The main decorative features were three tall windows with ornate grilles and the four decorative panels immediately below them. These panels were in bas-relief showing various couples in dramatic tableaux – dancing, kissing, etc. The sculptor's name does not seem to have been publicised and no signature was engraved but the style and theme recall the contributions of Newbury A. Trent to the front of many Gaumonts. This was almost the only instance of such work appearing on the front of an Odeon, however. The panels were floodlit from underneath at night, along with the rest of the upper frontage. The local council disliked coloured neon lighting and refused to allow any neon to be installed. Odeon kept badgering but as late as May 1939 the council reiterated its disapproval.

An awkward procession of rising foyer spaces was necessary to enable patrons to reach the stalls as well as the balcony. The auditorium was rather dull and undistinguished. Like the exterior, it had no resemblance to earlier Odeons. Perhaps the cinema had already been designed before Oscar Deutsch took the lease? Perhaps Andrew Mather was brought in by Deutsch to modify J. Raworth Hill's work? (This is not the Joseph Hill who designed Surbiton, even though the unusual curved corners of the proscenium arch are reminiscent of the earlier cinema.)

Andrew Mather's other contribution to the year's openings was the Odeon at **Chingford** in east London. Its flamboyant exterior in cream-grey terracotta has excited some architectural historians. David Atwell has described it as "a remarkable building with astonishing verticality in its design, dominated by a splendid tower" and notes its "sensational art deco lines". Richard Gray has referred to "a magnificent tower in reconstructed stone, with stylised figures near the summit supporting the central channelled section". In no way does its detailing correspond to the Odeon style and it is clearly a pre-designed scheme that Odeon took over.

The entrance was set down a side street, so the tower helped draw attention to it. The auditorium extended back diagonally (with the peak of the pitched roof visible as one approached from the main road). The entrance hall was peculiar, with a staircase placed at an awkward angle up the middle, leading to

Odeon Guildford. In the auditorium, there is a suggestion of lowered blinds with tassels attached within the rounded recesses above the front side exits, and plaster tassels are featured directly below in swag formation. Further tassels were suspended from the corners of the main light fitting over the circle!

Odeon Chingford. The Odeon name sign is awkwardly placed – the letters might have looked better fitted within the sections. Odeon flags are flying from the two poles. The globe light fittings of the auditorium are another old-fashioned touch in a dreary setting.

Odeon Barnet. The exterior design of this takeover scheme leads to two main name signs of equal size being placed at each side rather than the usual one in the centre. The individual letters are more extended in shape than usual. Note the neon piercing the shadow on the vertical sign at right. The guard rails suggest the open-air balcony was accessible from the upper foyer. The octagonal "O" shape of the windows above the framed stills is a coincidence. The poster between the entrance doors is a curious feature.

Odeon Shirley. The main Odeon letters on the frontage were two feet high.

the raised rear section of the semi-stadium auditorium (no balcony overhang). This auditorium was dreary and old-fashioned with a curved ceiling reminiscent of early picture houses plus front side exits that protruded awkwardly and ostentatiously into the auditorium. It was a let down after the exterior. But it did introduce a new and shortlived extension of "branding" in that the seat standards at the ends of each row carried the Odeon name diagonally, slightly raised and highlighted in colour. The same standards were also installed at Sudbury but apparently nowhere else. Quite why Odeon didn't retain the idea for regular use is a mystery. (Gaumont-British regularly used "GB" on its standards.)

At **Barnet** in Hertfordshire, an area which had interested Odeon earlier, construction started on a cinema outside the town centre on the Great North Road with a large car park at the rear. This was going to be a County cinema for the promoters of the existing Hermitage at Hitchin and County at Hertford, including the builder John Ray and architect Edgar Simmons. Then in March 1935, the name "County" was covered over on the large billboard at the front of the half-completed hall and the name "Odeon Theatre" was painted in huge letters on one side of the roof facing uphill towards the town centre. Oscar Deutsch took over with enough time left for the circuit pattern of carpet to be laid and Odeon clocks placed on the side walls – here, for the first time, the letters on the clock face were changed from ODEON and THEATRE (replacing all twelve numerals), to THE (in place of 11, 12 and 1) and ODEON (8, 7, 6, 5 and 4) with four thick dashes for the remaining hours, this becoming standard at all subsequent Odeons. Plans for an organ at Barnet were cancelled but the seating in alternate red and blue upholstery seems to have been ordered before Odeon came in.

The cinema's exterior was strikingly similar to that of the County at Hertford while the interior also retained a great deal in common, including the same style of laylight in the ceiling and acoustic wallboards in place of plaster on the side walls and ceiling. In 1938 Simmons and Ray teamed up on another cinema, the Dominion at East Barnet, which had an auditorium with a very close resemblance to that of the Odeon. Such duplication in the same area was very odd: it must have been hard at times for Barnet picturegoers to remember which cinema they were in...

Besides consolidating his representation in the West Midlands, the Odeon at **Shirley** in the Solihull area of Birmingham was another example of Oscar Deutsch's early policy of providing new areas of housing development with cinema facilities. As previously mentioned, it was originally announced at the same time as the Warley Cinema, to be a sister theatre called the Shirley Cinema, both designed by Roland Satchwell. W. W. Turner – whose company suppied the 1,156 seats – was one of

Odeon Southgate. The vertical name sign on the corner is lit up in neon at night, unlike the horizontal one over the entrance.

the directors. The opening in April is said to have been delayed because Lily Deutsch could not decide on the colour scheme for the auditorium.

In contrast to the Warley, Roland Satchwell remained the sole architect of the Shirley theatre and it opened with the Odeon name. There were shops to each side of the entrance and parking space for no less than 300 cars at the rear. The entrance to the cinema certainly claimed attention through a tall recess with a large window and the use of buff-coloured faience in contrast to the brick elsewhere, but the dull treatment demonstrated how much more exciting was A. P. Starkey's approach to such wide, low frontages. Besides the red neon on the name sign, there was 360ft. of green neon outlining the shape of the building.

The auditorium was on semi-stadium lines, dominated by a rectangular trough suspended from the ceiling with concealed lighting directed at the ceiling. The side walls had elaborate super-ficial decoration with a perpendicular emphasis and curtained windows high up. The reason for the windows was that Oscar Deutsch had agreed that the cinema would serve as a public meeting hall for Shirley when one was required (although some authorities demanded windows so that cleaners could work in daylight).

Southgate, in north London, was another scheme in an area of rapidly expanding population fuelled by the extension of the Piccadilly line of the London Underground. ABC had opened a large Ritz on Bowes Road nearby in New Southgate. Odeon appeared in Old Southgate, taking over a scheme designed by the prominent theatre architect, Bertie Crewe. This was rather heavy externally (it did not take up the challenge of Charles Holden's amazing station, opened in 1933) and also rather plain inside. The auditorium was notable only for stylised figures over the front side exits and in panels along the side walls of the centre and rear stalls although it did feature, by each side of the proscenium arch, the first instance in an Odeon of vents in a discreet honeycomb pattern of small round openings rather than a covering of decorative grillework.

Schemes... merely schemes

Oscar Deutsch was busily adding sites in 1935, but certain schemes – like an Odeon for Chiswick, west London, by George Coles and one for Cowes, Isle of Wight, by Andrew Mather – seem to have been quickly dropped. He was particularly interested in the south west of England and asked Harry Weedon to investigate the possibilities. In April 1935, Weedon dispatched a newly appointed assistant, Robert Bullivant, to the area.

Bullivant has recalled: "Not long after I joined Harry Weedon, he phoned me at about nine o'clock one Friday evening and asked me to be at the Madeira Hotel, Falmouth, at noon the following day to meet a man who would show me around the derelict Falmouth Brewery which was thought to be a suitable site for an Odeon cinema. While I was in Cornwall and Devon, I was also asked to inspect other sites, details of which would be given to me by my contact at the Madeira Hotel. After a stop for breakfast in Exeter, I reached Falmouth by noon on the Saturday and before I returned to Birmingham on the following Thursday I had inspected and partially surveyed sites in Falmouth, St. Austell, Camborne, Redruth, Yeovil, Barnstaple and Taunton.

"The name 'Odeon' was a talisman. Town clerks and borough surveyors were happy to meet us on Saturdays and Sundays and at any time of the day or night. The willingness of the town clerk or borough surveyor to give up their weekend was typical of a general desire to co-operate and remove any obstacles which might be in our path. There were two exceptions to this almost universal rule: the local cinema proprietors who had enjoyed a very profitable monopoly and the neighbours with genuine claims that the erection of a seventy-foot-high cinema would deny them light and air which they previously enjoyed."

In fact, Odeon was hardly a talisman as yet – the appeal was more the idea of a modern cinema. Certainly, some of the most stubborn resistance to Odeon's expansion did come from the south west of England, an area which was regarded as the stronghold of the independent exhibitor. At Barnstaple and Redruth, licensing committees seem to have favoured local operators and kept outsiders away, although a Gaumont Palace had opened in the former in 1931. There were many places in Britain where independent cinema proprietors were important figures in local business and politics and sometimes this seems to have influenced decisions to keep the major circuits out. Against this, many places were only too glad to have a new cinema to make them competitive with other towns and to bring in revenue on the rates.

Odeons were built to Weedon's designs at Falmouth, St. Austell and Yeovil – but not at Barnstaple in Devon or Camborne in Cornwall. In Barnstaple, Deutsch had proposed to spend over £30,000 on a Weedon Odeon seating 1,330 in Boutport Street, where the Gaumont Palace was located, but the magistrates refused a provisional licence. And Weedon's plans for a 1,000-seat Odeon on the site of the Commercial Hotel at the corner of Commercial Square and Trelowarren Street, Camborne, were abandoned in Spring 1936, probably because of the head start obtained by a local operator who started building the modern King's Cinema in September 1935.

Takeovers

The year's takeovers established the circuit in several larger towns and enabled it to concentrate on finding sites elsewhere, but the general standard and seating capacities of the acquired cinemas were sometimes unsatisfactory.

Most of the properties received little modification before being renamed Odeon. One exception was an old music hall not in cinema use – the Oldham Palace of Varieties – which was gutted and reconstructed internally. Another was the White Hall in Derby, a property that switched from ABC to Odeon on expiry of lease. After two months under Deutsch, it closed for five weeks of improvements and re-opened as the town's Odeon. Nevertheless, it seated only 913 and left the circuit in an inferior position to the new house that ABC built (the Regal with 1,840 seats) and the existing Gaumont Palace (2,175 seats). (The County circuit would take over the large Hippodrome, part of the Odeon circuit in due course, but this was never a satisfactory alternative.)

And when entry to Brighton, Sussex, was obtained via the seafront Palladium, Andrew Mather's practice was commissioned to completely modernise the narrow frontage and foyer before the Odeon name went up, thoroughly misleading patrons who found themselves sitting in an unaltered Frank Matcham variety theatre auditorium dating from 1888 (although it did have new seating and carpet in the circuit style). With 1,200 seats, this was too small for such a bustling centre, no match for Gaumont's huge Regent or ABC's vast Savoy, and it suffered booking problems. The recently-built Astoria had changed hands two months earlier, becoming a second ABC house in the resort. Whether this would have suited Deutsch better with its fringe location is debatable. But certainly the Palladium was only fit to be a stop-gap: Deutsch leapt at the chance to replace it with a better cinema later on.

The Regal Bath and Picture House Croydon never did live up to the image that Deutsch was cultivating with his new Odeons, being old-fashioned and on the small side, but they gave immediate access to important markets where it would have been expensive and difficult to find similarly well-placed sites and build from scratch. Even though they were extremely successful, the circuit could not achieve its full box-office potential with undersized halls. Bath, in particular, had a crowded, historic city centre which made new cinema building very problematical. The large, independent Forum was built on the edge of the centre. Odeon managed to lease the undistinguished but more central Regal, previously in Union hands. It seated only 863, but ABC suffered likewise with the elderly Beau Nash (1,088 seats).

The Lyceum at Taunton, Somerset, looked like a huge property from the outside but it seated only 678. Andrew Mather carried out some improvements but as an Odeon it was no match in size or location for the town's Gaumont Palace (1,476 seats).

The Royal at Torquay, Devon, was a former theatre with a low capacity (883 seats) that was outclassed by ABC's new Regal (1,600 seats).

The Lido at Islington gave Oscar Deutsch his first property in the inner London suburbs. It was out of the centre and an undistinguished hall but usefully located next to a police station in what was for many years a rowdy area. It was also one of the few cinemas of the period to have a fully rectangular screen with corners that were sharp rather than rounded.

Sometimes cinemas came in batches, requiring Odeon to take over undesirable properties along with those it really wanted. A case in point is its acquisition of the Hinckley and Dursley Theatres Company. The Regent and New Boro' at Hinckley in Leicestershire were of almost identical seating capacity (just under a thousand) but Deutsch's real plans initially focussed on a third cinema, then functioning as a dance hall, which he intended to replace with a modern Odeon designed by the Weedon practice. It was unlike Odeon to run two cinemas in a small town, let alone three, and in the end the idea of a new building was dropped and the New Boro' inherited the Odeon name. Also part of the deal was the tiny Victoria at Dursley, Gloucestershire, a 333-seater from which the Odeon name was withheld until reconstruction in 1948 after a fire.

Two very useful Hampshire properties came hand in hand: the Palace Andover and the Regal Winchester. The Regal was a recently opened cinema designed by Robert Cromie and superior to many new Odeons of the period. The older Picture House Winchester was also included but surplus to Odeon's requirements and closed.

The Morden Cinema at Morden, Surrey, was less than three years old when it passed into Odeon hands. Here the seating capacity was more than sufficient as a large site had been affordable in this newly developing area of outer London. The hall competed with the cinemas in Wimbledon and with ABC's Majestic Mitcham and later with the Gaumont at Rose Hill. Its location opposite the Northern Line Underground station was a great help.

Least worthwhile was the small Royalty in the holiday town of Broadstairs, Kent, which suffered out of season (and had competition from an older Picture House). It opened in October 1934 and Odeon took over for its first summer season. But the company had such a tough time that it was leased to an independent within three years, one of only two cinemas to leave the circuit in the 1930s. By then Odeon had much better representation in the area through a new cinema at Ramsgate.

The Odeon song

This was the year in which Odeon was first promoted in a song,

"Round the Corner", with the closing lyrics:

> Won't you meet me tonight
> Where your favourite pastime's right,
> It's round the corner at the O-de-on,
> Around the corner at the O-de-on

Clive Garner, the vintage record and film collector, writes:

"To my knowledge there were just two recordings of the Odeon theme song. The first record – 'Round the Corner', foxtrot with vocal chorus played by Billy Merrin & His Commanders (Cinecord OD1) – was recorded 7 June 1935 with Ken Crossley as vocalist. In 1935, Billy Merrin's Commanders, a well known Nottingham-based band of that period, was recording for the British Homophone Company that manufactured Cinecord records meant to be sold in the foyers of Odeon cinemas. It was a short-lived venture as there were only twenty-one records issued on this label and all but seven titles were also available on the company's Sterno label. The exceptions were the Odeon song and six titles recorded by GPO landline from the Odeon cinemas at Wealdstone, Haverstock Hill, Kingston-upon-Thames and Worthing, these all being organ solos by unnamed organists.

"The second version of the song – 'At the Odeon' Odeon Theme Song (Leslie Smith) (Odeon PO 54) – was recorded December 1936 by a studio group employed by EMI studios, either directed by George Scott Wood, Philip Green, or Harry Leader. I'm afraid I cannot identify the singer. This was a single-sided record not available for sale to the general public, bearing the trademark of the Odeon record company [quite separate from Odeon Theatres, with a registered trade mark of a temple and the Odeon name in rounded letters]. When I played this record recently on my weekly BBC Radio Merseyside 'Music and Memories' programme I had a letter from a lady listener who recalled it being played regularly as 'play-out' after 'God Save the King' at her local Odeon – I think she lives in Wrexham."

Bernie Weavers, an Odeon projectionist who started his career as a page boy at Shirley, confirms that the song was used as play-out after the National Anthem in the 1930s.*

---

* I am also grateful to Alex Gleason for his researches into this song, one version of which (they differ slightly) can be heard in the documentary *Odeon Cavalcade*.

1936: MAJOR EXPANSION

Odeon ended more than three months without an opening by inaugurating a cinema at Rickmansworth in Hertfordshire at the end of January. There was only one new addition in February at Newton Abbot in Devon but the pace of openings accelerated from March onwards to reach an astonishing total of thirty-two completely new Odeons by the end of the year (compared to fourteen openings by ABC and four by Gaumont – but, of course, these two major circuits were much bigger to start with.) Odeon originally trumpeted fifty-six new Odeons as appearing in 1936 (with fifty-one more in the planning stage), while Union threatened to build forty and Granada announced eight schemes. About 150 new cinemas were likely to open during 1936, according to *Kine Weekly* calculations, adding around a quarter of a million further seats. The Cinematograph Exhibitors' Association "limitation policy", primarily aimed at curbing Odeon, was clearly not working.

It seems new Odeons started up as soon as possible. There was no pattern: they often opened a couple of days apart, while the Odeons at Southall, Oldham (a major reconstruction) and Ramsgate made their debuts on Monday, Wednesday and Saturday of the same week. Takeovers were far fewer in number, the most significant bringing the Odeon circuit into Chesterfield, Ealing, Llandudno and Watford.

The thirty-two newcomers included many further suburban and small town halls (with several examples of Odeon's predilection for smaller seaside resorts that were of little appeal to Gaumont or ABC); but it also marked a trend towards entering larger markets such as Chester, Ipswich and Portsmouth. In addition, one completed cinema was sold off before opening and there were two other major conversions besides Oldham. In several instances, Odeon entered into direct competition with the Union circuit.

Oscar Deutsch was imbued with new confidence from his tie-up with the distributor United Artists, which was cemented in January 1936 and guaranteed a supply of important British and American films for the Odeons in the larger, more highly competitive situations he was now entering. In particular, it gave him the confidence to acquire the Alhambra Theatre in Leicester Square as the site for his West End flagship. Without a fixed supply of major new films, that cinema in particular would not have been viable.

At the same time, United Artists took a financial stake in the County circuit, creating the link that would eventually unite the two chains under Deutsch. Although Deutsch joined the board of County, the circuit's Swiss founder Charles J. Donada continued as managing director and the two companies remained separate, forming what was described as an alliance.

Weedon Odeons

Oscar Deutsch's faith in Harry Weedon after Kingstanding was made abundantly clear when the Weedon practice designed ten Odeons of 1936 and redesigned the interiors of two acquired properties. The new Odeons were all of outstanding design and included most of the year's heavyweights (in terms of location) – Chester, Harrogate, Lancaster, Scarborough, and Sutton Coldfield.*

In addition, to quote Robert Bullivant, "Harry Weedon was responsible for vetting, on behalf of Oscar Deutsch, plans for cinemas prepared by many other architects, and in some cases, vetting developed into an almost complete redesign." Plans were certainly sent to the Weedon office but, apart from the initial case of the Warley interior, only two examples of a redesign are known (Peterborough, Swiss Cottage) and it is inconceivable that Weedon would have criticised the work of such eminent figures as George Coles and Andrew Mather while it is apparent that many taken-over schemes continued to be unadapted to the circuit style in order to save money or time.

The Odeon at **Sutton Coldfield,** to the north east of Birmingham, was set back from the main road with its own access road, fringed by grass banks and trees, with a large car park at

---

* Although the Weedon practice was becoming increasingly involved in Odeon work, it remained active in other fields: houses, petrol stations, factories, etc. In contrast to the eclectic output of most firms, it largely designed work in the modern style, including a house that has been listed Grade II: Villa Marina on The Promenade, Craigside, Llandudno, built for Harry Scribbans and depicted in *Building* (February 1937). It looks nothing like a miniature Odeon.

Odeon Sutton Coldfield. The trees and other greenery at the outer edge of the site between the access road and main roads are a significant factor in the continuing enchantment of this view. The corner was originally occupied by two cottages and the ghost of a former inhabitant has appeared to cleaners in the right hand stalls area on several occasions. (Reproduced by permission of English Heritage. NMR.)

Odeon Sutton Coldfield. Main foyer and balcony foyer, both with circuit settees. Combed plaster adds some interest to the entrance hall and walls of the auditorium. (All reproduced by permission of English Heritage. NMR.)

the back which helped overcome its position half a mile south of the town centre (it was actually at Maney, a district of Sutton Coldfield).

Here, J. Cecil Clavering devised the perfect solution for a corner entrance in contrast to the centre entrance of Kingstanding. Opened nine months after Kingstanding, in April 1936, Sutton Coldfield had a brick slab tower enclosing a fin in standard buff-coloured tiles, on the top of which (as at Kingstanding) the word CINEMA appeared in red on both faces, reinforced by neon and visible from some distance around. The curving corner with projecting canopy seemed to bind the slab tower to a faience-clad wall set at right angles with a rounded end that enclosed a staircase from the circle and helped conceal the side of the auditorium. A red Odeon name sign in slightly extended letters was mounted on this face which carried a light green band at the top edge, just under the coping, that extended round the curve. Another faience-clad wall to the left of the tower, facing the main road, displayed a larger name sign (in squarer design with bevelled golden-yellow edge) as well as two parallel green bands near the top. Windows in sets of five punctuated the faience, the tall lower ones serving the double-height main foyer.

The exterior was a triumph of simplicity, at least the equal of Kingstanding, providing two of the very finest 1930s cinema exteriors in Britain, only two miles apart by main road.

The interior of Sutton Coldfield was intentionally less striking. By this time, a circuit style of sofas with chrome frames had become a standard feature and there was a row of these under the windows in the tall foyer. A series of pendant light fittings extended down the centre towards a full-height opening at the far end where a painting on the back wall showed a film camera on a tripod above actors in a costume drama. Stairs off to the right went up to a landing that overlooked the hall and led to the balcony through a small inner foyer. The auditorium was relaxing and unostentatious. The ceiling was confidently stepped down towards the proscenium with bands of concealed lighting, the side walls smoothly angled inwards with horizontal banding extending across ventilation openings.

The cinema was a considerable advance on the competing picture houses: the equally large Empress, then an independent hall, and the much larger Pavilion further south at Wylde Green, an ABC acquisition.

Clavering's next Odeon was at **Colwyn Bay,** opened just a week after Sutton Coldfield in plenty of time for the summer influx of visitors to the north Wales resort. The cinema replaced a building called Erskine Lodge and at the opening ceremony Odeon was congratulated on preserving many of the trees on the site (though they were not as much in evidence as at Sutton Coldfield).

This was another corner site but here the auditorium extended at right angles to the entrance, set back behind a curving parade of shops and flats. The low curved entrance projected further forward than the shops for greater visibility. The foyer extended straight back and the faience-clad side wall with Odeon neon sign and five tall windows, very similar to Sutton Coldfield, appeared on the other side here, a rather grand treatment for a side road. The buff-tiled slab tower was set back, built into the raised corner of the auditorium block with a broader, rounded front. A brick vertical projection carried the Odeon name rather than the word CINEMA. Four brick piers paralleled the slab tower. This was a striking variation on the Sutton Coldfield frontage, but not quite as satisfying in shape or in the disposition of brick and faience.

The inner entrance hall led to the stalls via stairs down in the centre and to the balcony via stairs up on each side. The auditorium was again rather plain and functional, with vertical bars predominating over the ventilation openings on the splay walls rather than the more extensive horizontal treatment at Sutton Coldfield. According to Tony Moss, CTA Chairman, there were plans for an organ as at some other seaside locations, but none was ever installed.

This large Odeon (1,706 seats) had been bitterly opposed by the proprietors of five existing cinemas who claimed that they had an average occupancy of only 28%. On top of that, it was poorly sited, away from the town centre.

"That never did very well. We ought never to have gone into there," Sidney Swingler has recalled. He related a story about the theatre's construction: "I had a phone call from William [Weedon] late-ish one night. 'I'm calling for you in the morning. We're going to Colwyn Bay. I'm in dire trouble and I don't know anybody who can get us out of it but you.' So he called for me in his Rolls and off we go to Colwyn Bay. They'd got the levels wrong. They started off with the wrong datum line. They used the plan for Harrogate for that. They'd got the front of the theatre with the foundations in and they were much lower than the pavement, so all the water from the existing pavement and the forecourt would go straight into the theatre. Anyway, they put it up a foot, I think. I went around to the Council and asked them whether they could lower the pavement – their pavement – which they did – eventually. There was still a very slight slope down. We put a grid all the way round. We had a step so that the foyer didn't flood. They never had any flooding trouble."

Despite such extra expenditure and partly because of its higher-than-average seating figure, this Odeon was one of the cheapest to build on a cost per seat basis (based on the total contract figure excluding the shops), a memo on the subject quoting a figure of £16.27. But Odeon's purchase a few months

Odeon Colwyn Bay. There is a line of red under the black rim of the low entrance.

Odeon Colwyn Bay. In the foyer view, a matching staircase to the balcony on the right is out of view. Here, as in the auditorium, the play of light on combed plaster provides much of the decorative interest. In a June 1936 article, Lily Deutsch declared the interior decoration to be her favourite to date. There are dressing rooms behind the splay walls.

later of the Winter Gardens, opened in 1935 as a cinema and theatre in nearby Llandudno, proved far more profitable than its Colwyn Bay venture.

After designing Sutton Coldfield and Colwyn Bay, J. Cecil Clavering shocked Harry Weedon with the announcement that he was leaving. He craved a feeling of security and had sat an examination for the Office of Works, part of the Civil Service. More than a year later, he received an offer of a post in Shanghai at about twice the salary Weedon paid him.

According to Robert Bullivant, Harry Weedon told Clavering, "Well, you're going to leave me in a terrible jam because I've just seen Oscar who's given me another ten sites to do." So Clavering arranged to delay his departure until he could be replaced. Weedon asked him, "Would you write back to your old [architectural] school and see if you can find anybody who's looking for a job?"

It was in this way that Robert Bullivant succeeded Clavering. Having gained a degree in architecture at Manchester University, Bullivant had worked for a diocesan architect in Oldham, adding flush-toilet blocks to ancient church schools until the money dried up in the Depression. He was advised by a professor at his architectural school that Clavering's job was available, applied, and was accepted. Aged twenty-four, he joined Weedon's office in late January 1935 at a salary of £6 per week. "I overlapped Cecil Clavering by about five or six months, probably a bit longer, certainly less than a year. So I took over a lot of Cecil's half-finished work with a style that was set, that Oscar accepted as the house style of Odeon cinemas." *

The Odeon for **Scarborough** in Yorkshire was one of the cinemas started by Clavering and taken over by Bullivant. (It progressed much faster than Sutton Coldfield and Colwyn Bay, and opened just before them in March 1936.) This was built away from the commercial heart of the town and the seafront but its site near the station ensured that it attracted the attention of every holidaymaker arriving by train. Odeon were even allowed to place a tower, carrying the name of the cinema vertically in neon, capped by rings of neon, in the middle of the road at the junction. There were five existing cinemas in Scarborough, three larger than the Odeon which was the only addition of the 1930s.

This Odeon had a similar exterior to Sutton Coldfield, contrasting brickwork and buff faience, but needed to accommodate a

* In 1972, Clavering recalled in a letter to Robert Bullivant: "I have no regrets about having left. I've had all the scope, the fun and the freedom I could have wished for at the Government's expense without any of the nagging worries and responsibilities of private practice. I've also done a great deal of private work, mainly factories, with a civil engineer who takes all the responsibility."

Odeon Scarborough. There is only one name sign on the building itself but the supplementary one on the pylon in the middle of the road is out of view. The canopy is state-of-the-art, incorporating three stepped lines of announcements.

Odeon Scarborough. This unusually ornate decorative scheme by Mollo and Egan included the screen curtains.

Odeon St. Austell. The slab tower carries no signage at all. Is that a symbolic representation of cactii above the entrance? The foyer view shows a standard design of Odeon doors which almost incorporates the trademark shape of the "O". On the very left of the foyer, note one of the ash stands with name attached that became a standard feature along with the settees. In the auditorium, the screen tabs' design was repeated at Redhill in different colours.

large restaurant above the entrance (which added £3,220 to the cost) and a three-storey row of shops and flats (£5,500) down one side. The result was a much taller, more compact building, with powerful presence – but not quite as well proportioned or as satisfying as Sutton Coldfield. It did not help that the large windows on the buff faience-clad side wall were shorter and wider than those at Sutton Coldfield. Undoubtedly, Sutton Coldfield (and Kingstanding) benefitted from more open and attractive surroundings – and less intensive use of a site – than Scarborough and most later Odeons.

The faience-clad fin carrying the message CINEMA was less dramatic set in a broader brick block, although its rounded vertical edge had a channel in red reinforced by neon. There was considerable use of horizontal colour bands in the faience: three bands above the name sign, as usual overlaid with neon; a thicker fluted green band between the heads of the large windows; three light green bands with attached neon just above the café windows; and two red bands across the upper part of the black base.

The auditorium at Scarborough abandoned the simplicity of Kingstanding or Sutton Coldfield. Instead, it boasted rich interior decoration by the team of Mollo and Egan, who previously contributed to the Odeon Surbiton and here persuaded Lily Deutsch to accept their proposal for a "rain forest" scheme. All the decoration represented luxuriant tropical vegetation, beginning with the colourful creepers and palm fronds of the screen tabs by Eugene Mollo, which seem to have initiated the series of striking designs that graced most subsequent Odeons (this particular design was repeated at Oldham and North Watford). The delicate stencil work of foliage nearer the proscenium opening was also the work of Mollo. The side wall panels with their repetitive pattern of branches and foliage prefigured Michael Egan's celebrated work at the Embassy Esher (but without the front lighting) while decorative bands extending across the ceiling updated the fruit bands on the barrel vaults of early cinemas.

The distribution of seats between stalls and balcony was unusual, with a far higher capacity upstairs than was customary. Typically, a cinema would have just over a third of its seating in the balcony but at Scarborough there were 765 seats, close to the 946 in the stalls. This required the provision of extra exits at the front of the balcony.

The Odeon at **St. Austell** was designed by the Weedon practice with P. J. Price the assistant in charge: "He was an architect's architect," declared Robert Bullivant. "He did very little on the administrative side. He preferred to be on the drawing board and he produced some very good work, but he hadn't got much ambition. He could have been made a partner if he'd carried on, but he wasn't interested. He just loved drawing and working on the board."

This Odeon attempted a sunny Mediterranean look in response to its Cornish coastal location, with an exterior in light coloured rendering rather than faience. There was a slab tower and an almost total absence of windows. The foyer was dominated by a large circular neon tube fitting within plaster moulding. The auditorium was rather daring, with a flat, completely plain ceiling, illuminated by concealed light at the rim, that sat like a lid (or did it give an impression of sky as in an atmospheric scheme?). The flat side walls here and in the foyer had trompe l'oeil fluting. The auditorium provided an early instance of plain ventilation openings, uncamouflaged by decorative grillework, although here they were comparatively inconspicuous over the front side exits.

Two smaller, locally owned cinemas survived the Odeon's arrival.

The two thorough conversions carried out by the Weedon practice during 1936 concerned the Palace Theatre of Varieties at **Oldham**, Lancashire, and the Victoria Picture House at Kettering, Northamptonshire. The Oldham Palace was brought to Oscar Deutsch by David Rosenfield, who located several northern sites for new Odeons. It marked Odeon's debut in the Greater Manchester area, which was never as densely covered by the circuit as Birmingham or London.

At Oldham, the exterior was little changed beyond the modernisation of the canopy and new entrance doors, but the interior was entirely reconstructed with the gallery being removed and a new lower ceiling installed. It was necessary to retain front balcony exits set into the splay walls. The fountain pattern of grillework over the front stalls exits was identical in design to that at the Odeon Kingstanding and here it recurred in the ceiling. All vestiges of the old orchestra pit vanished, leaving an unusually wide open space before the first row of seats.

Oldham was an unusual town in that it missed out on having a completely modern 1930s cinema. (In 1937, the Gaumont circuit carried out a conversion of another live theatre, creating a modern interior but only partially updating the exterior.)

At **Kettering**, the Victoria Picture House, an 850-seat former public hall, was closed for six months while both the interior and exterior were completely modernised. The rather brash new frontage concentrated on drawing attention to the cinema from a distance with the new Odeon name sign high up on the side wall, clear of adjacent buildings, reinforced by horizontal bands overlaid with neon tubing, and another smaller vertical name sign jutting out at first floor level. The actual front elevation was very plain, featuring a large window, slightly recessed.

An extra 240 seats were fitted into the narrow auditorium. Long strips of concealed lighting, deployed without quite the finesse of a George Coles scheme, extended along the side walls

Odeon Oldham. The frontage seems to have displayed only the initial letter and no full name sign until much later. The bricking-up of windows at first floor level is unfortunate. The design of screen tabs seen in the auditorium is the same as at Scarborough and later at North Watford.

Odeon Kettering.

and ceiling towards the screen, reinforced by further superficial decoration with a horizontal emphasis on the walls. For the first time in a Weedon scheme, the ventilation openings, both at the sides of the proscenium arch (a most unusual position) and along the side walls, received the unadorned "cheese grater" or "honeycomb" treatment.

Kettering already had an old cinema run by Gaumont and two independent halls. The Odeon proved no match as a building for the much larger and more prominent Regal, designed with flair by George Coles, which opened at the end of 1936. Kettering also gained another new cinema, the Savoy, in 1938, on the site of a burned-down older hall.

The Odeon at **Harrogate**, Yorkshire, was an almost exact copy of Sutton Coldfield, inside and out, with twenty-one more seats in the stalls and twenty-six more seats in the balcony. It might have been a nice idea for such an outstanding design to be repeated more widely but close duplication was rare in the 1930s if only because cinema sites varied so much in size and shape.[*]

Staff referred to Harrogate as "the garden" because the screen curtains depicted an owl on a branch against an enormous moon while the auditorium was painted in silver and pastel blues and greens to enhance the impression of a moonlit garden. (Sutton Coldfield does not seem to have had the same tabs and colour scheme but, if it did, the interior was not as bland as suggested earlier.)

When Harrogate's Odeon opened, the town already had a largish Gaumont hall and three locally run properties. ABC opened its Regal (apparently with one seat less than the Odeon) almost a year later.

Building Odeons in some historic cities proved particularly vexing. Not only was the modern Odeon look prohibited, but there could be other unexpected complications, as Robert Bullivant, the job architect for **Chester** and York, has recalled:

"At both Chester and York, work was suspended when excavations revealed most important evidence of Roman and earlier antiquities. At Chester, the first evidence of Roman settlement was found at a level more than twenty-five feet below Northgate Street and a survey of the drainage ducts cut by the Romans out of solid sandstone occupied Professor Newstead for over two months.

* The most notable example of repetition, of course, is seen in Theodore Komisarjevsky's interior designs for "standard" Granada Theatres, while the exteriors of the Granadas at Maidstone and Shrewsbury were very similar. The impressive Mayfair Whalebone Lane, South Dagenham, Essex, and the Towers at Hornchurch, Essex, by Kemp and Tasker were reputedly a close match inside and out. Various small town Regals by Harold Scott were very similar (but not otherwise noteworthy).

Odeon Harrogate. The only apparent differences from Sutton Coldfield are the small window halfway up the inner edge of the brick tower, the tall window set in the curve of the righthand extension to illuminate the staircase inside, and the steps at the exits at far left, seemingly caused by a sloping site. (See also front cover.) The auditorium appears to have been of identical design apart from adding a few more seats. The design of screen tabs was repeated at Reading. (Auditorium reproduced by permission of English Heritage.NMR.)

Odeon Chester. The strong banding of the foyer walls corresponds to the wooden dado in the auditorium. Note the unusual forward slant of the balcony front and, extending from the dado, the solid wooden front to the orchestra pit rather than the usual grillework.

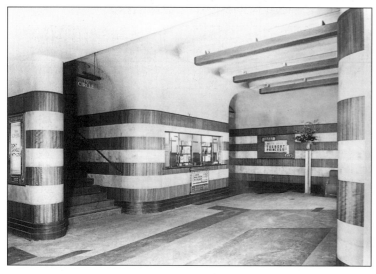

"Oscar Deutsch received news of the suspension of building work at Chester and at York without the reaction I had expected. He had been far more concerned by the unusual delay that had occurred before building work could commence. The planning authorities at both Chester and York had been very reluctant to consider an application for permission to erect a cinema within the area enclosed by the city walls.

"At Chester there were protracted negotiations for many months and innumerable sketch perspectives were prepared for submission to the [Royal] Fine Arts Commission. Eventually it became clear that the planning committee would be prepared to consider an application for a building in Northgate Street provided it did not look like an Odeon. Reluctantly, they agreed that the name 'Odeon' might be displayed but that the standard house style lettering should not be used. The Odeon sign was finally approved in Trajan lettering."

No faience was allowed and both buildings were faced entirely in brick. Bullivant recalled producing between twenty and twenty-four different designs over a year before he obtained approval at Chester and has denigrated the result as "the inevitable mishmash of committee interference."★

Despite much horizontal and vertical channelling and banding of the brickwork, the exterior at Chester did look rather ponderous with an oversized name sign in Trajan lettering on the corner tower. The auditorium displayed some flair in directing the eye towards the screen. It was dominated by a sloping ceiling of bands towards the proscenium carrying concealed lighting, ending with a final ribbed-plaster plunge on to the proscenium frame in the style of a Robert Cromie/Mollo and Egan interior such as that of the Ritz Chelmsford (1935). The front side wall treatment seemed rather messy with a tear-shaped recess for further concealed lighting and a back-lit decorative feature unconnected to a honeycomb of small vents immediately adjacent. The side walls further back were unusually plain and the ceiling treat-ment dominated the space in a manner reminiscent of the Grosvenor Rayners Lane.

Chester was crowded in terms of cinemas. Gaumont-British had got in early with a large Gaumont Palace adorned with a Tudor-style frontage, while ABC followed Odeon a year later with a very dull brick exterior.

When the Odeon at **Lancaster** in Lancashire opened, the town had six old cinemas, four of which had recently been taken over by the Union circuit. Although Union announced plans to build in Lancaster in 1937, the Odeon became the only significant

Odeon Lancaster. Here is a new screen tabs design, in which, barely visible at left, a gentleman in period costume is bowing to a woman under the drooping tree. The balcony front and side walls of the circle feature acoustic tiling. The balcony exits are unusually conspicuous. (Exterior from CTA Archive.)

★ At Chester, some of the Roman artefacts discovered on the site were put on display in glass cases set into one of the walls of the upstairs foyer where they remain on view.

modern 1930s cinema to appear in the town. The assistant in charge of the scheme was W. Calder Robson.

Set at a 45° angle to the auditorium, the wide frontage of the Odeon, incorporating a row of shops, was once again clad in buff-coloured faience (with just two thin bands in colour high up on the fin tower) until joined by the brickwork of the auditorium as it curved round the corner. The fin now carried the Odeon name rather than the word CINEMA. The frontage offered a new feature of three narrow ribs angled from the facade to give a triangular profile (a device more often used – at Scarborough, Hanley and elsewhere – to relieve expanses of brick on side walls). The side wall treatment above the line of shops was reminiscent of Sutton Coldfield and Harrogate but the main name sign was not as well positioned. The odd shape of the site resulted in balcony patrons having to cross the foyer to buy tickets, then turn back and use a staircase that rose behind the first of the shops.

The auditorium was distinctive, with accentuated front exits from the balcony and a band of pierced, boldly decorative grillework starting over the front stalls exits and extending across the ceiling. The main lighting was from concealed bands across the ceiling and around the proscenium.

The Odeon at **Bury,** Lancashire (assistant: P. J. Price), was the only modern cinema in the industrial town, competing with seven older and smaller halls. It was also the first completely new Odeon in the Manchester area, eight miles to the north of the city centre, following the Oldham conversion completed three months earlier.

Bury had a rather box-like exterior, the frontage almost entirely clad in faience. The auditorium was pleasant but the balcony front curiously failed to connect with the band of concealed lighting descending down the side wall. The clocks were placed unusually high above the side grilles.

The Odeon at **Loughborough,** Leicestershire (assistant: Arthur J. Price) was on a site at the edge of the town centre. Externally, it clearly resembled the Tower at West Bromwich, opened almost a year earlier, but had some bold and effective changes. In particular, it escaped the flat look of the Tower's front elevation and, for the first time in a Weedon building, the rectangular-shaped buff faience tiles were positioned in pairs in the basketweave pattern of Howitt's Odeons to form squares emphasised by thicker joints. The lines of green banding at West Bromwich were repeated across the top but the ends of the canopy were more rounded to correspond with the corners of the frontage and the first floor windows were incisively recessed between round-ended piers and enclosed by a further canopy above. The black base was intersected by conspicuous bands in strong green that continued across the piers between

Odeon Bury. The main Odeon sign is an excellent fit for the width of the box, but what use was made of all the space inside it? The screen tabs here, with sunny village setting, subsequently appeared in at least three more Odeons.

Odeon Loughborough. The name sign, in 4ft. tall letters, is spaced out to suit the wide frontage. The exterior was greatly enhanced at night by the neon installation of 366ft. of green tubing, 64ft. of red and 72ft. of blue, plus further neon under the outside upper edge of the canopy. The name sign also carries superimposed neon, as did a smaller sign (not visible) on a side wall. All this and floodlighting, too, from the top of the canopy!

Right: Odeon Loughborough. This simple and elegant auditorium has the most whimsical design of screen tabs, repeated at Epsom, Exeter and Swiss Cottage.

Below and lower right: Odeon Falmouth. The exterior is not quite finished. Note the brick wall behind that hides the roof. In the auditorium, the plain side walls are covered in acoustic tiling. The design of screen tabs was seen again at Hanley in 1937.

entrance doors which were recessed like the windows above. The way that various recesses contrasted with and balanced the projection of the two canopies made this one of the most satisfying of Odeon exteriors.

The auditorium at Loughborough was simple and effective, its ceiling light fittings and side wall grillework recalling Clavering's interiors. The screen tabs here were particularly delightful, showing an Odeon along Sutton Coldfield lines nestled in a mountainous landscape, a humorous response to stories of early Odeons in the middle of nowhere.

Loughborough had three existing cinemas run by the local C. K. Deeming circuit which retaliated by having its more centrally placed Empire rebuilt as a modern cinema to the designs of A. Hurley Robinson, doubled in size, with a very impressive, if narrow, modern frontage in a jazzed-up Odeon style, incorporating cream-coloured tiles and an angled central tower feature.

Besides handling St. Austell, P. J. Price was also in charge of the other Odeon in Cornwall, at **Falmouth.** This had a fine frontage with a well-judged integration of rounded and straight planes. It was in buff faience relieved by thin horizontal colour bands at regular intervals. The auditorium was ultra-modern with linear bands of concealed lighting pointing towards the screen in a flat ceiling which gave the impression of being supported by slanting columns at each side. A pattern of small holes made the ventilation openings almost invisible.

At Falmouth, the fast expanding Union circuit had acquired the existing three halls in January 1936 and apparently planned to add a new Ritz. But the opening of an Odeon at the end of the year put paid to that idea.

Andrew Mather

Like Weedon, Andrew Mather handled ten Odeons of 1936, all in the south of England. But several of these were initially designed for other promoters and only one of the sites – Portsmouth – was of front rank significance. The work of Mather's practice sometimes fitted the Odeon style but had often been designed with some other client's tastes in mind and was little altered when Odeon came in.

Several schemes were acquired from A. E. Abrahams. These included cinemas, initially designed in late 1934, for Eltham, south east London (probably Eltham Hill, possibly Well Hall), and two in Kent at Ashford (originally to be a Regal) and Sittingbourne.

In two instances, Mather's practice showed that it could deliver the modern Odeon look with much the same élan as Harry Weedon and T. Cecil Howitt.

At a roundabout in the **Well Hall** area of new housing estates at Eltham in south east London appeared an Odeon with a low but eye-catching exterior. The curved glazed tower, which recalled the De La Warr Pavilion at Bexhill and enclosed the staircase to the balcony, was neatly linked to a sweeping canopy. Buff faience on the side wall, above the entrance and along a descending parade of shops contrasted with a neatly stepped auditorium block faced in brick which took advantage of the natural slope of the site. The customary black base to the faience here was minimal, although the columns between the entrance doors were faced in black tiles. A circular outer foyer had the Odeon name in green mosaic on the terrazzo floor in front of a round paybox. The inner ground floor foyer had mirrors with etched glass figures and film motifs. The larger window on the side of the building provided daylight for the circle foyer.

The auditorium was most effective, with concealed lighting in bands across a stepped-down ceiling and porthole-like light fittings and ventilation openings on side walls which were decorated with horizontal bands leading towards the screen. The absence of decorative grillework on the splay walls made it seem a little stark although there was a band across the ceiling just in front of the proscenium arch. Rather unusually, there was a flurry of lattice-like plaster decoration on the back wall of the balcony as well as a laylight in the nearby ceiling.

This outstanding Odeon was the work of Horace Ward within the Mather practice (although Mollo and Egan worked on the decorations). Ward died soon afterwards from tuberculosis. Lily Deutsch noted that the cinema was decorated throughout in shades of one colour only, described as champagne gold.

Almost as splendid, inside and out, was the Odeon at **Ramsgate**, Kent, one of several Mather schemes opened in coastal locations during this year. Ramsgate had five cinemas or theatres equipped for films, but the Odeon was the only newcomer of the 1930s. The exterior shone in sunlight with its essential rounded corner and vast spread of tiles in opaque glass (not faience, but looking much the same), yellow-buff in colour above canopy level, much darker lower down. The entrance block and the attached parade of shops and flats were two storeys high with the taller auditorium set across the site behind. A slab wall extended at right angles from the auditorium to divide the cinema entrance from the shops and flats. This had the word CINEMA set into it on both sides, leaving the Odeon name to appear on the two faces of an attached vertical sign.

The attractive auditorium was boldly streamlined with bands across the ceiling and splay walls, extending across the proscenium columns and the main curtains. Concealed lighting around the rim of the ceiling and behind the proscenium must have added a touch of magic to this interior. As in so many Mather Odeons, the job architect remains unidentified.

The Odeon at **Rickmansworth** in Hertfordshire seems to

Odeon Well Hall. Note the surprisingly small main Odeon sign, matched by a vertical one on the side wall. This shadowy image makes it impossible to see the flower troughs at each side of the entrance or the prominent and unusual sign reading ODEON THEATRE *under the canopy, just above the entrance doors.*

Odeon Well Hall.

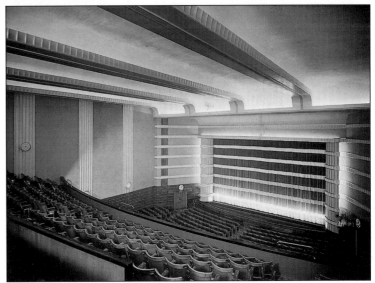

Above: Odeon Ramsgate. There is an extensive side wall to the left with strip windows. The screen tabs incorporated ethereal figures and seem to have been unique to the cinema.

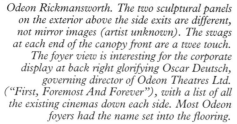

Odeon Rickmansworth. The two sculptural panels on the exterior above the side exits are different, not mirror images (artist unknown). The swags at each end of the canopy front are a twee touch. The foyer view is interesting for the corporate display at back right glorifying Oscar Deutsch, governing director of Odeon Theatres Ltd. ("First, Foremost And Forever"), with a list of all the existing cinemas down each side. Most Odeon foyers had the name set into the flooring.

have been designed for the circuit. It went into competition with an existing independent hall, the Picture House. The January opening was delayed for two days by the death of King George V. The site, between the High Street and the town stream, was so waterlogged that an elaborate system of piling was required. The brick and stone frontage is reported to have been redesigned in a traditional style to blend with the area and gain council approval (although an adjacent parade of shops and flats built as part of the scheme was far more modern in appearance). There was a very shallow canopy over the entrance because of the narrow pavement. A tower advertised the Odeon's whereabouts. Two bas-relief panels of reclining females above the side exits and a row of stone urns along the parapet were old-fashioned touches for an Odeon.

The auditorium was designed on the semi-stadium principle with the rear section above the entrance hall. The treatment seemed heavy and outmoded for 1936 while the proscenium opening had a utilitarian look reinforced by the elimination of an orchestra rail (the first of several Odeons to do away with this).

Mather's Odeon at **Faversham,** Kent, took the notion of blending in with a historic town centre to a Tudoresque extreme. Built at a very low cost, it was a late addition to the Tudor cycle established rather more elaborately at the Beaufort in Birmingham (1929) and the Gaumont (now Odeon) Salisbury (1931).

This had a narrow exterior in stone with leaded windows of coloured glass flanked by panels of masks and strapwork. The canopy seemed to rest on grotesque female figures inspired by the genuine late 16th century ones on the house next door. The roof of hand-made tiles incorporated a central steeple with an iron weather vane topped by a motif of a cameraman shooting a film.

The stadium auditorium (with the modest seating capacity of 729) continued the historic theme: lantern-shaped light fittings hung from an arched roof crossed by bands of decorative plaster-work while side walls suggested timber-framed panels displaying crests, bas-relief animals and flowers, plus jarring Odeon clocks in standard octagonal frames.

The cinema opened a little more than a year after the town's Argosy, where architects F. E. Bromige and Leslie Carter had provided Faversham with an ultra-modern auditorium, its ceiling plunging down to the screen and curving back over the side exits. No Odeon interior was ever this audacious. Between them, the Argosy and Odeon brought about the closure of the town's old Gem cinema.

Another low-budget Odeon at **Littlehampton,** Sussex, had a ponderous stone frontage with urns mounted on the front edges of a concave recess above the entrance and canopy. A row of shops had only recently been built across the front of the site

Odeon Faversham. There are two vertical name signs here rather than one horizontal one.

Odeon Littlehampton. The sculptural panel of a naked male figure with a lyre was lit up in one colour while the recess behind was floodlit in another. The brightest feature of the auditorium is the screen tabs, their design seemingly unique to this cinema.

and were retained as far as possible, their stone facing dictating the use of stone by Mather. The curved, faience-clad recesses of the Odeons at Sudbury and (see later) Bromley had an impact sadly missing here.

Mather's Odeons of this period had a bad habit of downgrading the route to the most expensive seats in the house. At both Faversham and Littlehampton, the balcony seats were reached by a staircase through a doorway off to one side of the foyer. And at Littlehampton the balcony was entered on one side rather than in the centre.

The auditorium at Littlehampton was rather plain and boxlike, relying primarily on concealed lighting around the edge of a ceiling recess to provide house illumination and comb effects on plaster to enliven the walls. The balcony barely overlapped the rear of the stalls and, rather unusually, contained ninety-four more seats than downstairs.

Littlehampton had two existing cinemas, the Regent and Palladium. In the 1930s, the town had 10,181 inhabitants – a very low out of season population to support three cinemas with a total of 2,300 seats – but all three survived on the summer swell of holidaymakers.

The Odeon at **Deal**, Kent, was the first example of a Mather exterior faced in large slabs of vitrolite, here coloured peach and black with horizontal bands in green. This was much cheaper and quicker to affix than faience tiles. Although it could work on very large exteriors, it did create a crude impression at Deal.

The stadium-style auditorium was more richly detailed than Littlehampton but with the same use of concealed lighting around the edges of the flat ceiling to provide the principal illumination. Here the Odeon clocks directly faced the audience, mounted on the end of the splay walls.

With a population of 13,680, Deal already had three picture houses. The small 300-seat Plaza closed six months later but the town retained three cinemas into the 1950s.

The Odeon at **Ashford** in Kent was a takeover scheme with a traditional brick and stone exterior and a determinedly old-fashioned interior but it did have one unusual feature. Designers never seemed to make any allowance for the Odeon clocks so that they usually looked awkwardly tacked on. But here the splay walls on each side boasted not one but two octagonal shapes on each side, those nearest the screen neatly accommodating the obligatory clockfaces.

This was a largish Odeon with 1,570 seats. Sidney Swingler recalled that it was "experimentally utilitarian" and "had to be cheap" although the cost according to Odeon records was about average for the number of seats. It competed for business with the smaller Cinema and Palace until the latter closed down in 1939.

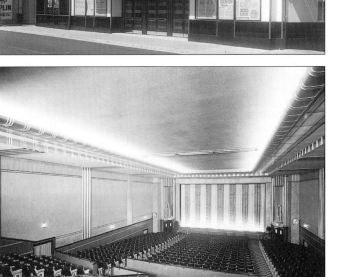

Odeon Deal. Note the small name sign on the tower.
The entrance to the car park is at right.

Odeon Ashford. This is one of a small number of Odeons to have
small name signs mounted on each end of the canopy.

Odeon Newport, Isle of Wight.

Odeon was the only one of the three major circuits to open a cinema on the Isle of Wight. The island had three towns with populations of around 10,000-11,000 – Cowes, Newport and Ryde. Deutsch seems to have contemplated building in each of them in turn through schemes presented or developed by Andrew Mather, before finally settling on Newport. In June 1935, as previously mentioned, he was toying with a scheme for Cowes, the port and holiday resort on the north coast. Cowes had two small cinemas operated by the local Isle of Wight Cinemas chain. No modern cinema was ever built there. For Ryde, the resort and main port of entry from the mainland, Mather designed an Odeon to appear between 21 and 23 Cross Street and seat 962 (670 stalls and 292 balcony). This had a long and narrow entrance passage leading to a wide inner foyer and auditorium beyond, with an exit passage at the screen end leading to the High Street. Plans were dated 28 October 1935. The scheme was announced in *The Cinema* of 18 March 1936 and listed in the *Kinematograph Year Book* as being "in course of construction" from the 1936 to the 1947 edition! The island's own circuit had two small cinemas in Ryde while another company built the large Commodore in Star Street, which opened in August 1936 and undoubtedly caused Odeon to drop its plans.

Newport, the main commercial centre located in the middle of the island, was the most sensible place to be, as the Odeon could draw audiences from all over the island. There were two older cinemas here, but Odeon faced a modern rival from 1938 when the existing Medina cinema (named after the local river) was replaced with a new cinema of the same name promoted by the owner of the Commodore Ryde. The other small cinema, owned by Isle of Wight Cinemas, remained open and a three-cornered fight for audiences extended into the early 1960s.

The Odeon at Newport showed the Mather output at its dreariest. The corner entrance was stultifyingly bland with its curved expanse of plain brickwork, but the horizontal banding of the side walls at ground level, continued across the rounded columns between the entrance doors, lent a modern touch to the lower regions. Inside, the unusual shape of the top of the proscenium arch added a modicum of interest to the auditorium.

At first glance, the Odeon at **Herne Bay** in Kent might seem a further candidate for rapid dismissal – but it was an excellent example of small town cinema, even if it paid little or no obeisance to the Odeon style. With another exterior in brick and stone, the cinema was exposed to view on three sides and attractively handled, especially compared to others like the Odeon on the Isle of Wight. Mather's unidentified job architect built up the corner to raise the Odeon sign and two flagposts, and introduced an eye-catching vertical panel of decorative metallic grillework featuring the octagonal O of the Odeon trademark as a sun shining over clouds below. The pitched roof of the auditorium was well hidden and the rear of the building, exposed to public view, was neatly handled with its own Odeon sign.

The auditorium had long interior-lit panels down each side just below ceiling level while the front side walls carried horizontal banding that, as at Ramsgate, linked up with the pattern on the main curtains. The front side exit doors extended slightly into the auditorium, incorporating the Odeon clock and concealed lighting for the pierced decorative plasterwork above.

The Odeon put pressure on the town's two existing cinemas in this holiday centre, both recently acquired by the Union circuit. In the same month as the Odeon opened, Union announced plans to improve the Casino on the seafront and in 1937 sought to close its Red Lantern outside the summer season. When ABC gained control of the Union circuit later that year, it shut down the Red Lantern for good, leaving the Casino and Odeon to fight it out into the 1950s.

The Odeon for **Portsmouth,** Hampshire, was the largest (with 1,824 seats) and consequently most expensive of the Mather Odeons of 1936. Along with Cardiff, Portsmouth was probably the most important (as well as the most competitive) market that Odeon entered in 1936. The Odeon would be followed by ABC's Savoy seven months later, while Gaumont's large Regent was the third major hall in town.

The Odeon's monolithic frontage was certainly impressive and broadly in the circuit style with its use of cream faience and wide green bands; but the rather dull inner foyer exhibited Mather's habit of relegating the balcony staircase to one side; and the auditorium design seemed extremely dated, like that of Ashford but more ornate – octagonal spaces awaited the Odeon clocks above each side exit, flanked by plaster mermaids, while to each side tall murals featured semi-abstract representations of such subjects as a film cameraman and a film projector.

The opening ceremony in December 1936 was performed by a local independent exhibitor, Councillor F. J. Spickernell, in his position as the Lord Mayor of Portsmouth. He had built the Regent and the Plaza Bradford Junction, both sold to Gaumont, and operated the large Tivoli Copnor and new Troxy Fratton. A year later, he would also officiate at the opening of the Odeon Southsea. What he really felt about blessing new competition is unrecorded, but at the original hearings for the Portsmouth scheme, the opposition counsel had stated that Odeon was "very much feared by the smaller people in the trade – they got the films first, and spoilt the market for their companies".

T. Cecil Howitt

During 1936, two further Odeons opened in the unmistakable style of T. Cecil Howitt. In fact, no cinema architect, other than

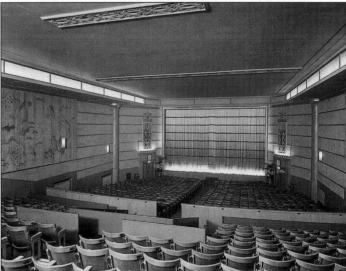

Odeon Herne Bay. The sea front is in the distance.
(Exterior view reproduced by permission of English Heritage.NMR.)

Odeon Portsmouth. The main name sign neatly surmounts the green vertical bands and neon strips spaced between them. The roof is in red Spanish tiles. Note floodlights mounted on the narrow canopy, the vertical name signs on the side of the tower and the unusually fussy neon overlay in lower centre.

F. E. Bromige, stamped his signature as clearly on his exteriors.

Clacton-on-Sea, the Essex seaside resort, had three small, old cinemas before two newcomers arrived in the space of two months during 1936: first an Odeon (with 1,214 seats), then the Century, designed by G. H. B. Gould (1,734 seats). The Century was a presentable building, approximating the Odeon style with curved entrance block and rectangular wings in light faience.

But Howitt's Odeon was a knockout – its colossal expanse of tiled exterior with flat-top tower daringly unrelieved by a window anywhere, the buff colour moderated only by thin green stripes across the top of the facade. The faience tiles were, as usual for Howitt, close-spaced in pairs to form a basketweave pattern of squares. Although it can hardly have pleased everybody, this must have been the town's most conspicuous and exciting 1930s structure.

The auditorium was extremely similar to that of Weston-super-Mare but offered more conspicuous grillework on the side walls and had a circular dome with concealed lighting over the balcony rather a rectangular recess which would have been more in keeping with the straight lines everywhere else.

Howitt's Odeon at **Bridgwater** was the only new cinema built in the Somerset town during the 1930s. Occupying the former cattle market, it was far larger than the town's other three cinemas, which included the Palace almost opposite, and made a strong impact, as at Clacton, because of its size and assertive appearance.

This Odeon was like a simpler, less elaborate version of the one at Weston-super-Mare, although it seated almost as many and (according to Odeon records) cost slightly more. With the auditorium extending parallel to the main road behind a parade of shops, it had an arresting flat-topped corner tower in buff faience, its mass relieved here by two slit windows in the side. The extension of shops and flats was faced in black glass at ground level and carried horizontal scarlet stripes overlaid with neon tubes at the stepped parapet. The mass of the auditorium, faced in yellow bricks, was rather too visible on the return side: this elevation might have been built up to conceal it.

The seating was in a stadium arrangement across a particularly wide auditorium with the side walls stepping only slightly inwards to narrow the proscenium end. The opening was far wider than at Weston-super-Mare but otherwise very similar, again including rounded, fluted columns on each side that seemed at odds with the rectangular treatment elsewhere. Again, the only grillework breaking up the side walls covered modest ventilation openings and had a repetitive swag-like pattern making it more elaborate than at Weston-super-Mare. A shallow octagonal dome with concealed lighting dominated the ceiling. There were sufficient stage facilities to enable a local dramatic company to

Odeon Clacton. This had a good location next to Woolworth's. The main Odeon sign is placed on the side of the tower to face the town centre. There was a shop set diagonally into the far corner of the site where the low extension did have the drawback of exposing the back wall of the auditorium to view.

Above, Odeon Clacton: foyer and auditorium.

Above: Odeon Bridgwater. Window boxes for the flats soften the mass of faience, along with the brightly coloured blinds of the shops. The line of foliage on the tower was a temporary opening adornment. The extension of the auditorium with the car park sign contains the upper lounge with a large window with stained glass features just out of view. The auditorium is decorated in broad bands of textured gold colour while the three coves of the proscenium arch display various colours.

present pantomimes here for several years (although only the standard two dressing rooms seem to have been provided).

George Coles

There was a gap of almost eighteen months between the opening of George Coles' Odeon at Isleworth and the five that arrived between August and October 1936. However, Coles had been working on at least one of the sites for nearly three years.

Coles now made his mark as an Odeon architect, designing interiors that were more striking than Weedon's, with some exteriors firmly grasping the circuit style and others with watered-down classical trimmings. It is not clear to what extent Coles relied on his assistants but the sheer volume of work and range of styles suggests a considerable amount of delegation, and one member of staff, Arthur Roberts, is said to have designed two (unidentified) Odeons.

The Odeon at **Southall,** Middlesex, was Coles' second contribution to the local cinema scene as he had designed the Palace around the corner in 1929 (later the Gaumont). Elsewhere, F. E. Bromige had devised the large Dominion of 1935, which became the town's ABC outlet, and there was also an earlier hall called the Gem.

The Palace presented an otherwise drab street with an invigorating and colourful outburst of Chinoiserie, but Coles did not take the opportunity to liven up his new site with a dazzling futuristic exterior. Indeed, he seemed hesitant to embrace the modern look in cinema exteriors, even in a place like Southall where there would have been no objection; but he was of an older generation and had made his name with ornate, traditional picture palaces.

Close-set buff faience was used to clad the Odeon's entrance block in which tall windows were flanked by pilasters with raised capitals that were emphasised by neon at night. The main Odeon sign sat above this area. The brick-faced auditorium extended parallel to the road, without the benefit of a parade of shops and flats to offset its bulk. A ponderous portico feature in stone was attached to the wall with an undersized secondary Odeon sign mounted above it. Faience extended across the entire frontage at ground level above a minimal black base, relieved mid-height by four narrow bands in green.

Odeon Southall. The two poster sites on the side wall are underwhelming. The auditorium's painted dado of squares and shadows is odd.

In contrast to the stolid exterior, the foyers and auditorium at Southall were thoroughly modern. The latter made considerable use of concealed lighting and bands running across the ceiling and down to the top edge of the proscenium opening in one of the architect's favourite devices. Further painted banding on the side walls also directed attention towards the screen. Niches in the splay walls were decorated with bizarre plant-like forms that could have strayed from Odeon's exotic rain forest curtain at

Odeon Ipswich. Right, the extensive use of neon along the side walls at canopy level was unusual. The rake of the stalls floor was helped by a sloping site.

Scarborough (the design of screen tabs used here has not been traced).

One of the most important additions of the year in terms of location, Coles' Odeon at **Ipswich,** the county town of Suffolk, followed the pattern of Southall's with a well-behaved exterior and contemporary interior; but here the historically sensitive setting, with the Ancient House a few streets away, dictated a more careful approach to the outside. Two walls were on full view with plain, tiled columns and spaced-out Odeon signs placed on the brickwork. The main entrance area was clad in buff faience with columns separating tall windows and carrying urns. A third name sign appeared above.

The lofty main foyer provided a startlingly modern contrast, with fluted black columns, geometric patterns in the rubber flooring, and steep central flight of steps to the balcony. The auditorium ceiling had a strong directional emphasis towards the proscenium, three bands crossing the cove before the wide proscenium opening. Bead-like fittings integrated with uplit cones were a striking feature of the side walls, along with unusually prominent light fittings further back.

This Odeon opened comfortably ahead of a Union scheme which provided Ipswich with a Ritz in January 1937. The town already had the Regent, part of the Gaumont chain, as well as five other halls. The Odeon, Ritz and Regent were all on the large side with 1,764, 1,689 and 1,775 seats respectively.

Oscar Deutsch had targeted **Bromley** in Kent, with only two small, old-fashioned Gaumont halls, as an ideal location three years earlier. "We did not have any easy job to find a site in Bromley. You cherish your ground very dearly, as we found out to our cost," he told the audience on opening night.

In October 1933, Deutsch optioned a site opposite Bromley North Station at the corner of Tweedy Road and Shurman Road. He instructed George Coles to prepare a scheme, which he did by the 24th of the same month. In February 1934, Deutsch advised several distributors that he was building an Odeon in Bromley. During that same month, Gaumont-British announced it was also building there – on a prominent corner in the High Street. The strong-willed C. M. Woolf, deputy chairman and joint managing director of Gaumont, demanded that Deutsch abandon his scheme as two big new cinemas for Bromley would be one too many.

Coles' plans were passed in March 1934 but in 1935 Deutsch decided on a larger site in another part of the High Street comprising a double-fronted shop with a large Amusement Park behind (formerly The Mart, an extension of the shop in front). Coles went to work on a difficult site: this was perhaps the most extreme Odeon example of the common practice in densely built-up town centres of securing a narrow foothold on the main

Odeon Bromley. The wings of the powerful frontage were dramatically outlined in neon at night, while the deep recess was floodlit. The placing of the main name sign at this low level was exceptional. The side wall of the auditorium, extending off to the left, can just be glimpsed.

Odeon Horsham. The screen tabs here featured an exotic forest setting repeated at Chorley.

street while building the auditorium on cheaper land some distance behind.

Odeon and Gaumont seem to have decided to proceed more or less simultaneously, with Deutsch's hall opening two months ahead of its rival. The Odeon was of standard 1,500-seat city capacity for the period but the Gaumont was a huge undertaking with over one thousand more seats. Suddenly, there were 4,075 extra cinema seats for local cinemagoers to occupy!

Coles' early plans of May 1935 showed a front elevation with classical detailing. This was scrapped by October 1935.★ It was essential to make the most eye-catching use of the limited frontage. Coles was urged by Deutsch to give it a more up-to-date look (like the Gaumont would have) and he responded magnificently with a modernistic scheme of a deep curved recess with rounded wings and an outwardly curving canopy with the name sign mounted on it.

Bromley's foyer had a central staircase leading up to the balcony and an auditorium that was surprisingly lofty and rather plain, with wavy patterns painted onto the side walls and the inner proscenium surround. The ribbed plasterwork crossing the splay walls incorporated ventilation openings and was reminiscent of Robert Cromie/Mollo and Egan's work at the Regal Wimbledon and elsewhere.

The Odeon that Coles designed for **Horsham,** West Sussex, was of more modest size, with 1,258 seats. The architect lived in the village of Mannings Heath, two miles south east of Horsham, and could take justifiable pride in his contribution to the local building scene. Here again Odeon were in competition with Union. The latter circuit had three small cinemas in the town and built a fourth, the Ritz, expecting to deter Odeon from proceeding with its plans. The Odeon opened nearly four months after the Ritz, with nearly two hundred more seats. It was a very expensive cinema, built at a cost of £33,555 or £27.19 per seat compared to an average of £20 (the Odeon at Newport, Isle of Wight, of similar size, opened ten days later, cost only £24,913). The two oldest Union properties in Horsham closed soon after the Odeon opened.

Like the town's Capitol and Ritz, the Odeon had a set-back entrance with a forecourt for patrons arriving by car, but here there was a pylon, illuminated from within and carrying a vertical Odeon sign that lit up in neon at night to draw attention to the building.

The foyers were inviting, with much use of horizontal banding and stencilled depictions of film-making, a stylised strip of film and modes of transport, etc. The auditorium had horizontal bands painted on the side walls and relied for interest on two

★ See David Atwell, *Cathedrals of the Movies,* page 151, where the two elevations are reproduced, along with a plan of the site.

Odeon Muswell Hill. A comparatively rare instance of the name sign being mounted on the canopy. The top of the frontage is brightly lit at night by horizontal bands of neon contrasting with the single neon tubes in the vertical channels. The ceiling of the auditorium has the most spectacular example of linear lighting in a George Coles' Odeon.

free-standing columns in niches in the splay walls, back lit and crowned by a light fitting.

Coles' major contribution in design terms to the circuit in 1936 was unquestionably the Odeon at **Muswell Hill**. This sedate north London suburb had two old cinemas when both Odeon and ABC set about building here. The Odeon opened in September 1936 and ABC's Ritz followed in December. Both were outstanding buildings architecturally and surprisingly capacious for the location: the Odeon accommodated 1,827 patrons while the Ritz had an even greater capacity with 1,997 seats. The two pre-existing halls closed.

The history of this Odeon was thoroughly researched (principally by Sue Heathcote) for a 1981 proposal by the Borough of Haringey to the Department of the Environment for the listing of the building (not then successful, but it has been listed since). The report was adapted for publication in *Picture House* (no. 3, Spring 1983) and these are extracts:

"George Coles was commissioned in 1935 by the Odeon organisation, through the Muswell Hill and Harlesden Property Company Ltd., to design a complex consisting of a cinema, shops and flats in Muswell Hill. Deutsch was interested only in his cinemas and a mixed development was agreed in order to raise finance, but as early as May 1937 the leases of the shops and flats were disposed of.

"A restraining factor on the development was the influence of St. James's Parish Church opposite the proposed site at the crossing of Fortis Green Road and Muswell Hill Road. The original plan had a large cinema entrance on the axis of the crossroads. Although the scheme was approved by the local planning authority, the Church formed a sufficiently powerful lobby to have the application for the vital licence refused by Middlesex County Council. A second scheme was drawn up which moved the cinema to its position as built at the far end of the block, round the corner away from the Church. A third and final plan was drawn up in November 1935 incorporating various improvements and revisions, including important formal changes to the vestibule and lobbies of the cinema and to the facade. No elevations have survived of the first or second stages and it has been suggested that these designs may have incorporated a tower in the cinema design and that the omission of this may have made extra monies available for spending on the interior of the cinema. [...]

"The exterior is essentially plain and straightforward but with an important interplay of dark and lit elements at night, in keeping with the importance given to night lighting effects in Odeon cinema designs. The curved and stepped facade of the cinema with cream faience facing and narrow fins is flanked by inter-penetrating blocks faced in black faience.

"Although each part of the complex functions separately, the articulation of the whole serves to focus attention on the cinema, using the curves and horizontality in the block of flats and shops to move towards the cinema. Horizontality is emphasised by the flat roof of the block, the concrete string courses, the rhythm of the windows, and the line of the cream faience below the flats. The faience is terminated on reaching the block faced with black faience flanking the cinema facade. After dark, the rhythm is emphasised as the black recedes from the cream on the cinema facade (originally lit and with red neon strips).

"Entrance to the main vestibule is via four sets of double doors (there are also a pair of double exit doors at each end of the facade walls). The curve of the facade wall is mirrored by the rear walls of the entrance vestibule. This is a double-height space, symmetrical in plan. Two pairs of broad columns at each side support the roof and carry the facade screen wall. An elaborate 'hinge' detail visually links these columns with adjacent walls, balconies and the sculptured ceilings to the vestibule and mezzanine (circle) lobby. Walls and ceilings all have a painted plaster finish. The entrance composition flooring has a geometric pattern, at the centre of which was originally positioned a small pay box. This geometric floorscaping in the access areas... and the general streamlining are directional as well as decorative features. A directional purpose can also be interpreted for the Art Deco light fittings.

"From the entrance vestibule a small circular lobby on the same axis leads to the stalls foyer. This lobby facilitates a single change of axis orientating the visitor toward the cinema auditorium. The foyer is rectangular with two columns and directional light fittings.

"The balcony foyer to the mezzanine level also has a circular lobby facilitating a change of axis. This is reached by two symmetrically planned flights of stairs rising from between the columns to the vestibule and turning to follow the line of curve of the rear walls up to the lobby. The lower landing of each stair leads also to the separate exit doors. The balcony foyer is larger than the one at ground level and originally accommodated a cinema café (there is also a kitchen and servery).

"The auditorium was... entered at two levels (with two entrances from the ground level foyer). In keeping with all Odeons, the auditorium is comfortably furnished and planned with excellent sight lines. The design features of the auditorium can be interpreted in a wealth of film symbolism. There is a long central segmented ceiling light running the full length of the ceiling from front to back which might be interpreted as a strip of film. The curves and columns along the side walls are like film reels and spools; and the stepped forms above the screen could be represented as camera shutters. The pattern in the

Odeon Muswell Hill. A view across the dazzling foyer.

plasterwork of the side walls, the balcony fascia and orchestra rail are an even more abstract expression of a machine aesthetic. The decoration contributed to the acoustic balance, disguised the vents of the plenum heating system, concealed the lighting, and gave a directional emphasis. Plasterwork and fabrics were originally in the house colours of cream, green and gold. The orchestra pit established a curve form and the minimum distance for good sight lines."

David Atwell, in *Cathedrals of the Movies*, refers to the "cash register" effect of Muswell Hill's "splendid interior" and to "the highest flair and imagination" in the design of foyer, circle stairs and auditorium ceiling. Richard Gray, in *Cinemas in Britain*, wrote: "Externally, the Muswell Hill Odeon had to behave quietly... but inside Coles created one of his most effective schemes. A superb double-height foyer, designed like a set from *Things To Come* [one of its first attractions], leads through rotundas at ground- and first-floor levels to the auditorium, where a lighting sconce plunges headlong from the back wall to the proscenium."

Other Odeons of 1936

After Oldham and Kettering, the third of the year's conversions gave Odeon an outlet in the centre of **Cardiff** in Wales, almost next door to the larger Olympia which became an ABC property. The New Imperial Cinema was a complete reconstruction of an older cinema on an enlarged site in 1934 for local entrepreneur Max Corne, but it closed again from April to September 1936 for upgrading to Odeon standards with plans drawn up by regional cinema specialist William S. Wort. The exterior was exceptionally narrow with a shallow canopy, on the ends of which two small name signs with neon were mounted, as had been done at Lancing. A much larger name sign was slapped across the vertical thrust of the upper two storeys. At the back of a long foyer, the auditorium seems to have had a slightly reduced seating capacity of 1,663. It looked slick and modern with art deco touches, inviting but not memorable.★

Howard Williams, another Welsh cinema architect, designed the Odeon at **Newton Abbot** in Devon. This had an out-of-the-way location in a corner of its own car park and was originally devised in 1933 for a promoter based in Torquay. It was a very

Odeon Cardiff. The dull exterior was part of an existing street frontage. This poor view of the auditorium gives some idea of the decorative treatment.

★ Odeon traded its acquisition of the New Imperial for a site in Bethany Square, Port Talbot. An Odeon Port Talbot was listed as "under construction" in the *Kine Year Book 1937* (and two succeeding editions) and surviving plans at the Weedon Partnership show that this was developed as a collaboration between Harry Weedon and local architect Thomas Gibb. The cinema was built and opened by Max Corne as the Majestic in January 1938, when its design was credited solely to Gibb. A takeover circa 1943 brought it into the Odeon circuit.

Odeon Newton Abbot. A rare Odeon where the frontage suited two Odeon signs rather than one. There seem to have been tightly curtained windows on the side walls. The architect's plans show a dressing room behind the right splay wall and an organ chamber behind the left side although no organ was ever installed. This was reputedly the only Odeon besides Perry Barr to have secondary gas lighting. (Auditorium view reproduced by permission of English Heritage.NMR.)

ordinary-looking building inside and out. The front elevation carried two name signs of equal weight placed vertically while there was a mock wood-panelled ceiling to the auditorium with art deco light fittings attached. Williams would go on to provide one of the most convincing imitation Odeon exteriors for the Plaza at Port Talbot, opened in 1940 (and now a listed building). The opening at Newton Abbot was delayed by a week to avoid clashing with a local operatic society's annual production. The town already possessed two small cinemas which survived the Odeon's arrival.

Corby, in Northamptonshire, gained its Odeon via an unusual arrangement with a local steel works anxious to attract and retain employees by providing them with a modern source of film entertainment (the town already had an old-fashioned hall called The Cinema). The population of 1,449 was set to explode from early 1935 as Stewart and Lloyds began to extract and smelt iron ore. In early September 1934, Oscar Deutsch announced a partnership with the company to build a modern Odeon on a site that had already been agreed. The industrial concern took a financial interest and was represented on the board of directors of the local Odeon company established for the venture. In other Odeons, local partners had often contributed sites but here there was talk of providing a subsidy to make the scheme viable.

Opened in March 1936 – hardly a rush job – Corby's Odeon was designed by a regional architect, Laurence M. Gotch. Of somewhat stiff appearance inside and out, it seated just over one thousand, less than the 1,500 originally envisaged. The facade was symmetrical, with a curved canopy that neatly echoed the cylindrical mass of faience above, while narrow colour bands inserted into the tiled areas were in the circuit style. The Odeon's arrival forced the closure of The Cinema in no time.

Yates, Cook and Darbyshire designed their last Odeon at **Wimbledon,** south London. The proprietor-manager of the existing Savoy cinema, H. Grafton Hutchinson, was persuaded to sell his building for demolition, clearing some of the space for the Odeon. As part of the deal, he was engaged by Odeon to assist at new openings and became the first manager at South Harrow and Wealdstone before returning to Wimbledon to take charge from day one. The new cinema also took in the former site of Ely's furnishing store and two members of the prominent local department store family, B. N. Ely and M. V. Ely, became directors of the local Odeon company along with the regular triumvirate of F. Stanley Bates, W. G. Elcock and Deutsch in his standard role as chairman and governing director.

The Wimbledon Odeon was a rather dull building inside and out, built at the opposite end of the town centre from County's far more imposing Regal. The ABC circuit ran the Elite while an independent operated the King's Palace, both nearer the

Odeon Corby.

Odeon Wimbledon. On the exterior, note the double thickness of the canopy, matching the side wall bands. and the decorative panels between the main windows. In the long and narrow auditorium, there are figures in bas relief in the decorative panels above the splay wall ventilation openings, too remote to be appreciated.

Regal than the Odeon. The tiny Princes gave up about the time the Odeon opened.

The Odeon at **Guide Bridge**, Ashton-under-Lyne, Lancashire, was built as the Verona to the design of prominent regional cinema architects Drury and Gomersall. This was a venture of local builders P. Hamer, inspired by their experience of erecting Odeons at Chester and elsewhere. Oscar Deutsch was anxious to add to his slim presence in the Manchester area and acquired the Verona just before opening, its name being hastily changed to Odeon.* In other respects, it looked nothing like an Odeon.

Designed by Roland Satchwell, **Stafford**'s Odeon was squeezed onto the most difficult site ever used for an Odeon. It was a mediocre building inside and out, so compact that Deutsch referred to it as the circuit's "drawing room cinema". The site resulted in less than a thousand seats with an exceptionally narrow proscenium opening, although one that allowed a good-size picture in the screen ratio of the period.

Deutsch proceeded with more than usual haste to see off a Union scheme for a Ritz, announced in March 1936. "The Odeon Stafford held the record for speed: it was put up in three months from scratch. They were still painting the exit doors at the opening party," Jossi Linz, who worked in Odeon's purchasing department, has recalled.

Dickie Dewes, head of the construction department at this period, has noted: "The Odeon Stafford – as originally built – had one highly unusual, possibly unique, feature. It had no back entrance. All the fuel for the boiler house had to be carried through the auditorium. A very small strip of land would have righted the position, but the owner refused to sell. I tried every possible approach, but failed. So we had to open without a back door and the moans from the manager about the damage to his seats and carpets from the fuel dust went up to the sky. The owner of the strip of land we needed was quite a pleasant character and when in Stafford I used to drop in and have a chat with him – still hoping. Years later, after the death of Oscar Deutsch and the end of the Second World War, the owner relented. I felt a terrific surge of relief when he agreed to sell and the theatre had an appropriate entrance for bringing in its fuel."

What certainly constituted a unique feature for an Odeon was the placing of the projection room at the rear of the stalls underneath the balcony. This was solely to permit the maximum number of seats upstairs, as the back rows extended in

* The company formed by P. Hamer – Verona Cinema (Guide Bridge) Ltd. – applied the proceeds of the sale to the construction of the larger Roxy at Hollinwood, Lancashire, which opened in December 1937 to the design of Drury and Gomersall. Unlike the Guide Bridge Odeon, the Roxy remains open to this day, subdivided into seven screens, and is still owned by Verona Cinema (Guide Bridge) Ltd.

Odeon Guide Bridge. The auditorium carpeting is not in the circuit design, the padded edge of the balcony is an anomaly, and the pleated curtains with their leaf design are most suited to an ABC hall.

Odeon Stafford. This cinema was attached to the existing pub at left. Adjacent buildings to right have been whited out. In the auditorium, the side extensions of the balcony front presumably allowed a few more seats to be added. The offbeat design of screen tabs seems to have appeared at this cinema only.

diminishing width right into the curved wall behind the entrance corner. The stairs to the balcony started on the left of the main foyer and brought patrons in on the left side rather than the centre.

Yet another odd feature about the Odeon Stafford, recalled by Sidney Swingler, is that it was forced to include a fish and chip shop in one of the two retail spaces at each end of the frontage – presumably to re-house a business on the original site. Fish and chip shops in the vicinity of cinemas were bad news as the smell of cooking had a habit of reaching the auditorium through the ventilation system. This type of business was normally prohibited from taking space in a cinema development.

Union's Ritz was never built and the Odeon became the only new cinema to appear in Stafford, competing with three halls owned by a local company that included the Picture House, which was very close to the Odeon at the edge of the town centre.

Takeovers

In 1936, new Odeons far outnumbered acquisitions. By far the most important deal, announced in September, was to take Odeon into Scotland for the first time through a new subsidiary, Odeon Cinema & Singleton Ltd., that would acquire a controlling interest in the Singleton chain. But final negotiations were drawn out and the ten cinemas only joined the circuit in March 1937.

Perhaps the year's most important single takeover was the Plaza at Watford, Hertfordshire. Although of outmoded design, this was very large, with an organ, and well sited to compete with the town's other major cinema, the fractionally larger Gaumont, when it arrived in 1937.

At Ealing in west London, the Avenue out at Northfields and the centrally placed Walpole came as a pair, sufficiently far apart to both play the Odeon circuit release. The larger Avenue took the Odeon name and added a real "atmospheric" (with tented ceiling rather than sky) to the circuit after the feeble in-house attempts at Weymouth and Lancing. The old-fashioned Walpole (built as a skating rink with exposed roof trusses) was announced in August 1938 as a likely candidate for rebuilding to plans by Andrew Mather but no firm proposals followed.

In north Wales, the huge Winter Gardens in the holidaying centre of Llandudno joined the circuit, although it would be some years before it took the Odeon name. It had opened in 1935 as a theatre with ballroom and café, adding some films in the summer season of 1936. This was one of David Rosenfield's several contributions to the growth of Odeon as his Brooklyn Trust, based in Manchester, acquired the property in October 1936, then turned it over to Oscar Deutsch.

The Regal at Skipton, North Yorkshire, had a modest 927 seats and retained its original name for many years after coming under Odeon ownership. The Palace at Bilston, in the Wolverhampton area, was slightly larger and inherited the Odeon name within a year. The Picture House at Chesterfield, Derbyshire, was a distinguished-looking cinema with a Tudor frontage and 1,559 seats. This fell into Deutsch's hands just a month after ABC's larger Regal had opened in the town.

Decorative Crafts

In May 1936 an Odeon subsidiary called Decorative Crafts was formed to carry out decorative schemes for the circuit, beginning with Bridgwater and followed by work at Loughborough and elsewhere. It seems to have been created to give Lily Deutsch a formal outlet for her involvement in Odeon design – by which they were "gilded by the Lily". The board of directors not only included Lily and Oscar Deutsch but also F. Stanley Bates and George Elcock, Harry Weedon and Odeon's technical chief, Sidney Swingler, while the managing director was George S. Hall. It was acknowledged that too many Odeons were being built for Decorative Crafts to handle them all, but in time the company intended to work on outside schemes as well, besides handling the maintenance and renovation of Odeons. Decorative Crafts certainly concerned itself with draperies, supplying colourful screen curtains in a variety of striking designs, following on from the example at Scarborough before the company was formed.[*]

Decorative Crafts appointed specialists such as the interior designers of Scarborough, Mollo and Egan, to work on Odeon schemes. An examination of several Weedon plans for Odeons show that they were highly specific about the exteriors but vague about the decorative aspects of the interiors. The undated plans for Harrogate refer to a "free area" at the fresh air inlets on the side walls forward of the balcony front. Plans for the Newport Odeon (25 September 1936) carry the annotations "See Decorative Crafts drawings for interior decoration" along with "See Acoustic Specialist drawings for position of pax tiles". The contract plans for Norwich (19 February 1937) simply indicate an opening for extract grilles 7ft. by 13ft. on each side wall and, further forward, "wall recessed for decorative treatment by specialists" together with a more general annotation that the decorative treatment of ceiling and walls would be found on specialists' drawings.

Robert Bullivant once remarked to me that several decorative schemes would have been submitted for Lily Deutsch's consider-ation and, when the meeting was held to make a choice, he would place his favourite in the most prominent position or the best light and this would usually be the one accepted by Mrs. Deutsch.

And Odeons That Never Were

Firstly, the one that got away. The Odeon for **Northwood Hills** to the north west of Harrow, was designed by A. D. (Douglas) Clare, who died aged 47 on 8 July 1936 while the cinema was nearing completion.[*] It was fully prepared for a September 1936 opening but remained mysteriously shut. In mid-November, the building was sold to the Shipman and King circuit which opened it as the Rex on 28 December, mounting their name sign directly over the Odeon one. (Cinema manager Arthur Hawkins remembers an occasion in the late 1940s when the Odeon sign reappeared, giving him the impression that Odeon had taken over the cinema – in fact, the Rex sign had been temporarily taken down.)

Such last-minute changes of ownership were not unknown: Granada sold its fully completed Manchester cinema to Gaumont in 1935 and purchased the Plaza Sutton just before opening (although the original promoter handled its first few days of operation). Odeon made successful offers for virtually completed properties, as at Guide Bridge, but did not relinquish any other cinema besides Northwood Hills.

So why was the Northwood Hills Odeon sold? I suspect that film booking problems arose from the nearby presence of Shipman and King's Astoria and Rivoli cinemas in Ruislip. S&K probably sought to bar the Odeon from playing concurrently the new releases that the Astoria and Rivoli normally played. Once S&K acquired the cinema, there was no bar and almost always the Rex took the same programme as either the Astoria or (less often) Rivoli, which was usually the Odeon release of the week. (An alternative possibility for the S&K takeover is that it might have agreed not to build on Odeon's toes somewhere else in exchange for acquiring Northwood Hills, but the few known unrealised S&K schemes do not fit this line of thought.)

As in previous years, several Odeon schemes surfaced in the architectural and film press that never went ahead. Early in the year came a scheme for Station Road, Wigan, Lancashire, to seat 2,000. This was probably the site on which Union built its

---

[*] Screen tabs (in the style seen at Lancaster and elsewhere) were supplied to at least one outsider, the New Cinema at Coten End, Warwick – which had an excellent Odeon-style exterior, although entirely in brick, by architect Ernest S. Roberts. As it opened in 1940, perhaps the set was originally made up for an uncompleted Odeon.

[*] A. D. Clare was in partnership with J. Stanley Beard on such cinemas as the Palace Kensal Rise, London (1931), the Plaza West Wickham, Kent, and the Luxor Eastbourne, Sussex (both 1933), and with Beard and W. R. Bennett on the Forum Ealing (1934). Going into practice on his own, Clare was responsible for the Winter Gardens at Ventor, Isle of Wight (which recalled the De La Warr Pavilion at Bexhill and which never showed films).

Odeon Northwood Hills. Exterior in September 1936 (courtesy of Bruce Peter), before becoming the Rex. Shipman and King remembered to take the Odeon name off the clockfaces in the auditorium, which hardly suggests an Odeon with its unusual ceiling design.

Ritz. It was closely followed by an Andrew Mather scheme for Hoe Street, Walthamstow, north London, that seems to have remained as a possibility until the outbreak of World War Two. Later in the year Odeons were proposed for Tontine Street, St. Helens, Lancashire, and for Godstone Road, Caterham, Surrey.

Other schemes were shot down at hearings for a provisional licence. The case of the Odeon planned for West Bromwich has been detailed previously. At Tottenham, north London, Oscar Deutsch was intent on providing a very large Odeon at the junction of High Street and Scotland Green to the designs of George Coles – the local planning authority rejected three separate applications and then became quite annoyed at Deutsch's persistence, declaring the subject closed for good. However, this was the year of a battle at Bournemouth, described in the next chapter, where it took four attempts to succeed.

Odeon was embroiled in a court case in July 1936 over plans to build at Gosport, Hampshire. The company had bought a site in Walpole Road, then sold it at a profit to a local circuit, Portsmouth Town Cinemas, which opened a Ritz there in March 1935. Odeon then became interested in two further sites in the town, but it was alleged that the company had given an undertaking not to build there when it sold the first site. The evidence was unclear and no court order was made. Perhaps, as in the case of Seaford, Oscar Deutsch withdrew as a matter of courtesy and good will, since no Odeon appeared.

1937: THE PEAK YEAR

This was not only the peak year for new Odeons, with thirty-seven being added, including the flagship Odeon Leicester Square, but also the year when the greatest number of existing cinemas were taken over – thirty-six, including four to be replaced by big new Odeons.

Although both the major rivals – ABC and Gaumont – were also at a 1930s building high, their combined total of openings did not equal Odeon's figure. And no other circuit ever came anywhere near matching Odeon's feat of opening fourteen cinemas in a little over six weeks, from Crewe and South Norwood on the same day, 16 July, to Wolverhampton on 11 September. Even more amazingly, eleven of these came from the Weedon practice – nine opened within less than a month (14 August-11 September) at Bolton, Boston, Burnley, Exeter, Morecambe, Peterborough, Radcliffe, Swiss Cottage and Wolverhampton – and they were almost all of outstanding quality. Weedon completed only five other Odeons during the rest of the year but these included the collaboration with Andrew Mather on the Odeon Leicester Square.

Odeons were also becoming much larger. Oscar Deutsch had clearly stopped believing that even 1,500 seats were usually sufficient. Cinemas seating 1,700 to 1,800 were now frequent, while others were around 2,000 seats or higher. A few smaller Odeons with 1,000-1,200 seats still appeared, mostly in country towns.

In contrast to Harry Weedon's flurry of activity, the George Coles practice designed only four new Odeons but they were major accomplishments (a fifth was an outside job taken over). He was also busy completing four cinemas for other clients, including Hyams and Gale's colossal Gaumont State Kilburn.

Besides working on Leicester Square, Andrew Mather's practice provided seven other Odeons of the usual varying quality, at least two being originally prepared for other promoters.

During this year Deutsch acquired six sites for new Odeons in Scotland. In addition, plans for Blackpool were approved but delayed. Most of the other locations where Odeons would build before World War Two had been chosen. Sites seem to have been accumulating at a rate far faster than the Odeon organisation could handle them, leading to considerable delays (Deutsch moved a few doors to somewhat larger London offices at 49 Park Lane during the year, although principal administration remained in Birmingham).

Much time was consumed when Odeon went public in July, offering shares in Odeon Theatres Limited which had been formed to buy out seventy-three of the separate local Odeon companies and take over thirteen recently purchased cinemas.

Harry Weedon

Some of the problems of designing the Odeon at **York** were mentioned jointly with those concerning Chester in the previous chapter. Regarding York, Robert Bullivant adds: "Negotiations were equally protracted. It was made clear that any application for a cinema on a site within the city walls would be firmly rejected. Eventually approval was given for the development of a site outside the city wall." Even then the building had to be toned down. "As at Chester, they were only prepared to consider an application for a building which did not look like an Odeon."

The site had been occupied by the Crescent Café and Dance Salon. Excavation revealed items of archaeological significance, as noted in *Cinema & Theatre Construction*, August 1936: "A few weeks ago remains, consisting of Roman pottery, bronze objects and foundations, were discovered by workmen on the site of the Odeon, Chester. Now comes the news that workmen have found specimens of Roman and medieval pottery at York. One of these discoveries, a vase, is pronounced by Dr. Walter E. Collinge, keeper of the Yorkshire Museum, to be an extremely interesting find, being a mask or face vase assignable to the fourth century. [...] The specimen has been generously presented to the Yorkshire Museum by Mr. Deutsch, and placed amongst the collection of Roman antiques."

Externally, the Odeon resembled Chester by being entirely in brick with the name sign in the "more refined" Trajan style of lettering. York's exterior was the more impressive of the two: the brickwork varied in colour with intricate banding while the round-ended two-storey extension with ground-floor shop was highly Odeon-like. The authorities allowed the use of neon to highlight the building at night.

Odeon York. Yet to be added on the left of the exterior is a two-storey parade of shops culminating in a rounded corner at right angles to that on the right. In the auditorium there are attractive cloud-like patterns in the orchestra rail. The side wall above the grillework has a pleasing linear arrangement of acoustic tiles. (Circle foyer view reproduced by permission of English Heritage. NMR.)

The balcony foyer displayed a high-level frieze of figures in costume interspersed with film crew members and studio equipment. The auditorium looked relatively straightforward with typical use of cove lighting in a descending ceiling, the striking feature being the rather jagged design of the grillework on the side and back walls and ceiling. But, in its original colour treatment with its screen curtains, it had considerable impact. CTA member James Bettley, who attended this Odeon in the early 1950s and later worked there, writes: "A chief projectionist I knew in the 1960s had been an apprentice based at York Odeon at the time of its opening. He remembered Harrogate as being referred to as 'the garden', Scarborough as 'the rain forest' – and York as 'Hades'! At York, the auditorium colour scheme was black, red and gold against cream and the striking screen curtains showed two mythical beasts grinning at the audience and approaching centre stage complete with spiked heads and fearsome claws." The design, which I had mistaken for squabbling cats, does not seem to have repeated elsewhere. Bettley also recalls the way terminating bands from the side wall treatment enclosed dark fluted columns at the sides of the prosce-nium arch, near their bases, to direct attention towards the screen, and he provides a vivid description of the way lighting was used in the early 1950s:

"The first of the three ceiling coves contained green bulbs which bathed the area above the proscenium whereas the side vertical coves contained red bulbs giving the ante-proscenium walls a rosy glow. The two ceiling coves further from the stage shed white light across the ceiling sections in front. The con-clusion of the feature film in this cinema was invariably spec-tacular. The screen curtains with their mythical beasts, created by appliquéd satin of black, gold and red on a silver ground, would close as footlights and batten bathed the scene in vivid red (usually). Once these curtains met, the house tabs would follow them in as the proscenium bay lighting came up. The house curtains were of maroon velvet with two horizontal copper-coloured satin bands near the bottom – the lower one slightly the deeper. Once these tabs met, the house lights would come up and the green circuit would be introduced in the footlights, changing the colour on the tabs from red to golden amber."

This is presumably the lighting scheme originally designed for the cinema, or something very similar. Besides showing cinemas coldly devoid of patrons, black-and-white architectural photo-graphs cannot take into account the contribution of variable colour lighting to completing the atmosphere of an auditorium. It must have done much to improve the duller Odeon interiors.

The York Odeon arrived in February, eight months before ABC's larger Regal, while the year also threw up a third new cinema, the Clifton, on the northern outskirts of the town. Curiously, Gaumont never built here but ran three old halls.

Odeon Hanley. The vast expanse of brick side wall is well handled and hides the roof – the windows mark the long main foyer and balcony lounge. This style of screen tabs was earlier seen at Falmouth.

Four further venues also competed for the cinemagoer's attention.

The **Hanley** Odeon, which served the seven towns of the Potteries in Staffordshire, had an awkward site with a narrow corner entrance leading to an auditorium set at right angles some distance back. It replaced the Grand Theatre, which had been destroyed in a fire some time after becoming a cinema in February 1932. Architect Cedric Price recalls that his father, Arthur J. Price, was in charge of this scheme and had a rabbit added to the design of the screen tabs.

A curving corner entrance terminated in a small slab tower at the boundary of the narrow site where it stood rather incongruously next to a much lower and older property. The rounded-ended tower was clad in buff faience made up of rectangular tiles placed vertically, culminating in what looked like a high-level observation deck for a thin member of staff. Faience in basket-weave pattern covered the corner above canopy level with a thin green band near the top, as usual reinforced by neon, while a recessed window was inserted into the curve.

Decoratively, the auditorium was on the dull side. It was one of the first Odeons to do away with the orchestra rail, leaving an unusually large expanse of carpeted floor. The balcony was very steep for a cinema while the rear ceiling of the auditorium had to be even higher to allow the projection box to be set over the balcony rather than at the back (as was customary in an Odeon). This permitted the seating to extend further back but the Odeon still held only 1,580 – on the low side for such a large catchment area. The main immediate competition in Hanley was Gaumont's large Regent, the even larger independently-run Palace and ABC's smallish Capitol. Gaumont also had the small Empire while a Roxy (independent) completed the opposition.

Wrexham in Denbighshire, Wales, had three existing cinemas, plus two more at nearby Rhos. Its Odeon was an eye-catching addition with buff faience covering an unusually low and wide entrance block totally lacking in windows above canopy level. The horizontality contrasted dramatically with a tower and projecting slab in faience. The slab carried the cinema name on both faces.

Odeon Wrexham. The parade of shops are part of the scheme (the two furthest units temporarily advertise the Odeon's opening). The design of screen tabs seems to have been unique to this cinema.

The semi-stadium auditorium was rather dramatic for an Odeon with bands of concealed lighting across the ceiling that faced back rather than forward and six front-lit decorative horizontal bands on the splay walls leading towards the screen. The assistant of record for the scheme is Budge Reid but the splay wall treatment is so reminiscent of Mollo and Egan's work at the Majestic Rochester (1935) that it must represent the first of their contributions through Decorative Crafts to the Weedon output of the year.

In May, the Odeon at **Yeovil**, Somerset, offered another forceful exterior with a brick fin, carrying the cinema name, emerging from a central faience-clad tower; but overall this

Odeon Yeovil. The flower beds considerably improve the approach. The inner foyer shows the cinema's pedigree with images of Crewe (drawing), Sutton Coldfield, Chester, Weston-super-Mare, Kingstanding, and an unbuilt scheme. Some of Eugene Mollo's vivid murals decorated the outer foyer.

frontage seemed a little top heavy and box-like. The cinema was rather out of the way up a side street, on a sloping site alongside a timber yard. The slab tower faced the town centre where the Gaumont and small Central were already established. Green bands traversed the faience tiles at ground level, above the black base, as well as highlighting a slightly protruding area with tall windows marking the inner foyer. Although the Weedon office made its usual admirable effort to hide the roof, economy was evident in an exit on the far side with a corrugated iron roof.

As at Wrexham, the job assistant was Budge Reid, with Mollo and Egan credited for the dramatically different design of the auditorium. Eugene Mollo set out to show the latest development in Holophane lighting, the moulded contour system which had been devised by R. Gillespie Williams and which was under consideration for the forthcoming Odeon in Leicester Square. The upper proscenium surround and ribs across the ceiling were covered in concave discs or domes, made of fibrous plaster but sprayed with cellulose, to reflect different colours projected onto them by hidden floodlights. The lighting made graduated changes and the entire ceiling became, according to one description, a "transparent and glimmering mass of light". A diagonal line divided light from shade: below it, the carpets and seat upholstery were deliberately dark in colour while the adjacent walls were given a non-reflective treatment and the lighting kept to a minimum. The ventilation openings on the splay walls were reduced to a discreet square of sieve-like openings.*

Budge Reid was again the job assistant on the Weedon Odeons at **Crewe**, Cheshire, and **Dudley**, Worcestershire – two near-perfect expressions of the circuit style. Externally, both featured deep recessed main windows between rounded piers with green banding in buff faience and further green strips at ground level above the black base. Crewe had a brick tower and fin splitting the frontage between cinema entrance (with buff faience cladding) and parade of shops and flats (much as had been done at Ramsgate). Dudley had an undivided frontage with a splendid array of curves including the corners of the brick auditorium behind.

Crewe was on the small side in terms of seating capacity (1,129 seats in stadium plan) and had a finely proportioned auditorium with decorative grillework clearly emanating from Mollo and Egan. It was the first and last 1930s cinema in town, competing with ABC's Empire and four other halls.

Dudley's auditorium was slightly plainer with patterned

---

* The cut-away side wall treatment appeared again a week later with the opening of the Gaumont Rose Hill (Carshalton) in Surrey and towards the end of the year at the Odeon North Watford (both Mollo and Egan without reflecting discs) as well as at the Davenport at Stockport, Cheshire, in mid-year (reflecting ribs and squares, no Mollo and Egan).

Odeon Crewe on 29 July 1937, three days after opening. The treatment of the shops and flats is very similar to Wrexham. The cinema's deeply recessed windows recall Loughborough. In the auditorium, acoustic tiles cover much of the side walls. The proscenium frame is back lit. The screen tabs' design was repeated seven months later at Spalding. (CTA Archive.)

Odeon Dudley. As at Yeovil (and earlier at Warley and elsewhere) flower beds enhance the approach to the cinema. The letters of the name sign line up with the five windows below.

Odeon Dudley. The sloping front to the balcony is a nice touch, though not without precedent.

grilles over ventilation openings set flush into the side walls and small areas to catch reflective lighting at each side of the proscenium opening.

With 1,876 seats, the Odeon was by far the largest cinema in Dudley, and more than a match for the three Gaumont properties (Regent, Criterion and Empire), some independents, and the two modern halls opposite, the Plaza and the live Hippodrome.

The Odeon at **Radcliffe** was a small and rather odd addition to the circuit in industrial Lancashire, two miles from Bury where the circuit was already established. Radcliffe already had three cinemas run by a small circuit that remained in business undercutting the prices of admission at the Odeon.

This was one of only two Weedon Odeons intentionally designed and built on the cheap (at two-thirds of the cost of the similarly-sized Crewe), but it still exhibited the company flair. It had a simplified but effective exterior with central use of faience and rounded corners in brick while the semi-stadium auditorium featured an abridged example of Mollo and Egan-style decorative grillework on the splay walls. The assistant in charge was W. Calder Robson.

The Odeon for **Boston**, Lincolnshire, harked back to earlier Weedon schemes. Its exterior was close to those of Loughborough and the Tower West Bromwich, while its interior seems (from the photographic evidence) to have been a little tepid. This was another handled by Budge Reid.

Other architects were adopting the Odeon style. Two or three months before the Odeon arrived in Boston, a local company opened the Regal, which had a faience-clad frontage with rounded corners, too brash for a Weedon job, by regional architect A. J. Thraves; but its exhilarating, streamlined auditorium certainly outclassed the Odeon. This was designed for the company owning the two existing cinemas in Boston to stand up to the threat posed by outsiders. Following Odeon, the Union circuit had announced a plan to build a 1,646-seat new cinema. The *Kinematograph Weekly* (11 June 1936) painted a nightmare scenario by which Boston (population: 16,597) could have ended up with five cinemas seating around 6,280 people, calculating that, if every man, woman and child went three times weekly, there would still be 17,000 unoccupied seats every week. Fortunately, Union's scheme evaporated but Boston still ended up with four cinemas.

The main elevation of the Boston Odeon displayed a new approach (never repeated) to the treatment of faience tiles in basketweave pattern. Whereas normally the joints were thickened around each pair of tiles to bring out the squares they formed, here the emphasis was reversed: the basketweave effect was highlighted by thickening the line of mortar between each pair of tiles. It was not an improvement.

Here, too, black-tiled piers between the recessed windows

Odeon Radcliffe. (Auditorium view
reproduced by permission of English Heritage.NMR.)

Odeon Boston. The colour bands (overlaid with neon and name sign
across the top of the frontage) are green, as are those across the black
base. The higher narrow openings between the columns are not windows
but slatted ventilation openings, somewhat like Weybridge. There are
four flower beds built into the steps on each side. In the auditorium,
the screen tabs' design was an original, although the lower part was
similar to York.

seemed more of a decorative addition than a structural feature, recalling those on the back walls of recesses at Bognor Regis and Colindale.

The auditorium design was rather barren with ribbed plaster-work enclosing the proscenium and bands across the ceiling with concealed lighting. There was a rectangular recess over the rear circle (reminiscent of Weston-super-Mare) with stencilled decoration in green and yellow lit up from the rim. It is a distinctly odd Weedon Odeon that calls to mind the work of so many rival architects.

The Bolton and Burnley Odeons were major ventures that opened a week apart in August 1937 in industrial Lancashire. **Bolton** (assistant: W. Calder Robson) seated 2,534, making it by far the largest Odeon to that date, the first to seat over two thousand. It had an imposing, almost intimidating tall frontage in buff faience with deep recessed windows and short green horizontal bands on the faience extending round the corners, accentuated by neon. The extra height and the unrounded upper corners of the entrance block denied it the streamlined smoothness of Dudley.

The auditorium was designed to reflect coloured lighting, not only from the concave discs on each side of the proscenium opening but also from the vertical ribbed surfaces elsewhere. The large capacity of the balcony necessitated extra side exits at the front of the circle. The rare addition of a Compton organ with illuminated jelly-mould console was in response to the Christie organ at the large Lido cinema, which had been opened five months earlier by the regional John Buckley circuit. (The Lido cheekily added the slogan "Nulli Secundus" – "Second to None" – to its advertising the week the Odeon opened.)

We have an invaluable record of the impact that a new Odeon made from the reminiscences of Leslie Halliwell about the forty-seven cinemas of his Bolton childhood, as recalled in the book *Seats in All Parts* (1985):

"Late in 1936, men began to clear a slum site in Ashburner Street, on the town centre side of the wholesale market and close to the less used of Bolton's two railway stations. It would have had to go before long, as its ramshackle and smelly old mill cottages provided too great a contrast to the new million-pound civic centre, all neo-Victorian vastness and inconvenience, which had been built two hundred yards away. But there was high excitement when gossip reported, and the *Evening News* confirmed, that the site was booked for a flagship cinema in Oscar Deutsch's rapidly spreading chain of sleek modernistic Odeons, an amenity with nearly three thousand seats, a car park, and a balcony café. Well, it took them twenty years to pave the car park, and the café was long notorious for serving the toughest buttered crumpets for miles around, but the rest of

Odeon Bolton.

Odeon Burnley. There appears to be a separate front stalls entrance with its own canopy to the left. The screen tabs with elephant seem to have been unique to this site. (Foyer view reproduced by permission of English Heritage.NMR.)

the dream came true, and for many months the unvarying hobby of Bolton's unemployed was to watch it rise from the surrounding squalor, brick by brick and tile by tile. Progress was sure but infuriatingly slow: so slow in fact that a rival project [the Lido], conceived and announced several months later, contrived to open first."

Halliwell attended the opening Saturday: "The décor was undeniably sumptuous. My first impression, after I got my breath back, was of rounded corners everywhere, without a right angle in sight. The immensity of the red velour curtains; the cunningly concealed lighting; the great golden honeycomb grills on each side of the screen; the green octagonal clocks in which the letters THE ODEON took the place of numerals; all these played their part in the magnificence of that massive decorated space. It was more overwhelming than being in St. Mark's Church, or even Manchester Cathedral. But as I later discovered to be the case with all Odeons, the design was in fact simple to the point of austerity. There was nothing that could catch dust. The foyers and corridors were laid with rubber tiling in green and black abstract designs, with just a touch of red; and even the toilets had a smooth severity which counterpointed the general grandeur. Henceforth, Bolton's older halls with their plaster cupids and decorated pillars would seem tawdry indeed."

The **Burnley** Odeon (assistant: Robert Bullivant) was one of several built on sites obtained by David Rosenfield. It was not quite as big as Bolton but seated well over 2,000. Its exterior with fin tower carrying the Odeon name was another outstanding demonstration of the house style.

The plans called for a cultural touch in the upper foyer, an oil painting called "The Seasons", but its inclusion is unconfirmed. The auditorium was unexceptional, with another instance of side exits at the circle front. The illuminated grillework, unusually high on the side walls, looked like a tame version of Mollo and Egan's work with its repetitive festoon curtain theme.

Like Bolton, Burnley was not lacking in cinemas – only in modern ones. There were around fourteen halls when the Odeon appeared, including a Temperance Cinema and nine operated by New Empire (Burnley) Limited, a circuit that had already had its fortunes dented by the new Odeon at Radcliffe.

In **Exeter,** Devon, the Odeon designed by Robert Bullivant had a towering frontage dominated by four ribbed vertical bands in light tiles which carried neon tubes. A most unusual and elaborate canopy had raised features that lined up with the soaring bands. Three tall windows admitted daylight to the lofty foyers.

The auditorium was also arresting with its interaction of plunging lines and the somewhat twee touch of two different groups of five medieval figures in bas relief high on a curve in the side walls, the lowest characters being helped up the slope.

Here, too, was another, more practical, innovation for Odeon: curtain lighting incorporated into the balcony front.

Exeter provides a dramatic illustration of the problems that could arise from the speed at which Odeon sometimes worked. It was claimed that building was completed in thirty-six weeks, a probable record for that part of the country. Robert Bullivant recalled: "The haste with which cinema sites were acquired by joining five or six sites together did not give the lawyers adequate time to make the necessary searches – a genius for improvisation was sometimes necessary to continue building around the unsuspected rights of tenure or of access which had only come to light when the building had been well advanced... The structural steelwork was almost completely erected before it was discovered that a neighbour enjoyed the right to take water from a standpipe which was situated in the middle of what would eventually be the centre aisle of the stalls. The removal of the standpipe involved expensive and protracted negotiations. Neither side would give way and the seats and carpet were being installed round the pipe before a settlement was reached."

And Bullivant remembered a further property dispute: "There was a shop next door that sold cigarettes and so on – and the owner was obviously being helped by solicitors to squeeze as much as he could out of the Odeon people. His little shop had space over the adjoining shop Odeon had bought – and he said he had rights to this and it meant Odeon couldn't pull it down. So we actually propped it up until about a week before the opening day and then dropped it down at the last moment. He was always having bricks dropped into his yard. He got quite a bit out of it in the end."

The Odeon followed a Gaumont Palace (1932) and ABC's Savoy (1936) to give the town full representation by the major circuits. Three small cinemas seem to have given up the ghost around 1937 but a second Gaumont hall and an independent persevered.

At **Morecambe**, the Lancashire seaside resort, the Weedon office (assistant: W. Calder Robson) refreshed the usual elements of a corner entrance with a quirky and playful, clef-shaped "observation deck" high up the frontage (Hanley had a similar feature in its slab tower). The auditorium made bold use of a repetitive decorative pattern on the side walls in vertical rather than horizontal bands.

The Odeon was not ideally positioned and had substantial competition from more than six rival halls, including Gaumont's Tower, and from the Empire when it opened in 1938 for live shows and films.

Harry Weedon had the unique experience among cinema architects of concluding two projects simultaneously when the Odeon at **Peterborough,** Northamptonshire, opened on the

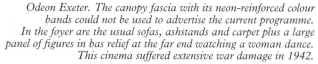

Odeon Exeter. The canopy fascia with its neon-reinforced colour bands could not be used to advertise the current programme. In the foyer are the usual sofas, ashstands and carpet plus a large panel of figures in bas relief at the far end watching a woman dance. This cinema suffered extensive war damage in 1942.

same day as Morecambe. The original architect was Roland Satchwell whose plans for this cinema, well out of the town centre, were approved in October 1935. However, his work was revised by the Weedon office which took sole credit for the completed building.

The weak exterior was little altered from Satchwell's original scheme. Such details as the wide windows and mouldings around them, and the decorative flourish above the parapet distance this from a regular Weedon exterior. The auditorium had some bold undulating curves and horizontal banding to relieve a rather bland scheme. The cinema opened two months ahead of the town's Embassy, designed for dual cinema and live use. Gaumont had the well-placed but old-fashioned Broadway and there were five other picture houses in the area.

The Odeon **Swiss Cottage**, north London, brought the Harry Weedon team to London, to revise or replace a Robert Cromie scheme developed for a company called Eldorado. Basil Herring was the assistant in charge. This was the largest London Odeon to date, with 2,115 seats, although it would be quickly overtaken by both Leicester Square and Edgware Road.

On the exterior, the lack of faience and the reliance on red brick certainly suggested Cromie rather than Weedon. The construction of a full fly tower was quite exceptional and the inclusion of a Compton organ a rarity. The decoration of the auditorium was flamboyant by Odeon standards and may have been a Mollo and Egan scheme retained. The curvaceous sweep of the orchestra rail and its jazzy decoration were also atypical. But this cinema's location in a sophisticated suburb (with no immediate competition but not far from the Haverstock Hill Odeon) may have encouraged a more deluxe treatment than normal. It would certainly be a top moneymaker for the circuit.

At **Wolverhampton,** Staffordshire, the exterior of the Odeon (assistant: P. J. Price) pulled some highly successful variations on standard features to create one of the best later facades. This had a tall, wide, rather flat frontage in which the only curving element was the canopy – rounded at one end, terminating in a mind-your-head underside scroll at the other. The horizontal banding all the way up the corner, of cream faience accented in red, had not been seen before. The slab tower was black-tiled with a brick core, and was not used to carry an Odeon sign. Black tiles with green bands enclosed the tall windows to the side of the entrance. The use of both red and green was exceptional, and both colours also appeared elsewhere on the facade.

The large auditorium might seem on the bland side but what must be taken into account, as described at York, is the effect of the changing colours of the principal lighting, concealed in the stepped ceiling and side walls. Bands across the ceiling and down the side walls carried repetitive decoration in a manner

Odeon Morecambe. There is an element of seaside "fun architecture" in the curving corridor added to the frontage.

Odeon Swiss Cottage. The screen tabs here featured an Odeon in the mountains – and a Swiss cottage.

Odeon Peterborough. The individual tiles are in basketweave pattern. The placing of the main name sign on the canopy is comparatively unusual. (CTA Archive.)

reminiscent of the barrel-vaulted ceilings in early picture houses.

Overall, this was not quite a match in design terms for the town's amazing Gaumont Palace (1932), although it had a more central location. One of W. R. Glen's ABCs, the good-looking Savoy, opened three months after the Odeon, giving the town a full complement of modern major circuit houses as well as numerous older halls.

At **Rhyl**, the coastal resort in Flintshire, the new Odeon had encountered fierce opposition. This was understandable, as the local Rhyl Entertainments company had three cinemas in the town, including the large Plaza, was building an equally large new Regal (on a site near the proposed Odeon), and seemed to be doing more than enough to cater for the cinematic needs of locals and holidaymakers. The Odeon not only disturbed a monopoly position, with all the advantages of reduced film hire, but it threatened huge over-capacity, especially out of season.

Nevertheless, the Odeon scheme had the support of Rhyl Ratepayers Association and 5,879 signatures had been gathered in favour of the application for a provisional licence before the licensing meeting on 13 March 1936. Representing Odeon, Neville Laski declared that people did not like monopolies, while E. T. Rhymer argued the case for the existing cinema interests. When the Council found in favour of Odeon, there was a storm of cheering and applause from the six hundred people who had packed the meeting.

As Robert Bullivant recalled: "The local cinema proprietors challenged the decision of the licensing justices to grant a provisional cinematograph licence and a public inquiry was held in the town hall with barristers representing both sides. Every seat at the inquiry was occupied and crowds blocked the streets outside awaiting the verdict. Harry Weedon spoke and explained why we were providing another cinema and he got rounds of applause. The decision to uphold the granting of a provisional licence to Odeon Theatres was celebrated with fireworks, two brass bands and dancing in the streets." Odeon's publicity department was on the ball!

However, the construction of the Odeon Rhyl was far from troublefree, as Bullivant, who designed the scheme, explained: "The building had only been going for about a fortnight when I received a phone call at about midday from the building manager of Bryants, who were doing to the job, to say that the foundation excavations were flooding. I said, 'Absolute nonsense!' So I got in my car and drove straight up to Rhyl and took a look and they were as dry as possible. The building control chap was in the local pub so I went and had a pint with him and I said, 'You're pulling my leg.' And he said, 'Well, you wait half an hour and then come out and have a look.' Of course, it was tidal. This thing was filling up with water in the afternoon and

Odeon Wolverhampton. There is another Odeon sign just visible on the top corner of the building.

then by the evening it was empty. It was entirely a tidal case. The soil investigation had been inadequate. At neap tides high water rose above the bottom of the stalls ramp. We managed to get round it by having a totally different set of foundations which we re-designed.

"I think we were the laughing stock of North Wales because building in that area was very dangerous. It had been underwater about 500 years before. But it was a good site [in terms of location].

"The whole district rode like a quilt on a subterranean porridge of primeval forest. The quilt could support a carefully distributed load but if the quilt was pierced it was a long way down to a bearing stratum. For years afterwards we took check levels between the floor of the cinema foyer and a bench mark on an adjoining railway bridge. The readings were not too alarming – assuming that the railway bridge was not subsiding also.

"Rhyl was one of those jobs which was a series of problems. Others went perfectly, no problems, and yet a place like Rhyl...! For instance, adjoining the cinema we were building was a pub approached by a driveway along the side of the cinema and the builder had got some scaffolding at the side of the cinema. A coach full of people came to the pub and hit the scaffolding which fell and killed one man. We damaged the pub and they weren't clever enough to take out a case against us. They replaced the thing themselves.

"I remember the inspection was being made a fortnight before the opening day, and it had been raining heavily prior to that. When we went up on the roof to have a look, we found that the roof was like a series of lakes. The structural steel was not strong enough to support the weight of the water on the roof. The structural engineer admitted full responsibility and said he wanted to admit this to the press. We said, 'Not on your life, sir! We've got to open in a fortnight!' And we damn well did open in a fortnight. An open truck on the railway has a bar going across underneath to strengthen it, and this is what we did to strengthen this roof rather than having to pull it all off and start again." ★

As finished, the Odeon Rhyl had an accomplished exterior with its curved entrance, leading to a circular outer lobby, backed by

★ Before his death, Robert Bullivant had not identified the Odeon at which another difficulty occurred but it might as well be added here while on the subject of problems: "Less than a week before the opening the Licensing Justices Committee asked for additional work before they would release the licence. Among other items, they earnestly demanded that open metalwork balustrades to staircases leading up from the stalls foyer to the circle foyer should be filled in with modesty panels. Additional labour was brought onto the site immediately and work went on continuously for eighty or ninety hours to ensure that the opening ceremony could proceed as arranged."

Odeon Rhyl. There were red horizontal bands on the faience around the main Odeon sign. As usual, the side wall hides the roof. In the auditorium, note how the circle front has been extended forward at each side. The lower octagonal openings below the clock faces mask the public address speakers. (Exterior from CTA Archive.)

a squat tower with rounded top in vertically channelled faience carrying neon tubes. The auditorium seems to have been designed in association with Mollo and Egan with its deep horizontal bands of front-lit repetitive decoration on the splay walls. Space is reported to have been left for an organ as this was a seaside town, but none was ever installed.

Rhyl gained the unusual distinction for a town of its size of having three outstanding cinemas, as both the Plaza and Regent were the work of Sidney Colwyn Foulkes with auditoria of greater intricacy and interest than that of the Odeon. The town was certainly over-provided with cinemas and Rhyl Entertain-ments' oldest property, the Cinema Royal, closed for five months in 1938, re-opening for the summer season and then closing for good on 4 February 1939, having been sold to Woolworth's for the site of a new store, part of a distinct national trend in which expand-ing retail chains took over surplus cinemas.

The last of the year's Weedon schemes to be completed was the most prestigious and important of all the Odeons – the new London flagship, the Odeon **Leicester Square.** The collab-oration with Andrew Mather's practice was the only time the two offices combined forces.★ It was the first project in London and the south east on which Weedon worked and Oscar Deutsch's insistence on the creative input of the practice he most trusted led to Weedon staff moving into Odeon's old suite of offices at 7 Park Lane in late 1936 to take it on, adding schemes for Swiss Cottage and Hendon.

The Odeon Leicester Square was built on the site of the Alhambra Theatre and adjacent property. The Moorish-style theatre's days had long been numbered. It had been expected to close on 20 August 1933 after a season of ballet, to be replaced by a £750,000 Palace of Amusement with dance floor, beer garden, garden restaurant, solarium, gymnasium and swimming bath, designed by Edward A. Stone. A later scheme promised a vast amusement palace called the New Century. The Alhambra continued as a music hall until 1 September 1936, after which Oscar Deutsch took possession. The close ties with United Artists led to the Othello sequences for *Men Are Not Gods,* its new drama with a live theatre setting, being filmed there on Sunday 8 October. The theatre was demolished around November. It is worth observing that had there been a preservation movement

for places of entertainment in those days, the Alhambra would unquestionably have been saved and Oscar Deutsch would have had to look elsewhere.

The site, including the adjacent Turkish baths, cost Odeon around £550,000. It stretched 220ft. between Leicester Square and Charing Cross Road and was 120ft. wide.

Everyone fretted and argued over various designs until, in March 1937, Oscar Deutsch and his fellow directors piled into a seven-seat Daimler with a shorthand typist and secretary, and stopped in a London park so that they could thrash it out with no risk of interruption. The final scheme is said to have been principally the work of a Mather staff member, Thomas Braddock. Cedric Price recalls that his father, Arthur J. Price, worked exten-sively on the building from Weedon's side.★

The cinema was constructed over seven months at a cost of £232,755, or £110 per seat – four times that of other major Odeons (of course, it had the advantage of being able to charge West End prices which were three to four times higher than those of other Odeons). The work finished behind schedule: the original intention had been to open with a major new British picture from United Artists, *Knight Without Armour,* but the delay led to the substitution of one of UA's top Hollywood releases (albeit with stars of British origin), *The Prisoner of Zenda,* on the night of Tuesday 2 November.

The agreed key to designing the exterior of the Odeon was to make it the complete opposite of the rest of the circuit by replac-ing the use of biscuit-coloured faience tiles with slabs of polished black granite. There were approximately two hundred of these, each 6ft. by 5ft. and 2ins. thick, similar to the panels of glass that Mather was placing on other Odeons. The scheme originally called for a 150ft. tower to carry the name of the cinema but the height was reduced to 120ft. to comply with a planning limit introduced in Victorian times and still in force (but often waived

★ Odeon publicity stated that Andrew Mather had already made an impact on the other sides of Leicester Square: on the south with the Leicester Square Theatre and adjacent offices (where Mather's practice was based); on the west with the Automobile Association offices; and, on the north side (working for Frank Matcham), the Empire cinema. Mather's involvement with the Empire does not seem to be substantiated elsewhere.

★ There are sketches and detailed drawings of more than a dozen different exterior schemes in the RIBA Drawings Collection, donated by the Weedon Partnership. None are close to the cinema as actually designed but all have a tower feature on the left, while the use of black granite (or black Belgian marble) as the facing material is indicated on many, and most have an unusually large area for announcing the pro-gramme in changeable lettering, either on the side of the tower or above the entrance. Sculptural features suggested for the frontage included a series of panels depicting drama through the ages, pierced panels fronting a high balcony, and figures placed vertically to each side of a fin (cf. Gaumont Palace Cheltenham). Some detailed drawings by Robert Bullivant use illuminated glass combined with neon tubing at the top of the tower, an idea that he would later push through at Bradford. One auditorium scheme shows five boxes at the back of the circle, obviously for visits by royalty and other notables.

Odeon Leicester Square. Three different schemes from 1936. Lily Deutsch is seen with the model (courtesy of the National Museum of Photography, Film & Television, Bradford – Daily Herald Archive).

Below: Andrew Mather, the prolific cinema architect who collaborated with Harry Weedon on the Odeon Leicester Square.

Odeon Leicester Square. Exterior by day and by night.

since 1956).* In height, the tower was reminiscent of that originally planned for the Warley by T. Cecil Howitt. The whole was outlined at night in neon, becoming an outstanding British expression of German "night architecture".

The exterior seemed commanding but aloof – and undeniably impressive. There were two name signs on the front of the tower, one horizontal and one vertical, sharing the initial letter. The vertical sign was more widely spaced than the horizontal one, to reflect the height of the tower, but its spacing never looked quite right. The lettering here was in the circuit style but had double lines of neon in red and blue against opal, recessed into the outline of the individual letters. To the right of the tower, huge letters were mounted on bars in front of a large recess announcing the current attraction and lit up at night in neon.** The pitched roof of the cinema was entirely hidden from view by the tall frontage and surrounding buildings.

The rear of the site came out on Charing Cross Road where there had been a subsidiary entrance to the Alhambra. Odeon built a 40ft.-deep, ten-floor office block there called Alhambra House, for which the principal architect was Eric Lyons. This was partly to produce additional income and partly to hide the fly tower, as the cinema had full stage facilities. A 20ft.-wide passageway at the southern side of the building extended from Leicester Square right through to Charing Cross Road, providing an exit way from the side doors of the cinema and access to the stage. It was built over at each end, enabling a standard Odeon name sign to be mounted on Charing Cross Road.

The entrance on Leicester Square had twelve doors with plate-glass etchings by Bainbridge Copnall of dancing figures and animals to represent the four seasons and the elements. Immediately above these doors appeared a 37ft.-long moving sign carrying neon-lit letters one foot high, a new device that would be installed at many later Odeons.*** The sign was just below two lines of slotted letters which carried programme information in the old-fashioned way. Higher up, the recessed windows to the balcony lounge were surmounted by a bronze canopy that carried the Odeon name on the front (in the same style as on the tower) and a wavy neon pattern on the underside.

After the spectacular exterior, the main and balcony foyers were rather grand and formal – no doubt to avoid any risk of giving offence on special occasions. The wide ground-floor foyer was carpeted rather than covered by rubber, and the pattern in the central area was far more regal than the standard circuit design. The walls were wood-panelled (suggestive of an ocean liner interior like that of the Queen Mary) while modern light fittings were placed in the coffers of the ceiling. In the front left corner were the doors to the royal retiring room in the basement.

The balcony was reached by a staircase on the left side which divided at the half landing. Two bas-relief panels designed by E. J. Doudney were displayed on the side walls of the upper stairs to the balcony.

The compact nature of the site did not permit the ideal arrangement of a central staircase leading forward to the balcony but it seems a lapse that a matching staircase was not provided on the other side of the entrance hall, despite the space that would be lost. Perhaps this lack of symmetry reflects Mather's involvment in the scheme – as previously noted, many of his schemes had one-sided balcony access whereas Weedon supplied double staircases in such circumstances (and had done so here on one early plan).

The balcony foyer was huge for reception purposes and richly appointed with extensive wood panelling. The usual Odeon fittings were absent – the carpet was another "quiet" design, the settees were of a more conventional shape (although covered in one of the standard designs), the ash stands lacked the Odeon name, and the clock was not of the octagonal variety.

But after the conservative treatment of the foyer areas came an auditorium which was wonderfully innovative – by far the most intricate and impressive of any the circuit created.

There were 2,116 seats (1,140 in the stalls and 976 in the circle), making it the third largest Odeon yet opened, after Bolton and Burnley, and with one more seat than Swiss Cottage. The seats here were all covered in a leopard skin pattern unique to the cinema: more than one small boy was gobsmacked at the thought of so many leopards being hunted, although in bright light they were very synthetic looking. In yet another exception

---

* Richard Gray suggests that the planning authorities did not want the tower to be visible, oversailing the National Gallery, when viewed from the south side of Trafalgar Square.

** This very expensive method of announcing the current attraction was not used at any other Odeon but it did not need changing every week unlike the similar displays at Gaumont's New Victoria. In fact, Gaumont were very keen on changeable neon letters and mounted them on the front of several Gaumont Palaces.

*** This sign had been tried out at another unidentified cinema to test its suitability for Leicester Square. All of the 100-plus letters could be quickly and separately plugged into the electrical circuit by any member of staff standing on a stepladder from one position by simply advancing the endless conveyor belt a little at a time. It was claimed that the letters

could be completely changed in twenty minutes, which made it eminently suitable for last-minute announcements. The sign could also be fitted with caricatured heads of famous film stars and other symbols, and had the advantage of carrying more than twice as much information as stationary letters as well as drawing attention by its movement.

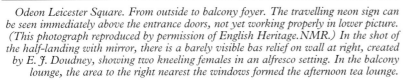

Odeon Leicester Square. From outside to balcony foyer. The travelling neon sign can be seen immediately above the entrance doors, not yet working properly in lower picture. (This photograph reproduced by permission of English Heritage.NMR.) In the shot of the half-landing with mirror, there is a barely visible bas relief on wall at right, created by E. J. Doudney, showing two kneeling females in an alfresco setting. In the balcony lounge, the area to the right nearest the windows formed the afternoon tea lounge.

to circuit practice, the seats were not the same throughout the house: those in the balcony were specially designed on springs with the backs padded with Dunlopillo while those in the stalls were of a standard design, the metal frames painted to look like woodwork. Sensibly, given the loud pattern of the seat covers, the carpet was in a plain, old gold colour.

The ceiling was crossed by bands of fibrous plaster which carried on down the side walls and concealed lighting as well as ventilation openings. These gave way to semi-circular coves just above the proscenium arch. As the main film ended, the auditorium would first light up from the semi-circular coves, then from each of the coves across in sequence through to the back. The lights would dim in reverse sequence before the curtains parted.

The artist Raymond Briton Riviere contributed striking sculptural features in plaster to each of the side walls of four naked female "surfers" riding a wave formed of an upward extension of the wood-panelled dado. According to Richard Gray (in an article, "The Flying Ladies of Leicester Square"), the figures "leap towards the rays of the sun (delineated by plaster semi-circles reaching nearly to the edge of the proscenium). Backlit by a rising electric sun and entwined by garlands, the figures symbolise the miracle of light, making film possible."

The figures looked very similar, obviously based on the same model, but the two groups were arranged slightly differently, with the third lady on the right side looking back.* The ladies were not solely decorative but concealed ventilation openings and the public address system.

A Compton organ was installed, with the console on a rising lift in the centre of the orchestra pit. This console was specially designed with curving, wave-like sides that echoed the splay walls of the auditorium and that were, as usual, lit up from within by changing colours. As Tony Moss has noted (in *Picture House* no. 11), "The magnificent Compton organ installed in the Odeon had the distinction of being the only one in a British theatre with five keyboards (manuals)... The organ's original 17 ranks of pipes contained some unusual stops for a theatre organ, e.g. 'Geigen' (a smaller version of the Diapason which brings the traditional church tone to the organ) and 'Posaune', a reed stop that is supposed to sound like a trombone. As one of the resident organists said, it is really more of a concert organ and, as such, it is one of the finest in the UK. It was opened by James Bell, who came from the Carlton Liverpool. He was not very well-

Odeon Leicester Square. The figures on the side wall, floodlit for this photograph (reproduced by permission of English Heritage.NMR).

---

* Riviere's widow, Tana, named the inspiration for the flying ladies as Annette Mills, who went on to present the children's television series *Muffin the Mule* in the 1950s. Riviere was in his late twenties at the time, working for White Allom, the company that handled all the fibrous plasterwork and decorations at the Odeon.

Odeon Leicester Square. The auditorium in all its original splendour. For a view across, see photograph facing title page.

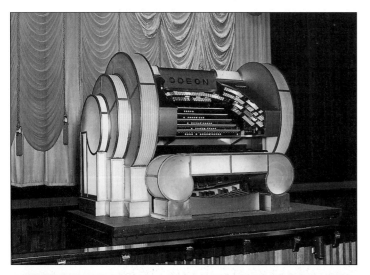

*Odeon Leicester Square. The organ and the safety curtain
(latter reproduced by permission of English Heritage. NMR).*

known and it is puzzling that one of the big names was not chosen to open this singularly prestigious organ."

The pit as a whole could be raised level with the stage to enlarge it. The organ console could be elevated even higher and rotated. There were two sets of parting curtains: the stage one in blended shades of gold and festooned, the screen one in white and silver designed for colour lighting from the balcony front. An iron safety curtain was also installed with a vivid montage painted on it of an audience in high-backed chairs watching scenes of music and dance being photographed by two cameramen, along with rolls of films, two spotlights and corner images of modes of transport: cars, public transport, planes and ships.

The projection room was enormous and had three projectors so that performances could carry on with the minimum of delay if one failed. A back-up print of the feature film was held.

Perhaps the Empire had the best location in the West End, on the north side of Leicester Square. But its frontage was nowhere near as conspicuous as that of the Odeon with its tower that looked particularly splendid from the Piccadilly Circus direction, advertising its presence to the milling crowds. These two cinemas became the best in the West End, although they did not have first choice of the whole range of new films and were tied to particular distributors.

George Coles

George Coles' Odeon at **Bury St. Edmunds** was his first since Horsham nine months earlier and his second and last in Suffolk following Ipswich. It had a tall, narrow, arresting frontage with two curved wings, outlined at night by neon, that incorporated glazed towers with horizontal bars seemingly inspired by the work of F. E. Bromige. Unusually, and a little awkwardly, the main name sign was mounted vertically on the end of a central slab tower. This frontage can be compared to the narrow entrance of Bromley, but here it had to be taller to hide the auditorium closer behind. Even by Odeon standards, the auditorium was rather plain. Although it seated a modest 1,289 people, it was almost twice the size of both the town's much older cinemas.

Coles also handled the much larger Odeon at **Bournemouth** in Hampshire where Oscar Deutsch settled for a site in the Lansdowne district on the eastern edge of the town centre, a half-mile away from the heart of entertainment. This was, in fact, Deutsch's first really big scheme, pre-dating Leicester Square: a £100,000 development to include not only an Odeon (with just under two thousand seats) but forty-five flats and eighteen shops (comparable to Haverstock Hill but on a larger scale). Such integrated developments were rare in this country though commonplace on the Continent.

The other two major circuits were to be found on Westover

Road where Gaumont's large Regent and ABC's even larger Westover (opened two months before the Odeon) competed in close proximity, along with the live Pavilion Theatre across the road. The Odeon's location allowed room for a slip road in front and a large car park behind, whereas the Regent and Westover lacked parking facilities of their own.

The town and its environs had a dozen further cinemas and the Odeon scheme only went ahead after a huge battle. A provisional licence was refused on four occasions between June and August 1936. A publicity campaign was mounted to win public approval, with a whole page advertisement in the local newspaper and a display on a huge hoarding outside the site in Christchurch Road to show how tastefully the project had been designed. Ratepayers were circularised with leaflets and reply-paid envelopes to gain their support for a project that, it was pointed out, would contribute handsomely to council coffers through local taxes. All fourteen existing cinemas had opposed the Odeon and Deutsch even went so far as to promise that any of them could play the same film as the Odeon at the same time. Permission was finally granted and then the race was on to complete the Odeon in time for the summer holiday seaason.

When the cinema was ready to open in early August, there was an attempt to delay the issuing of the licence until September, by which time the holidaymakers would have departed. But the licence was granted and twenty minutes later an aircraft appeared over the town bearing huge streamers that announced the opening of the Bournemouth Odeon the very next day.

The cinema was completed before the flats and shops. These dominated the frontage when it was finished. Bruce Peter observes: "The design of the flats was rather timid. These could have been much more flamboyant in a seaside town and helped to advertise the cinema." Still, the reticence did help to emphasise the cinema entrance, set in the middle with a slab tower in buff-coloured faience that contrasted with the brickwork everywhere else. The tower had name signs on each side across the top and vertically on the projecting edge.

As if to make up for this modest exterior, Coles brought tremendous verve to the foyers and auditorium. The upper foyer was a *tour de force* of streamlining, the auditorium a vigorous exercise in sharply stepped surfaces that cunningly integrated the ventilation openings and concealed the lighting. The back and rear side walls were covered in square acoustic tiles incorporated into the design. The overall effect might have seemed too harsh and geometric for some tastes.

In contrast to Bournemouth, Coles' Odeon at **Woolwich,** south east London, was highly conspicuous externally, with its entrance block and one side wall of the auditorium on display and clad in buff faience tiles along with a lower wall that enclosed a small

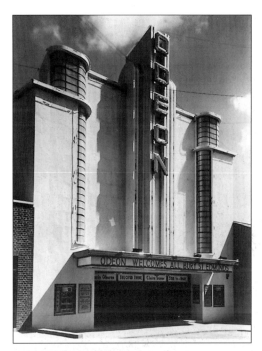

Odeon Bury St. Edmunds, with lay-by in front for cars to drop off patrons.

Odeon Bournemouth. The town centre is some distance to the right of the exterior. The screen tabs here were in the style introduced at Lancaster.

Odeon Woolwich by day (reproduced by permission of English Heritage.NMR). Further Odeon name signs were mounted on each side of the entrance block but not on the slab tower itself. Note the unusual extension of canopy lettering along the wall enclosing the car park (which is advertising a film report of the cinema's opening). See overleaf for night view and auditorium.

Odeon Woolwich.

car park. This Odeon needed to make an impression to compete with the lavish Granada directly opposite, which had opened six months earlier. The Granada had 600 more seats and a modern exterior in brick leading to a cathedral-like interior in complete contrast to that of the Odeon. Elsewhere, ABC showed films at a former live theatre, the Hippodrome, while four independent cinemas also plied for business.

At night, the Odeon achieved a sensational impact, its entire length outlined in horizontal bands of neon. The only windows were those virtually hidden by the canopy and the vertical lines in the rounded end of the slab tower (sometimes used for advertising at night) and in the corresponding extension at the screen end.

In the auditorium, the principal lighting was indirect. The elaborate decoration of the side walls was dominated by a wide, illuminated floral frieze that curved down on to the side exits, one of several features displaying the linearity favoured by this architect. The upper outer edge of the proscenium bowed forward in an elegant curve and concealed further lighting. Other illumination came from coves across the ceiling.

At **Acton,** in west London, Coles delivered another assertively modern Odeon, in complete contrast to his 1931 Savoy at East Acton, which had become an ABC house, as well as to Acton's much older Gaumont hall, the Globe. The Odeon opened just three weeks after the independent Dominion with its dazzling design by F. E. Bromige.

The Odeon's somewhat flat exterior in buff faience was the lifted by an exhilarating tower feature. This rose from the rounded corner as a slab in a deep concave curve with the Odeon name attached to the front edge, the letters spaced within curving bands.

The auditorium featured linear lighting in both the ceiling and side walls, and a fluted, cove-lit proscenium arch, while a flamboyant touch was the backlit circular features on each side wall.

After buildings like Woolwich and Acton, it becomes increasingly clear that George Coles had his own particular approach to an Odeon style. Not for him the interplay of brick, faience and glazing on frontages. He was, as Bruce Peter puts it, "more concerned with facades than volumetric composition." He arranged vast expanses of buff-coloured faience with no enrichment from basketweave patterning and an absolute minimum of interruption for windows, only rarely adding colour bands to the tilework. Even the black bases were as minimal as possible. The result was work even more severe than that of A. P. Starkey or T. Cecil Howitt. Auditoria – and often foyers as well – were also boldly conceived. Besides his fondness for linear lighting on the side walls and/or ceiling, he would often deftly fit the ventilation openings into horizontal bands rather than deal with them as separate, more conspicuous features. He rarely introduced the

Odeon Acton. The horizontal name sign across the frontage doesn't fit in with the vertical channelling.

Odeon Edgware Road. The deliberately mottled look of many faience exteriors is particularly evident here. (Exterior reproduced by permission of English Heritage.NMR.)

wood dados that added a look of quality to most of Weedon's work. In his best Odeon work – which most would regard as Muswell Hill and Woolwich – Coles delivered cinemas that had stylistic impact throughout (in contrast to the deliberately muted nature of most Weedon interiors).

One of Coles' many commissions from smaller companies was the Rex in **Edgware Road,** just a mile north of Marble Arch. However, this huge undertaking for R. Sokoloff and Harry Pearl of Essandee Cinemas passed to Odeon shortly before completion. Only £831 was spent on further outfitting, including Odeon signs in place of Rex, and the cinema opened with an organ and with carpet in a different pattern from the circuit's own. Seating 2,370, it was at the time the second largest Odeon after Bolton.

As it happened, the building had a frontage rather in the Odeon style, if unlike any other Odeon, with buff faience tiles placed vertically rather than horizontally to emphasise the height of the rather narrow frontage, and a complete absence of windows above canopy level.

The entrance replaced an older building and was set back from the adjoining properties leaving blank end walls on each side. The frontage peaked with a thin slab tower carrying the Odeon name on each side, visible from some distance along the straight Edgware Road.

The foyers had a streamlined appearance not far removed from the Odeon look, although the uplights on the staircase to the circle had no parallel.* The auditorium was much too lofty to suit the circuit with none of the streamlining of Coles' Odeons of the period. The fountain-like side wall decorative features seemed rather old-fashioned and the ceiling treatment looked ponderous.

This cinema brought Odeon into direct competition with Gaumont's Grand and other independent halls, while ABC opened a large Regal around the corner in Harrow Road some ten months later.

Andrew Mather

Andrew Mather's practice was now firmly set on using large vitrolite panels on Odeon frontages rather than faience tiles. As at **Lowestoft,** Suffolk, this could result in a rather crude box-like effect. Here the panels were placed vertically above canopy level between darker, narrow horizontal bands carrying red neon. (Within days of opening, the colour of the neon was changed at the request of the Town Council as it was said to be distracting motorists.) Here, as occasionally elsewhere, an Odeon sign was mounted on the canopy, clashing with one placed vertically on the small tower. In a manner reminiscent of the later Uxbridge Odeon but on a much smaller scale, the entrance corner was left open, around a supporting column with striped tiles matching the wall treatment at ground level.

The main foyer had an attractive island paybox and wide staircase on the lefthand side to the balcony. The upper walls were decorated with cartoon-like sketches drawn on cloth by Bainbridge Copnall showing various forms of racing and sporting activity.

The site sloped downwards, aiding the rake of the auditorium. This was rather ordinary with old-fashioned sidewall grillework on top of which sat a small bas-relief figure of a naked female, with others in different poses mounted high on the side walls above circular light fittings. The ceiling descended with the troughs carrying concealed lighting facing the audience rather than the proscenium. The curving wood dado and ribbed plasterwork by the sides of the proscenium added a more modern touch, along with the simple treatment of the orchestra barrier.

As a resort and busy fishing port, Lowestoft was well placed for cinemas with five independents and ABC's smallish Marina. The Odeon would be its only new cinema of the 1930s – Union proposed a Ritz at the same time as Mather submitted his plans in April 1936 but never proceeded.

The Odeon **Forest Gate** can only have been an inherited scheme as it bore no resemblance to the circuit style. It joined the older Queen's (an ABC house almost adjacent) and two smaller independent halls in serving this populous area of east London and was the nearest Odeon to the major centre of Stratford, a mile away along the Romford Road.

The stone frontage featured sculptured figures of Pan just above canopy height and bas-relief panels higher up while diminutive flagpoles sprouted an Odeon "O" at their base to each side of the main name sign. The auditorium was well composed but dreary, with ornate grillework in the ceiling.

The Odeon at **Aylesbury,** Buckinghamshire, was originally prepared for A. E. Abrahams and Mather's plans were passed in March 1936. The owner of the town's two existing picture houses, London and District Cinemas, had already experienced the competition of new Odeons at Epsom and Woolwich, and responded that same year by having its Pavilion modernised. The Odeon that arrived in June 1937 bore few of the circuit hallmarks. The rectangular frontage was faced in light stone-coloured vertical panels of opaque glass with intervening strips in green of the same material (whereas in true Odeons the colour bands were horizontal) while four projecting ribs, each with two

---

* As Bruce Peter notes, they were a feature of many contemporary London Underground escalator shafts, e.g. Southgate. Incidentally, many of the Underground station interiors paralleled the Odeon exterior look with buff tiles relieved by red or green colour stripes, e.g. Gants Hill.

Odeon Lowestoft. The rather crude frontage looks lower than it actually is. A further name sign appeared across the top of the short tower feature on the other side. The windows at first floor level have vertical blinds that blend in with the rest of the frontage. In the foyer, the simple pattern of the floor and the globe light fittings are not as unusual as the sporting sketches. A backlit sign to the circle at the head of the stairs is barely visible. The design of screen tabs had first been seen at Bury and would reappear at South Norwood and Llanelly.
(Foyer reproduced by permission of English Heritage. NMR.)

Odeon Forest Gate. The three-part canopy is unusual. A further Odeon sign can just be glimpsed on the side wall. The stand in the corner of the proscenium is an oddity.

strips of neon on the outer edge, added some impact, terminating underneath the canopy in an obtrusive fashion.

The main entrance hall was spacious and delightful with a round-fronted paybox set into steps, side staircases to the balcony and quintessentially 1930s wide-spaced signage indicating stalls and circle.

The auditorium offered an odd melange of decorative elements and plain surfaces with concealed illumination from coves across the stepped-down ceiling that faced the audience.

It is possible to underestimate the Mather Odeons of this period. The Odeon at **South Norwood,** near Croydon, was a much more impressive building than it looks in the photographs on page 148. It helped that it was the one really modern 1930s building in a very drab area.

There were two small, old-fashioned cinemas: the New Gaiety gained a facelift and a new name (Astoria) a few months before the Odeon opened, and the Central carried on as before. The London and Home Counties branch of the Cinematograph Exhibitors' Association strongly opposed the Odeon, arguing that it would put the Astoria and Central out of business, but both survived into the mid-1950s.

The Odeon's frontage was nicely proportioned with a gentle curve and plain cladding in vertical strips of cream-coloured vitrolite above a black base. It certainly registered as being in the Odeon style with its horizontal bands in jade green which carried neon tubing. The corners of the facade showed that the sheets of glass were pliable enough to curve and took the cinema away from the blocky, rectangular look of other Mather buildings faced in the material. The decorative grillework in the large central recess partly covered windows to the balcony lounge.

The main foyer was low and uninspired but the auditorium was very appealing. The ceiling seemed to float on concealed lighting at the rim. The ribs on the splay walls and on the ceiling above the proscenium arch guided the eye towards the screen, borrowing a favourite device of many Cromie/Mollo and Egan cinemas. The seven rows of seven small vents in the side walls were in the octagonal shape of the initial letter of the Odeon logo and of the clocks lower down. This cinema looked better without the fussy stencilled decoration further back on the side walls.

Mather's Odeon in **Penge,** a mile and a half away from the South Norwood Odeon, started life just five days after it. Here the immediate competition consisted of an old Gaumont property, the King's Hall, and a live theatre.

Externally, the Odeon Penge made every effort to be noticed with a strong juxtaposition of vertical and horizontal elements, both reinforced by green bands. Yet again opaque glass replaced faience tiles and there was an absence of windows. Its illuminated towers recalled the Palais Stoclet in Brussels.

Odeon Aylesbury.

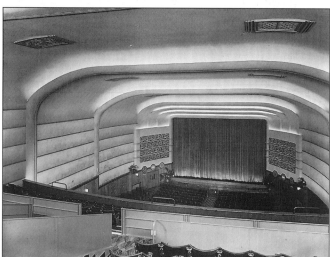

Odeon South Norwood. A small vertical Odeon sign can be seen high up on the end wall. This faced Norwood Junction railway station a few yards away. There was a small car park for fifty vehicles at the back. The screen tabs here were the same as at Bury, Lowestoft and Llanelly.

Odeon Penge. In the exterior view, note how one glass panel at top right has been broken revealing the stud lights behind. The canopy is unusually short. There are green bands across the black base. A car park was located to the left.

The inner foyer with its octagonal-shaped island paybox seemed unusually small while the weak auditorium again featured bands of concealed lighting which faced the audience. There was repetitive grillework on the splay walls with vertical bands across, below which three octagonal shapes appeared side by side: one taken up by the standard clock, the second enclosing an exit sign, and the third looking unhappily blank (but almost certainly accommodating the speakers for the public address system). Frontlighting of the grillework in the full Mollo and Egan manner would have been an improvement.

In December 1937, Odeon at **Southsea,** Hampshire, a residential and holiday district of Portsmouth, supplemented Mather's Odeon in the town centre. This was on an awkward site with a very long entrance hall leading to an auditorium some distance behind. Mather's office had faced a similar problem at Portsmouth but here opted to follow George Coles' approach at Bromley with two towers, vertically channelled to take neon, a curved central recess and the principal name sign mounted just above canopy level. Unfortunately, the design lacked the finesse that seemed to come so naturally to Coles and registered as ponderous.

The auditorium was more successful with its bold sidewall curves and dramatic concealed lighting of the area around the proscenium opening.

The other two major circuits were already established here: ABC with the Apollo, Commodore and Gaiety (the latter two soon relinquished to independents), and Gaumont with the Plaza at Bradford Junction. There was at least one other hall.

Apart from Leicester Square, Mather's most important contribution of the year was the Odeon at **Brighton** on the Sussex coast. This cinema was originally commissioned by H. H. Weingott, to be known as the Forum, but was identified as an Odeon scheme by June 1936 and submitted for approval in January 1937. It occupied an excellent site in the centre of Brighton, on the "tripper track" between the railway station and sea front. Next door was the S.S. Brighton, opened in 1934 as a swimming pool and converted the following year to an ice rink. With its tiled frontage, colour bands and canopy, it was a conspicuous reminder that other entertainment facilities besides cinemas adopted the streamlined 1930s look.

Oscar Deutsch already had an Odeon in the town, the former Palladium a short distance away on the sea front, which Mather had partly modernised in 1935, but this was not large enough to secure major first-run films. Taking over the Forum scheme solved the problem and gave him a modern cinema that would be far more inviting to contemporary audiences.

The frontage had been designed in light-toned faienceware with coloured bands and a black base and this, of course, fitted

Odeon Southsea. The adjacent land was never built on in the cinema's lifetime. Some of the space formed a cinema car park. In the auditorium, the orchestra rail is a solid barrier. The restful design of the screen tabs was repeated at Norwich.

Odeon Brighton. Next door, to the left, can be glimpsed the side wall of the S.S. Brighton. The auditorium introduced a new design of screen tabs repeated at Peckham and Luton.

in nicely with the Odeon style. In other respects, it was dramatically and powerfully different, although the six projecting ribs in the centre, carried over onto the roof, recall those of Aylesbury, itself not originally an Odeon scheme. The main Odeon sign might have been squeezed within the six vertical ribs but, instead, two matching signs were placed on the symmetrical wings, as at Barnet in similar circumstances. The right-angled banding at each side added strength to the facade, especially when emphasised by neon at night. The weak points were the placing of old-fashioned curlicued grillework between the ribs and the rungs and cone-like finials above them.

In the auditorium, the canopy connecting the splay walls had dramatic impact with its line of inner-lit circular openings and the concealed lighting of the proscenium area was effective but there was no great atmosphere.

Other Odeons of 1937

The Odeon at **Sittingbourne,** from the practice of F. C. Mitchell, was a rather plodding affair inside and out. This small-town Kent cinema seems to have been originally designed in 1934 for A. E. Abrahams. By 1937, Mitchell was doing more interesting work for London and Southern (which fell into Odeon's hands during the year). Sittingbourne already had two small cinemas and an Odeon with 1,593 seats proved excessively large.*

In industrial Lancashire, **Warrington's** Odeon was designed by area specialists Drury and Gomersall and had an elaborately detailed, lavish auditorium which nevertheless suggests why the duo have been irreverently dubbed Dreary and Gomersall. (For a more appreciative view of the practice, see Dennis Sharp in *The Picture Palace.*) This was the first new cinema in the town for many years but it was followed a few months later by Union's larger Ritz. ABC had the small Grand and around nine independents fought over the rest of the cinematic pie.

A. P. Starkey and his associate Frederick Adkins returned to the fold with the Odeon at **Reading,** Berkshire. Seating 1,704, this was their largest cinema. Located at the edge of town, down a side street, it was next to the Palace Theatre which Oscar Deutsch had acquired in October 1935 together with the adjacent building site (on which the Odeon appeared) and car parking space. (The Palace lost a side passage to the Odeon but continued as a live theatre in other hands.) The County circuit was already

* In March 1938, Odeon successfully appealed against Kent's assessment of £1,300 in council rates by revealing that, in its first year, the cinema had taken £11,000 at the box-office and paid out £10,200 in operating costs including £5,269 in film hire, leaving £800 excess for capital costs, etc. The Odeon had been assessed at £1,300 and this was reduced to £780. The company admitted that the cinema had seating in excess of demand.

Odeon Sittingbourne. The design of screen tabs inaugurated here reappeared at Hereford, Motherwell and East Ham.

Odeon Warrington.

Odeon Reading. The Palace Theatre was next door to the left. On the right, the frontage extends beyond the slab tower over the entrance to the car park to provide some kind of lounge area. Owls featured on the screen tabs of other theatres but this particular design seems to have been unique. (CTA Archive.)

established here with the Pavilion (near the Odeon) and the more centrally placed Vaudeville, both operated in partnership with a local company; ABC ran the Central; an independent had recently opened the Granby; and other cinemas operated in surrounding districts.

Perhaps hoping to impress Oscar Deutsch with their adaptability, Starkey and Adkins abandoned their earlier look in favour of a good stab at the Weedon style with an exterior in biscuit-coloured faience tiles arranged in basketweave pattern, a slab tower in darker tiles, minimal windows and smooth corner curves. The architects even paid attention to the back of the building which (as Bruce Peter pointed out to me) was good enough to have been the front of many cinemas up north!

The auditorium was simple: its most original features were the cove-lit bands on the lower splay walls with dot and dash perforations and the orchestra rail with wave-like slanting metal strips punctured by round openings (the latter supplied and possibly designed by Swanser & Son). If Starkey harboured hopes of becoming a principal Odeon architect again, he was to be disappointed. This would be his final contribution to the Deutsch empire.★

Hereford was another battleground between Odeon and Union. The latter had been operating the Garrick and Kemble for some time in competition with the independent Palladium. When Odeon arrived in April 1937 with a modest 1,133-seater designed by Roland Satchwell, Union retaliated by opening a modern Ritz of similar size nine months later.

Satchwell gave the Odeon Hereford an exterior with stone facing that blended anonymously into the historic town. The site had formerly been a judge's lodgings and S. W. Clift was a

★ Starkey and Adkins seem to have found further cinema work hard to come by, but they were associated with two cinemas which opened in 1939, one in 1940, and one scheme that was never built. In 1939, the excellent Crescent at Leatherhead, Surrey, opened as a combined effort of Starkey, A. E. Richardson and C. Lovett Gill while the practice received sole credit on its second cinema at Wealdstone, a thorough reconstruction of the tiny Herga, and its plans for a cinema at Westerham, Kent, progressed as far as receiving approval from Seven Oaks Rural District Council in February of that year. In 1940, Starkey and Adkins completed a combined office block and cinema at Banbury, Oxfordshire, the latter opening as the Regal. Starkey died on 6 August 1946. "Behind a quiet, almost excessively reticent manner, he had an unusually flexible and inventive mind, which continually sought new solutions to old problems. At the same time, all his experiments were tempered and controlled by an acute and logical reasoning which would never permit extravagances, and a taste which was sound and refined", remarked the author of his obituary in *The Builder*. Frederick Adkins took over the practice on finishing wartime work for the government, and by 1974 was a partner in the London practice of Hardy Cochrane Adkins Associates. He died in 1986.

Odeon Hereford. The five bands with concealed lighting over the proscenium extend dramatically across the ceiling to end in pointed diamond shapes. The screen tab design is repeated from Sittingbourne with different colours. The curtained side exits are unusual.

director of the scheme. There was an extraordinarily long foyer leading to the auditorium where the architect provided long tongues of concealed lighting in the ceiling that considerably enlivened the setting. As previously mentioned, Harry Weedon had taken over the design of the Odeon Peterborough from Satchwell. Weedon also became involved in problems with Satchwell's interior scheme here (there is a cryptic reference to "ceiling collapse at Hereford" in Robert Bullivant's notes, undated and unexplained at the time of his death). The Odeon Hereford was Satchwell's final work for Oscar Deutsch, but not his final work in the Odeon style.*

The number of architectural practices working on Odeons was being whittled down. Whinney, Son and Austen Hall popped back with two last Odeons – at **Epsom,** Surrey, and **Harlesden,** north London. Both had brick towers with flat tops, the one at Epsom grudgingly conceded by the council which insisted upon no faience but narrow bricks with stone dressings.

At Epsom, the foyer and auditorium were simply dull. In April 1935, Odeon were said to have been interested in an earlier site in the area, near Stoneleigh Park station (probably where the Rembrandt cinema was built in 1938), but this was far more central. The Odeon competed with a lesser circuit's lavish Capitol (1929, Robert Cromie) and with a small independent that closed in April 1938 (because of road widening).

Harlesden offered a far more arresting exterior than Epsom, with a low, curved corner extension faced in buff-coloured faience carrying an Odeon sign above a line of windows. There was a dynamic tension between the faience-clad horizontal elements and the vertical thrust of the brick tower with its flagpole. There were suggestions of the Worthing exterior in the extension and tower but with nowhere near the same impact. The auditorium was straightforward with splay wall recesses displaying thermometer-like columns.

The Odeon dismayed the independent Picardy and Coliseum

---

* Satchwell carried on as a prolific cinema architect, often working on schemes involving S. W. Clift and becoming a director of the owning company. Among his later output was the Beacon at Great Barr, Birmingham, opened on 6 March 1938. Although almost entirely faced in brick, it had an unmistakable Odeon look with Howitt-style flat-top tower and a curved section faced in cream faience with green bands above the entrance doors which carried the cinema's name in Odeon-style lettering. And his Avion at Aldridge, Staffordshire, opened on 26 September 1938, was a close imitation of the Warley Cinema, clad in light faience with green bands at the top, lacking only the tower feature. The crude handling of detail on both exteriors serves to point up the superiority of the Weedon and Howitt practices. Satchwell was described to this writer by Sidney Swingler with evident disdain as "a pantomime architect".

Odeon Epsom. The vertical sign on the tower looks particularly ill-fitting and was repeated on the right-hand side. The back wall faced the station and carried advertising for the cinema. The interior design has been attributed to Winifred Evans. The screen tabs here featured the Odeon-in-the-mountains design

Odeon Harlesden. This gives a clear view of one of the most frequently used designs of screen tabs.

and hurt ABC at their large but old-fashioned Willesden Hippodrome. Indeed, four months after the Odeon opened, the owner of the Picardy declared that five local cinemas had each lost one third of their business. This argument was used to fight ABC's efforts to build a new cinema in Harlesden and Odeon was happy to participate in the opposition now that it was on the other side.

Despite having taken over the large Plaza cinema in the centre of Watford, Hertfordshire, Oscar Deutsch also acquired Lou Morris's Ritz **North Watford** late during its construction on the St. Albans Road. Plans by Norwich architect J. Owen Bond had been passed by the licensing authority on 19 February 1936. Largely completed by the time Odeon (North Watford) Ltd. was registered in October 1937 to purchase the cinema, it opened as the Odeon at the end of the following month. Although the takeover might have been agreed some weeks before the registration of the company, there was no time for any major modifications – not that any were needed, as it was a most attractive building. (It seems that Deutsch had earlier toyed with this outlying area of the town as plans by architect Major W. J. King for an unbuilt cinema on the corner of St. Albans Road and the Watford By-Pass were at one stage linked to Odeon.)

The cinema had a wide frontage in brick with some stone dressings and five tall windows. It was the interior design and decoration by Mollo and Egan that made the cinema remarkable. The entrance hall and circle lounge were vividly decorated, with a stylised "orchard panel" upstairs. The auditorium displayed the new approach, previously examined at Yeovil, of splitting the side walls diagonally, here with bands across the ceiling carrying concealed lighting and extending down the side walls (as at the Gaumont Rose Hill). Much of the side wall was left daringly plain with concentrations of rich decoration around the side exits, under the balcony and alongside the proscenium. There was also a series of small round vents discreetly placed over the proscenium arch. The balcony had a rippled fascia that added yet another distinctive touch.

Takeovers

In May 1937, Odeon gained a controlling interest in the Entertainments and General Investment Corporation which owned, controlled or managed the fifty-four cinemas of the County circuit. Oscar Deutsch joined the board, with C. J. Donada continuing as managing director. It is clear that County continued to function on its own under Donada's leadership. Had it been otherwise, the best cinemas would have had their names changed to Odeon. Sidney Swingler has confirmed that the two chains were not really amalgamated until a few weeks before the Second World War. Following the failure of a stock issue (sabotaged by

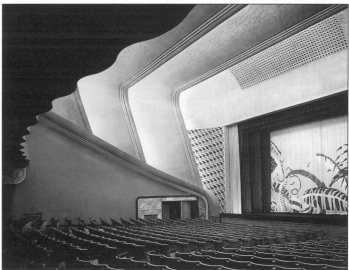

Odeon North Watford. Odeon had time to add the circuit style of carpet and its own design of screen tabs (seen earlier at Scarborough and Oldham).

Union), County's days of expansion were over – only a trickle of new cinemas already in the pipeline followed. Odeon avoided building in competition with County. An £80,000 scheme for a 2,492-seat Odeon in Plymouth, Devon, had been designed by P. J. Price in the Harry Weedon office for a site on Union Terrace, Union Street, at the junction with Station Road. The site alone cost £50,000. This would have been between County's Regent and the Gaumont Palace. It was dropped in February 1938 because the vast Regent, with 3,254 seats, was more than sufficient for an outlet.

Two important circuits were taken over by Odeon to become fully part of its operation.

With the acquisition of the ten cinemas of the Singleton circuit, which came into effect on 8 March 1937, Odeon entered Scotland and became a national circuit. (ABC, of course, had its roots in Scotland and Gaumont were well represented there. As for Northern Ireland, the only major circuit taking any real interest was Union, although Gaumont controlled one large, important cinema in Belfast. Odeon had no plans to build there in the 1930s.)

In Scotland, Odeon had previously developed plans for a cinema in Edinburgh which was never built. Discussions with George Singleton had been dragging on for a couple of years. The intermediary was George Archibald, the United Artists representative on the Odeon board. Born in Glasgow, he had been the projectionist or manager of the Paragon in the tough Gorbals district of the city when Singleton purchased it as his first cinema in 1920. Archibald soon left to manage other cinemas before becoming a film salesman in Scotland, then worked on a film trade paper in London before joining United Artists in 1933 as company secretary with a seat on the board.

The Paragon was the worst cinema on the Singleton circuit. It was a conversion of a church which still retained its pews instead of seats, so that its capacity varied according to how many patrons could be squeezed in. Sidney Swingler remembers having the tyres of his car let down when he visited. It has been said, laughingly, that Oscar Deutsch never saw the Paragon or any of the Singleton cinemas before they were bought and so he was taken for a bit of a ride – but Glaswegians were avid filmgoers and, while the Paragon hardly lived up to the Odeon image (and was not often advertised as part of the circuit), it made a lot of money. And Singleton had built some large, modern cinemas that were valuable additions to the Odeon circuit. These included three in the Glasgow suburbs: the Broadway Shettleston, Commodore Scotstoun and Vogue Rutherglen. He had very recently opened the Vogue at Dundee while continuing to operate the Empire, a former live theatre. His other cinemas included the older Pavilion Picture House in Airdrie, the Empire

Coatbridge to the east of Glasgow, and the Cinema Falkirk and Kings Hawick. This still left Odeon without a screen in the centre of Glasgow or anywhere in Edinburgh. The deal included a site for a new cinema in Melville Street, Falkirk, which Odeon dropped. It seems that initially a merger had been proposed between Deutsch and Singleton, which would have created a company called Odeon Cinema and Singleton Ltd. to run the chain with George Singleton a member of the board. But Singleton went his own way and used the proceeds of the sale to start a new circuit that wasn't permitted to directly compete with any of the cinemas he had sold but which included the huge new Vogue Govan (separately, Singleton built the Cosmo art house in the centre of Glasgow).

Along with its Singleton coup, Odeon pursued seven schemes of its own for new Scottish cinemas, all to be designed by Andrew Mather's practice which set up an office at 102 Bathgate Street, Glasgow. Odeon (Scotland) Ltd. was registered in February 1937, then in September local companies were formed to build cinemas at Ayr, Bridgeton, Falkirk (its own site, not Singleton's), Hamilton, Motherwell, Partick and Townhead. Only the schemes at Ayr, Hamilton and Motherwell were completed. The others (plus a later proposal for Springburn in the Glasgow area) were stopped by the outbreak of war and are included in more detail in an overall list of such schemes at the end of the 1939 chapter.

The acquisition of London and Southern Super Cinemas was another mixed bag. Headed by Arthur Cohen, L&S had built several large cinemas named Ambassador and taken over other existing halls in mainly prosperous areas. In the Bristol area, it had the Ambassador at Bedminster and another Ambassador under construction at Kingswood by its regular architect of the period, F. C. Mitchell. In the Portsmouth area, it had the Ambassador Cosham. In the Slough area, it had the Ambassador at Farnham Royal. In Hounslow, it had the Ambassador out at Hounslow West as well as the Dominion in the town centre. In London, it operated only the old Super Bloomsbury, on the fringe of the West End, having relinquished the Ambassadors at Hendon and Stoke Newington. Out in Surrey, two cinemas at Woking – the Astoria and Plaza – were in its portfolio as well as the Capitol at Walton-on-Thames. Up north it ran the Regal Rotherham but its recent hold on the Empire Normanton, Derbyshire, seems to have expired. There was an isolated screen out west: the Tredegar Hall at Newport.

Besides taking the Kingswood scheme to completion, Odeon gave the green light to an L&S project for Hayes, Middlesex, which opened under the Ambassador name in December 1938. The company owned Andrew Mather's scheme for Stoke Road, Gosport, Hampshire, which he had earlier placed with Odeon. In accordance with Deutsch's agreement not to compete in Gos-

```
OSCAR DEUTSCH ESQ.                                    SBS/DD/BS/"T"


RE: SHOPS.                                    1st.October 1937


                    We give you below, particulars regarding
shops:-

         Blackpool ........... None
         Bradford ........... 5
         Doncaster .......... 4  - Showrooms first floor
                                   Stores second floor.
         Hackney Road ....... 4
         Hendon ............. None
         Middlesborough ..... None
         Newcastle on Tyne .. 4
         Peckham ............ None
         Plymouth ........... 5
         Sheffield .......... 4 and offices

         Ayr ................ 2
         Camberwell ......... 4
         Canning Town ....... None
         Clapton ............ None
         Downham ............ 4
         Falkirk ............ 8
         Glasgow Townhead ... 2 and showrooms
         Glasgow Bridgton ... 3
         Hamilton ........... None
         Highgate ........... 1 or 2 - not definite.
         Kennington ......... None
         Leeds .............. 5
         Luton .............. 4
         Manchester ......... None
         Mile End Road ...... None
         Motherwell ......... None
         Partick ............ None
         Southport .......... None
         Swansea ............ None
         West Bromwich ...... None
         Westbourne Grove.... 6

                                           CONTINUED
```

```
OSCAR DEUTSCH ESQ.                            1st.October, 1937
```

```
                    So far as the following sites are
concerned, we are communicating with the Architect to
see whether they can give us the required information;
although on telephoning some of them this afternoon,
they are not at the moment, able to do so.

                         Addiscombe (W)
                         Barking
                         Cambridge.
                         Carlisle
                         Clapham
                         Fulham Road.
                         Grantham (LM)
                         Hastings
                         Kings Norton
                         Lewisham
                         Lincoln High Town
                         Liverpool
                         Manor Park (West Ham)
                         Mill Hill
                         Newcastle under Lyme
                         Oxford
                         Park Royal
                         Poplar
                         Shepherds Bush
                         Sheerness (LM)
                         Shoreditch
                         Stamford Hill
                         Stockton on Tees.
                         Stoke Newington
                         Thorpe
                         Twickenham
                         Walsall
                         Walthamstow.
```

This window into the Odeon circuit's plans at the beginning of October 1937 shows the huge expansion programme of that time. It covers cinemas at the planning stage, the first of which opened at Peckham in June 1938. None of the the cinemas on the second page (above right) were built, although some would have proceeded but for the outbreak of World War Two. No details have come to light about the schemes for Hastings, Lewisham, Liverpool, Newcastle under Lyme, Park Royal, Poplar, Shepherds Bush, Stockton on Tees, Twickenham and Walsall while Lincoln High Town is only known to have been designed by T. Cecil Howitt. The letters (LM) stand for Lou Morris, an entrepreneur well known for selling his schemes who was already active in Sheerness, but the (W) after Addiscombe is a puzzle. There is further information about other schemes at the end of the 1939 chapter.

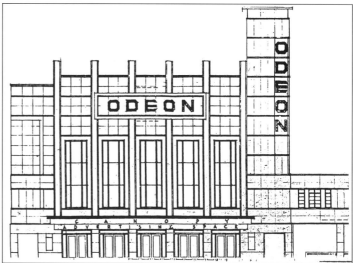

Left: three unbuilt schemes. Top, Odeon Plymouth in a perspective sketch by Eric Smith of the Weedon staff. Centre, Odeon Leeds (RIBA Library Photographs Collection). Bottom, Odeon Newcastle-upon-Tyne.
Above: the original 1937 scheme for the Odeon Westbourne Grove, revised and built post-war (courtesy of D.W.C. Sparke).

port, this was sold to Portsmouth Town Cinemas which already ran the Criterion and Ritz there (it was built as the Forum and opened in January 1939). In June 1937, after the takeover, L&S were reported to be planning a new cinema at Attercliffe, a district of Sheffield, but nothing more was heard of it.

An Andrew Mather scheme for a 1,704-seat Odeon in High Street, Slough, was transferred from Odeon to L&S in December 1937 but marked "dead" with the date 2 May 1938 in Odeon files. The opening of the Granada Slough two months earlier was probably the decisive factor. Odeon thereafter regarded L&S's Ambassador at Farnham Royal as its outlet for the Slough area and would not let cinemas in Slough play its circuit release first run.

L&S retained its separate identity as an Odeon subsidiary: no L&S cinema was renamed Odeon in Deutsch's lifetime. The new cinemas at Kingswood and Hayes (Middlesex) opened as Ambassadors.

Odeon also made some individual acquisitions during 1937. One of the more interesting was the Grosvenor at Rayners Lane, Harrow, purchased five months after its opening. This was so close to the Odeon South Harrow that it normally had to play the Gaumont release. Another very new cinema taken over was the Pavilion at East Dulwich, south London.

With no representation in Manchester, Odeon gained an important foothold through its purchase of the very large West End at Whalley Range, two miles south west of the city centre.

Two cinemas passed from the small General Cinema Theatres circuit to Odeon – the New Pavilion, Kensal Rise, north London, and the Plaza, West Wickham, Kent. Two long established north London cinemas, the Bethnal Green Foresters and the South Hackney Picture House, joined the circuit on the same day in June, whether through joint ownership or coincidence being unclear.

Other halls that went into the Odeon fold included the Astoria Prestwich; Picture House Dunstall, Wolverhampton; and Central Stourbridge. The Theatre de Luxe brought Odeon into Gloucester. This was achieved through Odeon (Broadstairs) Ltd., a company that was largely inactive as the Broadstairs theatre had been leased to an independent. Seating over one thousand, the Theatre de Luxe was deemed of adequate size for the circuit and it took a serious fire to set in motion plans for its replacement by a new Odeon.

However, four inner London properties were obtained specifically to be demolished for new Odeons: the Queen's Theatre, Peckham; the New Boleyn Electric Theatre, East Ham; the Savoy (ex-Empire) Camberwell; and the Kennington Theatre. The war prevented the latter being replaced. Several other schemes announced this year were dropped or delayed. A curious one, dating from February 1937, was for a second Odeon for Norwich on top of the scheme realised in Botolph Street in 1938: this was in Thunder Lane on the outskirts of town. A list of Odeon's future plans in October 1937 is illustrated, but this one had vanished by then.

It became clear by early 1937 that Oscar Deutsch was intent on establishing Odeon as a full-scale national rival to ABC and Gaumont. Not only had he moved into Scotland, not only had he set about building a huge Odeon in the heart of the West End, but he had made a firm decision to establish Odeons in the major provincial city centres. This was an enormous step as the sites were very expensive and the cinemas themselves more costly, being much larger than average.

In June 1936, Odeon sought to lease from the council a site in Newcastle at the corner of Pilgrim Street and City Road (south side) by Tyne Bridge. It was not an ideal location, away from the commercial heart of the city, but followed Deutsch's philosophy that people would make a point of going to an Odeon wherever it was. The council weighed up the proposal, worried about the extra traffic the cinema would create, but granted a lease in September. Harry Weedon's office then drew up plans for an Odeon to seat 2,042 (1,352 stalls + 690 balcony) with four lock-up shops and an underground car park that would double as a bombproof shelter for a full house of patrons. In March 1937 the Odeon was publicly announced, with construction work scheduled to start in August.

In April 1937, Odeon purchased the Albion Brewery site from Leeds Corporation for £54,590. This fronted onto Woodhouse Lane, Merrion Street and Wade Lane, and Robert Bullivant in the Harry Weedon office devised a scheme to seat 2,628 (1,626 stalls + 1,002 balcony) and cost £250,000. Five shops and a café were to be included.

And in July 1937, the trade learned of Deutsch's plans for Manchester, another Weedon design to seat 3,000 or 3,300 at a cost of £250,000, on the site of a warehouse in Chepstow Street.

All three of these schemes were bad news for Paramount, which had very large and, by now, somewhat old-fashioned cinemas in each city centre. This clearly prompted dialogue between Deutsch and David E. Rose, the British head of Paramount, over the possible sale of these cinemas or the Paramount circuit as a whole. The talks were kept secret and Odeon's suspension of real progress on these three projects contributed to conjecture over its financial state.

1938: SLOWING DOWN

In 1938, the number of new Odeons was down by ten to twenty-five (with two further cinemas opened by the London and Southern subsidiary*). ABC was close behind with twenty-two openings (as in 1937) although Gaumont, already well represented in most key locations, added only five.

The Odeons occupied the usual combination of major towns (Bradford, Bristol, Leicester), smaller towns and suburban locations, but seating capacity was on the rise. Ten of the cinemas had around 2,000 seats or more. Only two seated under 1,300 and both of these opened very early in the year. Three of the London Odeons (Peckham, East Ham, Deptford) were built on the sites of older cinemas or theatres.

What is significant about the Odeons appearing from 1938 onwards is that they were all the work of Weedon, Mather or Coles – except for one contribution by another valued practice, that of T. Cecil Howitt.

In general, cinema building was slowing down for a number of reasons. Saturation was being reached, and in many areas over-seating was apparent. In Middlesex it was noted that twenty schemes had been approved but by November only four were proceeding. Even for a circuit like Odeon, which could build anywhere with the certainty of a steady supply of good new films, there were few major locations where it was not already established or did not have a site waiting to be used. Sidney Swingler identified Wigan and Blackburn as the two places where the circuit could not find anywhere to build (although an Odeon site at Wigan fell through in 1936, as mentioned earlier). Edinburgh and Liverpool are even bigger areas where Odeon seem not to have made any firm plans.

In fact, Oscar Deutsch was now planning expansion abroad. In January 1938, he announced that he would extend the Odeon circuit to "two Empire colonies and one foreign country". It soon became clear that he had his eyes fixed on Canada, and in the autumn of 1938 Harry Weedon was dispatched to look

* These were the Ambassadors at Kingswood, Bristol, and at Hayes, Middlesex, both designed by F.C. Mitchell without reference to the Odeon style except that the vertical name signs in each case were in Odeon lettering and Hayes did frame its auditorium clocks in an octagonal shape.

over cinema design in North America. According to the *Motion Picture Herald* (3 August 1938) Deutsch was actively negotiating to build or take over a group of cinemas which would concentrate on showing United Artists pictures. The foreign country in which Oscar was interested was France. Then, back at home, he began to gingerly explore a takeover of Gaumont that would combine its huge circuit with that of Odeon under his leadership.

The greenlighting of Odeon schemes was delayed by the problems associated with finalising the first year's accounts as a public company (see chapter "A Romance of Finance"). This led to fewer Odeons coming on stream later in the year, especially from the Weedon office. A further hold-up to major schemes at Leeds, Manchester and Newcastle was the continuing possibility of acquiring the existing Paramount cinemas in their place.

By the autumn of 1937, British cinema construction in general was suffering delays from a shortage of steel and other essential materials as the armaments industry seized on supplies in response to the increasing likelihood of war. This fear put a dampener on further investment, especially in film production, and the idea of air raids worried smaller enterpreneurs less well cushioned by a wide spread of cinemas, especially those based in London (see *Gaumont British Cinemas* and *The Granada Theatres* regarding Hyams and Gale's nervous sale of cinemas under construction at Holloway and Kingston upon Thames).

This may have been the period recalled by Sidney Swingler when Oscar Deutsch very reluctantly assented to the use of bricks from Belgium, as he (like most cinema promoters) sought to use British materials wherever possible.

Following a dispute over payment, John Maltby gave up photographing Odeons after covering Balham. The work was taken over by the Salisbury Photo Press whose photography was excellent but whose negatives (unlike Maltby's) were destroyed by enemy action in World War Two so that later Odeons have often had to be illustrated from copies and secondary sources.

Harry Weedon

The Odeon at **Norwich**, Norfolk, opened in early February after a postponement occasioned by the non-arrival of some technical

equipment. This 2,054 seater, with Basil Herring as the job architect of record, was well out of the commercial centre, on the northern edge of the town. (Even so, it was described on plans drawn up in February 1937 as "Norwich Central" to distinguish it from the shortlived Odeon scheme further out of town in Thunder Lane.)

The Odeon wasn't entirely necessary as the allied County circuit had the Carlton, almost as large, in the heart of town about three quarters of a mile away. In addition, ABC had the Regent and Hippodrome while Gaumont operated the Haymarket and there were around eight other halls in the area owned by local circuits.

In design terms, the Odeon was far superior to the Carlton. It had a restrained facade (superior to one of similar shape at the Odeon North Watford) which featured a flat central area clad in buff faience tiles laid horizontally, surrounded by brickwork, and windows recessed between black piers and lighter horizontal bars. Neon was confined to the main name sign and the edge of the canopy which extended the full width of the frontage but was set back at each side. There were colour bands in the black base.

The lively auditorium displayed a banded wood dado, eliminated the orchestra rail, and offered a conspicuous amount of decorative grillework unusually keyed to the top corners of the proscenium arch.

Chorley in Lancashire gained two large modern cinemas – the Plaza in 1937 and the Odeon in February 1938 – to complement four older properties seating 800-900 each, making for a rather crowded market with around 6,250 seats available for a town of 30,795 people.

The Odeon (assistant: P. J. Price) was very recognisably in the circuit style. A slab tower, tiled in black and enclosed by brickwork, carried the Odeon name. The main section of the frontage, in buff faience, featured four piers between three tall windows. These were rather clumsily positioned, one half-absorbed by the tower, another abutting the rounded corner of adjacent shops and flats, while their excessive height forced the main name sign to be mounted on the parapet.

The auditorium was semi-stadium with horizontal banding of the side walls and jazzy front-lit decorative grillework, either designed by Mollo and Egan or following their example.

The centre and rear of the auditorium were lit by suspended art deco fittings, introducing a move towards direct lighting by the Weedon office. There certainly were problems associated with lighting concealed in coves. It quickly lost its intensity because of nicotine deposits on the bulbs, especially when it was directly above the seats rather than around the proscenium. Troughs in the ceiling could be reached from the void but it required dangerous high ladders to re-lamp those extending down side walls while chandeliers could, of course, be lowered from the void for maintenance.

Odeon Norwich. The name sign is finely positioned on the exterior. In the auditorium, the screen tabs design repeated that of Southsea. The rectangular grilles just above the dado before the proscenium arch cover the speakers of the public address system.

Odeon Chorley. The design of screen tabs was earlier seen at Horsham.

Odeon Spalding. The large poster on the side wall with the usher and torch is designed so that only a small area needs replacing to advertise the current programme. The rounded corner carrying windows at far left improves the appearance while the far corner of the side wall at right has been built up to help hide the roof. In the auditorium, the carpeting does not seem to be of the usual circuit style - perhaps a money-saving alternative? The screen tabs design was first seen at Crewe.

At **Spalding**, Lincolnshire, as earlier in Boston, regional architect A. J. Thraves did a capable job of designing an imitation Odeon with his 1937 Prince's (later Savoy) in cream faience with green bands and vertical ribs, rounded corners and tower. The 1,350-seat auditorium was less Odeon-like but effectively simple, relying on coves of concealed lighting.

Spalding's real Odeon (assistant: Basil Herring) was smaller (1,208 seats) and less well located, out of the town centre in a residential area although prominently visible on the London Road. It replaced a building called Haverfield House. The location had prompted thirty-eight house owners in the vicinity to oppose it, presumably fearing noise from the car park and a drop in the value of their property. However, 2,300 Spalding people signed a petition in favour of having an Odeon.

This followed Radcliffe as the second and last low budget Odeon handled by Weedon. It cost £22,760 or £18.84 per seat (whereas the Odeon Erith, opened two days earlier, with just thirty-eight more seats, cost £27,996 or £22.47 per seat). Here buff faience, in basketweave pattern with horizontal green bands reinforced at night by neon, was confined to a squat, curved corner entrance clasped by lower brick wings. The two columns under the canopy between the entrance doors were faced in black tiles (also in basket-weave pattern) but the cost-cutting showed in the plain brick side walls. The bricks did not seem to be of the usual quality and the stepped roof was left visible on the side facing the main road.

The semi-stadium auditorium was simply but effectively designed. Economy precluded the customary wooden dado and orchestra rail while there was much reliance on combed plaster-work to provide an enriched look, combined with areas of acoustic tiling on the side walls. The bands of concealed lighting across the ceiling faced the audience.

The Odeon at **Newport**, Monmouthshire, replaced the long and narrow Regal cinema, two adjacent shops and a warehouse behind, as well as taking up a vacant plot on the corner of Clarence Place and East Usk Road. It was situated out of the town centre but opposite the Gaumont circuit's elderly Coliseum, with ABC's large and better sited Olympia forming the principal competition among another half-dozen halls. (London and Southern, an Odeon subsidiary, operated the Tredegar Hall, a former public hall.)

The job architect at Newport was Arthur J. Price and the Odeon was an accomplished re-working of the corner entrance style created by J. Cecil Clavering at Sutton Coldfield, adding brick piers, possibly suggested by Colwyn Bay, to the wall of the slab tower. The faience-clad side wall gave a horizontal rather than vertical emphasis to its windows and highlighted most of them with a surround of black tiles (an idea first introduced at

Odeon Newport. Out of sight at left, just beyond the windows set into a curve, lies a recess with a tall window illuminating stairs down to the side exit. The main railway line between Paddington and South Wales is on an embankment just behind the cinema and during quiet moments in a film steam trains could sometimes be heard. (No interior views were taken by Odeon's photographer, John Maltby, and no others of the period have been located. CTA member David Daykin recalls that the screen tabs showed trees, fields and a stream or river. A later interior view will be featured in the second volume of this history.)

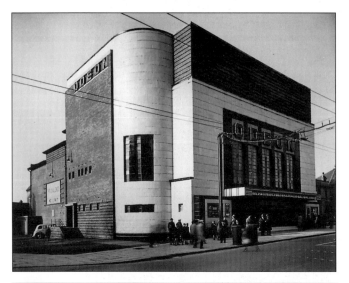

Odeon Llanelly. The black faience base of the exterior incorporated thin green bands. The squashed scroll treatment of the canopy ends is unusual. In the auditorium, the cove lighting in front of the proscenium is not on and the four smaller light fittings in the same style as the two visible are out of sight across the back of the balcony. The Odeon clock appears in an unusually high position and there may be a neon strip in the vertical feature fronting the rather ponderous splay wall grillework. The cluster of shiny vertical bands at the edge of the proscenium opening may have been designed to reflect coloured lighting.

Wolverhampton). Both the black and the buff tiles were set in basketweave pattern.

The auditorium also had similarities to Sutton Coldfield with concealed lighting in coves across the ceiling and thin horizontal bands across ventilation openings on the side walls. But here the bands carried a more eye-catching repetitive decorative design and the splay walls were dramatically different – recessed with the back edge leaning forward and featuring simple ribbed plasterwork at the same angle plus concealed lighting.

Arthur J. Price (1901-53) has previously been noted as the job architect at Loughborough and Hanley, and one of the team at Leicester Square. According to Robert Bullivant, "Arthur Price wasn't with us very long. He was a very strong-minded chap who lost us a very important job – not a cinema job. He told the client he didn't know what he was talking about." His architect son Cedric Price recalls that he was involved in the later Blackpool Odeon with W. Calder Robson and left to do his own work, designing two factories, at Hythe in Hampshire and Poole in Dorset, for Scott Payne's power boat company before World War Two when he joined the Marines. After the war, Price was an architect for various government ministries.

The next Weedon Odeon was deep into Wales at **Llanelly** (now Llanelli), built on the site of the Greenfield Working Men's Club with P. J. Price as the assistant in charge. There were six or more existing cinemas in town but this was the first and last major circuit house.

Externally, the design seemed a little top-heavy, with channelling of the upper brickwork on the front elevation doing little to relieve its obtrusive mass although the main name sign was skilfully positioned above five vertical windows on the main frontage with a black surround reminiscent of Wolverhampton and Newport. A subsidiary name sign was neatly recessed into the side wall where brick gave way to faience (the latter in basketweave pattern).

Here at Llanelly the trend to direct illumination of the auditorium was particularly clear with six light fittings suspended from the ceiling. This was a dull, poorly co-ordinated interior with an exceptional expanse of plain ceiling curving down to contain one band of cove lighting at the meeting with the splay walls.

"Too plain and bare" was the criticism made by the local planning committee of Robert Bullivant's exterior scheme for the Odeon **Leicester,** Leicestershire, but they nevertheless passed it in October 1936. It's curious that the Odeon should then have taken nearly two years to appear but perhaps the answer lies in the candid remarks of W. G. Elcock at the opening in July 1938: "We tried for three years to find a site in Leicester. It is a most difficult proposition to get a site of sufficient size to build a theatre of over 2,000 seats, so we had to sacrifice a central position

Odeon Leicester. Boards like this (top) sprung up on every Odeon site before and while building was in progress. (Leicestershire Museums, Arts and Records Service.) The copy image of the completed exterior (the best available) makes it impossible to see the basketweave pattern on the side wall, but the three lines of neon higher up are distinct. In the foyer, the sweeping curves in the rubberoid flooring add to the impact. The auditorium is a mish-mash of features. It lacks the customary wooden dado and, in the balcony, incorporated forward side exits reflecting the high number of seats. Ventilation grilles are neatly incorporated into the slanting balcony fascia but contrast horribly with the fussy decorative band on the side wall below. The octagonal decorative feature above the clock covered the public address system.

for size." The company may have been hesitating in case a better site came to light. Built on a curve in Rutland Street, the Odeon had a corner entrance that could at least be seen from part of the city centre. The ABC circuit had found more prominent space and opened its 2,414-seat Savoy in June 1937.

The Odeon's tall frontage would not be considered "plain and bare" by today's standards (although it was in starkly modern contrast to the fine Victorian office building just beyond it). Enclosed by brick wings carrying the usual staircases, the splayed-out corner entrance was eye-catching, with the main Odeon name sign mounted high up to be seen from afar. The building made a powerful impression at night with parallel neon bands set in the brick channels to each side of the main name sign, in the brick channels lower down on the left wing, and over the high green bands crossing the faience-clad side wall. The curving entrance canopy, the outer edge of the piers between the windows and the vertical ribs directly above the windows also carried neon.

The exterior lacked the lighter touch of Harrogate or Colwyn Bay, but this was because so much was being packed into the site, which had seating for 2,182 patrons. The treatment of the brick walls of the auditorium on full view along two side roads was in the very best Weedon manner, built up to hide the roof in contrasting colours of brick, with channelling to add interest at upper and ground levels.

Reached through a circular outer vestibule, the entrance hall was very uncharacteristic with much use of cylindrical light fittings and at least one figurine on a pedestal on the landing overlooking the main foyer which would have been more at home in a niche at one of W. R. Glen's ABCs of the period. The auditorium offered a riotous juxtaposition of elements dominated by curvaceous sweeps of plaster bands on the side walls that played with the idea of the cutaway effect seen at Yeovil and elsewhere. The decoration at each side of the proscenium opening seems to have been designed to reflect coloured lighting and was, at an upper level, fitted with light bulbs that faced out – a novel touch indeed.

Oscar Deutsch, who attended most openings, was at Leicester's, along with Harry Weedon. "There was a strong bond of affection and mutual respect," Robert Bullivant has noted. "When Deutsch suggested that a decorative frieze in the circle foyer was extravagant, Weedon was so disconcerted that his ebullience temporarily deserted him. I had great difficulty in persuading him to stay for the opening ceremony. I have no doubt that Deutsch believed that mild criticism from time to time could be highly efficacious and reminded architects and others who were employed by him that they must never relax." (It is possible that this anecdote should refer to York rather than Leicester.)

Leicester opened in July. It was almost five months before

Odeon Bradford. The distinctive glass tower was lit up in red and green. The surrounding faience is in basketweave pattern (elsewhere it is set horizontally). A travelling sign like that at the Odeon Leicester Square was installed on the canopy above the entrance doors. An ancient clock tower is partly visible behind the Odeon tower. In the auditorium, the octagonal decorative feature above the clock is repeated from Leicester and seems jarring.

another Weedon Odeon made its debut, again the work of Robert Bullivant. The largest so far in seating capacity, this was the 2,713-seater at **Bradford,** Yorkshire – the first major city centre cinema to open there since the New Victoria in 1930 (with 3,318 seats). ABC followed with a 2,021-seat Ritz in 1939, so that each of the major circuits was strongly represented. With a population of 450,000, Bradford was a key site for the Odeon circuit and the cinema's £65,000 construction cost (£23.96 per seat) was then second only to Leicester Square (but exceeded by Blackpool later). There were nearly forty central and suburban halls competing for the picturegoer's attention.

Built very centrally, close to the New Victoria on the site of the former Central (textile) Mills and shops, the Odeon experimented with a tower in glass bricks enclosed by faience. This must have stood out dramatically when lit up from within by red and green neon, although glass bricks were not used in any later Weedon schemes.* There seems to have been no supplementary external neon to outline the shape of the building. Art deco chandeliers in the lofty balcony foyer were visible through a huge window above the entrance. An attached parade of shops and flats was clad in black tiles at ground floor level and cream-coloured faience above with four bands in colour across the top. The glazing bars of the windows at first and second floor level reinforced the horizontal emphasis. The site was steeply sloping, which aided the rake of the stalls.

As at Leicester, the auditorium at Bradford was distinctively different from any other Odeon but it displayed considerable uniformity, linking the side walls to the ceiling through fluting. The side walls graduated in colour from a silver finish at the back to a gold colour at the proscenium arch to blend in with the gold stage curtain. Unusually, the ceiling seems to have been in darker tones. The main decorative features were the identical, specially commissioned full-relief sculptures mounted on each splay wall, featuring five figures in a pyramidal formation (the artist is not known). Here was a further instance of direct auditorium lighting from suspended fittings, supplemented by the concealed illumination of the proscenium surround. A little surprisingly, no organ was installed.

George Coles

The Coles practice delivered two particularly memorable Odeons at **Erith,** an inner industrial part of Kent on the River Thames, and Balham, a predominantly working class district of south London.

* As previously noted, Bullivant had proposed using glass bricks for the tower of the Odeon Leicester Square and they had also been employed to good effect on the tower of the Bristol in Birmingham (1937, architect: Hurley Robinson).

The Erith Odeon, on the site of an old hospital, entered into competition with two small independents and a moderate-size Union house recently remodelled in anticipation of the Odeon's arrival. It had a low seating capacity of 1,246 but looked enormous as it dominated a triangular site, presenting a flat wall of faience at the apex with a curved corner from which a 65ft.-high tower arose and swept back with the letters of ODEON slotted vertically within sections (a variation on the device introduced at Acton). On the main flanking wall, continued use of faience, especially at ground level, helped bind the entrance block to the auditorium.

Then came a marvellously streamlined foyer with an octagonal light fitting over octagonal paybox, and a splendid auditorium where backlit horizontal bands on the splay walls directed attention towards the screen as did somewhat less emphatic bands, looking as though they had been squeezed from a tube, that extended down the ceiling.

The much larger **Balham** Odeon opened on Easter Monday at the top of Balham Hill – really at Clapham South, midway between the centre of Balham and Clapham and some distance from rival picture houses. It was the only modern cinema in the area (Balham had two old Gaumont halls and one ABC; Clapham had one Gaumont hall and one independent), although Granada had opened a major new cinema further away at Clapham Junction and its Tooting flagship was within reach.

The frontage of the Odeon Balham was uncompromisingly modern and bright – a powerful symmetrical composition, curved at the front corners with sharp corners further back, the two sides joined together by a central tower and by the main Odeon name sign, half floating in the air. The tower had a slab projecting vertically, carrying horizontal Odeon name signs on each side, visible for miles away from this high point. A first floor café required more substantial fenestration than most Coles exteriors, but the line of windows skilfully reinforced the design.

The exterior led to one of Odeon's best and most spacious foyers, with a fine central staircase carrying patrons to the circle and café past one of those pink mirrors widely used to flatter the complexion of patrons.

The auditorium may have lacked the screenwards thrust of other Coles interiors and stumbled a bit with the bald display of acoustic tiles in the centre side walls; but it had a cool, lofty elegance with its double-height wood-panelled dados smoothly integrated into the proscenium surround and through the enriched edges to the twin coves of concealed lighting around the proscenium. The prominence of the wood dado is particularly noteworthy in that Coles' Odeons usually featured less expensive plasterwork, often with trompe l'oeil banding. The fronds and other foliage painted above the foyer staircase and on the proscenium surround were a curious attempt (seen at many

Odeon Erith. On the exterior, Coles employs the widespread device of thickening joints to create an impression of squares from each pair of rectangular tiles. The use made of lettering on the canopy edge is rather feeble. The clocks in the auditorium are further back than usual (and don't, as yet, agree on the time). The design of screen tabs had graced at least four earlier Odeons.

Odeon Balham. The faience here is presented as one solid mass with the barely noticeable variation of two bands of vertically arranged tiles lined up with the central windows and ribbed tiles carrying neon in line with the top edge of the canopy. The windows bring daylight into the café area.

Odeon Balham continued.

Odeon Brentwood. The faience tiles on the frontage are arranged vertically rather than horizontally as at Balham, and have a more mottled effect than usual. The screen tabs seem to have been unique to this cinema.

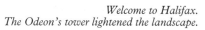

Welcome to Halifax.
The Odeon's tower lightened the landscape.

other Odeons) to soften the scheme – lost, of course, in later redecoration.

In May 1938 came Coles' more modest Odeon for the small town of **Brentwood** in Essex (which already had two independent cinemas). This carried one of his plainest, most conventional exteriors, but one that still clearly identified it as part of the circuit. Windows were prominent between four plain pilasters carrying double lines of neon.

The low entrance hall may have been unexciting but above it stood a circle lounge with ceiling dominated by a huge ring of art deco lighting complementing a smaller central fitting on an otherwise plain surface.

Then there was the long, narrow auditorium with its amazing streamlining, featuring linear lighting along the side walls and ceiling. The side wall strip came to a firm conclusion over the clocks and side exits while the strong lines down the ceiling largely gave way to a stepped curve just in front of the proscenium, reinforced by a circular light fitting set flush. Coles did away with any decorative treatment of the proscenium arch or niches in the front side walls, while ventilation openings were skilfully worked into the general design.

The **Halifax** Odeon was not in the same league as these preceding Odeons – but then this large northerly project (with 2,058 seats) wasn't designed for the circuit. Coles was originally engaged by Nat Cohen and J. Rafer, and received local council approval of his plans in late 1936, just before the opening of the Regal Kettering which he designed for the same partnership. There is an unmistakable resemblance between the two cinemas' exteriors: one recess with convex glass brick feature at Kettering becomes three side by side at Halifax.

The Yorkshire town was awash with cinemas – ten, in fact – before the Odeon arrived. The site was about a quarter of a mile from the entertainment nexus at Ward's End where the ABC circuit's Regal, opened less than three months after the Odeon, faced the Picture House (the main Gaumont circuit outlet) and a live theatre, with the Electric cinema and other entertainment venues in close proximity. ABC's progress with the Regal seems to have given Cohen and Rafer worries over booking films and encouraged them to sell out during construction.

The Odeon occupied a particularly difficult site at one end of the town centre, where it replaced slum property. The land sloped down to the main road and the screen had to be placed at that end because the foundations were of solid rock. The entrance was placed halfway along the side road nearest the town centre. This resulted in side entry to the stalls and a long extension of the foyer to the balcony staircase. A lower, corner entrance would have entailed an impossibly long, rising foyer extending the length of the auditorium. The space left at the bottom corner of

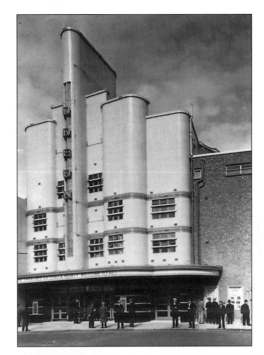

Odeon Deptford. The brickwork to the right ended in a curve and enclosed the wide main staircase to the balcony.

the site was taken up with a ground floor extension and a tower feature that carried the Odeon name on both sides and could be seen from Ward's End. Detached from the main entrance, the tower was perhaps an addition to the original scheme once it passed to Odeon, being the only part clad in buff faience tiles. However, the tower also drew attention to large expanses of unattractive brick wall behind – it would have been far better to have enclosed this area or tiled it over. Another Odeon sign was rather awkwardly perched on the front edge of the canopy and spaced out.

Trough light fittings in the main foyer were rather old-fashioned although the directional markings in the rubber flooring were cleverly extended up the stairs to the balcony. In the balcony lounge, the recesses inside the glass brick features were rather awkwardly cut off from public access by long seats placed across them.

The auditorium was not in Odeon style, although very impressive in its own right with an exceptionally wide proscenium. The ceiling was much higher than Odeon liked with the projection box placed over the rear of the balcony rather than at the back of it. There was strong decorative interest on each side wall from the two large bas-relief figures (females in similar poses but different costumes) with concealed side lighting. The figures bear a passing resemblance to the more stylised ones in Black's Regal Sunderland (1932).

Coles' Odeon for **Deptford** in inner south east London was unmistakably designed for the circuit. The faience-clad frontage was reminiscent of Woolwich with its central slab tower and tall vertical window set into its front edge. The attachment of the name sign appeared awkward – and why wasn't another sign attached to each side of the tower at the top? The ponderous treatment of the glazing bars on a large number of windows and the spotty effect of air vents detracted from the clean impression that Coles obtained at Woolwich and elsewhere. And here, for once, Coles introduced green horizontal bands on which neon tubes were mounted, but the two parallel strips were wide and obtrusive. There was something forbidding, even unwelcoming, about this frontage. The black base extended to canopy height around the entrance doors and also carried colour banding.

The large auditorium, too, was disappointing. A series of light fittings directly attached to the ceiling pointed towards the screen without the same impact as the continuous strips elsewhere. The plain side walls were heavily reliant on trompe l'oeil fluting for interest. Splay wall niches weakly enclosed plants.

Replacing the old Palladium cinema on an enlarged site, this Odeon certainly demonstrated that the circuit had no qualms about establishing itself in the roughest areas. Across the road stood the Broadway while the small independent Palace was nearby. Deptford merged with New Cross to the west as a

Odeon Shannon Corner. This featured a slip road, like many of Coles' schemes. Not visible, the mass of faience on the far return wall of the entrance block had two vertical channels, interrupted by a small window, descending to canopy level. The auditorium side walls are flat with horizontal banding painted on. The balcony front is tilted.

release area for new films with Gaumont's New Cross Kinema providing the most substantial competition.

Shannon Corner, New Malden, Surrey, represented a very out-of-town location for a 1938 Odeon, reminiscent of the early years and of cinemas like the Odeon Tolworth which was three miles away on the same Kingston By-Pass. But the new cinema's site was highly accessible to motorists and Malden was the only borough in Greater London without a cinema following the demise by fire of the Plaza at Christmas 1936.

Externally, Shannon Corner was sleek and modern. It looked in some ways more like the work of Weedon than Coles. A slimline tower carried the Odeon name with a line of neon at the edge while there was an unusual feature (reminiscent of Hanley and Morecambe) in the glazed corridor at the top of the rounded corner. But the flat facade on a brick box to the right of the tower was pure Coles, even with its windows: these would have been deeply recessed in a Weedon frontage. Three lines of narrow colour banding were introduced to the mass of faience cladding at ground level above the black base, as at Southall.

The foyer spaces were rather dreary and the auditorium only mildly interesting. It made a strong feature of linear laylights in the ceiling which undulated down towards the screen. The side walls had strong trompe l'oeil horizontal banding and rather conspicuous ventilation openings in the splay walls with horizontal and vertical sections that clashed. The balcony front was sharply angled back. High wall lights and two circular lights over the front stalls did not sit comfortably with the laylights.

Shannon Corner proved to be the last Odeon completed by Coles although the practice had further schemes in progress as listed at the end of the next chapter. The dull exterior sketches seen for some of these reinforce the impression given by Deptford and Shannon Corner that the Coles practice had lost its audacity: perhaps some key figure had left?

Andrew Mather

The major happening during 1938 within this practice was the death in London's Guy's Hospital of its head on Friday 4 November, aged 47. Andrew Mather was widely known to have been ill for months. Oscar Deutsch, W. G. Elcock and F. Stanley Bates all attended the funeral where Deutsch voiced a warm tribute to "my friend and colleague". The practice had more than a dozen Odeon schemes under way and in development, and it continued unabated under the leadership of Leonard Allen until sometime during World War Two, its completed buildings being credited to "The late Andrew Mather". (Allen worked on some postwar Odeons in his own name.)

The Odeon at **Eltham Hill,** in outer south east London, opened in April – the first Mather addition to the circuit since

Odeon Eltham Hill. The car park was directly behind. In the auditorium, the suspended lights by the decorative grillework clash with the attached fittings elsewhere while the four columns by the grilles have incongruous Ionic capitals. The obtrusive round openings at the edge of the inner proscenium cover the speakers for the public address system and could have been better placed.

Odeon Peckham. The cinema sparkles between two drab older buildings and was spectacular when outlined in neon and floodlit at night. Note the box for moving lettering under the canopy. The auditorium view is the best available from the period.

Odeon Hackney Road. Shadow obscures a surprisingly small name sign on the upper part of the vertical and the large name signs set in the recess just below the roofline on both elevations. A travelling neon sign is located under the canopy. The tall windows down the side street mark the balcony foyer. The auditorium shot reveals a new design of screen tabs.

December 1937. Set just outside the town centre, this had a very conspicuous but boring facade clad in sheets of cream and black glass with terracotta intervening at canopy level. It made the first use of an improved form of glass with a granulated surface to reduce shininess and combat the objection that it was too reminiscent of fitted bathrooms. The foyer was wide and spacious, leading to a well-proportioned semi-stadium auditorium which was extremely pleasant without being inspired.

This was an odd undertaking by Deutsch as the Odeon Well Hall lay only just over half a mile away and so the two cinemas could not normally play the same programme. But the argument may well have been that it was a good place to put a cinema and, if there was going to be one, it might as well be run by Odeon. In fact, it played the rival Gaumont release and with ABC's Palace in Eltham High Street gave the district the full spread of major circuit programmes.

Replacing an old theatre, the Odeon at **Peckham** in densely populated inner south east London stood about two miles away from the Deptford Odeon. It was in immediate competition with three older Gaumont halls and an independent. The frontage was eye-catching with two wings and a wide rectangular recess comparable to the early Odeons of A. P. Starkey. Here, though, the central space had four free-standing columns mounted at the front, which carried the cinema name. It is possible that patrons were allowed into this area from the circle lounge since railings were placed along the front. The facade above canopy level was faced in granulated glass in cream-yellow traversed by wide horizontal bands in jade green. These carried on across the columns as well as along the back of the recess, and cut through two upright bands in a darker shade of the same colour to each side of the recess. The black base was crossed by narrow green bands.

As at Eltham Hill, the interior was agreeable in an unassuming way. The auditorium did not look vast, yet it seated well over two thousand. The main light fittings were suspended from small concave domes down each side of the ceiling, while the proscenium arch was cove-lit. The inward curve of the side walls was neatly matched by the stepped descent of the ceiling.

Mather's Odeon for **Hackney Road** was another huge addition to the thickly inhabited inner London suburbs, this time north of the Thames. It was more than a mile by main road from the centre of Hackney (where Odeon operated the smallish Picture House) and nearer Hoxton and Bethnal Green (where the Foresters was an Odeon takeover). It had no major competition in the immediate area, although the small Shoreditch Standard had bitterly opposed its coming. Externally, it had a minimalist approach to the circuit style and looked ultra-modern with its shining expanse of light yellow vitrolite in horizontal bands. The exceptionally wide auditorium, seating just under two thousand,

Odeon Ayr. This rain-drenched view from autumn 1942 ventures slightly outside the period of this book but is the only early exterior image available. Inside, fancy screen tabs have given way to a side-opening festoon. The slight intrusion of front side exits into the auditorium is old-fashioned.

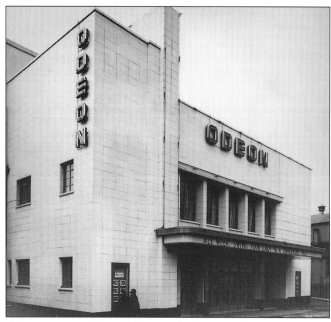

Below and lower left: Odeon Motherwell. Still raining in Scotland. Here the Odeon sign is better placed, neatly aligned with the windows. The light fittings of the auditorium are in clashing styles. Cove lighting of the proscenium opening is absent. This design of screen tabs was also seen at Sittingbourne, Hereford and East Ham.

Odeon Hamilton. Another wet day in Scotland. The horizontal name sign seems to have been positioned too high.

was on the plain side apart from thin, close-set metallic-looking bands on the side walls which extended from the circle front and curved back under the balcony, covering ventilation openings.

This was the year that Andrew Mather's first Scottish schemes came to fruition. All three were uninspired, built at low cost to seat around 1,800 – but they certainly offered better viewing conditions than most of the opposition and few cinemagoers would have known that they were being shortchanged in terms of what Odeon could offer down south.

There were at least five cinemas operating in **Ayr,** the resort town on the west coast of Scotland, when the Odeon opened, but only one was of recent construction (the small Ritz). Green's had a huge Playhouse, there was an atmospheric Orient, and Gaumont operated the Picture House. The Odeon had a tower to compete for attention with the statue of Robert Burns that faced it from the square outside, but this lacked the rich detail of the similar shaped feature at Portsmouth. The foyers and auditorium were well planned but made no great impression.

The Odeon at **Hamilton,** in the centre of industrial Lanarkshire, competed with ABC's Regal (a recently reconstructed house with 200 more seats than the Odeon), Gaumont's smaller and elderly La Scala, and four other halls, one of which (the Roxy) joined the Regal and Odeon in a tight cluster. The Odeon's entrance block was clad in cream faience with a modest slab tower (no name sign) and recessed windows at first floor level, and so it was recognisable in the circuit style. No photographs of the original interior have come to light but from later examination it seems to have been spacious and inviting.

At **Motherwell,** another heavily industrial town in Lanarkshire, the Odeon was separated by only an exit passage from Gaumont's pre-World War One Pavilion. ABC had a miserable-looking Rex, recently re-built from a theatre, and a more central, smaller La Scala. The Odeon's half-hearted tower feature was dwarfed by the auditorium behind but the foyer was deftly handled with circular island paybox and the auditorium was more than adequate.

By far the most notable work to be completed by the Mather office in 1938 emanated from Keith P. Roberts. He had worked under W. E. Trent at Gaumont on such London-area cinemas as the New Victoria (1930), Gaumont Palace Lewisham (1932) and Gaumont Bromley (1936). Joining the practice of Leslie H. Kemp and F. E. Tasker, he had a major hand in the cubist but Odeon-like exterior of the Havana Romford (1936) besides working on the Union Dunstable (1937) and Ritz Hereford (1938). He was primarily responsible for five Odeons that appeared between late May and mid-October 1938, as well as three in 1939.

First came the Odeon at **Redhill,** Surrey. It was constructed on piles over a brook and had a driveway leading up to a wide flight of steps at the entrance. A pylon with vertical Odeon sign advertised the cinema at the start of the drive, close to a bridge under the adjacent railway. The flat top of the facade, mounted on rounded piers, recalled T. Cecil Howitt's towers. The front elevation was clad in faience tiles rather than glass, perhaps to facilitate the introduction of porthole windows which also appeared further round each curved corner.*

The auditorium had laylights across the ceiling, three circular slatted openings in the ceiling in front of the proscenium arch and cove lighting of the splay walls. The narrow ventilation grilles, in parallel lines like grating, were a feature of other Mather Odeons, including Hackney Road. Bruce Peter suggests that the slant of the panels in the wooden dado and of the back edge of the cove lighting echoed the angle of the seat backs.

Redhill already had two small cinemas, of which the nearby Picture House was forced to close. The main competition came from Reigate, under two miles away, with its Majestic and Hippodrome, both part of the Shipman and King chain.

Keith P. Roberts' Odeon at **Uxbridge** refreshed the entertainment scene in this small but expanding Middlesex town with the first new cinema since the remarkable Regal in 1931. The slightly smaller Regal was promoted by A. E. Abrahams and later taken over by the Union circuit (along with the town's older Savoy). The Odeon was an Andrew Mather scheme originally developed for Abrahams in late 1936. By the time it was ready to open, Oscar Deutsch found himself in competition with the ABC circuit as the new managers of Union after its financial collapse. (There were also public shows in the RAF Cinema at the camp in the town.)

The Odeon's site was half a mile away from the Regal, at the other end of town, "opposite the trolley-bus terminal at the bottom of the High Street" (as its opening press advertisement advised cinemagoers). Oscar Deutsch was on hand to celebrate not only the opening but his twenty-first wedding anniversary – nothing like combining business with pleasure.

The exterior design was restricted by an unusual requirement to provide offices over the entrance. These formed a highly original and limiting feature at first and second floor level but Roberts opened up the ground floor by curving the cinema entrance and adjacent shops round to an entrance set further back, leaving a corner pillar to support the building. This created space for a sheltered pavement and driveway for cars to drop off patrons. An Odeon sign was mounted in widely spaced letters on the narrow canopy rather than higher up. The offices were included in the night-time lighting scheme, the lines of windows being emphasised by neon.

* The first plans for Redhill were drawn up by J. J. Joass. He is given no credit after Andrew Mather's practice took over.

Odeon Redhill. A moving sign is mounted on the front edge of the canopy. It seems a mistake to have the Odeon sign perched on the edge of the large window rather than higher up. The name sign high on the side wall advertises the cinema to passengers on passing trains. There are further unilluminated portholes around the curve on each side of the frontage. In the auditorium, the orchestra pit is solidly boxed in. The design of screen tabs was the same as at St. Austell. (Auditorium courtesy of Bruce Peter.)

Odeon Uxbridge. The entrance doors are set well back under the canopy in deep shadow. There is a travelling sign set into the front of the canopy. Inside, the view from the balcony foyer shows the stylised historical mural on the back wall of the stairs while in the auditorium the screen tabs design was previously aired at Wolverhampton and, seemingly, Chester. (Top right, from the scrapbook of Keith P. Roberts via Bruce Peter.)

Odeon East Ham. A travelling sign is half installed below the canopy.

Odeon East Ham. In the foyer views (courtesy of the late Keith P. Roberts), note the honeycomb pattern on the radiators and the stylised covering of the settees. In the auditorium, the design of screen tabs had been used at Motherwell and at least two other Odeons.

Only a corner tower containing an exit staircase enabled Roberts to really advertise the cinema by attaching a shiney black-tiled vertical that descended all the way to ground level with the Odeon name attached to each side and a flagpole on top. (Many of the characteristics of a full-fledged Odeon frontage in the Weedon style were to be found in Uxbridge on the wide frontage of Randalls' department store.)

The Odeon had a circular foyer with central paybox. The back wall of the stairs to the balcony featured a mural of Uxbridge's history. The auditorium offered a curious sequence of curved laylights placed centrally in the descending ceiling while the splay walls carried straight horizontal grillework between illuminated recesses. Lower down, the architect's love of porthole openings was in evidence alongside the Odeon clock as well as in the barrier to the orchestra pit.

The very large Odeon at **East Ham,** in north east London, was located on the Barking Road quite close to the even larger Granada which had opened in 1936. Three cinemas in the centre of East Ham included the Premier Super, a vast Gaumont property. ABC cinemas were all around – at Barking, Upton Park and Manor Park – and Barking also had the huge Rio dating from 1935.

The exterior of this Odeon made a startling departure from conventional cinema design (as well as the biggest possible contrast with the early Boleyn Electric Theatre which it replaced).* It was so forward-looking that it could easily be mistaken for a 1950s building. Vertical Odeon signs mounted on black tiles faced each direction at the sides of a large recessed window. A third Odeon sign, perched on top of the window (as at Redhill), was redundant and eventually removed. The glass lights in the flat roof over the recess were a striking feature on a cinema frontage, although used on buildings by Berthold Lubetkin and Joseph Emberton and earlier in 1938 on the canopy of the Regal cinema at Walton-on-Thames.

Like the frontage, the foyer with its simplicity of line was way ahead of its time. The huge window through which daylight flooded the lofty foyer made this perhaps the airiest of 1930s' cinema foyers while a huge laylight may have produced a similar effect after dark. With its side staircases to the balcony meeting in a bridge over the stalls entrance doors, the space formed a severe contrast to W. R. Glen's similarly arranged ABC foyers although the expanses of plain wall and ceiling were softened by decorative painting (with Roberts' approval?).

The auditorium, too, had an austere look, especially in the sharp car radiator look to the ventilation openings on the side

Odeon Luton. (Both courtesy of Bruce Peter.)

---

* The Boleyn had been first earmarked for replacement back in October 1936 when another architect, Cecil Masey, produced plans.

Odeon Luton. (Staircase and balcony foyer views courtesy of Bruce Peter and Tom Wade.) In the auditorium, the screen tabs repeat the design at Brighton and Peckham.

wall (echoing Uxbridge). The adjacent side wall was painted over with wave-like patterns. The dado, in light wood rather than the darker tones normally favoured, extended to the proscenium opening and continued as the barrier to the orchestra pit, punctuated with porthole openings like the windows in the exit doors. The lighting scheme was dominated by uplit saucer domes in the ceiling and concealed illumination in the rim of the elegantly shaped outer proscenium opening.

Keith P. Roberts' Odeon at **Luton,** Bedfordshire, was built simultaneously with ABC's Savoy. The Savoy had a perfect position right in the town centre while the Odeon was built in the Bury Park district along the Dunstable Road – suggesting, not for the first time, that ABC were prepared to pay more for sites while Odeon would rely on its reputation and circuit attractions to draw patrons to less prominent locations.

One side wall of the Odeon's auditorium extended along the back of the pavement (the continuation parade of shops and flats seems to have been built at the same time). Despite a cladding of cream tiles at ground level, the huge expanse of brickwork on a main road seemed rather forbidding. At the cinema's entrance, a tower enclosed a single "O" in the trademark style – clearly sufficient to inform people of the cinema's identity. The main Odeon sign surmounted a window just above canopy level at the front bottom edge of a large recess. The back of the recess was covered by large, square cream-coloured glass panels separated by narrow red bands and interrupted only by a line of five small windows high up.

This frontage as a whole was blocky and angular – resolutely rejecting the streamlining of earlier Odeons. However, a report on the listing of the building (*CTA Bulletin*, May/June 1999), presumably quoting the listing notice, describes the facade as "a remarkably sophisticated piece of purist geometry, entirely lacking artistic references or art deco styling" while referring to the building in general as "the best remaining example of International Modernism applied to a cinema".

Certainly, the foyers and auditorium were impressive. The auditorium – "a good example of the best streamlined style of the time" – displayed sinuous horizontal curves which incorporated more radiator-like ventilation grilles, a line of saucer light fittings around the perimeter of the ceiling, and a set of circular lights along the upper wall. As at East Ham there was a dado in lighter wood which also fronted the orchestra pit with round openings. There was stencil-like, underwater-themed decoration of some of the bare surfaces.

The Odeon opened five days before ABC's Savoy with slightly fewer seats, but both were very large cinemas accommodating close to 2,000. Luton suddenly became grossly overprovided with cinemas. The newcomers immediately seized two of the top first-run releases while the Palace Theatre, as a Gaumont house, continued to take the third. The Union circuit had tried to deter further competition by building its Union Cinema with 2,104 seats after taking over three older cinemas including the large Alma. As it happened, by the time the Savoy opened, Union's problem had become ABC's through its takeover of the failed circuit. There were other independent cinemas, and the outlying Empire, close to the Odeon, gave up the fight just three days after its arrival.

The **Mile End** Odeon in inner north east London, a vast building again designed by Keith P. Roberts, opened five days after Luton. This was in direct competition with ABC's Palladium and the independent Coliseum, among others, while over a half mile away stood ABC's large Empire, a former music hall. The Odeon's impending arrival seems to have prompted demolition of the Empire and the construction of a modern replacement of the same name. While the Odeon had a seating capacity of 2,304, the Empire came close with 1,974 seats when it opened eight months later.

Unlike East Ham and Luton, this Odeon was very recognisably in the house style with its slab tower and rounded corner, its contrast of brick and cream glass, yet pared down to bare essentials without any channelling of the brickwork or black base. The tower had a projecting upper edge that anchored the flagpole as it had at Luton. An Odeon name sign was mounted both across the top and down the front edge. The curved corner carried a line of continuous windows above canopy level enclosing the lounge on the upper floor. Unfortunately, photographs of the interior are in short supply. Those of the auditorium show only the front stalls side walls with their rather extraordinary juxtaposition of grooved plasterwork, a panel of painted foliage punctuated at the screen end by three circular recesses, and a cheese grater pattern of ventilation openings alongside the proscenium. The sharp extension outwards of the side walls (so that mid-stalls exit doors face straight back) and the overhang of the front side exits were most unusual in an Odeon.

T. Cecil Howitt

T. Cecil Howitt made a mid-year contribution with the opening of his Odeon **Bristol.** With its large size (just under 2,000 seats), imposing exterior and excellent central location in a major town, this automatically became one of the key cinemas on the circuit. It replaced Fry's chocolate factory.

Like previous Howitt Odeons in the west of England at Weston-super-Mare and Bridgwater, this had a corner entrance but here the architect modified his rectangular towers to create a circular one with a flat top that sat directly on the main structure, protruding all round. Lower down, five narrow tile-clad piers

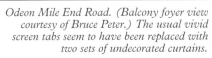

*Odeon Mile End Road. (Balcony foyer view
courtesy of Bruce Peter.) The usual vivid
screen tabs seem to have been replaced with
two sets of undecorated curtains.*

Odeon Bristol. This 1940 image of the exterior is the only early view to be located (courtesy of Les Lutner) and it conceals the considerable extent of faience-clad frontage around shops and offices to the left of the entrance. The name sign might have looked better more widely spaced directly over the five tall windows, or else more closely arranged in the centre. The poster on the right side wall has become a permanent advertisement for the Odeon Café and for the cinema as "THE HOME of Outstanding Entertainment". The overlap of foyer and auditorium shots, taken shortly after opening, is inherited from the original illustration in the book Odeon Cavalcade *in the author's collection.*

separated tall recessed windows. The frontage and side walls were clad in the usual buff faience tiles in basket-weave pattern with four narrow bands of green across the top. This may have lacked the subtle interplay of the best Weedon exteriors – the vast expanse of one flat, windowless side wall is a little oppressive – but it certainly demanded to be noticed.*

The entrance hall was circular while the octagonal double-height inner foyer was quite unlike anywhere else. It had ornate grillework featuring towers set into the gold-coloured walls and a promenade around at first floor level that led off to the balcony and to the area immediately above the entrance where a café opened six months after the cinema.

The auditorium was also very angular but in much the same manner as Howitt's earlier Odeons. The very wide proscenium opening was again framed by fluted columns and by parallel vertical bands on the splay walls that continued across the descending ceiling. Again the auditorium made strong use of combed plaster for decorative contrast but also sported two widely separated rows of small star-shaped lights set flush across the ceiling. In addition, there were ship and sea motifs on ornamental grillework on the back side walls. This interior was described as being in "pale gold bronze with shading of turquoise blue with silver relief on the side splays and columns". Although carried out by Decorative Crafts, it was emphasised that the Howitt practice had devised the decorative scheme.

The very high seating capacity of the balcony (894 seats compared to 1,051 in the stalls) dictated the provision of two staircases up to the central gangway and extra exits at each side attached to the balcony front. Odeon clocks appeared above these exit doors, the furthest back they had ever been, and additional clocks were placed directly below on the stalls floor to the side of exit doors there.

And a camp cinema

In *Memories of Kent Cinemas*, Martin Tapsell draws attention to a cinema at Lord Kitchener's Camp near Richborough in the Sandwich area of Kent: "With funds from the Odeon chairman Oscar Deutsch, refugees from Nazi Germany converted a derelict building into a 600-seat cinema. It opened as such in Deutsch's presence, during June 1938. Mrs. Lionel de Rothschild declared it open after the camp orchestra had played the National Anthem. Presumably the cinema closed as the refugees moved away from a likely invasion zone." Another source notes that the camp accommodated 3,500 German and Austrian Jewish refugees and suggests that Odeon built, equipped and operated the cinema.*

Takeovers

Odeon was not in an acquisitive mood this year, but it did obtain the large, atmospheric-style Riviera at Cheetham Hill to give it a second major property in Manchester (after the West End at Whalley Range), again close to the city centre but this time two miles to the north.

Odeon also took over a former live theatre, the Alhambra at Barnsley, Yorkshire, accepting a covenant that its name could not be changed. With two balconies, it was not ideal, and the company hatched plans for a new Odeon elsewhere.

It is usually difficult to determine whether new cinemas taken over by major circuits had proved successful and were sold on at a profit, or whether they had failed, often because of film booking problems, and had to be sold. The latter was certainly the case in Odeon's acquisition of the Embassy Gillingham which had opened in October 1936, designed by leading architect Robert Cromie for Fred White, a local entrepreneur. White ran into difficulties obtaining major films from the distributors and was forced to sell. Odeon is said to have rented the cinema for 99 years with no provision for increases, in which case the company was paying a peppercorn rent in later years.

The Clapton Kenning Hall in north London seems to have been acquired as part of a scheme for a new Odeon on an adjacent site. The Royalty Broadstairs was evidently such a problem to the circuit that it was leased out to an independent – with both an Odeon in much larger Ramsgate and County's Regal at Margate, it was very much surplus to requirements.

* A plaque on the outside wall, just to the left of the main entrance doors, that survived at least until October 1992, was headed by a cameo portrait of Joseph Fry and the dates 1728 and 1935 to each side, with an inscription below in capital letters: "Near this site for over 200 years J. S. Fry & Sons manufactured cocoa and chocolate before moving to Somerdale. A.D. 1935". The plaque disappeared after the Odeon was rebuilt internally and new slimmer tiles replaced those in basket-weave pattern on which it was originally mounted. I am indebted to Norman Walley for this information.

* Deutsch had also assisted a relative from Austria, Arnold Deutsch, who arrived in London in early 1934, joined by his wife a year later. Arnold sometimes went to Sabbath dinners in Birmingham with Oscar and his family and asked for Oscar's help to extend his visa. Oscar promised to find him work so that he could stay in Britain. However, in November 1937 he went off to Moscow. Oscar had no idea that Arnold Deutsch was a Russian agent who recruited twenty spies during his stay in England, including Anthony Blunt, Guy Burgess, Donald Maclean and Kim Philby. See *The Mitrokhin Archive – The KGB In Europe And The West* by Christopher Andrew and Vasili Mitrokhin (Allen Lane The Penguin Press, London, 1999).

1939: BEFORE THE WAR

The openings reduced to a trickle in the first eight months of 1939 before the declaration of war against Germany on Sunday 3 September proved to be an insurmountable obstacle to further completions. Some had been long in gestation: Hendon was first announced in March 1936 and plans approved by January 1937; work had supposedly commenced on Canning Town in November 1937.

These last seven Odeons came from the Harry Weedon and Andrew Mather stables, which also had others under construction. The war prevented T. Cecil Howitt from completing another of his occasional contributions at Doncaster while T. P. Bennett, the practice that had designed Haverstock Hill, would have to wait until long after the war to complete its second Odeon scheme at Highgate, north London.

On 31 March 1939, Weedon took Robert Bullivant, W. Calder Robson and Frederick H. Carter into partnership. The volume of work was there, encouraging Weedon to ensure that his most valuable associates stayed on. As partners, Bullivant and Robson publicly received "associate architect" credit for their work (Carter may have been an administrator: he does not feature as an Odeon architect).

Mather's output continued to be credited to "The late Andrew Mather". Three of the practice's four 1939 Odeons were designed by Keith P. Roberts.

Last openings

Five of the last Odeons were in the London area. From Weedon in February came one of two in the North: the Odeon at **Middlesbrough,** Yorkshire (assistant in charge: W. Calder Robson). It was the only major new cinema built there in the 1930s, and with 1,761 seats the largest on Teeside – both the Gaumont and ABC's Elite were older properties. In all, there were some fourteen competing cinemas in 1939.

Situated near the Town Hall, this Odeon had a simplified exterior in the circuit style, dominated by a black tower in the manner of Leicester Square but with small tiles and conspicuous light joints. A projecting flat top seemed to rest on 12ft.-high Odeon name signs (in a condensed version of the regular lettering) on all four sides. The tower was floodlit at night and, with all the signs blazing in neon, must have proclaimed the cinema's whereabouts superbly well.

Biscuit-coloured faience tiles covered the entrance block and the long side wall of the auditorium on the main road. Curves at the car park corner and where the auditorium wall met the entrance block moderated the severe appearance of the frontage. In a curious attempt to add some decorative interest, two piers clad in slightly darker tiles above the canopy enclosed some curled grillework and a small window. A tall window occupying the entire space would have looked much better. The flat expanse of tiles on the side wall called out for a more varied treatment: a basketweave pattern and colour bands would have helped. A name sign and poster plus scattered small windows were insufficient to relieve the blandness above the line of posters, still cases and exit doors at ground level.

Photographs of Middlesbrough's foyer and auditorium at the time of opening have proved elusive. Recent images show thorough modernisation, leaving only an unusual lip or canopy with scalloped edge over the proscenium (rather like that at the Gaumont Derby), which must have once carried concealed lighting; and an ornately decorated ventilation grille in a ceiling recess facing the back of the balcony. There were side exits via slips from the front of the balcony, reflecting a larger than average upstairs capacity achieved in part by the projection room being located over the back rows of the balcony.

In March came the Odeon at **Camberwell,** south London, a spectacular contribution by Keith P. Roberts and very arguably his finest cinema. Such was the infill of Odeons in the crowded inner London suburbs that it went up less than a mile away from the large Odeon at Peckham and only a mile away from the proposed Odeon Kennington. The Odeon East Dulwich (a takeover) was also close.

The Odeon Camberwell was the largest of the London Odeons with seating for nearly a thousand patrons in the balcony alone and for 2,470 in all. It was almost twice the size of ABC's Palace and seated more than Camberwell's further three cinemas put together. It overtook the long gestating scheme for a Florida

Odeon Middlesbrough. The car park can be seen to the left of the entrance along with the tall window of the balcony foyer. The cinema is attached to much older property at right. No auditorium view at opening has been located.

Odeon Dalston. No exterior view from this period has emerged and the auditorium shot is the best available. Later images will be included in the second volume of this history.

cinema, which finally opened in June 1940 as ABC's new house, the Regal, reputedly with 2,600 seats – even larger than the Odeon.

Built on the site of a live theatre and adjacent property, the Odeon stood at the V-shaped junction of two main roads, Denmark Hill and Coldharbour Lane. The entrance to the old theatre had been at the apex of the site, facing the heart of Camberwell, but this was now given over to a curving two-storey parade of shops which extended into ancillary space for the cinema as it enclosed the auditorium behind. Matching entrances to the cinema were provided at the far corners of the site along each of the two main roads, marked by towers (one of which cunningly concealed the outlet flue for the boiler) and connected by a radial entrance hall. This arrangement created a fan-shaped auditorium with a width at the back that would not have been possible the other way around. (Another notable cinema to feature two matching entrances was, of course, the London New Victoria, on which Keith P. Roberts worked in a junior capacity, but there the two sides of the site were parallel, not converging.)

The two towers were splendid eye-catchers with their glazed fronts which lit up at night. The towers and entrance blocks, together with the upper floor of the parade, were clad in large panels of light yellow vitrolite (a projecting edge enclosed the ground floor of the parade which was faced with black tiles). Set back, the brick bulk of the auditorium seemed comfortably remote rather than overwhelming and it was impossible to see the pitched roof of the auditorium from the street.

The long, wide entrance hall gained considerably from its gentle, elegant curve. In the middle, columns in polished black glass flanked the stairs to the balcony with a huge window of frosted glass at the first landing that hid the dismal view of adjacent property. The balcony landing was designed with equal élan.

The immense and well-proportioned auditorium was too bare for some tastes (there is an unsubstantiated story that Oscar Deutsch was so put off, he said he would never set foot in the place again). It was certainly very stark and functional apart from the wide band of flowery decoration painted on the side walls and across the ceiling. Roberts created an apparent lean towards the proscenium that straightened up in the bold honeycomb-like pattern of vents on each splay wall.* The round vents were echoed in the porthole windows of the doors below and in the

* Similar, far less conspicuous examples of this sieve-like pattern have been noted in earlier Odeons (Falmouth, Yeovil, etc.) but its bold presentation here can only be compared to that of the Gaumont Watford (1937), designed by Mollo and Egan with architect J. Owen Bond.

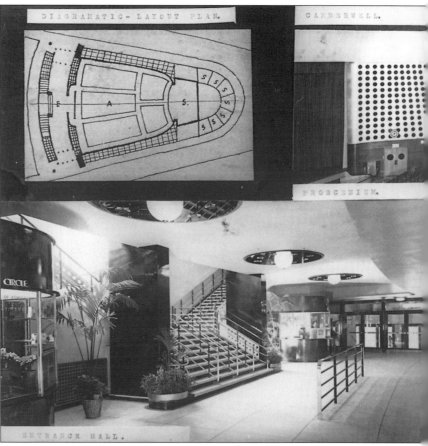

Odeon Camberwell. The exterior shows the Coldharbour Lane entrance.
A page copied from the album of Keith P. Roberts includes his sketch plan of the cinema
together with a view of the magnificent entrance hall and the side of the auditorium.

Odeon Camberwell. The view of the balcony landing shows Meccano-like staircase panels with round openings that correspond to auditorium features. The poor quality auditorium view is the best available from 1939 (CTA Archive).

slanting lines of circles on the side walls of the balcony, although the openings in the orchestra barrier were rectangular. The lighting was primarily direct, from fittings suspended from the ceiling. Like most Odeon architects, Roberts made no allowance for the clocks and they were rather crudely attached to four of the vents over the side exits.

Opened in May, the Odeon at **Dalston** in north London was another outstanding building from Andrew Mather's office but the name of the lead architect is not known (Keith P. Roberts declared that he was not involved). This project was fast-tracked (comparatively speaking), the acquisition of the site having been announced in January 1938 and a building tender accepted in August while many older schemes remained stalled. Dalston and the contiguous Stoke Newington area had a huge number of old cinemas (including Gaumont's Picture House), the Odeon's modern rival being ABC's fine 1936 Savoy Stoke Newington half a mile away (the small Classic Dalston was a recent reconstruction). The Odeon Hackney Road was a mile away to the south.

Built on an awkwardly shaped lot where two side roads met, the cinema was set back, facing the main Kingsland Road, leaving a triangular expanse of pavement in front. The main elevation was clad in small faience tiles in light yellow and had a short corner tower extending forward, to which the usual flagpole was attached.

The deftly handled auditorium (2,064 seats) had light fittings suspended from ribbed plaster panels in the ceiling and displayed simple but prominent grillework on the splay walls.

Designed by W. Calder Robson for Harry Weedon with the participation of Arthur J. Price, the Odeon for **Blackpool,** Lancashire, was the largest built by the circuit, seating 1,684 in the stalls and 1,404 in the balcony, making a total of 3,088.★ As in the case of the Palace Oldham and the Burnley Odeon, this was a site introduced by David Rosenfield, who was one of the local company's directors. The Odeon was the first and only large modern cinema built during the 1930s in the centre of Blackpool,

---

★ T. Cecil Howitt also drew up a scheme for this particularly important site, the only known example of two of the key practices competing for the same job (the Odeon Leicester Square was a collaboration between Weedon and Mather). Like all Howitt's later unrealised designs, his Blackpool proposal broke away from flat-top towers. The front elevation – in a rough sketch reproduced in the *CTA Bulletin*, vol. 21, no. 4, July-August 1987, page 7 – shows a canopy with a raised centre section over the entrance doors and first floor windows. This centre section was flanked by two slender columns carrying statues (more appropriate to one of Howitt's municipal buildings) while the Odeon name was mounted in widely spaced letters on the parapet. The design was perhaps too fussy for Blackpool. Howitt should have stuck with flat-top towers as Weedon's successful design had one.

Odeon Blackpool. The faience tiles outside the central recess were placed horizontally in pairs to create squares. Green bands can be seen in the black base as well as at the top. Unusually, the canopy edge carries neon tubing rather than a programme announcement. The entrance doors have a jazzy design. In the auditorium view, the screen tabs have a completely new and lavish design with swags. The huge seating capacity of the balcony required front side exits. Note the vents in the lower edge of the balcony fascia.

although the Union circuit had announced a scheme for a huge Ritz in the year it collapsed and ABC wanted to rebuild its Hippodrome.

The Odeon's cliff-like main frontage was a little more intricate than it looked at first glance, but the stepped recess in the centre, echoing a proscenium arch, might have been more effective had it been more pronounced. The use of convex tiles in the centre gave a fluted effect and the Odeon sign was neatly mounted in line with five tall windows. Three horizontal bands in green were introduced just below the parapet and these, as usual, were reinforced by neon at night.* The neon-outlined tower conveyed a blunt forcefulness while the brickwork on the side wall, stepped up to hide the pitched roof, received horizontal banding.

The low main entrance hall was exceptionally dreary with central paybox on the back wall and wide openings to both stalls and circle at each side.

Viewed from the balcony, the moulded edges of the stepped down ceiling and the stalactite-like light fittings provided an attractive and lively decorative scheme along with the flowery squares of grillework on the splay walls (probably contributed by Mollo and Egan) in two alternating patterns with an Odeon clock clumsily inset. The curving closely-fluted bays to each side of the proscenium seemed designed to reflect coloured lighting.

Because of the cinema's holiday location and the local competition of the Tower Ballroom, it was intended to add a five manual Compton as soon as possible. However, the organ was destroyed during the war when the Germans bombed a stationary goods train, apparently after it had reached Blackpool and was in sidings. Odeon installed the Conacher organ from the Ritz Southend in 1946.

At **Canning Town** in east London, near the docks on the north side of the Thames, Keith P. Roberts was confronted with an extremely awkward island site, the tip of which reached the main Barking Road. Excess space along one side and at an apex provided two small car parks. This very large property (2,240 seats) was half a mile out of the town centre in the direction of Plaistow, but in the midst of dense population and close to Gaumont's small and early Cinema. The Odeon's impending arrival spurred the owners of the Imperial on Barking Road, nearer the town centre, to internally reconstruct their building (originally a live theatre) and it re-opened ten days before the Odeon.

* This neon was installed by Pearce Signs, the company which had originated the circuit's distinctive style of name sign. It did not handle all the neon installations for the circuit but, by 1939, had done eighty-five, mostly in the South, including the Deptford and Peckham Odeons near its New Cross base and the Odeon Leicester Square.

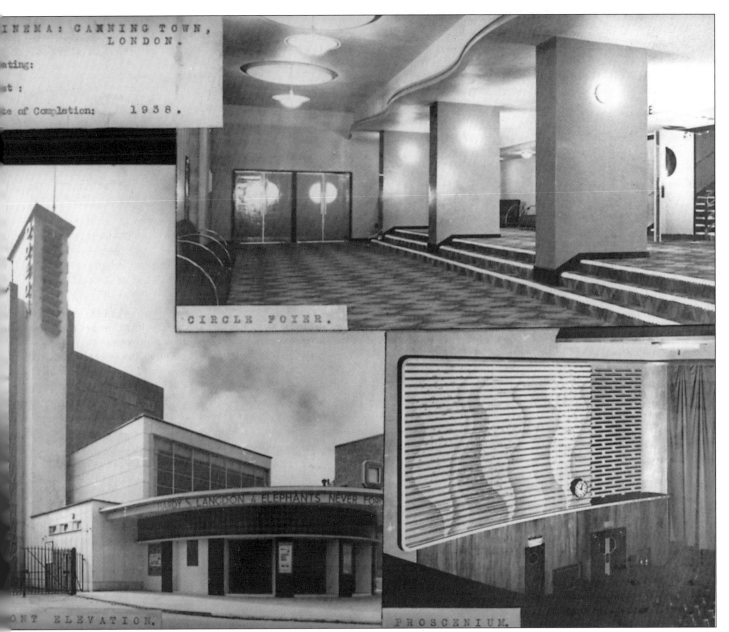

CINEMA: CANNING TOWN,
LONDON.

...ting:

...st:

...te of Completion: 1938.

CIRCLE FOYER.

HARDY & LANGDON ELEPHANTS NEVER FOR...

...ONT ELEVATION.

PROSCENIUM.

Odeon Canning Town. A page from architect Keith P. Roberts' album (the date of completion is wrong).
The iron gates to one of the small car parks can be seen at the left of the exterior view while the initial letter of
the name sign mounted on the canopy appears at the right edge. See also picture on Contents page.

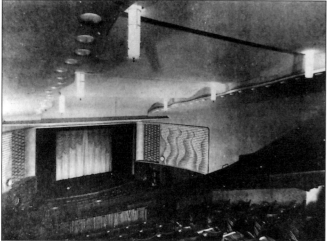

Odeon Canning Town. Inner main foyer view. Auditorium view is the best available but makes it impossible to see the round openings in the wooden barrier to the orchestra pit. (Both courtesy of Bruce Peter.)

The Odeon's exterior was clad in square cream faience tiles combined with black tiles around the entrance. There was a low curving outer entrance hall with an Odeon sign mounted on top to face Barking Road (the sign seems to have upset Roberts as he scissored it off in the cut-out of the exterior he kept in his album, which is reproduced on the Contents page). There was a tower, reminiscent of Dalston with its vents and flagpole, but taller and narrower, with vertical Odeon signs on each side.

The shape of the site encouraged Roberts to include a deep, lofty main entrance hall. It was similar to his East Ham foyer with its large window over the entrance and its structural columns at the head of the stairs, but it had pendant light fittings instead of a laylight. Foyers such as these (and the one at Aylesbury) certainly added a sense of occasion but were more a feature of ABC halls than Odeons.

The auditorium extended at right angles to the entrance and was rather more conventional than Camberwell. Principal illumination was provided by two lines of cylindrical fittings near the undulating edge of a shallow central recess. Close to this edge ran a curious series of large stud-like attachments. The curving splay walls incorporated ventilation openings in the design seen at Dalston.

Late in August came the Odeon at **Elmers End,** an area of Beckenham in the Croydon direction. Back in November 1935, Odeon had shown some interest in a site half a mile away in Elmers End Road, adjacent to Birkbeck station, but it was never used for a cinema. Why Oscar Deutsch still wanted to build in this area at this late date is a great mystery, although the Odeon's site had long been earmarked for a cinema: architects Dixon and Braddock submitted plans on behalf of General Cinema Theatres in November 1936. Odeon announced its acquisition of the site in July 1938 and placed contracts the following month, so this scheme was taken up late in the day and leapfrogged many others of greater potential in the pipeline. The location recalled very early Odeons like South Harrow or Wallington. Elmers End might just have warranted a low-cost 1,000-seater but instead here was an expensive Odeon with 1,518 seats. There had been considerable recent housing development in and around Elmers End and the site occupied a prominent position at an important road junction, but it could not compete with Beckenham itself – or nearby Penge, South Norwood, Croydon, Bromley, or even West Wickham, all with Odeons in easy reach.

At any rate, the Elmers End Odeon had added financial potential from an attached curving Odeon Parade of seven shops with flats above, which hid one of two car parks behind. And it was a handsome addition to the circuit as Keith P. Roberts designed the cinema and the parade with characteristic flair.

The exterior treatment of the cinema had some elements of

Odeon Elmers End. A narrow road to or from the car parks runs down the left side of the building. The back of the slab tower carried a line of large round ventilation openings across the top while a further Odeon sign was mounted horizontally on a buff-tiled wall just below. The first floor doors to the flats are stylishly shielded.

The view of the back of the main foyer shows the doors to the stalls at right, the stairs to the balcony at left. (Courtesy of the late Keith P. Roberts.)

Sutton Coldfield and of Roberts' work at Mile End. Buff faience tiles contrasted with the chocolate-brown terra cotta in the slab tower and in the columns between the entrance doors. The brick wall at right angles to the slab tower was left completely plain – Roberts did not favour the decorative additions of Weedon schemes. The vast curving window of the first floor had square panes of glass that corresponded to the squares on the slab wall. The horizontal Odeon sign on the upper part of this wall was well placed – unlike the one mounted vertically on the end of the slab, partly covering a recessed line of glass bricks.

The upstairs lounge was particularly spacious and bright in daytime with a fine view of Elmers End Green through its full-height continuous windows while it exercised an allure when lit up at night.

The auditorium was notable for the highly stylised grillework on the front side walls (faced in gold and silver with bright scarlet on the returns) and for the placing of the signs of the Zodiac on the bold pattern of squares covering the walls further back. The main illumination came from eight suspended light fittings, squatter than those at Canning Town. For once, the ceiling and side walls were not merged but treated as separate entities with a slight gap where they met, while the columns at each side of the proscenium opening also lacked any smooth link to the splay walls. Balcony fronts were rarely given much attention but here Roberts placed strong horizontal grooves, plus a wavy protruding lower edge (like that of North Watford) which would have caught the attention of rear stalls patrons. These undulations were picked up in the back edge of the splay wall grillework.

According to a report in the *Kinematograph Weekly* (10 August 1939), the next Odeon to open would feature a screen with a light rather than dark surround in which a colour image would "merge off the edge". It is unclear whether such a development was tried out at Elmers End.

Oscar Deutsch did not attend the Elmers End opening (Stanley Bates took his place) but he sent a telegram to be read out: "All success to the launching of the new Odeon, and I hope that all present will get a really good evening, bringing relief from the existing tension..."

He referred to the increasing likelihood of war which initially prompted him to cancel or postpone the opening of the Odeon at **Hendon,** north London, two days later. But he changed his mind and, on Monday 28 August 1939, the last pre-war Odeon made its debut. Deutsch was there to tell the audience that, in the government's mind, the cinema was of great value in troubled times and, because of this and his view that it should be "business as usual" during a crisis, the opening was taking place "in spite of Mr. Hitler". The film that night was a topical British spy thriller, *Q Planes*.

Odeon Hendon. In the exterior view there can just be seen at far left the end of a name sign mounted on the top of the back wall facing up Church Road towards the centre of Hendon.

The Odeon Hendon was handled by Robert Bullivant in the Harry Weedon offices, here working entirely in brick as at Chester and York. It was smaller than average (1,362 seats) and situated at an important crossroads in another area of Hendon from the Ambassador, part of the Gaumont chain, which had the better position by the tube station at the commercial heart of the district. (There was also a Classic repertory cinema in the area.)

Bullivant has recalled: "I have a suspicion that Hendon had been [originally] designed by someone else and a planning application had been submitted by a firm of contractors/ enterpreneurs called Berney and Marks before they flogged it to Oscar Deutsch. They were most anxious that it should be as economical as possible because not only were they putting up a major part of the finance but they were building it, too – employing tradesmen to do it. It was a very unsatisfactory job from every point of view. We had a London office and the chap in charge was giving us a certain amount of trouble. It was long-range instruction on what we wanted and I had to go down and spend a lot of time there."

Nevertheless, the Odeon Hendon showed the skill and craftsmanship of the best Weedon output. Here was an assured arrangement of slab tower, rounded corner (with splayed piers between tall windows as at Leicester), porthole windows, and highly presentable side elevations, even if the contrast of faience and brick was missing. A name sign was mounted across the ends of the corner piers and it is a pity that no further sign appeared on the tower or on the side wall above the tall windows as at Sutton Coldfield.

The auditorium from the balcony was dominated by large light fittings, but there was some concealed lighting behind the bands of horizontally ribbed plaster on the splay walls to illuminate the recesses and the sides of the proscenium opening. The slanting back of the splay walls added interest, along with the lively overlapping wheels of decorative grillework just below. The Odeon clocks were displaced to the edge of the proscenium, below the openings for the public address system. The orchestra rail was omitted.

Robert Bullivant has written: "As I returned from a site meeting at the Odeon Hendon, I was too involved with the problems of achieving completion ... to understand the significance of newspaper placards announcing that Germany and Russia had that day signed a non-aggression pact. The show had to go on and the invitations went out and the opening ceremony at Hendon was organised. I arrived at the cinema to find a mere handful of spectators, the auditorium less than a quarter occupied and at the reception, which always followed the showing of the film, few people remaining to enjoy the elaborate buffet which had been set up in the circle foyer. I drove back to my hotel through Hyde Park and I knew the show was over. The army were digging trenches under the trees. Four days later, Mr. Chamberlain announced that we were at War and on the following day the House approved emergency powers under which every cinema throughout the country was closed immediately."

At this time, the Weedon partnership was operating from four offices with a total of over 160 staff. "The practice had cash flow problems but Weedon's own financial problems were acute," Robert Bullivant has noted, explaining, "I had not realised at the time that he had been receiving half his fees from Deutsch in cash and half in Odeon shares. When all cinemas were closed, those shares became almost valueless and Weedon dared not put them on the market for fear of offending Deutsch and depressing their market value even further."

The cinemas soon re-opened and were joined by some new ones in the advanced stages of construction, especially during the first year of the "Phoney War"; but no Odeons were among their number. There were high expectations of finishing Doncaster and Worcester, and other projects at Highgate, Sheffield and Westbourne Grove seem to have been sufficiently advanced as to allow some hope that they might be completed (see "Schemes in progress" below). The rival ABC circuit geared up for the likelihood of war more successfully, opening eleven cinemas in 1939 (beating Odeon's yearly total of new builds for the first time) and managing to complete five in 1940.

Bullivant went to London after two or three months of war to close the Park Lane office. W. (Bill) Calder Robson, the youngest of the partners, left to take up a job in a factory producing military materials, then was called up into the Marines where he served with his good friend and former colleague, Arthur J. Price. Bullivant recalled: "Unfortunately, [Robson's] health was not too good and he never came back to us but died relatively young. We wanted him back but the war knocked him about too much."

Takeovers

The Odeon circuit's only takeovers of the first eight months of the year were two former live theatres: the Bedford Camden Town, north London, and the Empire Bristol, in late June, seemingly when the ABC circuit's leases expired. Both were closed in December and reverted to live shows under new managements. It is difficult to see why Odeon ever took them. Perhaps the Bedford was envisioned as the site of a new Odeon (although no plans were announced). There was no need for a second cinema in the heart of Bristol, but this may have come attached to the Bedford.

Schemes in progress

The following schemes were noted in company records as being "under construction" when war broke out:

DONCASTER, YORKSHIRE – Hallgate, corner of Wood Street. Architect: T. Cecil Howitt. To seat 1,690 (1,012 stalls + 678 balcony). This £60,000 scheme, announced in mid-March 1937, included four offices and a car park (entered from Wood Street on the side of the site). Previously occupied by a house used by the Doncaster Collieries Association, the site had been promptly cleared in August 1937. The builder, appointed in April 1939, was O. Miskin and construction finally started later that month. It was well under way with the steelwork in place at the outbreak of war. Auditorium seating and carpets had been ordered, at an estimated cost of just over £3,299, on 28 August 1939 while lounge furniture had also been arranged. Opening was expected in Spring 1940. Work eventually resumed in the 1950s to a modified design but stopped when the Ritz cinema across the road became the town's Odeon instead. Banks and a furniture store appeared on the site.

GLOUCESTER, GLOUCESTERSHIRE – Northgate Street. Architect: Harry Weedon. A £60,000 scheme to seat 1,650 (1,220 stalls + 430 balcony) taking in the site of the Theatre de Luxe, destroyed by fire. Provisional plans were approved in March 1939 but little seems to have been done here, as the remains of the old theatre were reported to have been cleared around 1960 for offices to be built.

HIGHGATE, NORTH LONDON – corner of Varley Road, Junction Road and Bickerton Road. Architect: T. P. Bennett & Son. This was a site leased from Abrahams Consolidated. The contract figure was £42,910 when the cinema was to seat 2,176 (1,212 stalls + 964 balcony) but seating had been reduced to 1,975 (1,150 + 825) by March 1939. Builders were appointed in May and the shell was half-erected at the outbreak of war. Work resumed in March 1940 after the Ministry of Supply gave permission for its completion. A roof was added but the building was requisitioned by the Ministry of Works for storage and as an air-raid shelter. Redesigned and opened post-war.

MORLEY, YORKSHIRE – Queen Street. Architect: Harry Weedon. Undated plans show 1,187 seats, semi-stadium: 860 front + 327 rear, later revised to 1,196 (864 + 332). This scheme was being put through London and Southern Super Cinemas although it would have had the Odeon name and a faience-clad exterior. Abandoned post-war.

SHEFFIELD, YORKSHIRE – Norfolk Street and Flat Street. Architects: Harry Weedon and W. Calder Robson. To seat 2,326 (1,502 stalls + 824 balcony) with four shops and block of offices. A contract was agreed on 22 July 1937 to lease the site for 99 years from the Local Authority with the work to be completed by 24 June 1938. Plans were approved in April 1938. The site was cleared by May 1938. Construction work was reported to have

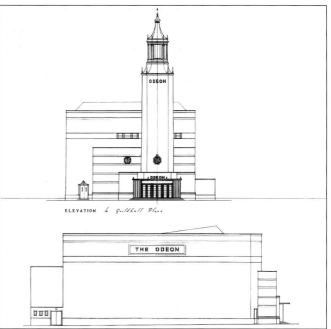

Two schemes by T. Cecil Howitt. Top: Odeon Doncaster. Above: Odeon Cambridge. The 100ft. high tower blends in with the town's historic spires and draw attention to its very central but somewhat concealed location. No faience would have been used: only brickwork with stone dressings. The tower and entrance doors were set off centre to be visible down narrow Guildhall Place from Guildhall Street by the Guildhall. The single-storey extension to the right is the waiting area leading to the stalls via doors in the right side rather than through the back of the auditorium. The auditorium extended straight back. (Both courtesy of Les Lutner.)

started in March 1939 although in June 1939 Sheffield Corporation approved amended plans (with construction to be completed by 1 April 1940) and in July the builders, C. Bryant & Son, were appointed. So far, Odeon had reportedly managed to avoid signing the actual lease or paying a deposit, but had paid the ground rent. Structural steelwork had been partly positioned when war broke out. Odeon received permission from the Ministry of Supply to complete this building in early March 1940 and work recommenced for a while without getting very far. After the war, Robert Bullivant in the Weedon Partnership redesigned the scheme. Most of the old steelwork had to be removed in April 1955 when work resumed because a new road now occupied part of the original site. The Odeon opened at the junction of Flat Street and Esperanto Place on 16 July 1956 without any accompanying shops or offices

WESTBOURNE GROVE, north west London – corner of Richmond Road. Architect: Andrew Mather. Announced October 1937, to seat 2,050, later 1,870. Builders were appointed and some work started in 1938. Permission was granted in early March 1940 by the Ministry of Works for construction to be completed but this did not happen. It was re-designed in the 1950s by Leonard Allen and opened then.

WORCESTER, WORCESTERSHIRE – Foregate Street. Architect: Harry Weedon, whose plans for the replacement of the Silver Cinema had been prepared by May 1937. The building contract was placed in June 1939. The 1,688 seats (938 stalls + 750 balcony) were actually being installed in late 1940 and a licence had been sought in January 1941 for an opening later that month or in February when, according to Dickie Dewes: "A rival cinema proprietor, in a sudden burst of patriotism, called publicly for the work to be stopped and the workers transferred to the war effort. The government survey which swiftly followed revealed that the building was of special suitability for munition purposes". It was requisitioned by the Ministry of Works on behalf of the Ministry of Aircraft Production to store special alloys in transit between Birmingham and Bristol, and a side wall was broken through to provide access to the adjacent railway station. (Odeon promptly acquired the St. Johns cinema, in an outlying part of town, to spite the opposition.) The building was de-requisitioned in 1948 and the design modernised before it opened as an Odeon in 1950.

Other schemes

Odeon records, including the list of sites dated 1 October 1937 (reproduced on page 157), show numerous further schemes from the late 1930s, none of which were completed after the war. The Edmonton and St. Helens listings that follow come from out-side sources, while there is also the matter of a site at Stepney, east London: in 1938, Viscount Tredegar sued Odeon over a broken agreement to lease a site there; the matter was settled in court on 1 June when Odeon, which had initially counter-claimed breach of warranty and misrepresentation, agreed to uphold the contract and make certain payments within fourteen days.

A Harry Weedon scheme for Newcastle-under-Lyme was noted as being "in abeyance" and the schemes for Leeds, Liverpool, Manchester and Newcastle-on-Tyne were in the same position while the alternative of taking over the towns' Paramounts was slowly explored (see next chapter).

It is impossible to say how many (or how few) of the following schemes would have been built under normal circumstances but, as a rough guide, those where more information is listed were the most active. (The dates of announcement given are usually the first spotted in the trade press: there may have been earlier reports elsewhere.)

ADDISCOMBE, SURREY. Architect: Andrew Mather. With the opening nearby of the Elmers End Odeon and the closeness to Croydon, it is hard to imagine this one taking off.

BARKING, ESSEX – corner of London Road, Linton Road and James Street. (This site seems to have been known as Blake's Corner.) Architect: Andrew Mather. To seat 2,118 (1,492 stalls + 626 balcony). Announced September 1937. Plans were approved March 1939, when Odeon sought a year's extension of the con-dition in the approval that it had to start building by a certain date. In mid-August 1939, Odeon's appointed contractors were unwilling to proceed because of the likelihood of war. Despite the acquisition of the Barking Rio in 1943, the scheme was apparently revived with a re-designed exterior in 1949 though never built.

BARNSLEY, YORKSHIRE – New Street, next to the Town Hall, and Pall Mall. Architect: Harry Weedon (assistant: W. Calder Robson). Announced March 1937. To seat 1,630 (1032 stalls + 598 balcony). Plans approved January 1938. (Odeon already had the former live theatre, the Alhambra, in the town.)

BRIDGETON, GLASGOW – 114 Main Street. Architect: Andrew Mather. To seat 1,916 (1,352 stalls + 564 balcony). Plans passed March 1938. Steelwork was reported being put in place at the declaration of war, then construction was suspended as Odeon listed no Scottish halls "under construction" in late 1939.

CAMBRIDGE, CAMBRIDGESHIRE – Guildhall Place, off Guildhall Street. Architect: T. Cecil Howitt. Plans approved 16 December 1937. To seat 1,500 (1,040 stalls + 460 balcony) with side exits at the screen end onto Corn Exchange Street and car park (exit onto St. Tibbs Row). Area later developed for Magistrates' Court and multi-storey car park.

CARLISLE, CUMBERLAND. Architect: Harry Weedon.

CATFORD, SOUTH EAST LONDON – Bromley Road and Whitefoot Lane. Architect: Andrew Mather. Actually in the Southend district between Downham and Catford and listed in October 1937 as being at Downham. Permission was refused by Lewisham Borough Council in November 1937 because part of the site was needed for widening Whitefoot Lane but was then granted by the London County Council in January 1938.

CLAPHAM JUNCTION, SOUTH LONDON – Falcon Road and Station Approach. Architect: Andrew Mather. Acquisition of site announced October 1937. To seat 1,700 (1,068 stalls + 632 balcony). The main frontage was on Falcon Road but Odeon acquired a former amusement arcade to provide an additional entrance from the busy pedestrianised passage or approach to the railway station.

CLAPTON, NORTH EAST LONDON – 233-243 Lower Clapton Road, corner of Powell Road and Kenning Hall Road. Architect: George Coles. To cost £48,000 and seat 1,974 (1,214 stalls + 760 balcony). Work was announced as starting soon in August 1938. (It seems likely that the scheme actually included the Kenning Hall Cinema at 229 Lower Clapton Road, if only to help provide a car park, which would explain why Odeon purchased this very minor property.)

DEVIZES, WILTSHIRE – St. John Street. Architect: Andrew Mather. An Odeon (the first in Wiltshire) was proposed in September 1938 but the start of work on the new Regal the following month for a local operator seems to have killed the scheme.

DOWNHAM, KENT – see Catford.

DUMBARTON, DUMBARTON. Architect: Keith P. Roberts for Andrew Mather. A 1937 perspective sketch survives of this Scottish scheme, which is probably one of the twelve that Odeon claimed in November 1938 to have planned.

EDMONTON, NORTH LONDON – Cambridge Road. Architect: Andrew Mather. 1,850 seats. Announced in January 1938 as a Mather scheme with no mention of Odeon, then linked to Odeon in March 1938, but it does not feature in later company records.

FALKIRK, STIRLING – High Street and Callendar Riggs. Architect: Andrew Mather. Site acquired by July 1937 at a cost of £9,000. The total scheme was to cost £38,000 and provide 1,759 seats. Plans passed March 1938 and a builder appointed. This was situated at the east end of the High Street facing a new bus station, and was a different site from that in Melville Street which came with the Singleton circuit takeover.

FULHAM ROAD, WEST LONDON. Architect: Andrew Mather.

GRANTHAM, LINCOLNSHIRE. Architect: T. Cecil Howitt.

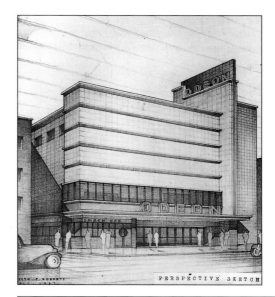

Top: perspective sketch for the Odeon Dumbarton, designed by Keith P. Roberts. (Courtesy of Bruce Peter.)

Above: the restrained design for the Odeon Oxford from Harry Weedon's office, with arches at each end serving the car park behind. (RIBA Library Photographs Collection.)

HASTINGS, SUSSEX. Architect: George Coles.

IRLAM O' TH' HEIGHTS, LANCASHIRE. Main road site. No architect named. To seat 1,750. Originally announced to open by May 1938.

KENNINGTON, SOUTH LONDON – Kennington Park Road, Kennington Park Place and De Laune Street. Architect: George Coles. The local company for this project was formed in December 1937. Site occupied by the closed Kennington Theatre. To seat 2,046 (1,310 stalls + 736 balcony) and cost approximately £50,000. This scheme was reactivated after the war but denied planning permission.

KINGS NORTON, BIRMINGHAM. Architect: Harry Weedon. (Weedon records suggest that only sketches, now lost, were prepared.) Probably not the Watford House site that Odeon were reported to have bought at the junction of Middleton Hall Road and Pershore Road South in June 1936 only to discover a restrictive covenant prevented the erection of business premises on the land (the house had already been demolished). Odeon withdrew a court application for the removal of the covenant on the day of the hearing in August 1936, most likely because it now had another site in mind: the Council school site at Kings Heath, which was in the same area and which Odeon were reported seeking in December 1936. Other new cinemas that opened in the area may have put Odeon off.

LEWISHAM, SOUTH LONDON. Architect: Andrew Mather.

LEYTONSTONE, NORTH EAST LONDON – High Road. Architect: Andrew Mather. Acquisition of site announced January 1938. To seat 2,037 (1,284 stalls + 753 balcony).

MANOR PARK, EAST LONDON – High Street North and Monega Road. Architect: Andrew Mather. To seat 2,072 (1,336 stalls + 736 balcony). Car park on opposite corner.

MILL HILL, NORTH WEST LONDON. Architect: Andrew Mather.

OXFORD, OXFORDSHIRE – St. Aldates. Architect: Harry Weedon.

PARTICK, GLASGOW – Dumbarton Street and Keith Street. Architect: Keith P. Roberts for Andrew Mather. To seat 2,080 (1,272 stalls + 808 balcony). The company to build this cinema was registered in September 1937. Some demolition was reported before the scheme was put on ice for unspecified reasons in April 1938, and it was evidently revived as Glasgow Corporation approved the plans in late September/early October 1939.

POPLAR, EAST LONDON – East India Dock Road. Architect: Andrew Mather.

ST. HELENS, LANCASHIRE – Tontine Street. Architect: Harry Weedon. Plans had been prepared at December 1936 but this one does not figure in the 1937 list, suggesting the site had been lost.

Drawing of Keith P. Roberts' scheme for the Odeon Partick, dated 1937. (Courtesy of Bruce Peter.)

SHOREDITCH, EAST LONDON. Architect: Andrew Mather. (This is not the Hackney Road Odeon, which opened in 1938, only half a mile from the centre of Shoreditch.)

SOUTHPORT, LANCASHIRE – corner of Albert Road and Leicester Street. No architect named, but probably Harry Weedon. On 2 October 1937, the Town Planning Committee rejected a scheme with 2,200 seats, commenting: "the elevation of the proposed building fronting to Albert Road would be a disfigurement by reason of its design and would injure the amenities of the neighbourhood". (Sounds like a great Harry Weedon scheme!)

SPRINGBURN, NEAR GLASGOW. Architect: Andrew Mather.

STAMFORD HILL, NORTH LONDON. Architect: Andrew Mather.

STOCKTON-ON-TEES, CO. DURHAM. Architect: Harry Weedon.

STOKE NEWINGTON, NORTH LONDON. Architect: Andrew Mather. This scheme would have been extraordinarily close to the Dalston Odeon which may have replaced it.

SWANSEA, GLAMORGAN – High Street. Architect: Harry Weedon (assistant: Basil Herring). A huge scheme to seat 2,463 (1,491 stalls + 972 balcony) (as announced September 1937) or 2,414 (1,421 stalls + 993 balcony) (later revision?).

TOTTENHAM, NORTH LONDON. Architect: Andrew Mather. Presumably the failed scheme of 1936 for a 2,000-seater at High Road, corner of Scotland Green, hoping to make a comeback. Mather's plans were approved in April 1938 (no client was mentioned) but applications for a provisional licence were repeatedly rejected. The last application in March 1939, vigorously opposed by existing cinemas and once again refused, was believed to have come from an operator other than Odeon.

TOWNHEAD, GLASGOW – Castle Street, corner of Roystonhill, and Garngad Hill. Architect: Andrew Mather. To seat 2,376 (1,678 stalls + 698 balcony). Two shops.

THORPE [not clear which Thorpe of several]. Architect: Harry Weedon.

WALSALL, STAFFORDSHIRE. Architect: Harry Weedon.

WALTHAMSTOW, NORTH EAST LONDON – Hoe Street. Architect: Andrew Mather. Plans submitted in March 1936.

Surviving Weedon index cards indicate work on an Odeon for the Weoley Castle district of Birmingham (the actual plans have disappeared), but there is no date to indicate whether this was an early or late scheme, and no other references have come to light.

In November 1938, Odeon claimed to have twelve more Scottish sites planned after its Hamilton theatre, but the above list includes only six.

There were reports in both *Today's Cinema* (4 October 1939) and *The Builder* (13 October 1939) that Odeon had acquired a site at 6/8 Rock Street, Finsbury Park, north London, from ABC for a new cinema. The former reported a denial by Odeon a week later. It seems highly improbable that Odeon would have wanted the site since it took over the Astoria Finsbury Park only a few weeks later, although an expression of interest might have put pressure on Paramount to complete the deal. The site remained with ABC.

Another casualty of the declaration of war was an Odeon headquarters in the centre of Birmingham designed by Harry Weedon to replace rented offices in Temple Row and others scattered about the city centre. It was during 1937 that Oscar Deutsch had first announced the building of Odeon House, at the corner of Cumberland Street and Broad Street. This would have included shops at ground level and a small private cinema on the roof. Although work was reported starting in May 1937, it only got underway shortly before war was declared. The steel frame was almost complete in September 1939 when Odeon moved to London. Robert Bullivant confirmed that it would have been an ordinary office building, not designed externally in the cinema style. (After the war, the site was acquired by Birmingham Corporation, and its Housing Department adapted Weedon's drawings to suit its own purposes, the finished building being called Bush House.)

While on the subject of unrealised cinemas, it may be of interest to note that Harry Weedon had taken on his first outside schemes since his close association with Oscar Deutsch began. In July 1939, his practice was announced as designing a cinema in High Street, Bromsgrove, south of Birmingham, for Raglan Theatres of Dudley, and in October a replacement cinema for the Plaza Bromyard, between Leominster and Worcester, for B. Longfield.

Although many existing cinema owners must have breathed a sigh of relief when Deutsch's future schemes were scuppered by the war, there were advantages in the other direction when Odeons were spared newer competition. For example, Mortimer Dent started work on a new cinema at Warley designed by Hurley Robinson, presumably for his rapidly expanding Danilo circuit, but work was suspended and never resumed. And ABC's long-delayed scheme for Harlesden seem to have finally got underway, only to be stalled for good. And, even if Odeon couldn't as yet open at Worcester, a scheme for a further new cinema which Odeon had opposed never got off the ground.

A ROMANCE OF FINANCE: THE PRE-WAR BUSINESS OF ODEON

Administration

Oscar Deutsch established his first London office around 1932. Noting that he chose premises in Park Lane rather than in regular film circles in Soho, this writer once implied that he sought a more respectable image than others in the film trade. This drew a detailed response from Dickie Dewes:

"The London offices of Oscar Deutsch (there were two in turn, both in Park Lane) could hardly be called offices in the generally accepted sense of the term. Little, if any, normal office work was done there. The accommodation was used by Oscar Deutsch, some of his Birmingham business associates, and senior members of staff when visits were paid to London. The facilities allowed for interviews, using the telephone, receiving mail and messages, and provided space for secretaries and typists who were with the party to type notes, etc.

"Without being dogmatic, I would have said the first of these offices was opened in 1932. Regular visits to London – perhaps only one a week – had commenced in 1929 but the number increased rapidly. Until the first office opened, an hotel was used for meetings and interviews. Some of the visits lasted two or three days, but some were for one day only and quite a lot were for half a day. These latter left Birmingham at 1pm and London on the return journey at 7pm.

"The half-day visit was extremely popular with Deutsch and George Elcock. Taylor or I often went with them. A typist would come down to New Street Station with us, and Deutsch would dictate until the express pulled out. Leaving at one o'clock enabled one to read the morning mail, dictate some replies, and deal with urgent matters. Then one could work on the train, spend four hours in London, and compare notes while having dinner on the train coming back. (Oscar Deutsch, of course, did not eat much on trains.)

"Often decisions would be taken during the journey and telegrams dispatched when the train stopped. If the express had passed Coventry, the next stop was Euston and there was no normal means of communication whatsoever. Our solution was to write the telegram on one of the forms always carried for the purpose. The money was added and the items made into a large

packet. The packet was then hurled on to the centre of the platform at Rugby or some other station as the express hurtled through. As you made the throw, you waved your arms wildly, shouted at the top of your voice and then pointed at the packet. Often one had the satisfaction of seeing several persons hasten towards the parcel. Sometimes it was swept away in the wind without being seen by anyone. There was a note for the finder saying, 'Please send this telegram and use the change to drink my health.' The truly wonderful thing about all this is that between seventy-five per cent and eighty per cent of these telegrams reached their destination safely.

"Deutsch used to stay at the Railway Hotel, Euston, and we sometimes took documents to him there. His visits to London were mainly for interviews in connection with financing arrangements.

"Deutsch was attracted by an advertisement announcing the opening of the Dorchester Hotel [on Park Lane], and he asked Taylor to obtain a brochure and tariff. The Dorchester opened on 21 April 1931 and from then until his death Deutsch stayed there whenever he visited London. This speedily brought him into association with the company that built the hotel – Sir Robert McAlpine & Sons – and with Sir Malcolm McAlpine, its chairman. The fact that Deutsch stayed at the Dorchester is the reason why Park Lane was chosen for both the offices which were used in turn. He had no actual objection to offices in Soho.

"The entire administration of the Odeon Theatres was carried out from Birmingham until mid-August 1939."

Other sources suggest that film booking needed to be done from London.

Finance

Each Odeon was built by a separate company with Deutsch, W. G. Elcock and F. Stanley Bates often joined as directors by a local businessman who contributed the site or was the builder of the theatre. These Odeons were linked by Cinema Service Ltd., which booked the films and provided other managerial support. Cinema Service also looked after Deutsch's earlier cinemas and acted as a booking agent for others in the early years.

Until Odeon had grown into a large and successful circuit,

Oscar Deutsch, holding cigar, and fellow directors F. Stanley Bates and George Elcock are pictured with Hollywood legend and United Artists founder-director Mary Pickford at the London Odeon offices in Park Lane.

the formation of separate companies for each cinema made it more attractive for a local site owner or builder to invest and become a director, knowing that he would not be affected if other Odeon companies should fail. Also, local directors were often men of influence who could help expedite planning and licensing consent. This approach was quite widely followed by other groups: each of the Granada Theatres was originally a separate company.

"Broadly speaking, the procedure became as follows", wrote Alan Wood in his book *Mr. Rank*. "[Deutsch] would buy a site and build a cinema, finance being obtained (from insurance companies, etc.) by creating a ground rent on the site, and selling a mortgage on the building. Preference shares might be issued to local people – perhaps to the actual builders who put up the cinema. The ordinary shares were kept by Deutsch himself and his associates."

And here, in more detail, is Robert Bullivant:

"By 1935 there were seemingly unlimited financial resources available for Deutsch to create a pre-eminent chain of cinemas in the United Kingdom. A separate limited company was set up for each projected Odeon cinema, and when an option on the site had been obtained, one building contractor was invited to price the Bills of Quantities and submit a Tender.

"In the early 1930s, it was not unusual that in a town of 150,000 to 200,000 inhabitants there had been only one or two major building contracts in the previous five years. Extensions perhaps to the Labour Exchange or the Post Office, a shop for Montague Burton with a billiard saloon on the first floor, or a garage for the local bus company. Large numbers of craftsmen in the building industry had been unemployed for long periods and builders would take on contracts at a loss in order to hold their organisation together and to keep some craftsmanship alive. Building was never cheaper than in the early Thirties.

"When the selected contractor had submitted his tender for the Odeon cinema, he was offered the contract at the tender figure, plus an agreed fee, if he would also agree that payment against all architects certificates would be postponed by six months or more. Because a £30,000 cinema in the High Street would be by far the biggest contract in the town, because the contractor wanted desperately to keep his craftsmen occupied for a few months, and partly because of the glamour of the film industry, such offers were rarely refused. The bricks and mortar of the partly completed cinema were the security for an advance from Eagle Star to pay the contractor's post-dated Certificates. For an initial investment of £100 to register the company, Oscar Deutsch had created another Odeon.

"To maintain the rate of expansion which Deutsch required and to ensure that all Odeons conformed, as far as possible, to the required technical standards and to the house style, he set up a unique construction team.

"The construction team was in two parts. Construction 'T', as the first half was called, was 'in house' and included specialists in sound and projection, acoustics, air conditioning, lighting, stage drapes, furnishing, publicity, sales, maintenance and other operational aspects of the exhibition side of the film industry.

"Harry Weedon was given responsibility for the other half of the team which was known as Construction 'A' and, although he continued to operate as an architect in private practice, we became so closely associated with the in house team that there was almost complete integration. Construction 'A' was responsible for site surveys, sketch schemes, obtaining statutory approvals, appointing contractors and specialists and for the administration, co-ordination and supervision of the whole contract."[*]

So many projects were in hand that a weekly report (no examples of which are known to survive) was issued under the headings:

Sites being investigated
Plans being prepared
Plans awaiting local or county approval
Plans approved
Plans out to tender
Buildings commenced
Building in course of construction
Opening dates

United Artists

Mention has been made previously of Odeon's tie-up with United Artists because of Deutsch's need to secure a line-up of quality features (especially British) to strengthen his position for further expansion. The two major circuits, Gaumont and ABC, made quality British pictures to show in their own cinemas to meet the quota imposed on exhibitors: these were only available to Odeon where they were not represented or on second run.

It seems to have been United Artists that approached Odeon in the first place, as the company was unhappy with its position in the British market. Of the two major circuits, Gaumont had continual tiffs with distributors in the early 1930s (see *Gaumont British Cinemas*, page 110) and was very selective in what it would take. ABC, too, was very choosy and favoured particular distributors. Like many companies, United Artists had established a West End showcase, in this case the London Pavilion, to

control the launch of its pictures, but this was not enough. As an American executive, F. M. Guedalla, reported in a letter to the New York head office in September 1935: "We also should have the possibility of using several hundred theatres in the Provinces not only for obtaining fair terms on which to show United Artists pictures therein, but also as means of counteracting terms which might be very arbitrary on the part of the big Gaumont-British Circuit and also the BIP [ABC] Circuit and any other big Circuits, particularly if as constantly contemplated, such Circuits should amalgamate." (Quoted in *United Artists – The Company Built By The Stars* by Tino Balio.)

As a distributor in Britain, United Artists was compelled to handle a percentage of locally-made films and, instead of settling for quota quickies, it had arranged for a stream of quality main features from two sources. It released the output of Herbert Wilcox's British & Dominions company which produced, among others, the acclaimed weepie, *Escape Me Never,* with Elisabeth Bergner in 1935. And it was the backer of Alexander Korda's London Films, beginning with the international smash hit *The Private Life Of Henry VIII* in 1933, an arrangement which in 1935 had delivered *The Scarlet Pimpernel* with Leslie Howard, *Sanders Of The River* with Paul Robeson, and *The Ghost Goes West* with Robert Donat. In addition, United Artists had top-quality American product from Samuel Goldwyn and 20th Century which had included *Clive Of India, Cardinal Richelieu, Les Miserables, The Call Of The Wild* and *Barbary Coast.*

The arrangement took some time to come about. It was during April 1935 that the news first broke of a plan to link UA with two British circuits, Odeon and County. UA's American head, Joseph Schenck, came to Britain in June 1935 to discuss the scheme. And it was in January 1936 that United Artists acquired a half interest in the Odeon circuit for the nominal sum of £50. Deutsch and his associates retained ultimate control by having the right to elect the chairman as well as half the directors, giving the chairman the casting vote in any equal split among the directors. Sidney Swingler remembered the deal as one by which United Artists also took shares in lieu of rental and felt it had been "a good tie-up for each". Deutsch became a director of United Artists' British subsidiary which gave him some inside influence there.

At this time, Charles J. Donada's County circuit was at least as important as Odeon with its large, new cinemas in such big towns as Colchester, Staines, Wembley, Wimbledon, Southampton, Margate, Southend and Chelmsford. United Artists did not propose a merger of Odeon and County, but the two companies avoided treading on each other's toes. One immediate result of the tie-up was that Korda's star Merle Oberon appeared in a number of advertising shorts for Odeon.

[*]According to a former chief projectionist at the Odeon York (as recalled by James Bettley), at the time of construction schemes were coded according to their cost: York was a "red" scheme while Harrogate and Scarborough were only "green" and there were also "blue" schemes assumed to be the most basic and economical to build.

Deutsch could now proceed to build a new Odeon flagship in London's Leicester Square, knowing that it would have suitable product to show through the premiere runs of United Artists' major releases (UA retained the small London Pavilion as a secondary house). Similarly, Odeons could now be built in the biggest provincial centres, assured of the product to compete head-on with Gaumont and ABC.

Consolidation and crisis

On 20 February 1937, Odeon Theatre Holdings Ltd. was incorporated as part of the floating of a public stock issue to raise £4 million for further expansion. It underwent a change of name on 3 June to Odeon Theatres Ltd.

The issue was first advertised on 4 July 1937, following a period during which few such launches had occurred. It prompted the Mayor of Bury St. Edmunds, on opening the town's new Odeon the following night, to refer to the growth of the circuit as "a romance of finance".

The directorate consisted of Oscar Deutsch (chairman and managing director), Hon. Peter Aitken, F. Stanley Bates, Sydney A. Bennett, W. G. Elcock, Edward C. Simmons, and two representatives of United Artists: Maurice Silverstone, an American who was the distributor's managing director, and George Archibald, a Glaswegian, who was a director and would soon succeed Silverstone as joint m.d. (with E. T. Carr). It was proposed to voluntarily liquidate eighty-six subsidiary companies (each formed for the construction or purchase of a cinema) and place their assets in the new Odeon Theatres Ltd. There were management agreements with further companies that owned seventy-one Odeons. A lot of money had been lost backing British film producers and advertising for the share offer promised, in capital letters, that THE COMPANY WILL NOT ENGAGE IN FILM PRODUCTION, EITHER BY ITSELF OR ANY SUBSIDIARY COMPANY. The authorised share capital of £6 million was divided into four million 6% Cumulative Preference Shares of £1 each and eight million Ordinary Shares of five shillings each. Issued share capital in early 1938 amounted to 1,465,000 Cumulative Shares and 850,000 Ordinary Shares.

At the beginning of 1939, a crisis almost brought about the compulsory liquidation of Odeon Theatres Ltd. A year of trading had long been completed and the publication of the accounts and the declaration of the first six-month dividend on part of the capital, the 6% Preference Shares, were considerably overdue. The accounts were in a terrible muddle because of the tangle of paperwork produced by the huge amount of consolidation.

"Under company law, it was a legal offence to pay dividends other than from profits or reserves apportioned for the purpose," noted Dickie Dewes. "Obviously, in its first year of trading, Odeon Theatres Ltd. had no reserves. In consequence, it could only pay the preference dividend from actual profits. Efforts to strike a trial balance and ascertain the actual profit were not achieved."

The company was paralysed. Distributors were not being paid and worried that rumours about the collapse of the company might prove true. Deutsch and many of his associates were confident that Odeon Theatres Ltd. had made sufficient profit to pay the dividend. But they had to prove it. And the job had to be done quickly. In conversation, Dickie Dewes likened the company to a ship above Niagara Falls. Unless immediate action was taken, it would go under and a receiver would sell it to the highest bidder. Here is his full account of the drama:

"The cash position was brittle. The formation had left the cash reserves still vulnerable. Creditors were obviously apprehensive. A minor detrimental happening might trigger off a cash crisis of damaging proportions. The only real safeguard was the prompt publication of the accounts and the declaration of a preference dividend. Wisecracks were beginning to be made in Wardour Street. Sarcastic remarks were appearing in some of the trade press. Certain of the dailies were becoming curious.

"Speed was imperative. The snag was that, so far, the accounting department of Odeon had not succeeded in finalising the accounts. They had not even managed to table a trial balance.

"To put it bluntly, the accounting department was a real shambles. It was the Achilles' heel of Odeon. The main reason was that the man who had been in charge for many years – a chartered accountant with a seat on the board of the parent company – was just not interested in this portion of his responsibility. He had simply deputised everything to staff who lacked the calibre to shoulder the various responsibilities, and indeed had no authority to do so.[*] I had suffered very badly from the deficiencies of the accounting department in the past. For instance, they held all the legal agreements appertaining to the properties and could seldom find any of them. They had not even anything in the nature of a master register.

"George Archibald, J.P., joint managing director of United Artists, was a member of the Odeon directorate, representing the United Artists financial investment. Archibald officially visited the head office in Birmingham on several occasions in quick succession – presumably at the request of the board. At this time he had the reputation of being the most unpopular renter the cinematograph industry of this country had ever

---

[*] In another reference to the crisis, Dickie Dewes stated clearly that "The Demon King of the Pantomime was director George Elcock". Seemingly, Oscar Deutsch was too close to Elcock to notice his shortcomings and no one else dared to criticise him.

known. He cannot have won any great popularity in Birmingham as he was stated to have asked 'a vast number of extremely awkward questions' – doubtless about the so far unproduced accounts.

"It was widely believed that Archibald then went back to the board and stressed that a man of sound accounting calibre and great drive must take charge of the Odeon accounting department without delay if disaster was to be avoided.

"Years later I sat next to George Archibald at a trade banquet. He had mellowed and was Lord Archibald now, and during the meal he recalled the crisis: 'The accounting department at Birmingham went round and round and simply could not produce the accounts. The position was set to blow up. The board of Odeon Theatres Ltd. was very concerned. We [the United Artists representatives] were given the fright of our lives. Nobody could say if the Odeon company had made a profit large enough to pay the preference dividend or not. Somebody said, "We cannot afford to wait. Pay the damn dividend and chance it." The majority of the board refused. The feeling was that if the dividend was paid and later proved not to have been fully earned, the resulting scandal would reflect not only on the company but on the personal reputation of every director.'"

To speed up the work, George Archibald borrowed modern accounting equipment from British Thomson-Houston, the Rugby-based manufacturers of Odeon's projection room equipment.* One of its staff, John H. (Henry) Davis, came to Birmingham to explain the machinery and get it functioning. Davis and his equipment made such a good impression on Oscar Deutsch, always interested in technological advances, that the prematurely balding Londoner was invited to stay and take charge as chief accountant. Born on 10 November 1906 and educated at the City of London School, Davis had worked as a chartered secretary for several industrial concerns. He had no direct experience of the film business, nor any particular interest in cinema when he accepted Deutsch's offer. He gave notice at BT-H and took up his new position during 1938.

Dickie Dewes continued: "The choice of John Davis for the new responsibility was not entirely popular. It was the first appointment of senior executive calibre from outside the circle closely associated with the Odeon venture from the earliest days, ten years before. Naturally, the appointment had been made by Oscar Deutsch, as chairman of Odeon, but strong rumours suggested that he had been influenced by United Artists and other financial interests.

"At Birmingham, J.D. was very much a stranger within the gates. He was felt to be closely associated with the United Artists interests and UA itself was viewed in many quarters as trespassing on the sphere of Odeon control.

"Immediately, J.D. interviewed every head of department and every senior executive. This was followed by a luncheon at the Queen's Hotel, Birmingham, at which he clearly outlined his plans and gave details of the special co-operation for which he asked to ensure the utmost speed. All present pledged their support.

"J.D. made adjustments to the working of the accounting department itself and the tempo quickened. Every possible hour was worked. The staff of all departments were marshalled to assist the accounting department in the evenings and at weekends. Some of the employees involved were not ideal material for accountancy purposes but it all helped and J.D. kept a bird's eye view.

"The trial balance – balanced. The effort to complete the accounts forged ahead. But would luck hold out? The nattering from Wardour Stret was growing louder. Press comment was be-coming more pointed. The board of the company was very perturbed.

"The view I firmly held was that with J.D. in control the crash of Odeon Theatres Ltd. was a high probability, but that without him the crash was a dead cert. A lot of others held much the same view.

"A rumour wafted through head office that J.D. had failed and that now was the ideal time for those to act who thought the company would be better off without him. It was suggested that the smallest item detrimental to his operation be widely publicised and that replies to J.D.'s requests for information should be delayed and supplied short and incomplete. The source of the rumour was never traced but some of us felt it a wise precaution to have a talk with our staffs. I do not believe the rumour did any real damage – J.D. was certainly more than capable of taking care of himself.

"J.D. spared nobody, but he spared himself least of all. One of his staff paid him this back-handed compliment: 'He's a perfect bastard but you can't say he doesn't know his stuff and he never dodges the column himself.'

"The accounts were finalised and published. The preference dividend was declared. There was a breathing space. The accounting department was not yet able to supply the current facts on

---

* These could be the same highly sophisticated machines that Odeon boasted about having among £15,000 worth of equipment in its accounts department in 1939: three Powers-Samas accounting machines, worth £3,000 each, which recorded such data as house receipts, purchases, sales, movements of stock, etc. by perforated holes in cards that could be automatically sorted at the rate of 400 per minute and placed in a tabulator which could read the information represented by the holes and translate it into a printed record with totals and balances as appropriate. It still required 160 members of staff to run the department and operate the equipment.

cash and financial obligations with the speed J.D. desired but he was steadily building up the operation. J.D. was actually ill but in the months that followed he came back to normal health and strength."

A preliminary statement of the first results of Odeon Theatres Ltd. was made in early September 1938 and covered the fifty-four weeks to 25 June 1938. Profits of £371,589 had been made and the results were described by the *Kinematograph Weekly* as "really excellent", noting that many of the newer cinemas had not been operating for the full period. After directors' fees, depreciation, loan interest and payment of the preference dividend, this reduced to £122,224. A 10% dividend on ordinary shares was proposed. John Davis was rewarded for his efforts with the position of Secretary and Financial Controller.

Odeon continued to set up individual companies to build each new theatre, often with a local director like the Mr. Vincent who provided the site at Yeovil, but the companies were subsidiaries of Odeon Theatres Limited, promoted and controlled by the parent company.

The Odeon-Gaumont merger scheme

All was not well at Gaumont-British by 1938. No ordinary dividends had been paid for some time. An audacious plan to combine the Odeon and Gaumont circuits under Oscar Deutsch was first discussed in late 1937 but rumours did not sweep the trade until October 1938. The complications seemed formidable, especially after a Board of Trade inspector was appointed in January 1939 to investigate Gaumont's tangled affairs, the same month that the merger scheme became public knowledge. John Maxwell, head of ABC, had previously optioned the key Metropolis and Bradford Trust shares which gave control of Gaumont but his attempts to take over had been thwarted by a veto held by a major shareholder, Hollywood's 20th Century-Fox, which had been worried that a combined ABC-Gaumont circuit would reduce competition and force down rentals in what was the biggest single overseas territory for American films.

Deutsch was more than willing to head an Odeon-Gaumont super circuit if and when financiers Philip Hill and Partners acquired the key voting shares on which ABC retained its option until October 1941. In an interview with *The Financial Times* (quoted in *Kinematograph Weekly*, 12 January 1939) Deutsch said: "The negotiations are being conducted by outside financial interests and I am taking no part in them. Any offer for the shares must be fair to the Gaumont-British and the Odeon shareholders. No discussions have taken place with Associated British regarding that company's option on the 51 per cent of the Metropolis and Bradford Trust voting shares. With regard

to the American objections of the past I have received assurances from high executives that Twentieth Century-Fox would welcome Odeon securing an interest in Gaumont-British. Any bid will first be addressed to Isidore Ostrer, chairman of Gaumont-British, for his own large holdings and then to the shareholders. I anticipate that an offer will also be made to Associated British for that company's 250,000 'B' non-voting shares in the Trust."

The *Kinematograph Weekly* seems to have been asked to emphasise that Deutsch was not directly involved. Its lead news story declared: "Oscar Deutsch is not taking, and has not taken, any part in the proposed merger, although should the deal materialise, thereby forming a huge circuit of more than 600 kinemas, he would automatically become chairman. Oscar Deutsch is making no official statement for the present, but it is authoritatively understood that in his opinion the proposed acquisition of Gaumont control by Philip Hill cannot be carried out immediately."

Philip Hill himself went off to Florida to confer with Fox's Sidney Kent as well as with Nicholas Schenck of Metro-Goldwyn-Mayer, which now shared the veto with Fox. As Deutsch himself recognised in April 1939, "The last word has to be said by Schenck and Kent." If they agreed, Odeon would proceed with its offer to Gaumont's shareholders. It seems that Schenck was not won over, although when Deutsch admitted that the deal was "postponed – at least" (i.e., if not dead), he put the blame elsewhere: "The international situation makes the time not exactly propitious for a big financial transaction of the kind." The continuing investigation by the Board of Trade remained a complication.

It is clear that Oscar would have been delighted to preside over the merged chains and that he would have been the best man for the job, but he had cleverly stayed clear of the negotiations and avoided damaging his reputation if they failed.

Openings

There is no doubt that the opening of almost every large new cinema in the 1930s was enthusiastically welcomed by a full house with invited guests in the front circle and an overspill crowd outside, the excitement fuelled by an elaborate publicity campaign. Of the major circuits, ABC played it cool by first opening for business in the afternoon with a minimum of ceremony. Gaumont, Granada and others went for a major splash, often hiring top stars to make a personal appearance – Gracie Fields was always a sensational draw. Odeon took a medium course, opening with a special evening performance featuring a British picture whenever possible. Lesser stars from the film would often make a personal appearance and Odeon's connection with Alexander Korda's London Films through United Artists proved useful in obtaining both the film and Korda's contract players.

A local dignitary (usually the mayor, Member of Parliament or chairman of the Council) performed the actual opening ceremony and invariably praised the look of the building and anticipated considerable success. A band (usually from the armed forces) played in the orchestra pit (as did the organist where an organ was installed) and a group of pipers often led the VIPs down the aisle through the auditorium and onto the stage. Oscar Deutsch made it a point to speak at the openings unless they were very distant or he was restrained by ill health, since his presence was a promotional asset and reinforced his leadership of the circuit.* (In his absence, Stanley Bates or George Elcock usually spoke on his behalf). The architect would also be in attendance. The films on opening night often comprised one or two shorts (usually a cartoon), a newsreel and a main feature. Perhaps the biggest cinema name to attend an Odeon opening was Charles Laughton who showed up in his home town of Scarborough, although George Formby appeared at Blackpool. The Indian boy actor Sabu went to Muswell Hill and to Uxbridge (where Anna Neagle was also a celebrity guest). A collection was usually taken on behalf of a local hospital or other charity. Anniversaries of the opening – "birthdays" – provided another opportunity for banging the drum.

Leslie Halliwell has described the opening of the Bolton Odeon: "Each seat on opening night had a gilt-edged programme waiting upon it, and no sooner had we absorbed this dazzling piece of showmanship than a mammoth all-glass Compton rose from the orchestra pit, changing colour as it came and radiating 'The Entry of the Gladiators' through a dozen strategically placed loudspeakers. [...] The première attraction, following a Mickey Mouse and the news, was *Dark Journey*, a moderately adult spy melodrama with Conrad Veidt and a new young star called Vivien Leigh. There were absolutely no complaints about it, except that we would have preferred a happier ending, but some of us wondered why it had been chosen in preference to the great backlog of spectaculars which the Odeon was known to have held in reserve."

Oscar Deutsch's desire to open Odeons with British films did not always work out, as recorded earlier at the Odeon Leicester Square. Sometimes a British film would be used for the opening night only, as at Uxbridge where it was advertised only as "Special Presentation of a Great British Production (By courtesy of London

Film Productions Ltd.)" and turned out to be Alexander Korda's Technicolor adventure *The Drum*. This was a Monday and for the rest of the week audiences anxious to view the new cinema had to watch a minor James Cagney film instead.

First-nighters at Harlesden were treated to the world premiere of the very minor *Talking Feet* with Hazel Ascot, the film's star and Britain's answer to Shirley Temple, in attendance along with supporting actor Dave Burnaby and director John Baxter. (The same film opened South Norwood two weeks later.)

Mondays and Saturdays were the favoured days for opening Odeons. Wednesdays were sometimes used, and even a Thursday on at least one occasion. There was no barrier to two Odeons opening on the same day, as has been noted on two occasions in July and September 1937.

For the launch of the Odeon Blackpool, second only to Leicester Square, the party of guests, accompanied by film star Conrad Veidt, joined their own special coach on a scheduled train from London on Friday and were entertained for the whole weekend of the Saturday opening, returning on Monday. George Formby joined in at the opening.

Not every Odeon opened to full-time operation. As late as 1938, Spalding started with matinees at 2.30pm only on Tuesdays, Thursdays and Saturdays, opening every evening at 6pm. It obviously had less potential than most, which ties in with its being such a low-cost theatre. Chorley's Odeon, with five competitors, had similarly limited matinees, on Mondays, Wednesdays and Saturdays, opening at 6pm otherwise.

Pricing and seating

In common with other cinemas, Odeons charged more to sit in the balcony than in the stalls, with two or three different prices in each area – it cost three times as much or more to sit in the front of the balcony as compared to the front stalls. For the exclusive premiere presentations at the Odeon Leicester Square, prices of admission started at two-shillings-and-sixpence and went up to eight-shillings-and-sixpence. But, for the run of Odeons, tickets cost from sixpence or ninepence and rose to two shillings or two-shillings-and-sixpence, the higher price range being applied to wealthier areas. Odeons usually offered reduced prices for weekday afternoon shows. The top price seats were bookable in advance.

It was one of the circuit's widely-trumpeted boasts that every seat in the house was identical and only its position governed the price charged to occupy it. All the seats did have padded arm rests, which was an unusual benefit for those in the cheaper rows, but what was not mentioned was that the legroom between the rows of seats increased along with the seat prices.

* He could occasionally let his sense of self-importance go to his head, such as when he had a record made, "Coronation Expression of Loyalty", in which audiences heard his expression of patriotism at the time of the coronation of King George VI and Queen Elizabeth in May 1937.

Typically, the front stalls, usually making up the first nine to a dozen rows, were 2ft. 6ins. back to back. (This became the minimum requirement of the London County Council in 1938.) The remaining rows in the stalls, usually fourteen to eighteen in number and often behind a gangway across, were 2ft. 8ins. apart. The most expensive seats, in the front section of the balcony before the cross-aisle, were spaced 2ft. 11ins. or 3ft. apart – except for the first row which was 3ft. 2ins. or 3ft. 3ins. to allow for the balcony front, and the back row which was also wider for some reason. The rear balcony seating was usually in rows 2ft. 11ins. apart, with an extra three inches in the front and back rows. Of course, the balcony also provided much better sightlines from the stepping of the rows as compared to the gradual rake of the stalls floor.

Screen width seems to have varied slightly in the larger Odeons from 20ft. at Middlesbrough to 25ft. at Norwich.

Oscar at the Odeons

Besides attending openings, Oscar Deutsch would also inspect his cinemas, as Dennis Williams, a young employee in 1940, has recalled:

"He'd try to visit every cinema once a year, but there were so many of them it was impossible to do that. I think I saw him on three occasions when I was doing relief work. He would always make an appointment and say, 'Is it convenient to come?' Of course, it had to be convenient. He would meet as many of the staff as possible to give them a little pep talk – and he was just as interested in meeting the cleaners as meeting the chiefs of staff. And he used to keep an eye open for any little thing that required attention – for example, a worn carpet or a nose on a stair that might have been a little dangerous. He'd always say, 'We'll arrange for a contractor to do it or you can get somebody locally to do it, and charge it to petty cash.' He was very particular about the efficiency and cleanliness of staff rooms and toilets and the areas where the public had access, but at the few cinemas that had restaurants he never seemed to be interested in the catering side at all. He'd always take the manager out to lunch and he would always stop and see the show. About a week later, you'd receive a memo thanking you for your hospitality with a little list of things that required attention. And he'd always preface this list with a request that he would consider it a personal favour if attention could be given to these points and he requested that, when the jobs listed had been completed, would the manager be kind enough to drop him a memo to say they had been done. Which was a very polite way to do it."

John Fernee adds: "Many of the operating staff that I have met at Odeons who remembered Oscar Deutsch spoke very highly of him, particularly his memory for their names. He always remembered, and addressed them by their Christian names, an unusual feature in worker-employer relationships before the war."

A highly favourable impression of an Odeon in its early years is given by F. R. Buckley in the Birmingham *Evening Dispatch* of 29 November 1935, part of a series of reports on local cinemas. He visited the Warley Odeon to be greeted by an all-pervading scent of carnations, "the only decent theatre perfume I have yet encountered". He remarked on the American system of usher training – "Warley, at your service, sir" was the standard greeting on the telephone – but he added that it worked. He observed that the front rows of the stalls, the sixpenny seats forty feet from the screen, were tilted back for a better view. He commented favourably on the air filters, the free cloakroom and the system of seat reservations. And he admired the elaborate festoon curtain with lovely colours that kept blending and changing. Of course, being in the vicinity of Oscar Deutsch's home, this Odeon would have been run to a particularly high standard.

An indication of the extent to which Odeon went to realise each cinema's potential is given by an account of a lunchtime conversation with Oscar Deutsch. 'Onlooker', the diarist of *Today's Cinema* (10 April 1937), reported that the Odeon chief had set up a "psychological and statistical bureau" and noted: "Work in this department is thoroughly to explore every district where there is to be an Odeon, reporting on the type of inhabitant, the type of programmes in other cinemas that attract the best business, and every detail that will help head office to select the best programme for that neighbourhood. Oscar Deutsch tells me he estimates this department has added at least an extra 20 per cent to the patronage that would have been obtained without it... Other departments are being developed on similar original lines. Among other things, he is planning to revolutionise the film poster, almost completely eliminating letterpress, and adopting the high standard set by national advertisers. The circuit, up or building, now comprises about 180 cinemas, and as he plans to have an Odeon in all the big centres, Oscar Deutsch will be head of a circuit of about 300 before 'letting up' on development."

The comments about variable programming make considerable sense, but Odeons generally all played the same main features as a circuit release and there was little scope for modification, except perhaps for second features and the Sunday revival bookings, or at Odeons with split-week bookings.

Booking

As the Odeon circuit gained strength, building larger cinemas in more important locations, so its booking power improved to the point where it became able to match the Gaumont and ABC circuits with its own weekly release of new films which would only play at other cinemas where there were gaps in the spread of the circuit. It is meaningful to talk of an Odeon circuit release from 1938 onwards when the chain included Scotland (through the Singleton take-over) and had opened its flagship cinema in Leicester Square, although not every film that premiered at the Odeon Leicester Square obtained an Odeon circuit release and, as the flagship usually held films for three weeks or more, many circuit programmes were first premiered at other West End cinemas like the Leicester Square Theatre.

Even in 1938, the existence of an Odeon in a town did not automatically qualify it for first run of all the films taken for a circuit release. In Brighton, a very crowded market, the circuit had the former Palladium, which had been re-named Odeon (with the tag "The House On The Front" to denote its location). With only 1,200 seats, this Odeon lost all the major attractions booked by the circuit to one or other of the ABC circuit's two halls in the town, the Savoy (2,567 seats) or Astoria (1,823 seats). Undoubtedly, these two more modern, larger cinemas could bring a bigger return to distributors, and even United Artists gave them priority. The Odeon premiered the weaker half of the new releases taken by the circuit, but had to take the top half as second runs if it played them at all. Some of the plums were too rich to bypass entirely. United Artists' *The Garden Of Allah* did two weeks at the Astoria in July 1937, then played a week at the Odeon about three weeks later. First National's *The Charge Of The Light Brigade* also played two weeks at the Astoria, then after a gap of about a fortnight did two further weeks at the Odeon. United Artists' major British picture *Dark Journey* played a week at the Savoy, then surfaced at the Odeon for a further week two months later.

The low status of this Odeon was further threatened by the proposed construction of a large new cinema nearby on West Street. This could very well have deprived the Odeon of any first-run product. Deutsch reacted by buying the scheme and opening it as a new Odeon. This did not help the ex-Palladium (which was soon sold to an independent operator) but the new Odeon was of sufficient size (1,920 seats) and stature to obtain every Odeon release on exclusive first run in Brighton.

Odeon also had an early purpose-built cinema on the outskirts of Brighton, at Kemp Town. This never qualified by location or size as a first-run house but usually played split weeks of films (Monday to Wednesday or Thursday to Saturday) about two months after their debut in the town centre. In situations like this, the Odeon would have automatic access to the circuit release at the appropriate time and would supplement it with other programmes for the other half of the week (exceptionally strong attractions like *The Garden Of Allah* warranted a six-day run).

In Croydon, Deutsch had an old property renamed Odeon, well located in the town centre but seating a lowly 1,280. Here, the Odeon had to play the circuit's top attractions concurrently with a nearby rival, the huge Davis Theatre (3,725 seats) or ABC's secondary hall in the town, the Hippodrome (1,250 seats). The Davis took the Gaumont release and in one instance played the Odeon's top feature, *Elephant Boy,* as the lower half of a double bill with *Lloyd's Of London. Dark Journey* played ABC's main Croydon house, the Savoy, at the same time as the Odeon. The small size of the Odeon remained a problem, partially eased when the circuit took over the Hippodrome and could play the same film at both houses, but some major films played both the Odeon and the Davis until the early Fifties. Given these problems with small seating capacities, it is easy to see why Oscar Deutsch increased the size of later new Odeons.

In certain locations where Gaumont or ABC were not represented, an Odeon could drop some of its weaker programmes in favour of top attractions booked to these other circuits. In Worthing, for example, the purpose-built Odeon had the upper hand over the locally-owned Rivoli and Dome while ABC, with just one outlet (the Plaza, leased in fact from Odeon) stuck religiously to its own weekly programmes. The two independent halls normally shared the Gaumont release but the Odeon Worthing took some of the plums away from the Rivoli, even though the latter had around 150 more seats. Being old-fashioned and not as centrally located, the Rivoli was less attractive to distributors who could expect to see better returns from the Odeon for films like *Snow White and the Seven Dwarfs.* * Had the Rivoli been owned by Gaumont, it would have held on to these programmes.

In a major city where Odeon had several large outlying cinemas but lacked a city centre outlet, its halls fitted into the established release structure. In Birmingham, a new film taken by the Odeon circuit would first play in the centre of town at a non-Odeon cinema like the Scala, Paramount or Futurist. A few weeks later, the Odeons at Perry Barr, Shirley, Sutton Coldfield and Warley would play the film, usually for six days and mostly in tandem with each other and with other cinemas far enough away from them not to be "barred" (bars were the arrangement by which one cinema barred others within the same immediate area

---

* The continuous performances of the time raised an occasional problem of patrons early in the day staying to watch a hit film more than once and blocking seats that could have been sold for the later shows. This problem would have been particularly acute in the case of *Snow White* with its short two-hour programme that allowed more screenings daily. Odeons generally ran this particular film three times in continuous shows starting at noon and ending at 6pm, then had two entirely separate evening performances.

from playing a film concurrently and for a minimum period of a few weeks afterwards). These Odeons were all big hitters, with large seating capacities. A further few weeks on, the film would dribble down to lesser, lower capacity halls like the Odeons at Blackheath and Kingstanding, usually for a three-day run. Such cinemas had come by their lower status in a variety of ways: they were too close to other, bigger Odeons to play a film concurrently; their catchment areas were insufficiently populous to support six-day bookings and a lack of rival cinemas meant that they could obtain other new releases as well. They took less money because they were so late in playing films and charged less for their best seats, while Blackheath only opened at 6pm on Tuesdays and Fridays.

The spread of Odeons was not sufficient to ensure a full release for the very biggest attractions and many titles were shared with the Gaumont circuit. These included outstanding British releases from United Artists such as *The Drum* and *The Four Feathers,* both with the added bonus of Technicolor.* There were locations such as Penge and Peckham where both Odeon and Gaumont had halls in direct competition, and it seems that the bigger or better hall (the Gaumont at Peckham, the Odeon at Penge) normally played the main release, leaving the rival to find something else (not a difficult task, as Gaumont had a 'B' circuit of surplus halls with its own release). However, the practice of combining circuits for major releases died down by the end of the 1930s.

As previously noted, in some areas Odeon itself (or the allied County chain) owned two outlets in close or direct proximity. In the Harrow area, the Odeons at Rayners Lane and Kingsbury almost always played the Gaumont release, leaving the Odeon release to the nearby Odeons at South Harrow and Colindale – but when there was an overwhelmingly popular Odeon attraction (often one being shared with Gaumont), all four cinemas played the film.

At Wimbledon, when both Odeon and Gaumont circuits took the same film, County's Regal seems to have played it, leaving the Odeon to find an alternative programme. In Guildford, County's Playhouse generally played the Gaumont release but CTA member John Hickey recalls that a strong Gaumont attraction would be switched occasionally to the larger and more modern Odeon while the Playhouse received weaker Odeon programmes such as Paramount's *Kiss The Boys Goodbye* in 1941. Similarly, the Odeon took a few top ABC releases away

from their normal outlet, the Cinema, including MGM's *Blossoms In The Dust,* either because the independently-owned hall was unable to agree terms or the distributor wanted the greater seating capacity of the Odeon.

In the absence of local competition from ABC, the Odeons at Haverstock Hill and Edgware Road sometimes combined the Odeon and ABC release in one bumper programme (*The Life Of Emile Zola* plus *The Sky's The Limit; Stage Door* plus *Artists And Models*). But once the Odeon Swiss Cottage opened, the nearby Odeon Haverstock Hill usually screened the week's ABC release. The Odeon Edgware Road lost its access to the best ABC releases once ABC's Regal opened around the corner.

The Odeon audience

Did Odeon create a more sophisticated ambience than its main rivals and, if so, did it attract a different, more up-market audience besides part of the existing core of cinemagoers? I suspect that there was not much difference in the appeal of a purpose-built Odeon, Gaumont, ABC or Granada cinema. All operated to high standards of programming and operation and would charge a wide range of prices of admission, with the best seats in the front of the balcony costing three or four times as much as the cheapest seats in the front stalls, so that each cinema catered for well-off patrons as well as those who had to count their pennies.

The May/June 1938 issue of *World Film News* contains a short study of cinemagoing in Muswell Hill, the outer London suburb which gained two large, brand new cinemas in the last three months of 1936: ABC's Ritz and the Odeon. The writer, Daphne Hudson, describes Muswell Hill as predominantly "better middle-class" but notes a different response to the two cinemas. ABC charged from sixpence to two shillings for admission; the Odeon started at ninepence and went up to two shillings as well. Perhaps the lower price at the Ritz helped create the difference in clientele that the writer detects (without ever identifying the cinemas by name):

"Each of the two large houses attracts a slightly different type of patron; there are few regulars in either case and all show considerable care in their choice of film. A picture which does not gain the approval of Monday night's audience might as well be written up as a failure right away. [Films started their runs on Mondays for six days.]

"At the cheaper cinema the greatest attractions are spectacle and action, rather than atmosphere and sentiment. The pace must be fairly fast, either swift or dramatic, or slick and funny – something refreshing after the humdrum of suburban life. *Educated Evans* was a great success here. Ginger Rogers and Fred Astaire were popular for a time, but enthusiasm waned as the novelty

---

* *The Four Feathers* did astonishing business. It broke the attendance and box-office records at the Odeon Leicester Square (where it played for eight weeks from 17 April 1939) while on the opening day at the Odeon Clacton in August 1939 the police had to be called to restore order after the doors were broken down by the crowds outside.

wore off. Perhaps their films were not 'meaty' enough for these filmgoers – they certainly like something to exercise their mental molars on. Newsreels, in moderation, get by with credit, and the *March Of Time* is considered by the manager to have a definite box-office value, though he does say that to show more than one 20 minutes' documentary in a programme would be bad policy. Similarly any form of moralising meets with a chilly reception.

"At the dearer house, tastes are a little different. Here we have a Mecca of the aged, who form a fair proportion of the inhabitants of Muswell Hill. A telling commentary on the nature of the audience is the enormous demand for deaf-aids which are installed. It has even been known for an old lady to request a cushion for her sciatica and accommodation for her pekingese! Retired gentlefolk, a considerable element in the neighbourhood, make the cinema a genteel form of recreation, and choose their films with care, boycotting anything with a doubtful title. They have no use for anything far-fetched or exotic. They like a good, sensible plot of medium pace. They like films about ordinary people like themselves, or historically familiar characters – Britishers like Clive and Rhodes, whose motives they can understand and admire. A tale with a true British flavour, though not necessarily of British production, goes down as well as anything.

"The most astonishing success was *Victoria The Great*. It attracted not only keen filmgoers, but many for whom its appeal was a personal or patriotic one. And a vast number had never, judging by their disconcerted manner, been inside a cinema before; but they remember Victoria, and overcame their prejudices against 'new-fangled amusements' in order to revive memories of times which had been their own. They hobbled forth, pushing each other in bathchairs, of which a considerable number were in evidence, and turning aside from the very brink of the grave to take a last look at the Grand Old Lady. Never had the cinema seen so large an audience, and certainly never had so great a proportion been over eighty years of age."

It is important to remember that every circuit cinema played a wide range of product. *Victoria The Great* would have played at the Ritz had it been given an ABC release. But would it have done so well? The Odeon had a café and a more central location, which may have counted in its favour. Like the Ritz, many suburban Odeons charged sixpence for their cheapest seats, although those at Colindale, Finchley, Kingsbury and Swiss Cottage also started at ninepence like Muswell Hill.

It is also worth observing that the art deco look of the Odeon Muswell Hill did not deter the genteel folk of the area. It would seem that Oscar Deutsch was right to believe in modern architecture: it went down well with all ages.

There is some evidence that Odeon's booking department were more receptive to "quality" pictures than other chains.

Pygmalion, the film version of George Bernard Shaw's play with Wendy Hiller and Leslie Howard, was such a success on Odeon circuit release in January 1939 that it gained a repeat run in June at all London Odeons when it scored at the box-office all over again. Trade commentator "Josh" Billings of the *Kinematograph Weekly* described the General Film Distributors' release as the "biggest all time turn up" and "the film of the year". He noted: "*Pygmalion* had to live down prejudice. Had the other circuits and the majority of independents displayed Odeon's acumen it would, undoubtedly, have created an all-time record. Its success as a reissue is proof. Released and reissued in the same year is, incidentally, a record in itself."

Both Swiss Cottage and Haverstock Hill Odeons would occasionally play subtitled foreign films as the supporting feature, upgrading the programme in a more "up market" area: Swiss Cottage played *Legions d'Honneur* and Haverstock Hill *Jouer d'Echecs* in support of the re-run of *Pygmalion* while audiences for W. C. Fields' *You Can't Cheat An Honest Man* also saw *Quai Des Brumes* at Swiss Cottage.

An instance of less highbrow but still innovative programming resulted from the huge popularity of Deanna Durbin's films for Universal, released by General Film Distributors. Odeon brought back six of her hit films for one day each in a special festival week that played the entire circuit in 1941.

And Odeon claimed to have taken a chance in giving the British comedy *It's A Grand Old World* (1937), starring the Northern comedian Sandy Powell, a booking throughout the entire circuit, not just in the areas where his accent and style of humour were most obviously acceptable. Its popularity everywhere led to further Sandy Powell films – *Leave It To Me* (1938), *I've Got A Horse* (1938) and *All At Sea* (1939) – being shown throughout the circuit to the mutual benefit of Odeon and the independent distributor, British Lion.

A rare insight into the barring arrangements of the industry comes from correspondence in the files of Sidney Bernstein, the head of the rival Granada Theatres chain.

In 1938, Bernstein wrote directly to Oscar Deutsch over problems that the newly opened Odeon Deptford was causing the Granada Greenwich. Bernstein alleged that the Odeon was attempting to bar the Granada from playing the same films and wrote: "...in these days when everybody is trying to restrict bars, and when we ourselves have agreed in the case of Tooting and Sutton to allow concurrency with you at Morden and Epsom, this new desire on the part of your film booking department is particularly unreasonable."

An unidentified member of Odeon's booking department informed Deutsch: "The distance from the Odeon Deptford to Greenwich is 1.7 miles, while the distance from the G.B.

[Gaumont-British] New Cross [Kinema] to Greenwich is 2.1 miles. The G.B. Lewisham [Gaumont Palace] to Greenwich is 2½ miles, and both these G.B. theatres bar Greenwich. Surely we, being the nearest, are entitled to the same privilege, and I have discussed this matter with Mr. Jarratt [Gaumont-British chief], who agrees that this is a fair and reasonable bar. It is understood, however, that should we book a film for Deptford which is not a circuit film, a concurrency should be allowed with Greenwich, but that all circuit films are entitled to bar. This has been agreed by Metro [MGM] and United Artists."

In April 1939, Odeon consented to a full concurrency provided that it received reduced terms from film distributors and the Granada Greenwich ceased including stage shows, which would give it an advantage. Bernstein responded in June 1939: "...in view of our film booking position we consider variety – which we introduced before the Odeon opened – is essential."

Deutsch replied that lack of good films might have compelled the Granada to run variety but that, if the cinema had access to all the Odeon circuit product, "then the only reason why you have to play variety would be removed". In fact, Odeon and General Film Distributors jointly insisted that the Granada Greenwich should not stage any variety when playing the Deanna Durbin hit *Three Smart Girls*. Bernstein replied that, under these circumstances, he didn't expect the Granada would play the film.

The long delay between the London premiere run and the general release of films vexed Oscar Deutsch. Opening his regular contribution to the *Kinematograph Weekly*'s New Year issue dated 13 January 1938, the Odeon chief wrote:

"Attainment as standard practice of an earlier release, and an appreciable advance, therefore, towards the idea of an immediate release, are achievements of 1938 to which I look forward with a certain amount of confidence.

"*Victoria The Great* opened the year auspiciously for those who believe in and have fought for a drastic shortening of the period between West End run and general exhibition.

"This magnificent picture broke records on the Odeon circuit. I definitely ascribe a big part of its unusual success to its early release. Essentially, *Victoria The Great* proved that a British picture of quality appeals with exceptional force to the British public; our early release of the picture meant that the picture-goer saw it while it was news.

"To me, almost as important as the fact that a great British picture has been made is that there should be facilities whereby the reputation created by an enthusiastic Press reception of its premiere presentation can be capitalised in all parts of the country. The moral of *Victoria's* success in the first days of the New Year is one which every British producer and renter [distributor] can draw for himself.

"Odeon's policy is definitely to work for immediate release as a general Trade policy. We cannot control renters' practice, or the practice of other exhibitors, but we shall do what we can by example.

"There is the greatest possible incentive to pioneer in this way in the fact that the relations between release dates and profits have now been shown to be direct and indisputable.

"In the first six months of 1938 Odeon theatres will run earlier releases to the extent of 50 per cent of their programmes.

"When I say earlier releases, I do not mean immediate releases. It is impracticable at this stage to arrange for a simultaneous provincial and suburban release directly after the completion of a West End run. We shall get as quick a release as we can and we shall try to shorten the period progressively."

Victoria The Great opened with a gala West End premiere at the Leicester Square Theatre on 16 September 1937 and began its London suburban Odeon release on 27 December. More typically, United Artists' *The Prisoner Of Zenda* opened the Odeon Leicester Square on 2 November 1937 and played there until 1 December but did not appear in the London suburbs until 14 March 1938. It was still fresh enough at the end of July 1938 to be the opening attraction at the Odeon Ayr.

Deutsch's partnership with United Artists meant that he could be assured of the earlier release of some UA pictures. These comprised half of Odeon's main features in the first six months of 1938, although the sharing of many titles with Gaumont meant that the rival circuit had to agree on the dates: *The Hurricane* ran at the Odeon Leicester Square for a remarkable seven weeks from 26 January to 14 March but didn't play London's suburban Odeons and Gaumonts until 5 September. Alexander Korda's *The Drum* played six weeks at Leicester Square (4 April-15 May) but didn't reach local Odeons and Gaumonts until 24 October. However, purely Odeon releases such as *Vogues Of 1938* and *Paradise For Two* made the jump from Leicester Square to North London suburbs in much shorter time – nine weeks and sixteen weeks respectively, still long enough for initial interest to fade, but of course it has to be remembered that a gap stimulated eager patrons to travel into the West End and pay the much higher prices.

Live

Odeons were normally provided with a shallow stage and two dressing rooms which were, at least in some locations, exceedingly tiny (Leicester Square as a special case had seven dressing rooms; the Odeon Newton Abbot claimed three). There were also orchestra pits or enclosures in most auditoria, although organs were rarely installed. Odeon was the least live-show minded of the major circuits although, according to one report, Oscar Deutsch was so impressed by the performance of Jack Payne and his band at the opening of an Odeon in the summer of 1936 that he arranged for them to tour the circuit.

In July 1939, it was decided to make the organ more of an occasional attraction and twelve of the full-time organists were dismissed, four being retained to cover sixteen cinemas one week in every four. However, it was announced that organs would continue to be played regularly at the Odeons at Leicester Square, Islington, Llandudno and Regal Rotherham. The outbreak of war probably reduced the use of organists even more.

A small stage was needed for announcements and for conducting the Saturday morning children's shows. Odeon went in for amateur variety on Friday nights before the Second World War at some cinemas but the extent of this has not been established. Certainly such nights were advertised for the Odeon Kemp Town, Rayners Lane (though not any others in the Harrow area), and South Norwood.

Saturday morning pictures

Like other circuits, Odeon ran regular shows for children on Saturday mornings. These were originally known as Odeon Children's Circles and had a set of seven 'rules' that included "Always respect old people and help them when you can", "Respect your parents and love your brothers and sisters" and (hardly a rule) "The Club is British, same as the Odeon, and we are all united under the one flag – The Union Jack".

In 1937 the Circles became Mickey Mouse Clubs. The concept of the Mickey Mouse Club originated in the United States where the regular film show (which including a Walt Disney cartoon) was supplemented by various character-building social and charitable activities such as picnics and fund-raising.

In Britain, United Artists distributed Disney cartoons and allowed cinemas to establish Mickey Mouse Clubs provided they included one of the Disney cartoons in every show. It was at the Odeon Worthing – as Terry Staples has noted in his book *All Pals Together* – that manager Sidney Parsons originated what became the rallying song:

> Every Saturday morning, where do we go?
> Getting into mischief? Oh dear, no!
> To the Mickey Mouse Club with our badges on,
> Every Saturday morning at the O - DE - ON!
> Play the game, be honest, and every day
> Do our best at home, at school, at play;
> Love of King and Country will always be our song,
> Loyalty is taught us at the O - DE - ON!

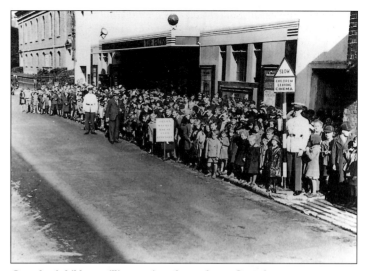

Crowds of children spilling out into the road on a Saturday morning for the photographer outside the Odeon Kemp Town, Brighton, circa 1938.

The song was accompanied by the words on the screen with a "bouncing ball" to keep the audience in time with the music.

Then the gatherings became known as Odeon Children's Clubs with the club song:

> Is everybody happy? Yes!
> Do we ever worry? No!
> To the Odeon we have come
> Now we're all together
> We can have some fun.
> Do we ask for favours? No!
> Do we love our neighbours? Yes!
> We're a hundred thousand strong
> So how can we all be wrong?
> As members of the O.C.C., we stress,
> Is everybody happy? Yes!

In Autumn 1937 all the gatherings reverted to being Odeon Mickey Mouse Clubs with Sidney Parsons adding additional verses to the song that emphasised caution in crossing the road and helping the less fortunate.

In August 1938, Odeon executive Richard Ford issued managers with a questionnaire to build up information about the 150,000 children attending Mickey Mouse Clubs at 142 of its cinemas. Managers estimated that fifty-five per cent of the members were boys, and that the age range went, at the widest guess, from three years to fourteen. They reported on the children's reactions to terrifying scenes as part of a 19-page survey issued in October 1938 that caused Onlooker in *The Cinema* (2 November) to comment: "You cannot escape the impression as you read the reports of these showmen that the atmosphere at these club gatherings is a very different one from that of a cinema manager giving a film entertainment to an ordinary audience. They have made the 'club' idea a very real thing. I expressed the view some time ago that Deutsch had done a work that, in its way, was comparable to that achieved by Baden Powell in the last generation, and I am becoming more than ever convinced that this estimate is not far-fetched."

Before long, some 170 Odeon cinemas were putting on Saturday morning shows. The club at the Odeon Acton had 1,600 members, of which seventy-five per cent would attend in a good week.

The clubs regularly issued "Charity commands" through the Chief Mickey Mouse, the manager of the cinema. These requested children to collect items for various appeals on behalf of local hospitals and charities. In one example, the Home for the Blind in Boston reportedly received washing materials to the extent of forty bars of 'common' soap, eleven tablets of toilet soap, twenty-one packets of Lux, fifty-one packets of soap powder, thirteen packets of soap flakes, thirty-three packets of starch, sixty-one packets of soda, sixty-five bags of blue, and three tins of Vim.

The Odeon Mickey Mouse Clubs and club song continued until April 1943.

Sundays

Odeon was as keen as other circuits to open on Sunday. Indeed, Oscar Deutsch had been at the forefront of the fight for Sunday opening in Birmingham during his two years as head of the Midlands branch of the Cinematograph Exhibitors' Association.

But where cinemas were closed to the public on Sundays, other activities could occur. The Odeons at Hereford and Wimbledon were used by local film societies to show foreign-language films such as *Kameradschaft*. And a former Shirley patron, Brian Bulgin, has recalled (*Focus on Film* no. 23, Winter 1975/6, page 13) "a small social/historical sidelight" with regard to his local Odeon: "In the mid-Thirties, Herbert E. G. Harvey, manager of the Odeon Shirley, near Birmingham, started a car club amongst patrons, which met monthly and undertook Sunday treasure hunts, picnics and visits to stately homes. I believe Oscar Deutsch viewed the idea favourably, but I don't know whether it spread. There was an enamel badge for the radiator – the familiar Odeon green 'O' provided the shape, the enclosed portion was Odeon terracotta split by a crimson bar on which the word 'SHIRLEY' was emblazoned. I can hardly imagine a cinema today having such a corporate sense of audience identity to enable any kind of club to be run – but there's always bingo." The idea spread and there were several more Odeon car clubs but their location has not been established.

Big screen television

With his enthusiasm for technological developments, Oscar Deutsch envisaged a major role for television in cinemas. Three companies were developing rival systems to present live events (in black-and-white, of course). EMI was running its own experiments and Baird had linked up with Gaumont to demonstrate its technology. The Scophony company, headed by S. Sagall, worked with Odeon and Deutsch was so keen that in March 1939 he was negotiating to acquire a financial interest in the company. The Scophony system had the advantage of using only normal voltages (whereas the cathode ray projection system of its two rivals required high voltages) and it developed the first large TV picture, 15ft. by 12ft.

The three systems presented the Derby live on Wednesday 24 May 1939. The Baird system was used at three Gaumont cinemas (including the London New Victoria), EMI put on a demonstration at its headquarters, and Oscar Deutsch issued invitations to see Scophony in action at the Odeon Leicester Square. *Today's Cinema* reported: "Odeon had a full house to see the event. [...] the lighting on the screen was brighter than anything previously achieved by Scophony, a system which has always been noted for its brightness. A fifteen foot screen was used, and on one or two 'key' shots as with Baird and EMI provided quality comparable with news photography. Transmission, however, still leaves much room for improvement."

It was unlike the trade press to be this critical, so there clearly were real problems. In fact, Sidney Bernstein of Granada sent his press officer, Ewart Hodgson, to view the Derby at the Odeon and report back to him. This private memo, dated the day after the event, shows how far the system had to go: "The results obtained were deplorably poor, definition was lacking and frequently the screen gave the impression of spirit photography. Another important fault was that so many of the incidents seemed to be photographed at half a mile range. In fact the picture presented was nothing like as good as the pre-war newsreels of, say, King Edward VII's funeral. The theatre, so far as I could judge, was not half full. The audience was completely bored and greeted with derisive laughter the commentator's line, 'Now here come the horses. Study the jockeys' colours carefully so that you can distinguish your favourite runner when the race begins.'"

However, *The Observer's* film critic, C. A. Lejeune, was among those invited and she thrilled to the immediacy of the moment, opening her following Sunday 'Films of the Week' column with a discussion of television, pinpointing its threat to cinemagoing, as demonstrated by the Derby coverage: "That instant of time in which Blue Peter streaked across the screen to the winning post was more exciting than Greta Garbo, Gary Cooper, or any gangster hold-up." She did not consider the possibility that the novelty might wear off.

The Odeon showed live the following evening, Thursday 25 May, the Armstrong versus Roderick world championship boxing match from the Harringay Arena in place of the regular film show. At one point a technical hitch removed the picture so that only the commentary could be heard, but fortunately vision returned at the crucial moment.

Undeterred, Oscar Deutsch wanted to install Scophony at a number of Odeons and was fully prepared to pay the BBC fees for supplying cinemas with material (the promoters of special events also required payment). The Odeon Swiss Cottage was to be the second Odeon to take Scophony but the war probably prevented this happening. Deutsch saw television as potentially providing a substantial part of the cinema programme: the news and supporting items, perhaps replacing the second feature with a live variety show. At this time, of course, home television sets were only within reach of the wealthy in limited transmission areas. Had cinemas included television material as described, it might have considerably delayed the spread of television domestically.

The Cinematograph Exhibitors' Association was worried but realised that opposition to big screen television in cinemas was futile when two of the major circuits were determined to go ahead with it.

WAR AND THE DEATH OF OSCAR DEUTSCH

Just before the actual declaration of war, blackouts were imposed to test the nation's readiness, giving a foretaste of the conditions to come. One in August 1939 applied from 10pm in Scotland and considerably cut cinema attendances but a midnight deadline in London did no harm. However, London too was badly affected by a blackout after dark on Friday 1 September 1939.

When war was declared on Sunday 3 September, all cinemas were forced to close from that day onwards as a safety precaution. In the absence of any enemy air attacks, people were frustrated at being denied access to their local cinema and it was quickly realised that the population needed entertainment to keep up its spirits. Cinemas in the "neutral" (not at high risk) and "reception" areas (to which children were evacuated) received permission to re-open from Saturday 9 September (although the Odeon Redhill only heard at 6.30pm that day). Cinemas in the "danger" areas were allowed to re-open on Friday 15 September but had to close by 10pm with those in the West End of London initially restricted to a 6pm shutdown. As blackouts became a nightly occurrence, Odeons advertised themselves as "the brightest spot in the blackout".

In the Ealing area, both the central Walpole and outlying Odeon played the circuit release and in the confusion following the outbreak of war in September 1939 shared the same print of *Idiot's Delight*. The chief projectionist at the Walpole was sometimes frantically peering from the roof for the cyclist bringing the next reel but just managed to keep the show running without interruption.

For some years, Oscar Deutsch had ensured that Odeon helped to prepare the nation for the likelihood of conflict. When in 1938 the Government started a campaign to increase recruitment into the volunteer Territorial Army, Deutsch assigned Odeon's public relations officer, Sir Michael Bruce, to put together a short film, *Territorial Cavalcade,* using documentary footage from the Boer War and World War One to show the Army's past work. This was personally financed by Oscar Deutsch and given a gala premiere at the Odeon Leicester Square in May 1938. It then played the entire circuit (as well as other cinemas wishing to screen it). Foyers carried extensive displays, sometimes for ARP [Air Raid Precautions] activities as well, and became

temporary recruiting stations while Territorial Army parades through towns and searchlight displays of anti-aircraft work in car parks were often arranged. Over 30,000 men had registered their names with recruiting officers in the foyers of Odeon cinemas by September 1938.

Odeon's chief also arranged for a huge poster for national service to hang from the tower of the Odeon Leicester Square and launched a scheme for training Odeon staff in ARP.

In April 1939, *The Cinema* trade paper was moved to comment: "Magnificent lead from Oscar Deutsch in national defence. Learn that all Odeon staff will readily receive permission to join any aspect of national service. Anyone going to territorial camp will get fortnight off with pay and arrangement will not affect summer vacation." Head office staff in particular took up the offer in considerable numbers. A Gaumont spokesman noted rather tetchily that it had begun encouraging its staff to train for national service before Odeon – but Oscar's publicity staff had done their customary wizard job of spreading the word about the circuit's initiatives.

In October 1939, Oscar Deutsch was so impressed by a Ministry of Information radio broadcast of an eyewitness account of a flight over the Siegfried Line that he had it re-played to audiences at Odeons with a radio set up in the centre of the stage under a white spotlight.

In November 1940, Deutsch encouraged his 7,500 employees to put some of their earnings into National Savings Certificates by making Odeon the first cinema concern to give a free certificate for every four that staff purchased through deductions from their pay – it was an offer promptly taken up by at least 4,800 of the staff.

Early in 1940, Oscar Deutsch decided to establish temporary headquarters outside London to avoid the threat of bombing. A large estate, Moor Hall, at Cookham on the Thames in Berkshire, was acquired for offices and living quarters for most of the staff, including the booking and accounts departments. A new headquarters was established in the old, disused County cinema at Marlow, Buckinghamshire (a later cinema of the same name having replaced it). In August 1940, staff moved into Cookham just before the first bombing raids and after nearly a year of apprehensive waiting.

Harry Weedon had become dejected by the drying up of cinema work, but he regained some of his old enthusiasm when Deutsch commissioned him to put the Cookham buildings into a fit state for occupation within a few weeks. (A year later, plans were passed to convert garages into additional offices.)

Food rationing had been introduced in 1940 and Oscar Deutsch's strict diet required a regular supply of milk. "One of the more unusual commissions which Weedon received from Deutsch was to negotiate building licences and all necessary permits and approvals to acquire and accommodate two Jersey cows in the paddock adjoining Deutsch's house at [5, Augustus Road] Edgbaston, Birmingham," Robert Bullivant recalled. "Weedon took this in his stride, including the appointment of a land girl to manage this unlikely smallholding."

In 1940, the Odeon chief startled the film trade with his proposal to open the Leicester Square flagship every Sunday afternoon (before regular opening hours) to offer free film entertainment for troops who happened to be in town. It was said that the idea originated with the Odeon's staff who proposed to give their services free, but it certainly gained Deutsch's full support. Staff at other West End cinemas immediately came up with similar proposals. The Cinematograph Exhibitors' Association didn't like the idea (servicemen would be less inclined to go to a paying show afterwards) but didn't dare oppose it in public. Instead, its representatives made an appointment to see Oscar on Monday 4 March and he was persuaded to drop the scheme although the CEA consented to one special show and there was soothing talk of "occasional" further shows.

The special show took place on Sunday 7 April 1940 and only people in uniform with tickets allocated by the War Office were allowed to enter. (Such was the demand that the War Office requested extra tickets, not appreciating that there was a limit to the number of seats.) Music hall performers gave their services free, followed by a film show.

Oscar was always ready to offer his cinemas for good causes. He arranged and hosted a private showing of propaganda films at the Odeon Leicester Square on the afternoon of 2 April 1940. In the summer of 1941, he allowed George Formby to have both the flagship and the Odeon Blackpool for fund-raising concerts for the Tank Fund, after which Odeon began its own Tank Fund concerts at the Majestic Wembley.

In October-November 1940, Deutsch strongly supported the Army Council's plan to create mobile cinemas for showing films to the troops and criticised the CEA and the Kinematograph Renters' Society for their opposition to the scheme. He released correspondence with the War Office and General Sir John Dill "in which it is made abundantly clear to my mind that the industry has behaved in a thoughtless and foolish manner."

At other times, Deutsch functioned as the industry's leading spokesman. On Wednesday 21 February 1940, presiding over a lecture given at the Royal Society of Arts by Oliver Bell, director of the British Film Institute, on "War-time Uses of the Film", Oscar took the opportunity to declare that "public demand for entertainment is greater than ever, in spite of – maybe because of – the blackout." He also gave Odeon a plug by noting that in one week the chain had collected over £10,000 for the Comforts for the Troops Fund. In late 1939, Oscar Deutsch had appeared on screen throughout the circuit to urge audiences to support the Odeon War Comforts Fund.

Deutsch became so prominent that he was jokingly described as running the Ministry of Entertainment. But he was perturbed when the notion was echoed in German propaganda broadcasts as Lord Haw-Haw attempted to arouse anti-semitic feeling by declaring that it was Burton's who made the soldiers' uniforms, Lyons who were feeding them and Oscar Deutsch who kept them entertained...

Last acquisitions

Odeon entered Coventry before the end of 1939 by taking over Charles Orr's circuit of five cinemas after the exhibitor retired from the business at the early age of 58. This brought the Scala, one of Oscar Deutsch's earlier houses, back under his control. The best of the batch – and the only justification for the deal, unless old friendships were involved – was the large and modern Scala. The deal seems to attracted no attention in the trade press and may have taken place before the war, even in 1938.

Oscar Deutsch's previously mentioned determination to establish Odeon in Leeds, Newcastle and Manchester, made fully evident in 1937, had worried Paramount with its large properties in each of the cities. This clearly prompted dialogue between David E. Rose, the British head of Paramount, and Deutsch over the possible sale or lease of Paramount's provincial cinemas to Odeon. This went on for more than eighteen months. Odeon made occasional announcements of impending progress at the three sites, to put pressure on Paramount and to move ahead if the talks should conclusively fail.

Odeon's scheme for Leeds had been temporarily postponed in April 1938. In August of that year the company stated that construction was about to commence. In November, a totally unrelated rival scheme was announced for a 2,000-seater with shops and offices on a nearby site. In March 1939, an Odeon spokesman declared that a start would probably be made on its site the following month, and demolition of an old brewery certainly began. The site had been cleared by September, but no structural work ever took place. Some of the space was being used for car parking. In Manchester, Odeon had switched sites by May 1938 to Oxford Street (where the Paramount and Gaumont were located), at the junction with Portland Street. This scheme was initially to be designed by Harry Weedon, then by Verity and Beverley, the practice which had handled the Paramounts.

As late as May 1939, David E. Rose strongly denied rumours that the entire Paramount chain outside the West End would be sold. However, the tone soon changed. The *Kinematograph Weekly* in August 1939 reported that Paramount felt the need to either sell or enlarge its circuit as it had insufficient booking power, and that the company had decided on the former course, retaining only its London showcases, the Plaza and Carlton. The trade paper also recorded that Paramount "recognises the growth of nationalistic feeling" and that expansion would not have been welcomed. The declaration of war temporarily stalled discussion and it was not until Thursday 23 November 1939 that Deutsch signed an agreement with Rose to take over seven of Paramount's cinemas from the following Monday on 35-year leases.

The seven were the three Paramounts that had been threatened by new Odeons at Leeds, Manchester and Newcastle plus the four Astorias in the London suburbs at Brixton, Finsbury Park, Old Kent Road and Streatham. Deutsch therefore abandoned his own schemes for Manchester, Newcastle and Leeds (where the site was turned over entirely to parking for the duration of the war), and the three Paramounts were renamed Odeons at weekly intervals in April 1940. According to Sidney Swingler, it was impossible to make a profit on the stage shows that accompanied films at the Paramount theatres, even if a hall was "packed to suffocation", and so stage staff, orchestras, bands and other acts were eliminated, retaining just the organists.

Negotiations continued for Odeon to acquire the remaining Paramounts at Birmingham, Glasgow, Liverpool and London's Tottenham Court Road where some degree of "tie-up" came into effect, possibly involving Odeon in day-to-day management of the four theatres. Deutsch was unquestionably anxious to acquire the three provincial halls which would crown his strong suburban representation in Birmingham and Glasgow and enable Odeon at last to enter the Liverpool scene (there had been a Harry Weedon scheme for a new Odeon on Merseyside but whether this had collapsed or was still a possibility is unclear: it had certainly not progressed to the same degree as the plans for Leeds, Manchester and Newcastle). In August 1940, David E. Rose was busy with Paramount's British production plans and Oscar Deutsch continued talks with Arthur Segal, the veteran exhibitor who had a financial interest in the Paramounts; but Segal died of heart failure in December and Deutsch was not able to pull off the deal in the remaining year of his life. One result of the link

Oscar Deutsch (right) and Paramount's British chief David E. Rose sign the contract by which Odeon takes over seven Paramount cinemas.

Odeon Bradford. Bomb damage in 1940.

with Paramount was that from September 1941 the company's pictures were nationally released solely through the Odeon circuit.

The imminence of war prompted an end to the wasteful practice of the Odeon and County circuits operating independently of each other (although there had been an increasing degree of liaison over the preceding two years). In mid-August 1939, Odeon took over the booking of films for County and its accounts department was set to be merged with that of Odeon. The move to Marlow and Cookham led to a full merger under Odeon's control.

The County circuit was a mixed bag of properties. Its own building programme had provided high quality cinemas that easily met Odeon standards and established it in Chelmsford, Margate, Nottingham, Southampton, Southend and other important centres. County had also built superior cinemas in prosperous smaller country towns in the south of England, like Camberley, Farnborough, Farnham, Fleet, Godalming and Marlow. Its takeovers now placed Odeon in such worthwhile locations as Aberdeen, Aldershot, Colchester, Folkestone, High Wycombe, Staines and Wembley. There was some degree of duplication, with Odeon gaining second (and even third) halls in such places as Guildford, Reading, Weybridge and Wimbledon.

In June 1940, the first County properties – the frontline Astorias at Folkestone and Southend – were renamed Odeons, followed a month later by the Regent Aberdeen. County's financial interest in the Regent Plymouth was bought by Odeon and it also was renamed in June 1940. The County at Marlow became an Odeon in February 1941 to accord with the move of London staff to the town and was the last cinema to take the name in Deutsch's lifetime. The headings in press advertising were re-designed so that the names of County and London & Southern's cinemas appeared in the trademark Odeon style of lettering accompanied by the words "An Associate Odeon Theatre".

Odeon had for some time been the third largest British circuit. The amalgamation with County still left it in third place with considerably fewer cinemas than Gaumont and ABC, but a much higher proportion of them had been recently built and it had a higher average seating capacity.

Attendances

After war was declared, Oscar Deutsch decided to keep all the Odeon cinemas open, despite the drop in attendances at many of them, as a matter of good will as well as an amenity for soldiers stationed near them and defiance of the enemy. Some Odeons benefitted from the evacuation of mothers and children from the cities (which had started just before the actual declaration of war) – the Odeon Horsham being a case in point.

(Cinemas like the Odeon Lewes were used as a "control centre" at which newly arrived children could be paired with their new families. An Odeon Welfare Department made a point of seeing that evacuees were introduced to local children at the Saturday morning Mickey Mouse Clubs.

At the second annual general meeting of Odeon Theatres in November 1939, Oscar Deutsch pointed to the valuable effect on building regular patronage that had resulted from an [almost] unbroken line of attractive films: *The Lambeth Walk, The Mikado, The Spy In Black, Good-Bye Mr. Chips!, Wuthering Heights, Nurse Edith Cavell, The Lion Has Wings, Stagecoach, Three Smart Girls Grow Up, Q Planes, Love Affair* and *The Four Feathers*. Deutsch declared that there had been no substantial drop in the "evacuation areas" and a natural increase in "reception areas" while many bright moonlit nights had helped overcome the difficulties of travelling in the blackout.

The war influenced the films that were booked. A topical French melodrama, *Double Crime In The Maginot Line*, was given a full circuit release with English subtitles from December 1939 as the top half of a double bill with a revival of the 1936 George Formby comedy *Keep Your Seats, Please*. And from January 1940, the Odeon circuit showed *Professor Mamlock*, a subtitled Russian drama about the persecution of an eminent German Jewish surgeon which showed the horrors of a Nazi concentration camp. It had been banned by the British Board of Film Censors shortly before war was declared for fear of provoking the Germans. It opened at the Academy Oxford Street under a special London "A" certificate just after the war started, and was a huge success. The BBFC then gave it a certificate (after the sound on a whipping sequence was toned down). It was the last foreign-language film to play the full Odeon circuit until *The Wages of Fear* in 1954.

Mamlock was followed shortly afterwards by *Hitler – Beast of Berlin,* a poverty-row exploitation feature that would never have been shown as a main feature under normal circumstances. It had been picked up by British Lion and played under its original American title, deemed too inflammatory for use there at a time when the United States was not in the war.

The Lion Has Wings was a rushed propaganda film starring Ralph Richardson and Merle Oberon, made by London Films for United Artists release, showing the outbreak of war and the preparedness of the Royal Air Force. Oscar Deutsch took steps for the film to be shown as quickly as possibly because it was of such topical importance. Bars were dropped, enabling it to become one of the top hits of the year, double-billed at Odeons from late November 1939 with a skating Sonja Henie in *Second Fiddle*. This was perhaps the ideal war-time combination: a stirring propaganda film and pure escapism.

In May 1940, Onlooker in *The Daily Cinema* commented: "You may remember that after the closing of cinemas at the beginning of the war, and the general setback of business for some time after re-opening, Deutsch was the first man to announce that cinemas had returned to something like normal takings. That statement was received with some scepticism by the trade at the time, but has been proved since to be a plain, straightforward utterance, ungarnished by mere optimism." Of course, Odeons may have been doing better than the opposition.*

It was noted that the London area was only slowly improving and some of the suburbs were particularly slow about it. This was during the period of the "phoney war" when none of the anticipated bombing raids had occurred. But it was impossible to remain optimistic that late spring and summer as Germany invaded northern France and Belgium, coming closer and closer to Britain, and Italy declared war on the Allies. People stayed at home to listen to the news, and attendances were further decimated in coastal areas threatened by invasion where mass evacuation had already taken place. In towns like Margate (where County's large Regal was situated) and Whitstable, attendances were down by three-quarters, resulting in huge losses. In towns like Folkestone, Deutsch shared the takings from his cinemas with exhibitors who were temporarily forced to close. However, in Southend, a town with far too many cinemas including two County properties, the less successful Ritz was temporarily closed in September 1940 while the larger Astoria remained open along with seven others – half the area's total number of halls.

In the West End of London, attendances fell to a trickle. The premiere of the thriller *Gaslight* with Diana Wynyard and Anton Walbrook at the Odeon on Monday 17 June 1940 was badly affected. Onlooker referred to "the brave show of an Odeon first night only getting by because Oscar Deutsch insisted on doing a little bit more in his tireless work for national causes. Nobody was in Leicester Square to watch the spectacle, no first night devotee fought for a seat in the farthest corner of the circle. Only the celebrities still swayed for a corner of the limelight. This week's occasion looks like being the last of its kind for many months to come." However, the diarist underestimated Oscar Deutsch. If reports are to be believed, just five weeks later when *The Grapes Of Wrath* was launched with a premiere attended by Oscar Deutsch at the Odeon on Monday 22 July, "milling crowds stormed the theatre" for "one of the biggest first nights ever seen" and a "host of celebrities were present".

* At its third annual general meeting at the Dorcester on 19 November 1940, Deutsch reported only a small decline in Odeon Theatres' profits to £473,481 (from £509,990). It had been decided to pass on an ordinary dividend in order to conserve financial resources.

The bombing of England by the Germans finally began on 13 August 1940 and intensified with the blitzing of London on fifty-eight consecutive nights from Saturday 7 September 1940 onwards, with the East End being particularly badly hit.

There were increasing air raid alerts. At the beginning of September, the Odeon Kingston reported: "The warnings have had a pretty considerable effect – business is rather worse than an old hot summer. We had two or three sessions last week during which audiences were present during warnings, and kept the theatre going for some hours after the last show. The spirit of the public is marvellous, and there is no vestige of alarm."

One effect was that many Odeon patrons went to matinees rather than evening performances. As the bombs fell in raid after raid after raid, West End business in particular suffered as cinemagoers were reluctant to make long journeys. In an attempt to persuade more people to attend evening shows at the Odeon Leicester Square, it was proposed to announce or relay any vital war development from the 9 pm news broadcast to the audience. The BBC readily agreed but Reuters and other news agencies refused, saying it would breach their exclusive contracts.

Attendances throughout the rest of the capital were very poor. At this time, all London cinemas were reported to be operating at a loss, and many closed temporarily (no Odeons, of course). The normally sure-fire box-office attraction of Deanna Durbin in *It's A Date* did so badly on release in September that Odeon re-booked it at Christmas. Cinemas were finishing at 9pm for a while, and times were rearranged so that the big film played first at the last show, allowing audiences to get home even earlier. The London County Council permitted cinemas to open earlier at 10.30am on weekdays and at 3pm (then at 1.30pm) on Sundays. Cinemas opened on Christmas Day 1940 following Sunday hours.

The gloom seemed to lift a bit in 1941. The old practice of Odeon sharing major films with Gaumont was revived for *The Great Dictator* and *The Thief Of Bagdad*. *The Great Dictator* was such a powerful attraction that it opened in Manchester at both the Odeon (ex-Paramount) and Gaumont as well as the locally-run Gaiety, and seems to have done good business at all of them in spite of heavy bombing. It was remembered as the biggest draw of the period at the Walpole Ealing, along with *Ninotchka*.

Odeon executive Wilfred Phillips stated in a press advertisement that Leslie Howard's *Pimpernel Smith*, a cunning update of *The Scarlet Pimpernel*, had taken more money in its north and south London suburban release in July/August 1941 than any film that Odeon had ever shown.

Saturday morning pictures were particularly badly affected by the bombing. By July 1941, the number of Mickey Mouse Clubs had shrunk to forty-five, almost entirely in the reception areas, with ten thousand members.

Bomb damage

Cinemas in general were so well constructed that they provided the best possible haven from air raids. The Odeon Redhill even had an air-raid shelter for 600 people under the building, which was fitted out with electric lights and seats for the elderly immediately war was declared.

Some Odeons that provided a conspicuous target for enemy bombers or a guide to major targets were elaborately camouflaged. By December 1939, the Odeon Norwich had been made "practically invisible" from the air by a camouflage expert. Two sides of the building were painted to suggest rows of houses. The roof was broken up by patches of colour. The back wall and the large car park at the rear were disguised with patches of red material to look like rooftops. The Odeon at Shannon Corner, New Malden, was another to be camouflaged as it was adjacent to an obvious target, the premises of Decca Navigation.

At the end of August 1940, the Odeon at Bradford, Yorkshire, was the first to suffer as a result of the bombing. The prompt action of the manager and staff restricted the damage to the screen end of the auditorium. One of the current attractions was *The Grapes Of Wrath*. It was sufficiently patched up to re-open on 11 November.

The flagship in Leicester Square had some near misses, as manager William H. Thornton recalled in a 1944 article:

"I do not think I shall ever forget the night of the first big blitz at my theatre. I was in the midst of a most important premiere [of *Lillian Russell*, on Monday 26 August 1940] and it promised to be one of real pre-war standard. The film was nearly at an end when the sirens sounded. We stopped the film for a brief interval and I went on the stage and announced that there had been a warning. Then, when the film was over and everyone realised that things were far hotter and much noisier than they had ever been before, they were most loath to leave, and, of course, we did not wish them to do so. Consequently, hardly anyone left the theatre and we had our guests until early the next morning. I wish you could have seen the Odeon Leicester Square as dawn appeared. Downstairs, in our reception rooms dowagers and debutantes together lay on cushions on the floor, covered in old drapes and anything that we could find to keep them warm and cosy. Upstairs in the lounge and on the settees, the men-folk sat, talking, or patrolling up and down, or helping in whatever way they could. Naturally, the staff remained throughout the night and looked after everybody in a truly magnificent fashion. They made tea and coffee and went from one of our 'house guests' to the next enquiring if anything could be done to make them more comfortable.

"From that day on firewatching came to stay at this theatre. Of course, it was long before firewatching was introduced officially in the country, but everybody felt that they would like to remain periodically and in turn, to see that no harm came to the theatre in which they worked. I shall always remember and always most deeply appreciate what I feel was an act of devotion and loyalty during those dangerous and difficult days.

"Two incidents stand out particularly clearly in my mind during this blitz period. On a night in October 1940 a land mine dropped in Leicester Square. Our vestibule, foyer, roof and large part of the auditorium were severely damaged. Our theatre was closed then for five weeks, and every day everybody was in to help with the cleaning up process and to do whatever they could to assist the workmen. Nevertheless, at the end of those five weeks no-one would have known what we had been through. Our huge black tower stood as strong and challenging as ever against the sky, and our Union Jack floated in the wind. We could not be beaten.

"I remember so vividly, too, on one of our bad nights climbing to the very top of the tower and looking over London. One could see for many miles round great fires burning in the centre of our city.

"Yet another time we had to face a 'hiding'. Once again our roof was damaged when a bomb was dropped a few yards from the theatre. Next morning the staff were in and everyone formed little working parties and patched up our torn roof with pieces of asbestos sheeting and tarpaulins. Two days later we were open once more."

At a lesser location, the Odeon Islington, CTA member Thomas Maxwell recalls his weekly visits: "As it was next to a police station, it had an air raid siren. During the Blitz when the night-time raids started, we would be sitting in the front stalls and every night at 10.30 the wailing started – low down, then the full alert. The programme ended at 10.45, so we had to walk home with the bangs, the huge flashes lighting up the streets, the planes and the bombs whizzing down and the anti-aircraft guns booming at Highbury."

The worst disaster to befall an Odeon occurred on Saturday 14 September 1940 during an early afternoon performance of a minor film called *It Could Happen To You* at the Odeon Kemp Town, Brighton. Manager Cyril D. Huxtable interrupted the film to give an air raid warning but the audience of nearly three hundred remained in place. Shortly afterwards, a lone German raider dropped twenty bombs, one of which landed in the right-hand front corner of the auditorium near the rows of sixpenny seats. Usherette Gladys Nash told Brighton historian John Montgomery: "It was the most horrible experience of my life. A bomb came through the roof and exploded in front of the screen. There were children all around me, dead." The number of young victims was increased because the Saturday morning Mickey

Odeon Kemp Town. After the bomb and after restoration. (Brighton and Hove Libraries.)

Mouse Club had been suspended and the remaining chapters of the serial transferred to Saturday afternoon performances. In all, fifty-five people were reported to have lost their lives in the cinema and immediate vicinity.

Oscar Deutsch promptly invited the staff to take a week's holiday at his expense in the country at Cookham, near the Odeon headquarters, and arranged for them to visit the set of *Major Barbara* at Denham Studios, where they were posed with the stars of the picture, Wendy Hiller and Rex Harrison, for a photograph that appeared in the Brighton press. Manager Huxtable was appointed to run the Odeon Marlow while the rest of the staff were temporarily assigned to the Odeon and Palladium in the centre of Brighton and to the Lido at Hove. Work started immediately on repairing and modernising the building to plans drawn up by Leonard Allen, successor to the original architect, Andrew Mather. The main steel girder, roof and ceiling all had to be replaced; all glass light fittings were removed and 400 new seats installed. Lily Deutsch selected a rose-coloured decorative scheme while Decorative Crafts supplied a colourful screen tableau curtain showing the "mountain pass" design and a front curtain in gold and silver festoons. The Odeon re-opened on Boxing Day, and Oscar Deutsch arranged an informal dinner for all the workmen involved to thank them for their efforts, a gesture that the Odeon press corps ensured was reported in the local press.

The following incident, related by Zoe Josephs, took place in the autumn of 1940: "A time bomb lodged beneath the Odeon Perry Barr, but it was defused. Oscar Deutsch, though desperately ill, had gold medallions struck for the bomb disposal squad, entitling the soldiers to visit any Odeon free at all times." These were lifetime passes and the trade press noted that Oscar had a "sentimental attachment" to the particular theatre – it was, of course, the first to be named Odeon.

One of the most modern Odeons, at Canning Town, east London, was closed by bomb damage on 2 October 1940, only fifteen months after opening. It re-opened five months later, then had to shut again after two months because of further bomb damage, never to re-open. This is probably the least-known Odeon because it had by far the shortest operating life. According to Sidney Swingler, "It was half on a raft and half on a 'stiletto' foundation, pushing columns right down into the ground. The raft was at the screen end. We used a break joint just in front of the balcony because we knew it wouldn't stay permanently – so, instead of having cracked brickwork which we'd have to stitch up after a while, we put a break joint in. A bomb fell and went underneath the raft part and it went off, smashing up the raft. The building didn't look damaged from the outside. The joint opened about four to five inches. It didn't look dangerous at all but the thing was likely to collapse."

In the same month, at the top of Balham Hill in south London, the very conspicuous Odeon (which had camouflaged its roof), had a narrow escape when a bomb destroyed the right wing of the frontage but spared the auditorium, enabling business to continue. One of the following week's attractions, a minor Hollywood feature, had the highly appropriate title *I'm Still Alive.* On the other hand, the Odeon Haverstock Hill was damaged beyond immediate repair on 7 November 1940 and remained dark for fourteen years.

Bombing raids on Kent resulted in the destruction of most of the frontage and a significant part of the foyer of the Royalty Broadstairs on 1 November 1940. Like the Odeon Lancing, this unimportant property had been taken over by a local operator – here Fred Salt, who still had the smaller Picture House. Ten years later the building was repaired and re-opened as an Odeon.

The Odeon Leicester had a lucky escape around this time. As related in February 1941 by Rita Cave, head of Odeon's press and public relations department: "[Leicester] had been almost free from bombardment until a couple of months ago, when it had a fierce attack on two consecutive nights. The Fire Chief warned the manager of the Odeon there that he could not possibly save the theatre, as a large factory within 50 yards was a sea of flame, into which 'Jerry' had dropped further bombs. At the last moment the wind changed, and the house was saved. The manager had a staff of 18, and every one stood by until the theatre was out of danger – some of them were on the roof watching for incendiaries and would not budge until ordered to do so. The manager stood by until 4.30am on that day and 4am the next. That is the spirit of every man and woman [working for Odeon Theatres]..."

Among the London & Southern properties, the already closed Super Bloomsbury was severely damaged by bombing in early 1941 and never re-opened.

On the night of 21 April that year, the Odeon Forest Gate narrowly avoided disaster when its neighbour, the Queen's, part of the ABC circuit, was destroyed by a land mine. Even so, the Odeon suffered enough damage to remain dark for more than three months. Three days later, the County circuit's Hippodrome at Devonport was so badly hit that it never functioned again.

On the Sunday night of 7 September 1941, four hours after a thousand people had watched the single 7.25pm screening of *Kipps* at the beginning of its four-day run at County's Regal Margate, a German bomber scored a direct hit on the auditorium and blew out the front windows and doors. The spot where the manager had been sleeping until a few nights before was crushed. Three staff on fire-watch duty escaped serious injury. Only the Regal and Parade had remained open in Margate, but the Regal's demise led to the return of the Plaza.

Odeon Balham. (Wandsworth Local History Service.)

Odeon Forest Gate, taken 29 April 1941. The near miss here destroyed the rival ABC house, the Queen's, which has part of its façade visible on the left. (CTA Archive.)

The Regal was almost certainly the cinema in the following story (as was customary during the war, the precise location was not revealed to avoid giving the enemy useful information). One cinema (among many) doing very poor business had been kept open on Oscar Deutsch's instructions to entertain servicemen but was flattened by a lone German raider's fire bombs. Deutsch informed the entire staff that they would continue to receive full pay for twelve weeks after which they could transfer to any other Odeon cinema of their choosing.

Oscar Deutsch, film promoter

Oscar Deutsch had always been an ardent supporter of British films. He advertised Odeons as "The home of British pictures" and prophesied that Britain would overtake Hollywood. In 1937, when the British quota of twenty per cent was reluctantly fulfilled by many cinemas, Odeon went out of its way to book domestic productions and some sites were reaching thirty per cent while Llandudno notched up forty-eight per cent of playing time for home-grown pictures. The likelihood of war caused major financing difficulties for British independent producers from 1938 onwards and Oscar Deutsch came up with an imaginative solution.

Odeon was restrained by its articles of association from involvement in film production but in early 1939 Deutsch secretly obtained the approval of the Board of Trade for a scheme whereby unmade films would be guaranteed a full Odeon circuit release on their completion. Deutsch and his advisers studied the story and casting and offered the guarantee only to films they were confident would be popular. Deutsch himself did not invest any money but the assurance of an Odeon booking made it much easier for producers to obtain finance from ever-cautious bankers. When news of the arrangement leaked out, it created a trade sensation.

A difficulty with Deutsch's scheme was that it might contravene the ban on "blind booking", i.e. booking films without an opportunity to see them. This ban had been brought in during the 1920s to protect exhibitors from having to take packages of films before they were made, but the fact that it was an exhibitor who proposed to willingly take the risk must have influenced the Board of Trade. Of course, such an arrangement denied rival exhibitors a chance to bid for the completed films and possibly offer better booking terms – but if the films wouldn't have been made without Deutsch's support, the point is not really relevant. Certainly, as long as Oscar could spot winners in the pre-production stages, he had found a way of helping Odeon to meet its quota obligations and make money.

"Almost a year ago I secured approval from the Board of Trade," said Deutsch at a luncheon in late January 1940 before the press show of the first film revealed to have been made with the Odeon chief's support. "I have it in writing that the Board do not consider this a breach of the advance booking clauses in the 1938 Quota Act. About half a dozen producers have availed themselves of this arrangement." The film was Grand National's production of *The Stars Look Down,* the coal-mining drama based on A. J. Cronin's novel, directed by Carol Reed and starring Michael Redgrave and Margaret Lockwood. The independent producer-distributor's joint managing director, Jeffrey Bernard, commented: "Mr. Deutsch has been a 'fairy godmother' to Grand National and he has already agreed that we shall make some more pictures."

Oscar was rewarded with a massive hit. *The Stars Look Down* opened at the Odeon Leicester Square on Monday 22 January and, despite the blackout and snow, created a war-time attendance record for the theatre to that date, with 27,702 paying customers in the first week and takings of over £1,100 on the Saturday night. The film drew audiences back to evening shows in the West End as well as to matinees. Its initial three-week engagement was extended to four weeks and its general release began a week later, an instance of when Oscar Deutsch was really able to fulfill his pre-war plan for a speedier general release. (*Stars'* success was so conspicuous it attracted snide comments from Lord Haw-Haw that it had not been faithful to the book.)

Today's Cinema (26 March 1940) reported how Deutsch "took over the spotlight" at a dinner at the Savoy the previous week, following a screening of a major new British spying drama, *Contraband,* starring Conrad Veidt and Valerie Hobson under the direction of Michael Powell. The trade paper's columnist, Onlooker, wrote: "These days the Odeon chief is something of a tonic to those who look sadly on the future of the business. Have seen Oscar speaking several times of late. Every time it is the same. Oscar gets to his feet, pulls his jacket into trim line, puts on a broad smile and proceeds to rout the pessimists. Now I can already hear you cynics muttering something about it being easy to talk. To which I promptly reply that Oscar is one of the few men who since the war have definitely cut the cackle and got down to the actual rescue of British studios. You all know by now of his sponsoring of *The Stars Look Down.* Although he didn't say so in as many words last week, shouldn't be surprised if *Contraband* had a similar Odeon circuit blessing. At any rate it is going into the circuit distribution and during the attractive booking week of Whitsuntide.* One of these days,

---

* *Contraband* had its premiere run at the Odeon Leicester Square from Monday 25 March 1940. Both film and cinema gained a huge publicity break when Winston Churchill attended a performance and his visit was splashed in the *Daily Mail* and other newspapers.

shall make it my business to ask Oscar just how many pictures have benefitted from his interest since the outbreak of war. One thing I know already, they have all been shrewd deals that have made good money for everybody who has had anything to do with them."

Oscar could perhaps try his audience's patience by his enthusiasm for speaking at every opportunity. There was a luncheon for Paramount's British production of *Quiet Wedding* in January 1941 when Onlooker reported: "O.D. made a little speech emphasising that the picture had been completed despite wholesale wartime difficulties. Somebody remarked to me afterwards it was a rather obvious thing to say; all the same we do tend to forget current difficulties in assessing the work of those who carry on through the war."

Deutsch moved on from guaranteeing producers an Odeon release to making his own financial investment in British filmmaking. One film he certainly made possible was the propaganda thriller *49th Parallel,* initiated and nearly half-financed by taxpayers' money through the Ministry of Information. Deutsch personally provided most of the remainder: £30,000, half the cost of production. The Michael Powell film showed Canadians joining the fight against the Nazis when a submarine crew takes refuge in their country. The production received a barrage of adverse publicity in both the national and film trade press following shooting delays caused by the defection of actress Elisabeth Bergner after expensive location filming in Canada and by having to work around the other commitments of stars Leslie Howard and Laurence Olivier. In November 1940, Oscar sought to defuse charges of extravagance and wasting public money by hosting a fork luncheon in the Odeon Leicester Square press room but he failed to satisfy several reporters who received no clear-cut answers to their questions and further criticised the venture in print.

In the summer of 1940, he was reported to have started a partnership with Lady Yule to finance pictures with the profits going to the Red Cross. They would be made by Lady Yule's British National Films, the first being a history of the Red Cross itself, scripted by Miles Malleson. This was never made, unless it turned into the short *Red Cross In Action* which accompanied *The Mark Of Zorro* at the Odeon Leicester Square and was shown by the entire circuit.

Tansa Films was formed in the spring of 1941 by Deutsch, C. M. Woolf (of General Film Distributors) and J. Arthur Rank to finance the film version of the romantic comedy play *Jeannie.* This starred Michael Redgrave and the stage sensation, Barbara Mullen. It was produced by Marcel Hellman and released by General Film Distributors through the Odeon circuit in the summer of 1941.

News leaked out of other Deutsch film projects, one of which was a big-budget picture about Christopher Columbus's discovery of America. Onlooker commented on 28 May 1941: "O.D. certainly keeps his epic plans to himself. In this instance I am assured on the authority of Sunday paper writer Ernest Betts that production will begin in a few weeks. Oscar has commissioned Rafael Sabatini [the well-known maritime author] to do the story and is thinking of location work in Spain. Well, it's a grand plan and Oscar is so engrossed in film production these days that I will believe anything about his plans. So many pictures have had some of O.D.'s discriminating financing these last few years that he can now be looked upon as one of Britain's big shot producers."

A further Deutsch project was a Technicolor picture about the RAF that would feature a night bombing raid. Onlooker was moved to complain (11 June 1941): "I don't know why it is, but Oscar generally imposes a ban of silence on all those engaged in his productions... work has been going on for some months."

Deutsch had good reason to keep quiet as neither the historical epic nor the air raid film was ready to go into production and both lapsed on his death. His practice was to keep projects under wraps until they were sure of proceeding or (as with the film *Jeannie* when Tansa was announced) already underway .

His last major production venture was his further partnership with Rank and Woolf to form British Film Makers, registered in July 1941. Announced in early November 1941, the company intended to shoot five films over the following year. It had already made much progress and its first picture, *The Day Will Dawn,* a war-time drama about the bombing of a German U-base in Norway, was in production at the time of Deutsch's death a month later.*

The end

By December 1940, it was apparent to insiders that Oscar Deutsch's precarious health was deteriorating, and he reduced his workload by resigning from the board of United Artists.

Deutsch delayed further treatment for several months until,

---

* One of Deutsch's sons, David, pursued a career in film production with some success. After starting as an assistant editor for Gainsborough, he worked for producer Sydney Box. He produced the Joseph Losey thriller *Blind Date* (1959) for Box and Independent Artists. He set up Domino Productions and made Clive Donner's black comedy *Nothing But The Best* (1964), the romantic drama *Interlude* (1968) and the bawdy period comedy *Lock Up Your Daughters!* (1969). He also produced John Boorman's first film, the David Clark Five musical *Catch Us If You Can* (1965). He was a co-producer of the Fred Zinnemann thriller *The Day Of The Jackal* (1973). He died in London on 13 December 1991 of kidney failure, aged 65.

in early June 1941, he submitted to a major operation at Cookham. "He has had a rather rough passage," noted the *Kinematograph Weekly*, adding that he was expected back in his office soon. "Oscar is certainly not seriously ill," said Onlooker.

Two weeks after the operation, Oscar was recuperating in Birmingham and planning a holiday. By mid-July, he seemed to be back at work. At any rate, he caused a minor uproar by cutting through negotiations between the Cinematograph Exhibitors' Association and the National Association of Theatrical and Kine Employees, giving all Odeon employees a ten per cent war time bonus (on top of an existing 7 1/2% bonus) to help them keep up with inflation and to encourage them to remain with the company at a time when it was very difficult to find enough staff. The CEA was furious because it was not given advance notice of his decision, because negotiations were being conducted on an area-by-area basis, and because it set a precedent which naturally delighted NATKE.

Oscar Deutsch sent out the invitations to the press show on Tuesday 29 July of the major new United Artists release, *Lady Hamilton*, and announced that the premiere at the Odeon Leicester Square would benefit the British Voluntary Ambulance Corps.* However, he seem to have started his holiday in Cornwall instead of attending the UA luncheon at Claridge's after the press show.

He did gain attention around this time by telling a newspaper columnist, "If it is possible, and the Government should make it possible, we should have newsreels twice and three times the present length." This drew the trade response that the Government should stay out of film industry affairs and that the proposal would leave no time for second features.

Even while convalescing in Cornwall, Oscar could not resist a spot of business, negotiating the purchase of the largest cinema in Cardiff, the Capitol. He returned home to Birmingham on 9 August and had a sudden and unexpected setback. This may have been related to the night when a bomb fell nearby and the blast blew him out of his bed, causing injuries from which he never fully recovered.

By mid-August, Oscar had seemed to be well on the mend. He was on the point of taking a train to London for the day when a sudden relapse occurred, too public to be concealed. Onlooker informed his readers in *The Cinema*: "... medical instructions are that, for a time at least, he must have no contact with business and concentrate wholeheartedly on the job of getting

really well... I gather that this relapse has been sudden and somewhat unexpected... even a short time after his convalescence began, Oscar was receiving a number of visitors from Wardour Street... [and] essential callers such as Will [Wilfred] Phillips... he probably found these friendly visits helpful... but he'll now have to take things very slowly indeed."

Two weeks later, telegram invitations were sent out by Deutsch's office for a luncheon with Sarah Churchill and Vic Oliver preceding the press show of their film *He Found A Star*. The Odeon chief provided a postscript: "Regret ill-health still prevents me being with you but hope to be back quite soon." At the luncheon, the film's producer John Corfield praised Oscar for his support of the industry and Vic Oliver declared, "Mr. Deutsch has done much for the British artist. I could tell numerous stories of wonderful acts by him."

Oscar's health did not really improve but there was one occasion that he could not – would not – miss. On Wednesday 8 October 1941, in defiance of doctors' orders, he returned to the public eye as joint host with C. M. Woolf of the luncheon to celebrate the opening – at last – of *49th Parallel*. It took place at Claridges after the 10.30am combined press and trade show at the Odeon Leicester Square and before the world premiere public screening there at 2.30pm. Deutsch presided at this major event where nearly 300 guests enjoyed champagne cocktails followed by oysters and forty-year-old liqueurs. Under close scrutiny, his bearing impressed Onlooker: "O.D. went through the ordeal of shaking hands with just about everyone that came into the room. Afterwards in his speech he demonstrated further the extent of his recovery. Sentiments were expressed in such a resounding voice that the microphone seemed hardly necessary."

Oscar must have been elated by the way the film had turned out. As written by Emeric Pressburger and directed by Michael Powell, *49th Parallel* was gripping entertainment and skilful propaganda that brought home the Nazi threat to north Americans (in the United States, it was released under the title *The Invaders*). With three major box-office names – Leslie Howard, Laurence Olivier and Anton Walbrook – and rave reviews, the film proved a phenomenal success from the outset – at the Odeon, the first weekend's takings smashed existing records despite reduced opening hours (but helped by a lull in enemy raids). Special free morning shows of *49th Parallel* were arranged for Canadian servicemen at Odeons near their bases. The production made a huge profit. (In fact, the filming in Canada had aroused considerable international interest and Columbia bought distribution rights outside Britain and Australia for what was reported as the biggest sum ever paid for a British film.)

Oscar's condition worsened in the following weeks and doctors kept him from doing anything that could be avoided. One last

* A rousing historical drama with a propaganda slant, *Lady Hamilton* ran for seven weeks at the Odeon Leicester Square and broke box office records for the war period at many cinemas on its general release from late September 1941. It was re-booked to many Odeons three months later.

idea that carried the chief's personal approval was the Odeon Hospitality Scheme by which Odeons in port towns displayed posters in French, Danish, Dutch, Polish, Norwegian and Greek inviting Allied and neutral seamen to spend an evening in the home of British families.

The option held by John Maxwell on the key Gaumont-British voting shares expired in October. Deutsch's deteriorating health clearly ruled him out as head of a merged Odeon and Gaumont chain. Instead of Odeon, it was General Cinema Finance, a corporation headed by J. Arthur Rank, C. M. Woolf and Lord Portal, that bought control of Gaumont by the end of the month. GCF had earlier invested in Odeon Theatres to the extent that J. Arthur Rank became a board member from January 1939.

It was Rank who, on Tuesday 2 December 1941, took Oscar Deutsch's place at the fourth annual general meeting of Odeon Theatres, held at the Dorchester Hotel. Deutsch expressed his sincere regrets at not being able to attend and a proposal to send him a message of good wishes was unanimously adopted. He was close to death in the London Clinic.

Rank reported that there had been over 100 million admissions to Odeon Theatres during the year under review and net profits had risen to over half a million pounds, although after the dividend was paid on preference shares and taxation and a reserve made against adverse future occurrences, only £22,000 was left and no dividend would be paid on ordinary shares. Rank sought to emphasise that Odeon was doing so well not as a result of the war but because of the maturing of its business as recently opened Odeons developed their full potential to draw customers. With Rank in charge, the occasion noticeably lacked the quick repartee that had been customary between Oscar Deutsch and shareholders.

Three days after the meeting, Oscar Deutsch died in the early hours of Friday 5 December 1941 at the London Clinic, aged 48.[*]

His body was transported to Birmingham for burial in the Jewish cemetery at Witton on the following Sunday morning.

The funeral procession detoured to pass by the first Odeon at Perry Barr where staff had assembled to pay their last respects and the Union Jack flew at half mast.[**] In the afternoon, a memorial service took place at the Singer's Hill Synagogue in Birmingham where Oscar had been warden and president. A further memorial service was held in London on the following Thursday, 11 December, at the Berkeley Street Synagogue where a rabbi from Singer's Hill described how much work Oscar had done on his regular weekends at home to further Jewish causes and to sort out the affairs of the local congregation.

The Cinematograph Exhibitors' Association had often opposed Oscar Deutsch, but its head, Sydney Lewis, made a warm tribute, describing him as "a man beloved by those who knew him well, admired by those who perhaps only knew him a little, and a little envied by those who did not know him much, but nevertheless underlying all was a deep admiration and affection."

As a leading County Cinemas executive, Ralph S. Bromhead knew Oscar well: "I was very fond of him indeed. He wasn't perhaps quite as strong or tough a character as one would have expected, but he was a good man in many ways. I remember him quoting Cecil Rhodes to me: 'So much to do and so little time to do it.'" Like most others, Bromhead had not been aware until the war years that Deutsch suffered from cancer and did not connect the Rhodes remark to his state of health.

Bromhead recalled: "Oscar Deutsch was very proud of a lot of the buildings. He would talk with enthusiasm about a new development on the frontage of one of his latest cinemas. The architectural side certainly appealed to him enormously. I don't remember him being proud of getting the queues in and out quickly and the actual mechanics of running a cinema." (There was a trade joke that if you put Oscar Deutsch and ABC's John Maxwell together in a room, you'd have the two men who knew least about running a cinema.)

Even as devout an admirer as Dickie Dewes was ready to admit that Oscar could be difficult in private: "He was exasperating,

---

[*] There are striking parallels between Oscar Deutsch and another much loved head of a cinema chain who died young – Marcus Loew. The American entrepreneur's unexpected death in his sleep at the age of 57 on 5 September 1927 had shocked the film industry. Physically like Deutsch – a small, bespectacled man of nondescript appearance – Loew created the pre-eminent American circuit of 150 movie theatres and the production-distribution colossus, Metro-Goldwyn-Mayer. According to *Variety,* he had opened twenty-eight new theatres in a single year and had twenty-four under construction at the time of his passing. Although he died from heart failure, Loew suffered from "a long disordered stomach" and had been seriously ill since the preceding winter but refused to stop working. Sources all describe Loew as a financial genius of the utmost integrity, a charismatic figure who was always approachable

and friendly, a man who inspired intense loyalty in his associates, a secret benefactor who shunned the limelight – in other words, a man like Oscar Deutsch.

A second, lesser parallel – but one much closer to home – was the early demise of a well-known Midlands cinema owner, Sol Levy, which shocked fellow exhibitors even though it followed several years of poor health. Levy's offices were below Oscar's in Birmingham when he died in July 1929 at the age of 52.

[**] In 1993, at the instigation of the Birmingham Civic Society, a commemorative plaque was placed in the former Odeon Perry Barr – then a Gala bingo club – by Oscar's oldest son, Ronnie, to mark the centenary of his father's birth.

but possessed some unusual quality which protected him against dislike. His decisions were unpredictable and he was irascible – extremely so. When working with him, one could only maintain tranquillity by keeping in mind the full picture [of his parlous state of health]. Then it was easy. He showed great strength of will in keeping the above tendency under strict control on formal occasions, and at interviews."

Robert Bullivant looked back with affection: "I was only twenty-four when I first met him. Deutsch suffered from cancer and underwent several major operations but he succeeded in keeping this from almost all his business associates. A year or so before he died I began to suspect that all was not well but for about six years I was quite ignorant of his condition. What sort of man was he? He was a quietly spoken, undemonstrative leader of men who commanded respect and often deep affection from most of us who worked for him. He was not more than 5ft. 2ins. tall, with a high-domed bald head and bright eyes which twinkled behind thick lenses. One wondered how he found the energy to work a sixteen-hour day seven days a week.

"Oscar had boundless energy. He had that remarkable quality of Churchill's, that he could take afternoon naps in the little bedroom behind his office and wake up after a couple of hours without any alarm clock and be prepared to work until two o'clock in the morning. He only needed three hours sleep a night.

"Deutsch was very devoted to his wife Lily and to his children. In 1941, we all assumed the cinema was indestructible. Had he lived, he would have fought very hard to keep his chain of Odeons open."

To one young employee, Oscar was an exemplary boss. Dennis Williams recalls: "When I was working at head office in 1940, he was very highly regarded by the staff and I never heard a word said against him. He treated everybody with the greatest respect whether he was a cleaner or an executive. His philosophy was that the company should look after its employees and inspire confidence – which he always did. If anybody had any problems, they could ask to see the boss and he'd always welcome them. And also he said, 'If you ever have any financial difficulties, come and see me because the company is quite prepared to make an interest-free loan to overcome your difficulty and you can pay it back when you're in a position to do so.' I personally can't remember an incident where that was ever effected but it was there if you wanted it. Also, he said to his managers, 'If you're in any financial difficulties, don't try fiddling the company's money. Try asking head office for assistance and assistance will be granted.'"

A junior in the booking department at the outbreak of war, George Pinches recalled not only the charismatic personality of Deutsch but again his generosity. When Deutsch learned that his staff in their new Cookham accommodation were going to provide themselves with a range of recreational facilities to use in their spare time, he immediately insisted on footing the bill.

To some extent, Oscar Deutsch was lucky in the opportunities that came his way, but it took extraordinary nerve and perseverance to seize them and expand at such an astounding rate. Looking at the Odeon empire at the time of Deutsch's death, Dickie Dewes commented: "I think there is every justification for calling it a great achievement. But it certainly wasn't carefully planned or systematically carried out. The background position was such, the obstacles so numerous, and the rate of increase in construction and takeovers so rapid that the approach was not to organise but to improvise – improvise – improvise – in a frantic endeavour to meet the requirements of the present. To my mind, this does not belittle the achievement, but it does make one marvel that the ship ever came within sight of port."

Another veteran colleague, Sidney Swingler, declared: "He had great personal character – a most likable and charming man. He had consideration for everyone who ever worked with him. He had great faith in people and they didn't have to report to him constantly. His attitude was such that you would have done anything in your job to be worthy of the confidence he had in you. He was magnetic in his personality and he had that flair of being able to organise things without doing a lot himself. He never fired anyone without giving them another chance – but they only had one chance."

Swingler summed up Oscar Deutsch by saying warmly: "He was a British gentleman." This is perhaps how Deutsch would have most liked to be remembered. He was intensely patriotic – in part a response to the opportunities this country had given him and his parents – and he took justifiable pride in what he had done to create work in the Depression. The *Kinematograph Weekly*'s obituary went as far as to state: "He can say, with Wren, 'If you seek a monument to me, look around.'"

Oscar Deutsch left an Odeon circuit of 258 cinemas. He had overseen the opening of 141 buildings. He had brought six of his earlier picture houses into the fold. He had added 111 existing cinemas. He had explored the prospect of running the huge Gaumont company as well as Odeon. He had begun to plan the building of Odeons overseas. It fell to another, less imaginative man - J. Arthur Rank - to complete Deutsch's grand vision and to reap the recognition it brought.

THE ODEON RELEASE 1938 - 1941

These are the films that received an Odeon circuit general release, listed in order of appearance. London West End premiere runs of main features would have taken place some weeks earlier, sometimes during the preceding year. (A record of films shown at the Odeon Leicester Square – most of which received an Odeon circuit release – was published in *Picture House* no 11, Winter 1987/88.)

Films listed in brackets were minor B features and were often juggled about, especially outside London. Double bills were also sometimes altered. Where no B feature is indicated, a "full supporting programme" of shorts was shown. Some Odeons did not play the circuit release because of proximity to other Odeons while some mixed Odeon programmes with other releases.

Films marked † were British (or British Empire) in origin. Distributors are abbreviated as follows:

AA	Anglo-American
BL	British Lion
BSS	British Screen Service
Col	Columbia
FN	First National
Fox	20th Century-Fox
GFD	General Film Distributors
GN	Grand National
IFR	International Film Renters
MGM	Metro-Goldwyn-Mayer
Par	Paramount
RKO	RKO Radio
SCD	Sound City Distributors
UA	United Artists
WB	Warner Bros

1938

Cafe Metropole *Fox* (+ The Lady Escapes *Fox*)
† Knight Without Armour *UA* [also Gaumont circuit main feature release]
(+ Crime In The Clouds *FN* or Westbound Limited *GFD*)

A Star Is Born *UA* [also Gaumont circuit main feature release] (+ White Bondage *FN*)
† Action For Slander *UA*
(+ Studio Romance *FN*)
†Gangway *GFD* [also Gaumont circuit main feature release]
(+ Michael O'Halloran *BL*)
Stella Dallas *UA* [also ABC circuit main feature release]
(+ Behind The Mike *GFD*)
†The Squeaker *UA*
(+ Wine, Women And Horses *FN*)
Vogues Of 1938 *UA*
(+ The Life Of The Party *RKO* or
†The Girl In The Taxi *ABFD*)
†The Sky's The Limit *GFD*
(+ Windjammer *RKO*)
52nd Street *UA* (+ †Leave It To Me *BL*)
The Prisoner Of Zenda *UA* [also ABC circuit main feature release]
(+ Carnival Queen *GFD*)
Artists And Models *Par*
(+ She Asked For It *Par*)
†The Rat *RKO* (+ Hideaway *RKO*)
Dead End *UA* [also Gaumont circuit main feature release]
(+ Bulldog Drummond Comes Back *Par*)
Stand In *UA* (+ Riding On Air *RKO*)
†The Return Of The Scarlet Pimpernel *UA* [also Gaumont circuit main feature release] (+ †The Last Adventurers *SCD*)
†Paradise For Two *UA* [also Gaumont circuit main feature release]
(+ West Of Shanghai *FN*)
†Young And Innocent *GFD* [also Gaumont circuit main feature release]
(+ Adventure's End *GFD*)
Make A Wish *RKO*
(+ Expensive Husbands *FN)*
Ebb Tide *Par* (+ Rhythm In The Clouds *BL*)
†The Count Of Monte Cristo *UA revival*
(+ She Loved A Fireman *FN*)

The Perfect Specimen *FN*
(+ Small Town Boy *ABFD*)
†Blondes For Danger *BL*
(+ Dangerous Holiday *BL*)
First Lady *WB*
(+ †Intimate Relations *ABFD*)
Something To Sing About *ABFD*
(+ Wallaby Jim Of The Islands *ABFD)*
†Mademoiselle Docteur *UA*
(+ †Melody And Romance *BL*)
She Married An Artist *Col*
(+ The Trial Of Portia Merriman *BL)*
†I See Ice *ABFD* [also Gaumont circuit main feature release]
(+ Murder In Greenwich Village *Col*)
I Met My Love Again *UA*
(+ No Time To Marry *Col*)
Various *UA* revivals
†Kate Plus Ten *GFD*
(+ Little Miss Roughneck *Col*)
A Slight Case Of Murder *FN*
(+ Mr. Boggs Steps Out *ABFD*)
†Kicking The Moon Around *GFD*
(+ Over The Wall *FN*)
†South Riding *UA* [also Gaumont circuit main feature release] (+ †Mr. Satan *FN*)
Jezebel *FN* (+ Blondes At Work *FN*)
The Hurricane *UA* [also Gaumont circuit main feature release]
Mad About Music *GFD*
(+ Midnight Intruder *GFD*)
Snow White And The Seven Dwarfs *RKO* [also Gaumont circuit main feature release]
†The Divorce Of Lady X *UA*
(+ Condemned Women *RKO*)
†Break The News *GFD*
(+ A Dangerous Age *FN*)
Nothing Sacred *UA* [also Gaumont circuit main feature release]
(+ The Lone Wolf In Paris *Col*)
†Thank Evans *FN*
(+ Women Are Like That *WB*)

†The Drum *UA* [also Gaumont circuit main feature release] (+ Thunder Mountain *ABFD* or Penrod And His Twin Brother *FN*)

Gold Is Where You Find It *WB* (+ Rascals *Fox*)

The Goldwyn Follies *UA* [also Gaumont circuit main feature release] (+ The Crime Of Dr. Hallet *GFD*)

†The Challenge *UA* (+ Swing Your Lady *WB*)

The Adventures Of Marco Polo *UA* [also Gaumont circuit main feature release] (+ Love, Honour And Behave *FN*)

Blockade *UA* (+ †Around the Town *BL*)

Crime School *WB* [Gaumont circuit main feature release] (+ Professor Beware *Par*)

Spawn Of The North *Par* (+ County Fair *Pathe*)

†This Man Is News *Par* (+ Penrod's Double Trouble *WB*)

†Sixty Glorious Years *RKO*

1939

†Pygmalion *GFD* (+ Sinners In Paradise *GFD* or Call Of The Yukon *BL*)

The Adventures Of Tom Sawyer *UA* [also Gaumont circuit main feature release] (+ Goodbye Broadway *GFD*)

The Texans *Par* (+ His Lordship Goes To Press *RKO*)

Algiers *UA* (+ Red Lights Ahead *BSS* or †Old Mother Riley In Paris *Butcher's*)

†Prison Without Bars UA (+ Bulldog Drummond In Africa *Par*)

Marie Antoinette *MGM* [also Gaumont circuit main feature release]

The Hounds Of Zaroff *RKO revival* (+ Men Are Such Fools *WB*)

Little Tough Guy *GFD* (+ Secrets Of An Actress *WB*)

There Goes My Heart *UA* (+ various)

Room Service *RKO* (+ Old Iron *BL*)

Men With Wings *Par* (+ Fugitives For A Night *RKO*)

†The Return Of The Frog *BL* (+ Mother Carey's Chickens *RKO*)

The Young In Heart *UA* [also Gaumont circuit main feature release] (+ Illegal Traffic *Par*)

†Stolen Life *Par* [also at some Gaumonts] (+ Personal Secretary *GFD*)

Little Tough Guys In Society *GFD* (+ The Higgins Family *BL*)

Letter Of Introduction *GFD* (+ Secrets Of A Nurse *GFD*)

The Cowboy And The Lady *UA* [also Gaumont circuit main feature release] (+ Disbarred *Par*)

Service De Luxe *GFD* (+ The Storm *GFD*)

†The Ware Case *ABFD* (+ Mama Runs Wild *BL*)

Say It In French *Par* (+ Arrest Bulldog Drummond *Par*)

Pacific Liner *RKO* (+ His Exciting Night *GFD*)

The Duke Of West Point *UA* [also Gaumont circuit main feature release] (+ Pirates Of The Skies *GFD*)

Topper Takes A Trip *UA* [also Gaumont circuit main feature release] (+ Strange Faces *GFD*)

King Of The Turf *UA* (+ Shadows Over Shanghai *GN*)

†Pygmalion *GFD revival* (+ I Stand Accused *BL*)

†The Mind Of Mr. Reeder *GN* (+ Beauty For The Asking *RKO*)

You Can't Cheat An Honest Man *GFD* (+ Newsboys' Home *GFD*)

What A Woman! *Col* (+ I Cover The Waterfront *UA revival*)

†The Lady Vanishes *MGM revival* (+ †The Drum *UA revival*)

†Trouble Brewing *ABFD* [also Gaumont circuit main feature release] (+ The Saint Strikes Back *RKO* or various)

†I Killed The Count *GN* (+ Fisherman's Wharf *RKO*)

Captain Fury *UA* (+ Twelve Crowded Hours *RKO*)

Elephants Never Forget *UA* (+ various)

Love Affair *RKO* (+ They Made Her A Spy *RKO*)

†Q Planes *Col* (+ My Son Is A Criminal *Col*)

†The Four Feathers *UA* [also Gaumont circuit main feature release]

Idiot's Delight *MGM* (+ Magnificent Outcast *RKO*)

Three Smart Girls Grow Up *GFD*

Stagecoach *UA* (+ Woman Doctor *BL*)

†The Lambeth Walk *MGM* (+ The Flying Irishman *RKO*)

†The Mikado *GFD* (+ Society Smugglers *GFD*)

†The Spy In Black *Col* (+ Tomorrow At Midnight *GFD*)

†Good-Bye Mr Chips! *MGM* [also Gaumont/circuit main feature release]

Wuthering Heights *UA* [also Gaumont circuit main feature release] (+ Undercover Doctor *Par*)

Nurse Edith Cavell *RKO* (+ Bulldog Drummond's Bride *Par*)

†The Lion Has Wings *UA* (+ Second Fiddle *Fox*)

Double Crime In The Maginot Line *UA* (+ †Keep Your Seats, Please! *ABFD revival*)

Winter Carnival *UA* (+ †What Would You Do, Chums? *AA*)

†Cheer, Boys, Cheer *ABFD* (+ †Soldiers Of The King *GN revival*)

The Underpup *GFD* (+ Big Town Czar *GFD*)

1940

†Come On, George! *ABFD* (+ What A Life *Par*)

Professor Mamlock *BL* (+ †Young Man's Fancy *ABFD*)

†Inspector Hornleigh On Holiday *Fox* (+ Quick Millions *Fox*)

The Man In The Iron Mask *UA* (+ †Full Speed Ahead *GFD*)

Husbands Or Lovers *Par* (+ †An Englishman's Home *UA*)

Frontier Marshal *Fox* (+ Boy Friend *Fox*)

The Light That Failed *Par* (+ †Mr. Chedworth Steps Out *ABFD*)

†Over The Moon *UA* (+ †Meet Maxwell Archer *RKO*)

†The Stars Look Down *BL* (+ Night Work *Par*)

The Great Victor Herbert *Par* (+ If I Had A Million *Par revival*)

†Laugh It Off *AA* (+ †Return To Yesterday *ABFD*)

Hollywood Cavalcade *Fox* (+ Too Busy To Work *Fox*)

The Housekeeper's Daughter *UA* (+ Television Spy *Par*)

Sherlock Holmes *Fox* (+ Arizona Wildcat *Fox*)

Eternally Yours *UA* (+ †The Chinese Bungalow *BL*)

Destry Rides Again *GFD* (+ †Mrs. Pym Of Scotland Yard *GN*)

Hitler – Beast of Berlin *BL* (+ Adventure In Diamonds *Par*)

†21 Days *Col*
  (+ The Gracie Allen Murder Case *Par*)
Under Two Flags *Fox*
  (+ Charlie Chan In Reno *Fox*)
†Contraband *AA*
  (+ Money Isn't Everything *BL*)
Tower Of London *GFD*
  (+ Legion Of Lost Flyers *GFD*)
Of Mice And Men *UA*
Road To Singapore *Par*
  (+ The Witness Vanishes *GFD*)
Geronimo *Par* (+ †Inquest *BL*)
He Married His Wife *Fox*
  (+ The Man Who Wouldn't Talk *Fox*)
Green Hell *GFD* (+ Slightly Honorable *UA*)
My Little Chickadee *GFD*
  (+ One Third Of A Nation *GN*)
The Invisible Man Returns *GFD*
  (+ Two Bright Boys *GFD*)
Safari *Par* (+ Desire *Par revival*)
Rio *GFD* (+ Call A Messenger *GFD*)
Typhoon *Par* (+ Calling All Marines *BL*)
If I Had My Way *GFD*
  (+ The Farmer's Daughter *Par*)
Little Old New York *Fox*
  (+ The Big Guy *GFD*)
The Grapes Of Wrath *Fox*
  (+ Young As You Feel *Fox*)
The Blue Bird *Fox*
  (+ Emergency Squad *Par*)
†Gaslight *AA* (+ The Covered Trailer *BL*)
It's A Date *GFD*
  (+ Danger On Wheels *GFD*)
Johnny Apollo *Fox* (+ High School *Fox*)
Lillian Russell *Fox* (+ Framed *GFD*)
†The Case Of The Frightened Lady *BL*
  (+ Alias The Deacon *GFD*)
The Ghost Breakers *Par*
  (+ Charlie Chan In Panama *Fox*)
I Was An Adventuress *Fox*
  (+ On Their Own *Fox*)
Dr. Cyclops *Par* (+ †Room For Two *BL*)
Shooting High *Fox* (+ Lady Be Gay *GFD*)
Star Dust *Fox* (+ Girl In 313 *Fox*)
†It's In The Air *ABFD revival* or
  †The Private Life Of Henry VIII *UA revival*
  (+ Oh! Johnny, How You Can Love *GFD*)
†Under Your Hat *BL* (+ Earthbound *Fox*)
New Moon *MGM*
  (+ Down Went McGinty *Par*)
The Last Outpost *Par revival*
  (+ Free, Blonde And 21 *Fox*)
Black Friday *GFD* (+ La Conga Nights *GFD*)

Buck Benny Rides Again *Par*
  (+ Queen Of The Mob *Par*)
It's A Date *GFD revival*
  (+ The Way Of All Flesh *Par*)
Young People *Fox* (+ Money To Burn *BL*)

1941
I Want A Divorce *Par*
  (+ The House Of The Seven Gables *GFD*)
A Little Bit Of Heaven *GFD*
  (+ Manhattan Heartbeat *Fox*)
Hired Wife *GFD* (+ †Pastor Hall *BL*)
They Knew What They Wanted *RKO*
  (+ Life With Henry *Par*)
Rhythm On The River *Par*
  (+ South To Karanga *GFD*)
Argentine Nights *GFD*
  (+ †You Will Remember *BL*)
Rangers Of Fortune *Par*
  (+ Dancing On A Dime *Par*)
The Great Dictator *UA* [also Gaumont
  circuit main feature release]
The Mark Of Zorro *Fox*
  (+ Yesterday's Heroes *Fox*)
The Thief Of Bagdad *UA* [also Gaumont
  circuit main feature release]
  (+ Slightly Tempted *GFD*)
The Man I Married *Fox*
  (+ The Girl From Avenue 'A' *Fox*)
A Date With Destiny *Par*
  (+ Too Many Girls *RKO*)
Christmas In July *Par*
  (+ Convoy *ABFD revival*)
North West Mounted Police *Par*
Escape *MGM*
  (+ Mexican Spitfire Out West *RKO*)
†Quiet Wedding *Par*
  (+ World In Flames *Par*)
Seven Sinners *GFD*
  (+ Charlie Chan At The Wax Museum *Fox*)
Arise My Love *Par*
  (+ I'm Still Alive *RKO*)
Trail Of The Vigilantes *GFD*
  (+ Rumba *Par revival*)
†The Ghost Of St. Michael's *ABFD*
  (+ San Francisco Docks *GFD*)
Second Chorus *Par* (+ †Crooks' Tour *AA*)
Back Street *GFD*
  (+ Sandy Gets Her Man *GFD*)
Victory *Par* (+ A Night At Earl Carroll's *Par*)
Chad Hanna *Fox* (+ Half A Sinner *GFD*)
Virginia *Par* (+ Rookies *GFD*)

†Love On The Dole *AA*
  (+ We're Not Dressing *Par revival*)
The Invisible Woman *GFD*
  (+ The Quarterback *Par*)
Nice Girl? *GFD*
  (+ †The Man At The Gate *GFD*)
Cheers For Miss Bishop *UA*
  (+ His Affair *Fox revival*)
†Pimpernel Smith *AA*
  (+ Texas Rangers Ride Again *Par*)
†Major Barbara *GFD*
  (+ I'm Nobody's Sweetheart Now *GFD*)
That Night In Rio *Fox*
  (+ For Beauty's Sake *Fox*)
The Lady From Cheyenne *GFD*
  (+ †Target For Tonight *ABFD*)
†Once A Crook *Fox*
  (+ Romance Of Rio Grande *Fox*)
Moon Over Burma *Par*
  (+ Golden Hoofs *Fox*)
†Jeannie *GFD*
  (+ One Night In The Tropics *GFD*)
Caught In The Draft *Par*
  (+ Murder Among Friends *Fox*)
†He Found A Star *GFD*
  (+ Secret Interlude *Fox revival*)
Lady Hamilton *UA*
One Night In Lisbon *Par*
  (+ The Leatherpushers *GFD*)
Hold Back The Dawn *Par*
  (+ Pirates On Horseback *Par*)
Billy The Kid *MGM*
  (+ Dance Hall *Fox*)
Man Hunt *Fox*
  (+ †Keep Fit *ABFD revival*)
In The Navy *GFD*
  (+ The Man Who Lost Himself *GFD*
Nothing But The Truth *Par*
Deanna Durbin Repertory Week:
  one day showings of (all *GFD*)
  Three Smart Girls/100 Men And A Girl/
  Mad About Music/That Certain Age/
  Three Smart Girls Grow Up/First Love
†49th Parallel *GFD*
Skylark *Par* (+ Accent On Love *Fox*)
Shepherd Of The Hills *Par*
  (+ †Friday The 13th *IFR* or various)
Kiss The Boys Good-Bye *Par*
  (+ Ride On, Vaquero *Par*)
Aloma Of The South Seas *Par*
  (+ West Point Widow *Par*)
Moon Over Miami *Fox*
  (+ Sealed Lips *GFD*)

ODEON OPENINGS AND TAKEOVERS: A CHRONOLOGY

This is a complete list, in order of opening, of all the cinemas that were built and/or opened by Oscar Deutsch and his associates, including all the cinemas that were opened as Odeons before the Second World War.

New cinemas are in larger type. Each new Odeon is styled "The ODEON Theatre" in accordance with company practice in opening brochures of the 1930s.

Cinemas in smaller type are those already operating which were taken over and directly operated by Deutsch and Odeon, or openings not directly related to the circuit.

The list does not include cinemas which were booked or managed by Deutsch's Cinema Service (which are mentioned in the text). Information in brackets refers to periods before and/or after Odeon/Deutsch ownership. Takeover dates refer, as far as possible, to when cinemas were first operated by Odeon/ Deutsch but, because of vagueness in sources, may refer to the date when contracts were exchanged or the change of ownership announced. Because of the large number of properties involved, it has not been possible to check every detail, especially of post-Odeon usage.

To stay in period, counties or districts are those that the cinemas were in at time of opening or takeover.

The quoted cost of cinemas is for basic construction and is primarily useful for comparison between buildings. Outfitting cost a further £6-7,000, depending on the size of cinema, with the majority of the cost being seating and carpeting.

In the forthcoming second volume of this Odeon history, the same information will be presented in alphabetical order by town, as in preceding volumes on the ABC, Gaumont and Granada circuits. The Odeon list will then also include the further cinemas taken over and opened up to February 2000 when the Rank Group sold Odeon.

1925

Monday 1 June: **CROWN COVENTRY,** Warwickshire – Far Gosford Street. (Opened circa September 1912, architect: J. H. Gilbert. 850 seats.) (Sold early 1928. Temporarily closed October 1940 by air raid damage. Closed October 1957 for modernisation. Re-opened 1 March 1958, renamed Paris. Closed January 1978. Re-opened 1978. Closed 25 March 1980. Re-opened 26 October 1980. Closed 21 November 1981. Riley's American Pool and Snooker Club in 2001.)

And **GLOBE COVENTRY,** Warwickshire – Primrose Hill Street. (Opened September 1914. Architect: J. H. Gilbert.) (Leased from 2 April 1934 to Charles Orr.) Taken back circa 1939. Closed 1 December 1956. (Ballroom. Mecca bingo club from circa 1963. Walkers bingo club from 1987. Closed 1989. TicToc entertainment venue from 1990.)

1928

Monday 1 October: **PICTURE HOUSE BRIERLEY HILL,** Staffordshire – High Street. Architect: Stanley A. Griffiths. Taken into the Odeon circuit 17 July 1935. 944 seats: 680 stalls + 264 balcony. Renamed ODEON January 1936. Closed 25 July 1959. (Demolished. Supermarket, initially Fine Fare.)

1929

Circa January: **SILVER WORCESTER,** Worcestershire – Foregate Street. The company to acquire the cinema was formed in January. (Opened 1919.) Taken into the Odeon circuit 17 July 1935. 739 (or 741) seats. Closed March 1939. (Demolished March 1939 and construction of an Odeon started on an enlarged site.)

1930

Monday August 4: **The ODEON Theatre PERRY BARR,** Birmingham – Birchfield Road, between Canterbury Road and Thornbury Road. Architects: Stanley A. Griffiths, Horace G. Bradley. Taken into the Odeon circuit on 17 July 1935. 1,638 seats: 1,160 stalls + 478 circle. 1,494 seats in 1961. Closed 3 May 1969. (Re-opened 14 August 1969 as Top Rank Club for bingo. Façade completely rebuilt around this time. Closed 19 February 1983. Taken over by Dale Leisure and re-opened 27 October 1983 as Perry Social Club for bingo. Taken over 1985 by Granada, renamed Granada. Taken over May 1991 by Gala, renamed Gala. Closed 5 April 1997. Disused in June 2001.)

1931

Thursday April 16: **ROYAL ALFRETON,** Derbyshire – High Street. Architect: Harry Clayton. Taken into the Odeon circuit

17 July 1935. 1,450 seats: 1,103 stalls + 347 balcony. Renamed ODEON circa 1936. Closed 30 May 1964. (Demolished April 1965. Boots store on part of site.)

November: **GROSVENOR BLOXWICH**, Walsall – High Street. (Opened 11 December 1922 on site of Electric. Architects: Hickton & Farmer. Renamed Grosvenor 11 December 1922.) Taken into the Odeon circuit 17 July 1935. Renamed ODEON. 939 seats. Closed 2 May 1959. (Flix nightclub. Youth club in 2001.)

Date unknown: **EMPIRE SEAFORD**, Sussex – Sutton Road. (Opened circa 1912.) (Subleased to Langdon Enterprises from March 1932. Destroyed by fire early 1 March 1939.)

1932

Date unknown: **PREMIER WESTON-SUPER-MARE.** (Opened pre-1914 as Electric. Closed circa 1931.) (Demolished January 1933. Part of site for new Odeon – see 25 May 1935.)

1933

Friday 2 June: **The ODEON Theatre WEYMOUTH,** Dorset – Gloucester Street. Architect: Harry Clayton. £1,800 conversion of former bus garage. Decorative scheme: Allied Guilds (John Jackson). 541 seats (one floor). (Taken over 10 December 1967 by Classic, renamed Classic. Renamed Cannon. Taken over 14 January 1994 by Picturedrome Theatres, renamed Picturedrome. 418 seats. Closed 31 October 1999. Children's play zone.) [Subsequent Odeon was Gaumont renamed.]

Monday 3 July: **The ODEON Theatre KINGSTON,** Surrey – 24/28 High Street. Architects: Col. James E. Adamson, Marshall & Tweedy. 1,516 seats: 990 stalls + 526 balcony. £34,016. Closed 15 July 1967. (Re-opened 10 August 1967 as Top Rank Club for bingo. Closed 9 August 1987. Demolished circa 1989. Site vacant.)

Saturday 5 August: **FRIARS CANTERBURY,** Kent – The Friars. Architects: Alfred & Vincent Burr. 1,291 seats: 878 stalls + 413 balcony. £20,811. Renamed ODEON 4 April 1938. Renamed FRIARS in 1938. Renamed ODEON 16 December 1955. Closed 17 October 1981. (Re-opened 8 July 1984 after extensive alterations as Marlowe live theatre, seating 993. Open in June 2001.)

Monday 4 September: **The ODEON Theatre SOUTH HARROW,** Middlesex – 337 Northolt Road, between Scarsdale Road and Wyvenhoe Road. Architect: A. Percival Starkey. 997 seats, stadium: 718 front + 279 rear. £10,874. Closed 12 February 1972. (Auditorium and foyer area demolished & replaced by Duncan House block of flats. Wings remain.)

Monday October 31: **The ODEON Theatre LANCING,** Sussex – 45/49 Penhill Road. Architect: unknown ("arranged by builder"). 691 seats (one floor). £9,600. Renamed REGAL 2 March 1936. (Taken over 7 March 1939 by B. E. Fortesque. Closed 23 March 1940. Taken over by Mrs. Merriman Langdon & re-opened 16 October 1941.) Taken back 30 August 1942. Renamed ODEON 25 March 1945. Closed 20 January 1952. (Taken over by Shipman & King and put up for sale without re-opening. Chromium plating works. Welding and engineering workshop. Regal House in 1996: auditorium area used by Ingleside Garage with new roof and entrance, plumbers' merchants Leamey's of Lancing in foyer area and former shop, offices on first floor and elsewhere.)

Date unknown: **SAVOY WIMBLEDON,** London S.W.19 – Worple Road. (Closed circa 1933.)(Demolished as part of site for new Odeon – see 20 April 1936.)

1934

Monday 8 January: **The ODEON Theatre WORCESTER PARK,** Surrey – Central Road, corner of Windsor Road. Architects: Yates, Cook and Darbyshire. 894 seats: 543 stalls + 351 balcony. £16,125. Closed 29 September 1956. (Supermarket, initially Macmarket, later International and Somerfield. Closed. Demolished 1998. Public library.)

Tuesday 9 January: **The ODEON Theatre TOLWORTH, Surrey** – Hook Rise, Kingston By-Pass Road. Architects: Yates, Cook and Darbyshire. 891 seats: 439 stalls + 452 balcony. £10,983. Closed 10 October 1959. (Demolished March 1961. Tolworth Tower – Marks & Spencer food store with office block above.)

Thursday 1 February: **The ODEON Theatre KEMP TOWN,** Brighton, Sussex – 38 St. George's Road, corner of Paston Place. Architect: Andrew Mather. £7,838 (adaptation of an existing structure). 958 seats, stadium: 556 front section + 402 raised rear section. Closed 14 September 1940 by bomb damage. Restored and re-opened Boxing Day 1940. Closed 5 November 1960. (Re-opened 1962 as bingo club. Sold 4 September 1972 to Boswell Concessions – Kemptown Bingo and Social Club. Religious centre: 'The City'. Demolished January 1986. Cavendish Court block of flats.)

Saturday 24 March: **The ODEON Theatre WORTHING,** Sussex – Liverpool Road. Architects: Whinney, Son & Austen Hall. £32,500. 1,531 seats: 1,076 stalls + 455 balcony). Triple from 6 June 1974, seating 450 in former balcony + 120 & 120 in former rear stalls. Closed 27 September 1986. (Listed Grade II Spring 1987. De-listed. Demolished late 1987. Part of shopping mall and offices.)

Tuesday 27 March: **ROTHBURY PORTSLADE,** Sussex – Franklin Road. Architect: George Coles. Adaptation of building planned and partly built as an assembly hall. 548 seats (one floor). Associated with Odeon at opening. (Locally run from start. Taken over by Langdon Enterprises. Taken over by Robert Gordon Cinemas. Closed 19 January 1964. Bingo hall. Radio House from 1983, extensively converted. Home of Southern FM Classic Hits in 1993.)

Monday 9 April: **The ODEON Theatre WEYBRIDGE,** Surrey – Queens Road, corner of York Road. Architect: A. P. Starkey. £14,300. 912 seats: 656 stalls + 256 balcony). Closed 31 December 1960. (Roman Catholic Church of St. Martin de Porres.)

Saturday 14 April: **The ODEON Theatre SURBITON,** Surrey – Claremont Road. Architect: Joseph Hill. Interior designers: Mollo & Egan. £28,000. 1,502 seats: 974 stalls + 528 balcony. Closed 8 February 1975. (Sapphire Carpet & Furniture Centre. Closed 1977. B&Q store. Closed. Demolished March 1999. Waitrose supermarket.)

Saturday 26 May: **The ODEON Theatre WALLINGTON,** Surrey – corner of Woodcote Road and Ross Parade. Architects: Yates, Cook & Darbyshire. £17,250. 925 seats, stadium: 574 front + 351 rear section. Closed 27 April 1957. (Auditorium demolished for Wallis supermarket. Whispering Moon public house from 1993, still retaining corner entrance.)

Wednesday 30 May: **The ODEON Theatre KINGSBURY,** London N.W.9 – 632/8 Kingsbury Road. Architect: A. P. Starkey. £14,941. 1,003 seats: 724 stalls + 279 balcony. Renamed GAUMONT 20 March 1950. Renamed ODEON 30 May 1964. Closed 9 September 1972. (Demolished except for wings. Supermarket, originally J. Sainsbury but Aldi in 2001 with flats and Fitness First health club above.)

Saturday 2 June: **The ODEON Theatre LEWES,** Sussex – Cliffe High Street. Architect: Andrew Mather. £14,023. 986 seats, semi-stadium: 518 front + 468 rear. Closed 2 October 1971. (Sold 20 April 1972 to A. L. Hawton. Demolished 1982. Shops and housing.)

Saturday 14 July: **The ODEON Theatre BOGNOR REGIS,** Sussex – 64 London Road. Architects: Whinney, Son & Austen Hall. £15,949. 920 seats, stadium: 592 front + 328 rear. (Leased to independent from 23 January 1971, renamed Regal. Closed 16 November 1974 to become Regal bingo club. Renamed Crown bingo club December 1987.) [Subsequent Odeon is part of Southcoast World holiday centre elsewhere.]

Saturday 29 September: **The ODEON Theatre HAVERSTOCK HILL,** Hampstead, London N.W.3 – 201 Haverstock Hill. Also known as ODEON BELSIZE PARK and ODEON HAMPSTEAD. Architects: T. P. Bennett & Son. Approx. £35,000. 1,544 seats, stadium: 652 front + 892 rear. Closed October 1941 by bomb damage. Restored, architects: T. P. Bennett & Son, and re-opened 13 December 1954, seating 1,466. Closed 23 September 1972. (Demolished. Budgens supermarket, and – later, through former adjacent shop entrance – Screen on the Hill, opened 9 November 1977.)

Monday 15 October: **The ODEON Theatre WEALDSTONE,** Middlesex – corner of High Road and Bruce Road. Architect: A. P. Starkey (assistant: Frederick Adkins). £23,566. 1,222 seats: 880 stalls + 342 balcony. Closed 4 March 1961. (Demolished in early 1970s. Marlborough House office block.)

Saturday 20 October: **The ODEON Theatre BLACKHEATH,** Worcestershire – Long Lane. Also known as ODEON QUINTON AND BLACKHEATH. Architect: Stanley A. Griffiths. £14,706. 1,228 seats, stadium: 796 front + 432 rear. Closed 19 November 1960. (Bingo club from 10 February 1967. Ballroom. B&Q DIY store by 1982. Demolished 1984.)

Monday 22 October: **The ODEON Theatre WELLING,** Kent – Upper Wickham Lane. Architect: George Coles. £21,580. 1,374 seats: 928 stalls + 450 balcony. Closed 22 October 1960. (Top Rank bingo club. Refurbished 1994, entrance heavily altered. Open in June 1999, renamed Mecca).

Saturday 24 November: **The ODEON Theatre CLEVELEYS,** Lancashire – Crescent West & Runnymede Avenue. Architect: George Tonge. £24,234. 1,156 seats: 900 stalls + 256 balcony. Closed 7 January 1961. (Live theatre from 1961 with dressing rooms added. Orion bingo from 1965. Open in 2000.)

Saturday 22 December: **The WARLEY, WEST WARLEY,** Warwickshire – Hagley Road West and Wolverhampton New Road. Architects: (exterior) T. Cecil Howitt, (interior) Harry Weedon (assistant: J. Cecil Clavering); Roland Satchwell. £33,185. 1,530 seats: 1,066 stalls + 464 balcony. Renamed WARLEY ODEON circa 1935. 1,506 seats in 1960. Closed 25 November 1961 for conversion to bowling alley. (Warley Bowl opened 3 September 1962. Closed 29 April 1970. Demolished early 1973. Office block.)

1935

Monday 28 January: **The ODEON Theatre COLINDALE,** London N.W.9 – Wakemans Hill Parade, 287 Edgware Road. (With attached shops, 279/295 Edgware Road.) Architect: A. P. Starkey (assistant: Frederick Adkins). £18,080. 1,005 seats, stadium: 726 front + 279 rear. Closed 24 September 1960. (Reopened by independent late 1967, renamed Curzon. Taken over 2 January 1972 by Classic, renamed Classic. Classic 2 opened 27 January 1973 in one half of rear section. Classic 2 renamed Tatler Film Club from 27 January 1974. Tatler reverted to Classic 2 from 2 April 1978. Both closed 4 July 1981. Colindale Snooker Club from circa 1986, open in 2001.)

Monday 11 March: **The ODEON Theatre KENTON,** Middlesex – 202 Kenton Road. Architect: George Coles. £28,905. 1,396 seats: 979 stalls + 417 balcony. Closed 25 March 1961. Demolished. (Waitrose supermarket & Brent House office block in 1993. Pick & Save supermarket in 2001.)

Wednesday 20 March: **The ODEON Theatre ISLEWORTH,** Middlesex – corner of London Road and Harvard Road.

Architect: George Coles. £31,268 (excluding shops). 1,408 seats: 994 stalls + 414 balcony. Closed 5 January 1957. (Isleworth Studios. Auditorium completely transformed. Closed.)

Monday 15 April: **The ODEON Theatre SHIRLEY**, Warwickshire – corner of Solihull Lane and Stratford Road, Solihull. Architect: Satchwell & Roberts (Roland Satchwell). £21,149. 1,156 seats: 768 stalls + 388 balcony. Part-week bingo. Closed 29 October 1977. (Full-time bingo from 10 March 1978. Closed. Demolished September-October 1985.)

And **PALLADIUM BRIGHTON**, Sussex – 85 King's Road. (Opened 6 April 1912 as Palladium cinema, former live theatre. 1,000 seats.) Modernised by Odeon, architect: Andrew Mather. Renamed ODEON 8 June 1935. Renamed PALLADIUM 28 November 1937. Closed 26 October 1940. (Taken over circa 1942 by independent. Closed 26 May 1956 by Compulsory Purchase Order. Demolished 1963. Part of site for Brighton Centre.)

Monday 22 April: **WHITE HALL DERBY**, Derbyshire – St Peters Street. (Opened 14 December 1914. 870 seats. Taken over circa January 1929 by ABC.) 913 seats in 1935. Closed 29 June 1935 for modernisation. Re-opened 3 August 1935, renamed ODEON. Closed 1 May 1965. (Demolished. British Home Stores.)

Monday 13 May: **The ODEON Theatre GUILDFORD**, Surrey – Upper High Street, Epsom Road and Jenner Road. Architects: Andrew Mather and J. Raworth Hill. £32,613. 1,623 seats: 1,145 stalls & 478 balcony. Triple from 19 August 1973, seating 452 in former balcony, 121 & 121 in former rear stalls. Fourth cinema in front stalls from February 1989, seating 320. All closed 12 December 1996. (Disused.) [Present Odeon is new multiplex elsewhere.]

Wednesday 15 May: **The ODEON Theatre BARNET**, Hertfordshire – Underhill, Western Parade, Great North Road. Architect: Edgar Simmons. £29,130. 1,553 seats: 1,010 stalls + 543 balcony. Triple from 10 March 1974, seating 543 in former balcony + 130 & 130 in former rear stalls. Grade II listed building from 13 October 1985. Fourth cinema in former front stalls opened 18 December 1992, seating 217. Fifth cinema on former stage opened 28 December 1992, seating 158. Open in June 2001, seating 528 + 140 + 150 + 193 + 158.

Saturday 25 May: **The ODEON Theatre WESTON-SUPER-MARE**, Somerset – The Centre, at Locking Road and Walliscote Road. Partly built on site of Electric/Premier cinema, demolished in January 1933. Architect: T. Cecil Howitt. 1,807 seats: 1,174 stalls + 633 balcony. Triple from 23 December 1973, seating 632 in former balcony + 110 & 133 in rear stalls. Grade II listed building from 21 August 1986. Fourth cinema opened in former front stalls, seating 268. Open in June 2001, seating 590 + 109 + 1230 + 264.

Monday 27 May: **ROYALTY BROADSTAIRS**, Kent - York Street. (Opened 15 October 1934, architect: P. V. Levett. 788 seats, stadium.) See 8 April 1938.

Wednesday 17 July: pre-circuit properties taken into Odeon circuit – **ROYAL ALFRETON, GROSVENOR BLOXWICH, PICTURE**

HOUSE BRIERLEY HILL, ODEON PERRY BARR and **SILVER WORCESTER** (see earlier for details).

Monday 22 July: **The ODEON Theatre KINGSTANDING**, Birmingham – junction of Kings Road and Kettlehouse Road, Birmingham 44. Architect: Harry W. Weedon (assistant: J. Cecil Clavering). £21,450. 1,292 seats: 968 stalls + 324 balcony. Closed 2 December 1962. (Re-opened 6 December 1962 as the Top Rank Club for bingo. Grade II listed building from 10 October 1980. Renamed Mecca. Open in June 2001.)

Monday 29 July: takeover of HINCKLEY AND DURSLEY THEATRES, comprising:

VICTORIA DURSLEY, Gloucestershire – Silver Street. (Opened circa 1918, adaptation of Victoria Coffee Rooms, architect: O. Wainwright.) 333 seats in 1939: 231 stalls + 102 balcony. Closed 24 January 1947 by severe fire damage early next day. Re-opened August 1948, renamed ODEON. Closed 30 October 1954. (Indoor market.)

NEW BORO' HINCKLEY, Leicestershire – The Borough. (Opened 4 or 11 April 1935 incorporating Old Boro' cinemas as foyer.) 967 seats: 658 stalls + 309 balcony. Renamed ODEON 1 January 1936. Closed 3 June 1961. (Demolished. Anglia Building Society offices.)

REGENT HINCKLEY, Leicestershire – Rugby Road and Lancaster Road. (Opened 11 March 1929, architect: Horace G. Bradley. Designed for theatre and cinema use, opened with live show.) 970 seats: 670 stalls + 300 balcony. Renamed GAUMONT 18 April 1955. 897 seats in 1967. (Taken over 2 December 1967 by Classic, renamed Classic. Closed 30 June 1968. Bingo.)

And **PALLADIUM HINCKLEY**, Leicestershire. Dance hall. (Former cinema, closed circa 1929.) Not re-opened as cinema.

Also (same day): **ROYAL TORQUAY**, Devon – 29 Abbey Road. (Opened 27 March 1933, former Theatre Royal.) Renamed ODEON 12 April 1937. 883 seats in 1939: 571 stalls + 312 balcony. Closed 27 October 1973 for twinning. Re-opened 24 March 1974, seating 360 downstairs + 309 upstairs. Closed November 1999. (Taken over by Merlin Cinemas, re-opened 11 February 2000 as Central. Downstairs cinema tripled in 2001. All open in June 2001.)

Wednesday 31 July: **REGAL BATH**, Somerset – 16 Southgate Street. (Opened pre-1914 as Picturedrome. Enlarged 1930, renamed Regal. Taken over by Union.) Renamed ODEON 2 December 1935. 863 seats in 1939: 714 stalls + 149 balcony. 779 seats. Closed circa December 1969. (Taken over 25 December 1969 by City of London Real Property. Demolished for shopping centre.)

Monday 9 September: **The ODEON Theatre CHINGFORD**, London E.4 – Cherrydown Avenue, Chingford Mount. Architect: Andrew Mather. 1,400 seats (approx.). 1,142 seats in 1967. (Taken over 10 December 1967 by Classic, renamed Classic. Closed 3 June 1972. Demolished. Wallis supermarket, later Gateway, Poundstretcher in 2001 – plus offices.)

Monday 16 September: **The ODEON Theatre SUDBURY TOWN**, Greenford, Middlesex – Odeon Parade, Allendale Road, Sudbury Heights. Later known as ODEON SUDBURY. Architect: A. P. Starkey (assistant: Frederick Adkins). £16,665. 1,009 seats, semi-stadium: 730 front + 279 rear. Closed 27 October 1956. (Frontage rebuilt, foyer and auditorium rebuilt within old walls and occupied by Starlite Bingo and Social Club. Sudbury Town Nursery School on ground floor and Starlite

Snooker Club above in 2001. Sudbury House offices at rear on Sudbury Heights Avenue within part of old auditorium.)

Tuesday 24 September: **LYCEUM TAUNTON,** Somerset – Station Road. (Opened circa August 1913, architects: Stone and Lloyd. Altered, architect: F. C. Mitchell, and re-opened 4 January 1932.) Renamed ODEON circa 1936. Improved in late 1930s, architect: Andrew Mather, 681 seats: 432 stalls + 249 balcony. 673 seats in 1967. (Taken over December 1967 by Classic, renamed Classic. Classic 2 added April 1970, seating 71. Renamed Cannon in 1985. Both closed 10 October 1990. Taken over by independent and re-opened 11 December 1992, renamed Plaza. Closed 25 August 1994. Demolished December 1998. Laverock Court block of flats.)

Monday 14 October: **The ODEON Theatre FINCHLEY,** London N.12 – 894 High Road, from corner of Mayfield Avenue to corner of Friern Watch Avenue, North Finchley. Architect: A. P. Starkey (assistant: Frederick Adkins). 1,296 seats, semi-stadium: 878 front + 418 rear. Closed 26 December 1964. (Garage and showrooms for Halls [Finchley] Ltd. Frontage largely rebuilt. Furnitureland.)

Mid-October: **PALACE THEATRE READING,** Berkshire – Cheapside. 1,200 seats. Music hall acquired with adjacent car park and building site used for new Odeon. Sold. (Live theatre use. Closed 1959. Demolished 1961. Office block.)

Wednesday 16 October: **The ODEON Theatre SOUTHGATE,** London N.14 – corner of The Bourne and Tudor Way, Old Southgate. Architect: Bertie Crewe. £26,130. 1,438 seats: 810 stalls + 628 balcony. Closed 7 September 1972. (Taken over by independent & re-opened 27 December 1975 as Capitol, stalls only. Circle part re-opened 1979. Closed 2 January 1981. Demolished 1982. Hobart House office block.)

Monday 21 October: **The ODEON Theatre SIDCUP,** Kent – Station Road. Architect: A. P. Starkey (assistant: Frederick Adkins). £23,163. 1,371 seats, semi-stadium: 1,029 front + 342 rear. Closed 16 October 1944 by war-time bomb damage to auditorium. Reconstructed, architect: Leonard Allen, re-opened 2 August 1954, seating 1,260. Closed 14 January 1961. (Reconstructed internally for Lamorbey baths, opened 1967.)

Monday 28 October: **MORDEN CINEMA,** Morden, Surrey – London Road and Aberconway Road. (Opened 8 December 1932, architects: J. Stanley Beard & Clare.) 1,638 seats: 1,110 stalls + 528 balcony. Renamed ODEON 30 July 1937. Closed 13 January 1973. (B&Q do-it-yourself centre. Demolished. Lady St. Helier pub and other shops.)

Also (same day): **PALACE OF VARIETIES, OLDHAM,** Lancashire – Union Street, Live theatre. Reconstructed internally and re-opened as Odeon - see 19 August 1936.

Wednesday 6 November: takeover from A. N. Kendall of:

PALACE ANDOVER, Hampshire – Junction Road. (Opened circa 1926, architect: F. Henshaw.) 867 seats. Renamed ODEON circa 1937. 760 seats in 1967. (Taken over 2 December 1967 by Classic, renamed Classic. Split for bingo and films, 114 seats. Films ended 29 September 1973. Bingo continuing in 1999.)

REGAL WINCHESTER, Hampshire – North Walls. (Opened 1933. Architect: Robert Cromie.) Renamed ODEON 29 December 1935. 1,132 seats in 1939: 816 stalls + 316 balcony. (Taken over 3 January 1971 by Star, renamed Cinema. Split for bingo in former stalls and Studio 1, 2 and 3 cinemas, opened 16 March 1972, seating 140 in former storage area + 107 & 112 in former balcony. Taken over by Cannon, renamed Cannon. Taken over 1988 by independent, renamed Cinema. Closed 26 January 1989. Entire building demolished February-March 1989. Flats.)

And **PICTURE HOUSE WINCHESTER,** Hampshire – 56 High Street. (Opened circa April 1914. 450 seats. Closed 14 June 1926 for enlargement. Re-opened September 1926.) Closed 28 March 1936. (Superdrug store in 1985.)

Tuesday 3 December: **LIDO ISLINGTON,** London N.1 – 276 Upper Street, corner of Florence Street. (Opened 27 September 1928, conversion of vestry hall. Architects: Gray and Webb.) Renamed ODEON circa 1936. 1,138 seats in 1939: 642 stalls + 496 balcony. Closed 21 January 1961. (Demolished. Petrol station.)

Circa December: **PALLADIUM DEPTFORD,** London S.E. - 22/22a The Broadway. (Opened June 1911 as Picture Playhouse, architects: Taperell and Haase, 585 seats. Renamed Broadway Picture Palladium 1916.) (Demolished as part of site for new Odeon - see 3 October 1938).

Circa December: **PICTURE HOUSE CROYDON,** Surrey – 108 North End. (Opened 21 April 1928, architects: Clayton & Black, 1,280 seats.) Renamed ODEON 11 September 1936. 1,220 seats: 744 stalls + 476 balcony. Modernised 1956: 1,115 seats. Closed 3 June 1972. Twin from 11 September 1972, seating 454 downstairs + 430 upstairs. Closed 31 October 1985. (Auditorium demolished Summer 1986 for shops. Entrance hall converted to shop.)

Date unknown: **PLAZA WORTHING,** Sussex – Rowlands Road, corner of Eriswell Road. (Opened 14 December 1933 by Lou Morris. Architect: Harry Weston. Interior designers: Mollo & Egan. 2,270 seats.) May never have been directly operated. (Leased to ABC from 5 February 1936. Closed 11 December 1968. Bingo.)

1936

Date unknown: **NEW IMPERIAL CARDIFF,** Glamorgan – Queen Street. (Opened 17 February 1911 as Picture Palace. Architect: Bertie Crewe. 792 seats. Renamed Imperial. Reconstructed and opened 27 August 1934 for Max Corne as New Imperial. Architect: William S. Wort.) Closed 25 April 1936 for alterations. Re-opened as Odeon – see 14 September.

Date unknown: **GRAND THEATRE HANLEY,** Stoke-On-Trent, Staffordshire – Trinity Street. (Former live theatre. Cinema from 1 February 1932.) (Demolished for new Odeon – see 13 February 1937.)

Wednesday 29 January: **The ODEON Theatre RICKMANS-WORTH** Hertfordshire – High Street. Architect: Andrew Mather. £15,869 (excluding shops and flats). 920 seats, stadium: 574 front + 346 rear. Closed 5 January 1957. (Taken over by Urban District Council. Demolished 1965. Offices: Union Carbide House, with car park behind.)

Monday 17 February: **The ODEON Theatre NEWTON ABBOT,** Devon – Wolborough Street. Architect: Howard Williams. £17,000. 958 seats: 708 stalls + 250 balcony. Closed 1 July 1972. (Car showroom. Demolished August-October 1983 for relief road.)

Tuesday 18 February: **AVENUE EALING,** London W.5 – Northfield Avenue, Northfields. (Opened 5 September 1932. Architect: Cecil Masey. 1,538 seats.) Renamed ODEON circa 1937. 1,530 seats in 1939: 1,054 stalls

+ 476 balcony. (Taken over 15 November 1981 by Panton, renamed Coronet. Closed January 1985. Sold 9 March 1987 by Rank Organisation to Cadant. Grade II listed building. Top Hat nightclub from May 1988. Listing raised to Grade II★. Taken over 1995 by Ealing Elim Pentecostal Church, re-opened as Ealing Christian Centre, open in June 2001.)

And **WALPOLE EALING**, London W.5 – Bond Street. (Opened 29 July 1912. 1,200 seats, one floor. Converted to roller skating rink circa 1919. Converted, architect: J. Stanley Beard, to cinema, re-opened 16 November 1925.) 1432 seats, one floor, in 1939: 1,233 front + 199 rear section. Closed 28 October 1972. (Carpet showroom. Music rehearsal studio. Demolished. Offices: Walpole House. Frontage saved and displayed in Mattock Lane nearby.)

Monday 9 March: **The ODEON Theatre FAVERSHAM,** Kent – Market Place. Architect: Andrew Mather. £11,522. 729 seats, stadium: 288 + 441 seats. 674 seats in 1967. (Taken over 2 December 1967 by Classic, renamed Classic. Taken over by Coral for films + bingo. Bingo only from 1 May 1974. Films part-week. Films ceased 8 June 1985. Full-time bingo. Closed. Grade II listed building from 22 March 1988. Some film use from August 1990. Re-opened 11 February 1994 as New Royal cinema, 448 seats. Open in June 2001.)

Monday 16 March: **The ODEON Theatre CORBY,** Northamptonshire – Stephensons Way. Architect: Laurence M. Gotch. £23,432. 1,042 seats: 770 stalls + 272 balcony. (Taken over by local independent, renamed Rutland Cinema, from 19 January 1969. Closed late 1969. Rutland Bingo Club. Furniture store from 1996. Chicago Rock Café from 5 November 1997.)

Sunday 22 March: **VICTORIA KETTERING**, Northamptonshire – Gold Street. (Opened 23 August 1920, reconstruction of Victoria Hall. 850 seats.) Closed 24 April 1936 for conversion into Odeon - see 19 September 1936.

And **PRINCESS PETERBOROUGH**, Northamptonshire – Lincoln Road, Millfield. (Leased out to Emery circuit from 9 November 1936.)

Saturday 28 March: **The ODEON Theatre SCARBOROUGH,** Yorkshire – Westborough. Architect: Harry W. Weedon (assistants: J. Cecil Clavering, Robert Bullivant). Interior decoration: Mollo & Egan. £38,700. 1,711 seats: 946 stalls + 765 balcony. Closed 21 October 1988. Grade II listed building. (Taken over 1989 by Alan Ayckbourn and partners. Converted and refurbished, architects: Osbourne Christmas, and re-opened 1 May 1996 as Stephen Joseph Theatre with two auditoria: 413 seats [theatre in the round] and 165 seats [cinema/studio theatre in rear of former balcony] Open in June 2001.)

Saturday 18 April: **The ODEON Theatre SUTTON COLD-FIELD,** Warwickshire – Birmingham Road at Maney Corner and Holland Road, Maney. Architect: Harry Weedon (assistant: J. Cecil Clavering). £32,000. 1,600 seats: 1,028 stalls + 572 balcony. Triple from 9 April 1972: 591 seats in former balcony) + 132 & 132 in former rear stalls. Refurbished 1984. Fourth cinema added 1987 in former front stalls with 330 seats with one mini-cinema reduced to 110 seats and new screen erected in front of balcony. Grade II listed building from 18 November 1998. Open in June 2001, seating 598 + 132 + 118 + 307.

Monday 20 April: **The ODEON Theatre WIMBLEDON,** London S.W.19 – 19 Worple Road. Architects: Yates, Cook and Darbyshire. £30,000. 1,501 seats: 924 stalls + 577 balcony. Partly built on site of Queen's/Savoy cinema. Closed 26 November 1960. (Demolished. Lidl store with office block.) [Current Odeon is former Gaumont renamed.]

Saturday 25 April: **The ODEON Theatre COLWYN BAY,** Denbighshire – Conway Road, corner of Marine Road. Architect: Harry W. Weedon (assistant: J. Cecil Clavering). £31,100. 1,706 seats: 1,128 stalls + 578 balcony. Closed 5 January 1957. (Taken over by Hutchinson's, split for stalls bingo and balcony cinema. Re-opened 8 June 1966 as Astra Entertainment Centre, cinema seating 578. Bingo closed 9 March 1986. Cinema closed 10 October 1986. Demolished circa 1987-1988. Block of flats: Swn Y Mor.)

Wednesday 20 May: **The ODEON Theatre WELL HALL,** Eltham, London S.E.9 – Well Hall Road at Rochester Way. Architect: Andrew Mather (assistant: Horace Ward). £30,818. 1,480 seats: 1,028 stalls + 452 balcony. Twin from 7 January 1973, seating 450 former balcony + 130 former rear stalls. (Taken over 1 November 1981 by Panton Films, renamed Coronet. Grade II listed building. Closed 13 January 2000.)

Saturday 23 May: **The ODEON Theatre LITTLEHAMPTON,** Sussex. Architect: Andrew Mather – High Street. £20,792. 970 seats: 438 stalls + 532 balcony. 918 seats in 1967. (Taken over December 1967 by Classic, renamed Classic. Part-week bingo. Closed as cinema 31 May 1974 or 1 June 1974. Taken over by Victor Freeman for full-time bingo, renamed Regal Bingo Club. Closed. Demolished 1984. Shops.)

Saturday 30 May: **The ODEON Theatre CLACTON-ON-SEA,** Essex – West Avenue, corner of Jackson Road. Architect: T. Cecil Howitt. £25,550. 1,214 seats: 746 stalls + 468 balcony. Closed 8 November 1975. Re-opened 4 April 1976 for summer season. Closed Autumn 1976. (Taken over 3 June 1977 by independent, renamed Salon. Closed 30 November 1980. Demolished 1984. Shops.)

Monday 29 June: **The ODEON Theatre GUIDE BRIDGE,** Ashton-Under-Lyne, Lancashire – Stockport Road. Built as Verona cinema and acquired shortly before opening. Architects: Drury and Gomersall. 1,164 seats: 834 stalls + 330 balcony. Closed 11 March 1961. (Roman Catholic church.)

Saturday 11 July: **The ODEON Theatre ST. AUSTELL,** Cornwall – Chandos Place. Architect: Harry Weedon (assistant: P. J. Price). £24,250. 1,274 seats: 806 stalls + 468 balcony. (Taken over 3 December 1967 by Classic, renamed Classic. Taken over 8 January 1978 by independent, renamed Film Centre. Triple from 16 April 1981, seating 605 in former stalls + 125 & 138 in former balcony. Rear stalls converted to two further cinemas from 24 May 1991, seating 70 & 70. Open in June 2001.)

Monday 13 July: **The ODEON Theatre BRIDGWATER,** Somerset – Penel Orlieu (now at corner of Mount Street). Architect: T. Cecil Howitt. £32,380. 1,525 seats, stadium: 931 front + 594 rear. 1,441 seats in 1967. (Taken over 10 December 1967 by Classic, renamed Classic. Subdivided for bingo in front section, two cinemas in rear. Classic 1 & 2 cinemas opened 22 January 1973, 250 + 250 seats. One Classic briefly renamed Tatler in 1973. Closed March 1983. Re-opened 9 December 1983 by independent, renamed Film Centre. Open in June 2001.)

Thursday 16 July: **REGENT BURNT OAK,** Edgware, Middlesex – The Broadway, High Road. (Opened 25 February 1929. Architect: George Coles. 900 seats. Balcony added and frontage rebuilt in 1932, architect: George Coles.) Renamed ODEON 30 July 1937. Renamed GAUMONT in 1949. Renamed ODEON 16 December 1962. Closed 12 February 1972. (Demolished. Shops and flats.)

Saturday 25 July: **The ODEON Theatre DEAL,** Kent – Queen Street. Architect: Andrew Mather. £22,300. 932 seats, stadium: 602 front + 330 rear. (Taken over 10 December 1967 by Classic, renamed Classic. Twin from 30 June 1972, seating 284 & 284. Closed 31 January 1985. Snooker hall. One cinema re-opened 11 September 1986 by independent, named Flicks, seating 173. Second cinema opened 27 November 1977 in former bar area, seating 99. Both open in June 2001.)

Monday 17 August: **The ODEON Theatre SOUTHALL,** Middlesex – High Street. Architect: George Coles. £39,144. 1,580 seats: 1,122 stalls + 458 balcony. Closed 25 February 1961. (Reconstructed internally and re-opened 14 August 1961 as Top Rank Bowl. Closed. Sold 9 July 1970 to MFI, converted to store. Queenstyle Carpet Centre in 1996.)

Wednesday 19 August: **The ODEON Theatre OLDHAM,** Lancashire – Union Street. £13,522 interior reconstruction of Palace Theatre of Varieties, former live theatre. Architect: Harry Weedon. 1,707 seats: 1,122 stalls + 585 balcony. Triple from 14 July 1974: 585 in former circle + 110 & 110 seats in former rear stalls. Closed 29 October 1983. Disused. Demolished 1992. The Link, Council Social Services building from 2000.)

Saturday 22 August: **The ODEON Theatre RAMSGATE,** Kent – King Street at corner of Broad Street. Architect: Andrew Mather. £32,482. 1,568 seats: 1,034 stalls + 534 balcony. 1,446 seats in 1967. (Taken over 2 December 1967 by Classic, renamed Classic. Split for stalls bingo and balcony cinema, seating 534. Second cinema replaced bingo from 30 June 1983, seating 256 in part of stalls. Both closed 17 October 1985. Demolished 1988, except for parade of shops and flats. Iceland store & car park.)

Wednesday 26 August: **REGAL SKIPTON,** Yorkshire – Keighley Road. (Opened 1929 as Morriseum. Renamed Regal 1932.) 927 seats in 1939: 618 stalls + 309 balcony. Renamed ODEON 19 June 1950. 872 seats in 1967. (Taken over December 1967 by Classic, renamed Classic. Taken over 29 January 1971 by Hutchinson circuit, renamed Regal. Split for stalls bingo + twin cinemas in old balcony, latter opened 18 June 1971, seating 150 & 150. Closed 10 September 1987. Bliss and The Vestry nightclub from December 1999.)

Monday 31 August: **The ODEON Theatre ASHFORD,** Kent – High Street. Architect: Andrew Mather. £31,350. 1,570 seats: 1,102 stalls + 534 balcony. Closed 30 August 1975. (Re-opened early 1976 as Top Rank Club for bingo. Renamed Mecca. Open in June 2001).

Wednesday 2 September: **PALACE BILSTON,** Staffordshire – Lichfield Street. (Opened 17 November 1921 as Wood's New Picture Palace. Architect: Hurley Robinson. Interior design: Val Prince. 1,400 seats. Renamed Palace.) 1,251 seats in 1939: 965 stalls + 286 balcony. Renamed ODEON 30 July 1937. Closed 22 February 1964. (Re-opened 5 March 1964 as Top Rank Club for bingo. Sold 2 September 1971 to Hutchinsons, renamed Surewin. Sold and renamed Cascade. Closed. Asian venue. Multi-purpose hall from 7 November 1999.)

Monday 7 September: **The ODEON Theatre IPSWICH,** Suffolk – Lloyds Avenue. Architect: George Coles. £36,301. 1,764 seats: 1,141 stalls + 623 balcony. Modernised 1959/1960. Triple from 9 November 1975, seating 609 in former balcony + 109 & 109 in former rear stalls. Closed 3 July 1982. (Top Rank Club for bingo. Renamed Mecca. Open in June 2001.) [Present Odeon is new multiplex elsewhere.]

Wednesday 9 September: **The ODEON Theatre MUSWELL HILL,** London N.10 – Fortis Green Road. Architect: George Coles. £30,329 (excluding shops, offices and flats). 1,827 seats: 1,217 stalls + 610 balcony. Triple from 26 May 1974, seating 610 seats in former balcony + 110 & 110 in former rear stalls. Grade II listed building from 6 March 1984. Open in June 2001, seating 610 + 134 + 130.

Monday 14 September: **The ODEON Theatre CARDIFF,** Glamorgan – 55 Queen Street. £14,663 conversion of New Imperial Cinema. Architect: William S. Wort. 1,663 seats: 1,135 stalls + 528 balcony. 1,200 seats by 1977. Closed 12 January 1980. Re-opened as twin, seating 643 in former stalls + 448 seats in former balcony. Closed 16 March 2000. [Later Odeon was new multiplex elsewhere.]

Saturday 19 September: **The ODEON Theatre KETTERING,** Northamptonshire – Gold Street. £18,000 reconstruction of Victoria Picture House. Architect: Harry Weedon. Interior decoration: Mollo & Egan. 1,090 seats: 740 stalls + 350 balcony. Closed 29 October 1960. (Top Rank Club for bingo. Closed, sold to Borough of Kettering. Demolished 1974. Shops.)

Monday 21 September: **The ODEON Theatre BROMLEY,** Kent – 242 High Street, also known as The Mart. Architect: George Coles. £35,191. 1,492 seats: 1,018 stalls + 474 seats. Modernised 1961. Closed for tripling. Re-opened 12 April 1976, seating 760 seats in former balcony extended over front stalls + 125 & 116 in former rear stalls. Cinema in former balcony and one in rear stalls closed 9 October 1988 to add additional cinema on former stage and in front stalls. Closed cinemas re-opened 16 December 1988, seating 402 with new screen & 98.

New cinema opened 3 February 1989, seating 273. Refurbished early 2001. All open in June 2001, seating 402 + 125 + 98 + 273.

Monday 28 September: **The ODEON Theatre HARROGATE,** Yorkshire – East Parade, at corner of Station Avenue. Architect: Harry Weedon (assistant: W. Calder Robson) (based on Odeon Sutton Coldfield: architect: Harry Weedon, assistant: J. Cecil Clavering). £31,750. 1,647 seats: 1,049 stalls + 598 balcony. Triple from 14 August 1972, seating 532 in former balcony + 108 & 108 in former rear stalls. Refurbished 1984. Fourth cinema added circa 1990, seating 259 in former front stalls with new screen in front of upstairs cinema and one downstairs cinema reduced to 75 seats. All open in June 2001, seating 532 + 108 + 75 + 259.

And PLAZA WATFORD, Hertfordshire – The Parade, High Street at corner of Albert Road. (Opened 29 April 1929. Architects: Emden, Egan. 2,060 seats.) Renamed ODEON 12 October 1936. 1,989 seats in 1939: 1,253 stalls + 736 balcony. Closed 30 November 1963. (Demolished. Cater's supermarket and Top Rank Suite above, both later sold and renamed: Presto and Bailey's in 1985, Multiyork store and Kudos nightclub in 2001.) [Later Odeon was former Gaumont renamed.]

Saturday 3 October: **The ODEON Theatre CHESTER,** Cheshire – Northgate Street at corner of Hunter Street. Architect: Harry Weedon (assistant: Robert Bullivant). 1,628 seats: 1,080 stalls + 548 balcony. Triple from 11 April 1976, seating 802 seats in former balcony extended over front stalls + 122 & 122 in former rear stalls. Two new cinemas opened 22 March 1991 in rear of upstairs cinema, seating 151 & 151, reducing existing cinema to 406 seats. All open in June 2001, seating 408 + 148 + 148 + 123 + 123.

Monday 5 October: **The ODEON Theatre STAFFORD,** Staffordshire – Newport Road. Architect: Roland Satchwell. £17,550. 956 seats: 535 stalls + 421 balcony. (Taken over 26 July 1981 by Hutchinsons, renamed Astra. Triple from 27 December 1981, seating 170 & 168 in former balcony + 435 in former stalls. Taken over 1988 by Apollo. Cinemas renamed Apollo. Downstairs cinema closed for bingo, then re-opened 1990. All open in June 2001, seating 305 + 170 + 164.)

Wednesday 7 October: **The ODEON Theatre HORSHAM,** Sussex – North Street. Architect: George Coles. £33,555. 1,258 seats: 766 stalls + 492 balcony. 1,240 seats in 1967. (Taken over 10 December 1967 by Classic, renamed Classic. Split for Mecca bingo in former stalls + two Classic cinemas opened 26 May 1972, seating 310 in former balcony & 110 in former restaurant. Cinemas taken over by Mecca, renamed Mecca. Cinemas closed 10 January 1976. Bingo closed. Demolished by November 1981. Office block.)

October: ALHAMBRA THEATRE LEICESTER SQUARE, London W.1. (Opened 23 December 1929 by ABC, former live theatre with some films featured. Taken over by Stoll. Variety use only from March 1931. Closed.) Not re-opened. (Demolished from November 1936 as part of site of Odeon Leicester Square - see 2 November 1937.)

Circa October: **QUEEN'S HALL Picture Theatre PECKHAM,** London S.E.15 – High Street. (Opened October 1910, former public hall and roller skating rink. 900 seats.) Closed 9 May 1937. (Demolished as part of site for new Odeon – see 1 June 1938.)

Saturday 17 October: **The ODEON Theatre NEWPORT,** Isle of Wight – Pyle Street and Town Lane. Architect: Andrew Mather. £24,913. 1,228 seats: 742 stalls + 486 balcony. (Taken over 1 January 1961 by Isle of Wight Theatres, renamed Savoy. Taken over 1969 by Star. Closed 18 December 1982. Demolished Summer 1984. Savoy Court flats above Daybell's Furnishings shop in 2000.)

Monday 2 November: **The ODEON Theatre HERNE BAY,** Kent – 4 Avenue Road. Architect: Andrew Mather. 974 seats, stadium: 518 front + 456 raised rear section. 814 seats in 1967. (Taken over 3 December 1967, renamed Classic. Renamed Cannon. Closed 8 October 1987. Demolished 1988. Flats.)

Saturday 7 November: **The ODEON Theatre LANCASTER,** Lancashire – King Street and Spring Garden Street. Architect: Harry Weedon (assistant: W. Calder Robson). £34,012. 1,592 seats: 950 stalls + 642 balcony. (Taken over 3 January 1971 by Star, split for stalls bingo and Studio 1 & 2 cinemas in balcony opened 12 August 1971, seating 260 & 260. Cinemas taken over by Cannon, renamed Cannon. Taken over July 1995 by Virgin. Taken over 2 May 1996 by ABC. Renamed ABC Cinemas. Open in June 2001, seating 250 & 246.)

Monday 9 November: PICTURE HOUSE CHESTERFIELD, Derbyshire – Holywell Street. (Opened 10 September 1923.) Renamed ODEON circa 1937. 1,559 seats in 1939: 991 stalls + 568 balcony. Closed 17 October 1981. (The Winding Wheel – meeting hall. Grade II listed building from October 2000. Open in June 2001.)

Mid-November: sale, before opening, of **ODEON NORTHWOOD HILLS,** Middlesex – Pinner Road. Architect: A. D. Clare. Circa 1,000 seats. (Opened Monday 28 December 1936 by Shipman and King circuit, renamed Rex. Closed 22 September 1973. Demolished. Somerfield supermarket.)

Monday 16 November: **The ODEON Theatre BURY,** Lancashire – Rochdale Road at corner of Clerke Street. Architect: Harry Weedon (assistant: P. J. Price). £32,500. 1,487 seats: 1,027 stalls + 460 balcony. Closed 24 October 1981. (Club use: Arena in 1988, Sol in 1998.)

Saturday 21 November: **The ODEON Theatre LOUGH-BOROUGH,** Leicestershire – Baxtergate. Architect: Harry Weedon (assistant: Arthur J. Price). £30,485. 1,625 seats: 1,029 stalls + 596 balcony. 1,452 seats in 1967. (Taken over 2 December 1967 by Classic, renamed Classic. Closed 12 January 1974. Bingo. Open in June 2001.)

December: **WINTER GARDENS LLANDUDNO,** Caernarvon – Gloddaeth Street. (Opened 25 March 1935 as live theatre & cinema. Taken over December 1936 by Brooklyn Trust, passed to Odeon.) 1,883 seats in 1939: 1,074 stalls + 809 balcony. Renamed ODEON circa 1943. (Sold to Hutchinson circuit 13 October 1969, renamed Astra. Open summers only. Closed circa October 1986. Demolished. Residential homes: Ormside Grange.)

Monday 14 December: **The ODEON Theatre PORTS-MOUTH**, Hampshire – London Road, North End. Architect: Andrew Mather. £36,997. 1,824 seats: 1,224 stalls + 600 balcony. Closed 10 September 1960 for modernisation. Re-opened 25 September 1960. Triple from 26 August 1973, seating 567 in former balcony + 132 & 132 seats in former rear stalls. Lower cinemas enlarged to 228 seats and 228 seats. Fourth cinema added 1990 in former front stalls, seating 250 with new screen in front of balcony upstairs and one rear cinema reduced. Refurbished December 1998. All open in June 2001, seating 524 + 225 + 173 + 259.

Circa December: **BARNET CINEMA**, Hertfordshire – 122 High Street, High Barnet. (Opened 26 December 1912 as Cinema Palace, one floor. Balcony added 9 October 1926, renamed Cinema. Redecorated July 1933.) 1,038 seats in 1939. Renamed GAUMONT 10 January 1955. Closed 8 August 1959. (Demolished 1961. Supermarket.)

Thursday 17 December: **The ODEON Theatre FALMOUTH**, Cornwall – Killigrew Street. Architect: Harry Weedon (assistant: P. J. Price). £24,305. 1,148 seats, semi-stadium: 707 front + 441 rear. 929 seats in 1967. (Taken over 17 December 1967 by Classic, renamed Classic. Closed 3 May 1970. Demolished. Tesco supermarket, open in 2001.)

1937

Date unknown: **NEW EMPIRE CAMBERWELL**, London S.E.5 – Denmark Hill. (Former Empire Theatre. 1,000 seats.) Closed 8 August 1937. (Demolished as part of site for new Odeon – see 20 March 1939.)

Date unknown: **KENNINGTON THEATRE**, London S.E. - Kennington Park Road, South Place and De Laune Street. (Opened 28 Febraury 1921, former live theatre. 1,347 seats. Part of United Pictures Theatres circuit from January 1928. Closed 1934.) Not re-opened. (Part of site for unbuilt Odeon - see chapter on 1939, list of Other Schemes.)

Monday 4 January: **The ODEON Theatre SITTING-BOURNE**, Kent – High Street. Architect: F. C. Mitchell. £28,720. 1,593 seats: 1,077 stalls + 516 balcony. 1,551 seats in 1967. (Taken over 2 December 1967 by Classic, renamed Vogue. Closed 13 January 1968. Bingo club. Classic cinema opened 9 August 1971 in former café, seating 111. Second Classic cinema opened in former balcony, seating 330. Renamed Cannon 1 & 2. Cinemas taken over 7 January 1997 by Picturedrome, renamed Picturedrome. Cinemas taken over in 2000 by Reeltime, renamed New Century. Open in June 2001 with Mecca bingo club on ground floor.)

Monday 11 January: **The ODEON Theatre WARRINGTON**, Lancashire – Buttermarket Street. Architects: Drury & Gomersall. £33,308. 1,635 seats: 1,059 stalls + 576 balcony. Triple from 14 September 1980, seating 576 seats in former balcony + 291 & 196 seats in former stalls. Closed 28 August 1994. (Demolished January 1995. Yates Wine Lodge.)

Saturday 23 January: **The ODEON Theatre LOWESTOFT**, Suffolk – London Road North. Architect: Andrew Mather. £33,113. 1,868 seats: 1,262 stalls + 606 balcony. Closed 25 April 1979. (Demolished 1981. W. H. Smith store.)

Monday 1 February: **The ODEON Theatre YORK**, Yorkshire – Blossom Street. Architect: Harry Weedon (assistant: Robert Bullivant). £40,500. 1,484 seats: 934 stalls + 550 balcony. Triple from 20 August 1972, seating 820 seats in former balcony extended forward to original screen + 111 & 111 seats in former rear stalls. Grade II listed building from 23 April 1981. Open in June 2001: 799 + 111 + 111 seats.

Saturday 13 February: **The ODEON Theatre HANLEY**, Stoke-On-Trent, Staffordshire – Trinity Street at corner of Foundry Street. On site of Grand Theatre. Architect: Harry Weedon (assistant: Arthur J. Price). £36,248. 1,580 seats: 1,036 stalls + 544 balcony. Modernised circa 1960: 1,401 seats. Closed 15 November 1975. (The Foyer pub in 1999.)

Monday 1 March: **The ODEON Theatre FOREST GATE**, London E.7. – Romford Road. Architect: Andrew Mather. 1,806 seats: 1,110 stalls + 696 balcony. Closed 21 April 1941 by bomb damage. Re-opened 4 August 1941. Closed 31 October 1975. (Snooker hall. Pot Black snooker in 1984, using former exit as entrance. Closed by 1994. Muslim centre in 2001: Minhaj-ul-Quran Mosque and Cultural Centre.)

Monday 8 March: **The ODEON Theatre READING**, Berkshire – Cheapside. Architect: A. P. Starkey (assistant: Frederick Adkins). £32,173. 1,704 seats: 1,210 stalls + 494 balcony. 1,413 seats by 1979. Twin from 14 April 1979, seating 410 in former balcony + 640 in former stalls. Car park sold for redevelopment. Lower cinema subdivided in 1989 into two cinemas, seating 221 & 221. All closed 25 November 1999.

And (same day): cinemas from SINGLETON CIRCUIT (announced September 1936), comprising:

PAVILION AIRDRIE, Lanarkshire – Graham Street. (Opened pre-1914. 1,092 seats. Taken over pre-1920 by Singleton.) (Taken over December 1967 by Classic, renamed Classic. Closed 27 September 1970. Demolished. Airdrie Sheriff Courthouse.)

EMPIRE COATBRIDGE, Lanarkshire – Main Street. (Opened pre-1921, former live theatre. 1,200 seats.) Renamed ODEON circa 1938. 1,140 seats in 1939. Closed 8 May 1971. (Sold to Burgh 19 October 1971. Shops.)

EMPIRE DUNDEE, Angus – Rosebank Street, Hilltown. (Opened pre-1914, former live theatre. Taken over 3 January 1927 by Singleton.) 1,090 seats in 1939. Closed 30 October 1957 by fire. (Sold 17 February 1967. Demolished.)

VOGUE DUNDEE, Angus – 46 Strathmartine Road. (Opened 21 September 1936 by Singleton. Architect: James McKissack & Son. Seats, stadium plan: 1,534.) Renamed ODEON June 1938. Closed 24 February 1973. (Demolished 1973. Safeways supermarket.)

CINEMA FALKIRK, Stirling – Melville Street. (Opened circa 1917 as New Cinema House, 580 seats. Taken over circa 1925 by Singleton. Renamed Cinema circa 1926.) Closed 22 May 1956 by fire.

PARAGON GORBALS, Glasgow – 403 Cumberland Street. (Opened 1912. 1,300 seats. Taken over November 1912 by Singleton. Reconstructed 1927, architects: A. V. Gardner and W. R. Glen.) Closed June 1958. (Demolished. Housing.)

KING'S HAWICK, Roxburgh – Exchange Buildings. (Opened circa 1922, former live theatre. Taken over circa 1929 by Singleton.) 1,288 seats in 1939. Renamed ODEON circa 1946. (Taken over 9 December 1967 by Classic, renamed Classic. Taken over 1 January 1971 by independent, renamed Marina. Partweek bingo by 1980. 750 seats. Closed. Nightclub. Closed by fire circa 1994. Demolished. Car park.)

VOGUE RUTHERGLEN, Glasgow – 58/60 Main Street. (Opened 29 January 1936 by Singleton. Architect: James McKissack. 1,741 seats.) Renamed ODEON 24 June 1938. Closed 12 October 1974. (Top Rank Club for bingo. Renamed Mecca. Open in June 2001.)

COMMODORE SCOTSTOUN, Glasgow – 1297 Dumbarton Road. (Opened 26 December 1932 by Singleton. Architect: James McKissack. 1,919 seats.) Renamed ODEON 24 June 1938. Closed 25 November 1967. (Bingo. Disused. Destroyed by fire 19 August 1976. Site cleared.)

BROADWAY SHETTLESTON, Glasgow – 19 Amulree Street. (Opened 5 June 1930 by Singleton. Architect: James McKissack. 1,640 seats.) Renamed ODEON 24 June 1938. Closed 25 January 1969. (Top Rank Club for bingo. Closed circa 1991. Demolished August 1995. Housing.)

Saturday 13 March: **The ODEON Theatre WREXHAM,** Denbighshire – Brook Street. Architect: Harry Weedon (assistant: Budge Reid). £28,600. 1,246 seats: 958 stalls + 288 balcony. Split-week films and bingo from 1972. Closed 15 May 1976. (Top Rank Club for full-time bingo. Renamed Mecca. Closed May 1999 in move to new premises.) [Present Odeon is multiplex elsewhere.]

Circa 20 March: **BOLEYN Electric Theatre EAST HAM,** London E. 6 – Barking Road. Closed June 1937. (Demolished for new Odeon on enlarged site.)

Saturday 17 April: **The ODEON Theatre HEREFORD,** Herefordshire – 6 Commercial Street, High Town. Architect: Roland Satchwell. £27,977. 1,133 seats: 788 stalls + 345 balcony. (Taken over 26 October 1975 by Brent Walker, renamed Focus. Taken over 3 June 1983 by Classic, renamed Classic. Closed 1 March 1984. Demolished.)

Monday 19 April: **The ODEON Theatre EPSOM,** Surrey – High Street. Architect: Whinney, Son & Austen Hall. £31,231. 1,434 seats: 1,016 stalls + 418 balcony. Closed 19 June 1971. (Sale to Four Millbank Nominees [Star West] completed 12 July 1971. Demolished. Sainsbury supermarket.) [Current Odeon is multiplex elsewhere.]

Wednesday 5 May: **GROSVENOR RAYNERS LANE,** Harrow, Middlesex – 440 Alexandra Avenue. (Opened 12 October 1936. Architect: F. E. Bromige.) 1,235 seats in 1939: 830 stalls + 405 balcony. Renamed ODEON circa 1941. Renamed GAUMONT 26 October 1950. Renamed ODEON 27 April 1964. 1,020 seats. Grade II listed building from 13 March 1981. (Taken over 1 November 1981 by independent, renamed Ace. Closed 16 October 1986. Listing raised to Grade II* 6 October 1988. Grosvenor Cine/Bar Experience with foyer as Ace Bar and auditorium as Studio Warehouse nightclub, both from 1991. Closed. Taken over circa 2000 by Zoroastrian Centre for Europe, church use.)

Monday 10 May: **The ODEON Theatre YEOVIL,** Somerset – Court Ash Terrace. Architect: Harry Weedon (assistant: Budge Reid). Auditorium decoration: Mollo & Egan. £31,461. 1,580 seats: 978 stalls + 602 balcony. (Taken over 1972 by Classic, renamed Classic. Triple from 2 November 1972, seating 600 in former balcony + 400 & 400 in former stalls. Renamed Cannon. Renamed MGM. Taken over July 1995 by Virgin. Taken over 2 May 1996 by ABC. Renamed ABC Cinemas. Open in June 2001, seating 575 + 239 + 247.)

And **FORESTERS BETHNAL GREEN,** London E.1 – 93 Cambridge Heath Road. (Opened circa September 1926, former music hall reconstructed, architect: George Coles.) 1,057 seats in 1939: 674 stalls + 383 balcony. Closed April 1947 to repair war-time bomb damage. Re-opened 10 October 1949. Closed 20 August 1960. (Demolished. Block of flats: Sovereign House.)

And **PICTURE HOUSE SOUTH HACKNEY,** London E.9. – 133/7 Well Street. (Opened circa 1913 as Picture Palace, 1,500 seats. Enlarged, front rebuilt, architect: George Coles, and re-opened August 1933, renamed Picture House.) 1,201 seats in 1939. Closed circa 1942 by bomb damage. (Furniture store until 1946. Derelict. Demolished 1959. Extension to Frampton Park Housing Estate.)

Monday 21 June: **The ODEON Theatre AYLESBURY,** Buckinghamshire – Cambridge Street. Architect: Andrew Mather. £29,370. 1,451 seats: 954 balcony + 497 stalls. Triple from 26 August 1973, seating 497 in former balcony + 99 & 108 in former rear stalls. Refurbished 1984. New screen in front of upstairs cinema from 1985. Closed 30 October 1999, seating 450 + 108 + 113. (Disused in June 2001.)[Current Odeon is multiplex elsewhere.]

Thursday 1 July: **PLAZA WEST WICKHAM,** Kent – 88 Station Road. (Opened 4 September 1933. Architects: J. Stanley Beard & Clare.) 886 seats in 1939: 616 stalls + 270 balcony. Renamed ODEON 15 May 1938. Renamed GAUMONT 18 March 1951. Closed 5 January 1957. (Demolished June 1961. Rosemallow House with Finefare supermarket, Boots etc. from 1971.)

And **PAVILION KENSAL RISE,** London N.W.10 – Chamberlayne Road at corner of Bannister Road. (Opened 19 November 1914. Architect: Cecil Masey. 1,500 seats.) 1,455 seats in 1939: 994 stalls + 461 balcony. Renamed ODEON circa 1940. 1,261 seats in 1960s. Closed 2 May 1970. (Sold 30 December 1970 to Toupata Management. Demolished. Garage.)

Monday 5 July: **The ODEON Theatre BURY ST. EDMUNDS,** Suffolk – Brentgovel Street and Well Street. Architect: George Coles. £25,635. 1,289 seats: 867 balcony + 422 stalls. (Taken over 4 October 1975 by Brent Walker, re-named Focus. Grade II listed building from May 1981. De-listed October 1981. Closed 30 October 1982. Demolished 1983.)

Monday 12 July: **The ODEON Theatre HARLESDEN,** London N.W.10 – Craven Park Road and St. Albans Road. Architects: Whinney, Son & Austen Hall. £36,376. 1,719 seats: 1,224 stalls + 495 balcony. Closed 15 April 1972. (Re-opened as Asian cinema, renamed Liberty. Concert/dance hall. Tara nightclub. Closed. Demolished August-September 1989. Odeon Court block of flats by February 1994.)

Circa July: LONDON & SOUTHERN SUPER CINEMAS circuit, comprising:

AMBASSADOR BEDMINSTER, Bristol, Gloucestershire – Winterstoke Road. (Opened 7 December 1936 by London & Southern, completion of stalled scheme, new architect: F. J. Mitchell.) 1,249 seats, stadium: 808 front + 441 rear. Renamed ODEON July 1943. Closed 22 July 1961. (Top Rank Club for bingo. Closed 1995. Winterstoke Tyre & Exhaust Centre in front of building, Alphabet Zoo Play Centre & Party Venue in rear.)

SUPER BLOOMSBURY, London W.C. – Theobalds Road (Opened 3 September 1921 as Victory. Architects: Ernest A. Mann & Victor Peel. 1,346 seats: 894 stalls + 452 balcony. Renamed Bloomsbury Cinema mid-1920s. Taken over November 1929 by London & Southern, renamed Super.) 1,373 seats in 1939: 918 stalls + 455 balcony. Closed November 1940 by war-time conditions. (Severely damaged by bombing early 1941. Demolished. Mercury House office block.)

AMBASSADOR COSHAM, Portsmouth, Hampshire – High Street. (Opened 8 March 1937 by London & Southern. Architect: F. C. Mitchell. 1,645 seats: 1,124 stalls + 521 balcony. Renamed ODEON 5 September 1944. Closed 3 July 1976. (Top Rank Club for bingo. Crown bingo in 2001.)

AMBASSADOR FARNHAM ROYAL, Slough, Buckinghamshire – Farnham Road. (Opened 17 February 1936 by London & Southern. Architect: Sydney R. Croker, in association with F.C. Mitchell. 1,315 seats.) 1,315 seats in 1939: 928 stalls + 387 balcony. 1,306 seats in 1961. Closed 10 February 1968. (Demolished. MFI store.)

CAPITOL FOREST HILL, London S.E.23 – 11/15 London Road. (Opened 11 February 1929. Taken over April 1929 by London & Southern. Architect: J. Stanley Beard. Leased out from August 1932. Leased or subleased by ABC from July 1933. 1,687 seats. Sold 6 December 1965 by Rank. Closed 13 October 1973 by ABC. Bingo club. Grade II listed building. Capitol pub from Spring 2001.)

AMBASSADOR HOUNSLOW, Middlesex – Bath Road, Hounslow West. (Opened 7 September 1936 by London & Southern. Architect: W. J. King.) 1,876 seats in 1939: 1,332 stalls + 544 balcony. Renamed ODEON circa 1945. Triple from 16 June 1974, seating 490 in former balcony + 114 & 114 in former rear stalls. Closed 7 January 1984. (Demolished January 1984. Supermarket.)

DOMINION HOUNSLOW, Middlesex – London Road at corner of North Drive,. (Opened 28 December 1931. Architect: F. E. Bromige. Taken over by London & Southern.) 2,022 seats in 1939: 1,460 stalls + 562 balcony. 1,908 seats in 1961. Closed 30 December 1961. (Top Rank Club for bingo from March 1962. Renamed Mecca. Open in June 2001.)

TREDEGAR HALL NEWPORT, Monmouthshire – 12/22 Stow Hill. (Opened October 1922, former public hall. Taken over circa 1929 by London & Southern.) 1,019 seats in 1939: 600 stalls + 419 balcony. Closed December 1945 for floor repairs. Re-opened 7 April 1946. Closed 29 March 1958. (Majestic Ballroom. Returned 16 September 1965 to Odeon division of Rank. Taken over by Star. Jesper Bar & Nightclub in 2001.)

REGAL ROTHERHAM, Yorkshire – Corporation Street. (Opened 22 December 1934 by Lou Morris. Architects: Blackmore, Sykes. 1,850 seats. Taken over 1 April 1935 by London & Southern.) 1,825 seats in 1939: 1,097 stalls + 728 balcony. Renamed ODEON 1946. Closed 29 November 1975. (Taken over by independent and re-opened 1 December 1975, renamed Scala, 728 seats, balcony only. Closed 23 September 1983. Entertainment centre. Ritz bingo club from 25 May 1989. Mecca bingo in June 2001.)

CAPITOL WALTON-ON-THAMES, Surrey – High Street. (Opened 23 & 26 December 1927 by Lou Morris. Architect: J. Stanley Beard. Taken over circa 1934 by London & Southern.) 1,015 seats in 1939: 725 stalls + 290 balcony. Renamed ODEON circa 1947. Closed 29 November 1980.

(Demolished. Screens at Walton in redevelopment, opened 25 September 1992. Open in June 2001.)

ASTORIA WOKING, Surrey – Duke Street. (Opened 5 December 1932 by London & Southern on site of Palace Theatre. Architect: F. C. Mitchell.) 1,172 seats in 1939: 880 stalls + 292 balcony. Renamed ODEON circa 1945. Closed 28 October 1961 for modernisation. Re-opened 13 November 1961. Closed 19 April 1975. (Demolished. Office block.)

PLAZA WOKING, Surrey – Chertsey Road. (Opened 1913 as Central. 780 seats. Enlarged, front rebuilt, architects: Wilfred Travers & Frank C. Spiller, and re-opened circa September 1926, 1,046 seats. Taken over circa 1929 by London & Southern, renamed Plaza.) 914 seats in 1939: 563 stalls + 351 balcony. Renamed GAUMONT 29 May 1950. Closed 13 June 1959. (Demolished. Supermarket.)

Monday 26 July: **The ODEON Theatre CREWE,** Cheshire – Delamere Street. Architect: Harry Weedon (assistant: Budge Reid). £30,034. 1,129 seats, stadium plan: 855 front + 274 stepped rear section. (Taken over 25 October 1975 by Brent Walker, renamed Focus. Closed 25 May 1983. Demolished. McDonalds and other shops.)

And: **The ODEON Theatre SOUTH NORWOOD,** London S.E.25 – Station Road. Architect: Andrew Mather. £31,562. 1,572 seats: 1,020 stalls + 552 balcony. Closed 20 February 1971. (Demolished. Safeways Supermarket.)

Wednesday 28 July: **The ODEON Theatre DUDLEY,** Worcestershire – Castle Hill. Architect: Harry Weedon (assistant: Budge Reid). £31,562. 1,876 seats: 1,234 stalls + 642 balcony. Closed 22 February 1975. (Sold 9 March 1976 to International Bible Students Association. Re-opened 1977 as church: Kingdom Hall of Jehovah's Witnesses. Grade II listed building from October 2000. Open in 2001.)

Saturday 31 July: **The ODEON Theatre PENGE,** London S.E.20 – 162 High Street. Architect: Andrew Mather. £30,980. 1,582 seats: 1,096 stalls + 486 balcony. Closed 4 September 1976. (Bingo club from 16 September 1976. Coral Bingo from 1978. Closed 12 March 1990. Demolished 1994. Wetherspoon's pub: The Moon and Stars.)

Saturday 7 August: **The ODEON Theatre BOURNEMOUTH,** Hampshire – Christchurch Road, Lansdowne. Architect: George Coles. £46,548. 1,978 seats: 1,336 stalls + 642 balcony. Closed 16 January 1974. (Top Rank Club for bingo. Gala Club for bingo in 2000.)

Saturday 14 August: **The ODEON Theatre RADCLIFFE,** Lancashire – corner of Foundry Street and Egerton Street. Architect: Harry Weedon (assistant: W. Calder Robson). £19,535. 1,138 seats: 822 stalls + 316 balcony. Closed 27 April 1957. (Liquorsave Discount Wines & Spirits. Kwik Save supermarket in 1998.)

August: **PAVILION EAST DULWICH,** London S.E.22 – 72 Grove Vale, Goose Green. (Opened 30 July 1936 on site of old Pavilion. Architect: A. H. Jones.) 1,288 seats in 1939: 792 stalls + 496 balcony. Renamed ODEON circa 1939. Closed 21 October 1972. (Sold 7 June 1973 to Divine Light

Mission. Palace of Peace, Indian temple. Taken over 1978 for warehouse use, renamed London House. Demolished Spring 2001.)

Monday 30 August: **WEST END WHALLEY RANGE,** Manchester – Withington Road and Dudley Road. (Opened 8 December 1930. Architect: John Knight. 2,032 seats.) Renamed ODEON. 2,031 seats in 1939: 1,507 stalls + 524 balcony. Closed 23 December 1961. (Top Rank Club for bingo from 1962, later Star Bingo and EMI. Closed circa 1980. Demolished 1986. Flats: Crystal House in October 2001.)

Wednesday 18 August: **The ODEON Theatre BOSTON,** Lincolnshire – South Square, off Market Place. Architect: Harry Weedon (assistant: Budge Reid). £32,600. 1,592 seats: 1,067 stalls + 525 balcony. 1,430 seats in 1967. (Taken over 3 December 1967 by Classic, renamed Classic. Split-week films and bingo by 1977. Taken over 2 December 1981 by independent for films & live shows, renamed Haven. Part-week bingo. Closed 27 May 1987 by fire. Demolished January-February 1999. Car park.)

Saturday 21 August: **The ODEON Theatre BOLTON,** Lancashire – Ash Burner Street, corner of Black Horse Street. Architect: Harry Weedon (assistant: W. Calder Robson). £49,500. 2,534 seats: 1,598 stalls + 936 balcony. Modernised circa 1960. Triple from 20 August 1972, seating 879 in former balcony + 148 & 148 in former rear stalls. Closed 8 January 1983. (Detripled. Re-opened as Top Rank Club for bingo. Renamed Mecca. Open in June 2001.)

Saturday 28 August: **The ODEON Theatre BURNLEY,** Lancashire – Gunsmith Lane. Architect: Harry Weedon (assistant: Robert Bullivant). £42,517. 2,136 seats: 1,404 stalls + 732 balcony. Closed 17 November 1973. (Demolished. J. Sainsbury supermarket.)

Monday 30 August: **The ODEON Theatre EXETER,** Devon – Sidwell Street. Architect: Harry Weedon (assistant: Robert Bullivant). 1,920 seats: 1,176 stalls + 744 balcony. Temporarily closed 2 May 1942 by bomb damage. Closed March 1954 to repair war damage. Re-opened June 1954. Refurbished late 1960s: 1,630 seats. Triple from 6 August 1972, seating 742 in former balcony + 119 & 118 in former rear stalls. Refurbished 1986. Fourth cinema added early August 1988 in former front stalls, seating 344, with new screen in front of upstairs cinema and second small cinema reduced to 105 seats. All open in June 2001, seating 744 + 119 + 105 + 344.

Thursday 2 September: **The ODEON Theatre MORECAMBE,** Lancashire – Thornton Road and Euston Road. Architect: Harry Weedon (assistant: W. Calder Robson). £37,605. 1,560 seats: 1,084 stalls + 476 balcony. 1,274 seats in 1967. (Taken over 16 December 1967 by Classic, renamed Classic. Closed 28 February 1976. (One Stop DIY store.)

And: **The ODEON Theatre PETERBOROUGH,** Northamptonshire – The Broadway. Architect: Harry Weedon. £34,755. 1,752 seats: 1,208 stalls + 544 balcony. Triple from 25 February 1973, seating 544 in former balcony + 110 & 110

in former rear stalls. Closed 23 November 1991. (Taken over by Peter Boizot, adapted [architect: Tim Foster] and re-opened 31 May 2001 as Broadway, seating 1,200 in stalls and balcony, for cinema, theatre, conference and concert use, with new Gildenburgh Art Gallery and Gaston Restaurant adjacent.)

Saturday 4 September: **The ODEON Theatre SWISS COTTAGE,** London N.W.3 – 96 Finchley Road (backing onto Upper Avenue Road). Architect: Harry Weedon (assistant: Basil Herring). £57,550. 2,115 seats: 1,281 stalls + 834 balcony. Modernised circa 1960. Triple from 25 February 1973, seating 742 in former balcony + 105 & 109 in former rear stalls. Latter cinemas enlarged to 152 & 155 seats. Three further cinemas opened 19 June 1992 in former front stalls, stage and upstairs foyer, seating 250 + 200 + 112 seats. Refurbished 1998 with new box-office. Open in June 2001, seating 715 + 111 + 220 + 120 + 154 + 156.

Saturday 11 September: **The ODEON Theatre WOLVER-HAMPTON,** Staffordshire – Skinner Street. Architect: Harry Weedon (assistant: P. J. Price). £37,432. 1,940 seats: 1,272 stalls + 668 balcony. Triple from 7 October 1973, seating 622 in former balcony + 96 & 111 in former rear stalls. Closed 4 June 1983. (Detripled. Top Rank Club for bingo. Renamed Mecca. Grade II listed building from October 2000. Open in June 2001.)

Saturday 18 September: **ASTORIA PRESTWICH,** Lancashire – Bury New Road, Sedgeley Park. (Opened 3 September 1931 by Emery circuit. Architect: Charles Swain. 1,699 seats in 1939: 1,108 stalls + 591 balcony. Renamed ODEON 20 September 1937. Closed 12 August 1961. (Lancastrian Bingo Club. Demolished. Lidl supermarket.)

Monday 11 October: **THEATRE DE LUXE GLOUCESTER,** Gloucestershire – Northgate Street. (Opened 17 April 1922. Architect: William Leah. 1,062 seats.) 1,014 seats in 1938: 668 stalls + 346 balcony. Closed by fire on night of 29/30 January 1939. (Site cleared 1959. Lloyds Bank, shops & offices.)

Monday 25 October: **The ODEON Theatre WOOLWICH,** London S.E.18 – Parsons Hill, now John Wilson Street. Architect: George Coles. £46,595. 1,828 seats: 1,178 stalls + 650 balcony. Modernised internally circa May 1964: 1,111 seats. Grade II listed building. Closed 17 October 1981. (Taken over by Panton Films, re-opened 14 July 1983 renamed Coronet. Twin from 6 July 1990 seating 678 in former balcony + 360 in former rear stalls. Closed 9 June 1999. Taken over by church.)

Saturday 30 October: **The ODEON Theatre RHYL,** Flintshire – Brighton Road and High Street. Architect: Harry Weedon (assistant: Robert Bullivant). £37,435. 1,408 seats: 862 stalls + 546 balcony. (Taken over 13 October 1969 by Hutchinson, renamed Astra. Triple from 24 April 1974, seating 750 in stalls + 250 & 225 in former balcony. Stalls converted to bingo. Grade II listed building from 4 January 1989. Taken over by Apollo, renamed Apollo. Cinemas closed October 1995. Disused.)

Tuesday 2 November: **The ODEON Theatre LEICESTER SQUARE,** London W.C.2 – Leicester Square. Architects: Harry

Weedon, Andrew Mather. (Architect for Alhambra House offices on Charing Cross Road: Eric Lyons.) On site of Alhambra Theatre. £232,755. 2,116 seats: 1,140 stalls + 976 balcony. Closed 15 October 1940 by bomb damage overnight. Re-opened 18 November 1940. Closed 14 November 1948 for war damage repairs. Re-opened 30 December 1948. Closed 13 May 1953 (one day) for wide screen installation. 2,068 seats. Closed 19 September 1967 for modernisation. Re-opened 27 December 1967, seating 1,994. Modernised December 1987-January 1988. Closed 13 April 1998 for modernisation. Re-opened 5 August 1998, seating 1,943. Open in September 2001.)

Monday 8 November: **The ODEON Theatre ACTON,** London W.3 – King Street. Architect: George Coles. £37,647. 1,870 seats: 1,230 stalls + 640 balcony. Closed 18 October 1975. (B&Q store. Closed January 1988. Demolished.)

Tuesday 9 November: **The ODEON Theatre EDGWARE ROAD,** London W.2. – 319 Edgware Road. Architect: George Coles. £831 (expenditure after building largely completed). 2,370 seats: 1,528 stalls + 842 balcony. Closed for subdivision. Re-opened 20 February 1968 with smaller Odeon cinema, seating 1,116, extending former balcony with new screen (plus Top Rank Club for bingo in former stalls area). Cinema closed 7 June 1975. (Cinema re-opened 24 March 1979 for Asian films, renamed Liberty. Closed. Bingo closed 1983. Market in stalls area. Auditorium demolished July 1990. Frontage demolished November 1994. Part of Church Street open-air car park.)

Monday 15 November: **PICTURE HOUSE DUNSTALL,** Wolverhampton, Staffordshire – Stafford Road, Bushbury. (Opened 19 November 1934. Architect: Hurley Robinson.) Renamed ODEON circa 1938. 1,338 seats in 1939: 990 stalls + 348 balcony. Closed 5 November 1960. (Top Rank Club for bingo from 16 February 1962. Sold to Hutchinsons 2 September 1971, renamed Surewin Bingo. Closed 23 September 1981. Demolished November/December 1981. Retirement flats.)

Monday 22 November: **CENTRAL STOURBRIDGE,** Worcestershire – 63/5 High Street. (Opened 16 May 1929. Architects: Webb & Gray. 1,500 seats.) Renamed ODEON circa 1938. 1,378 seats in 1939: 797 stalls + 581 balcony. Closed 16 June 1973. (Shop and other commercial use. Closed 1990. Demolished. Wilkinsons store by 2000.)

Saturday 27 November: **The ODEON Theatre NORTH WATFORD,** Hertfordshire – St. Albans Road. Architects: J. Owen Bond & Son. Interior decoration: Mollo & Egan. £32,000 (approximately) (taken over just prior to completion). 1,394 seats: 942 stalls + 452 balcony. Closed 30 May 1959. (Waitrose supermarket from 1961. Demolished 1989. Flats.)

Saturday 4 December: **The ODEON Theatre SOUTHSEA,** Hampshire – Highland Road and Festing Road. Architect: Andrew Mather. £35,232. 1,688 seats: 1,152 stalls + 536 balcony. (Taken over 20 November 1977 by independent, renamed Salon. Second cinema added circa February 1981, seating 400 in former rear stalls area. Both closed September 1983. Demolished 1985. Sports field of Craneswater Junior School.)

Saturday 18 December: **The ODEON Theatre BRIGHTON,** Sussex – West Street at corner of Little Russell Street. Architect: Andrew Mather. £48,000. 1,920 seats: 1,236 stalls + 684 balcony. Modernised 1969. Closed 17 April 1973. (Demolished April 1990. Family Assurance House block of offices from 1992.) [Previous Odeon was former Palladium, see entry for 15 April 1935. Current Odeon is replacement.]

1938

Monday 17 January: **EMBASSY GILLINGHAM,** Kent – Gardiner Street. (Opened 3 October 1936. Architect: Robert Cromie. 1,762 seats.) 1,744 seats in 1938: 1,276 stalls + 468 balcony. Renamed ODEON 16 March 1946. 1,534 seats in 1967. (Taken over December 1967 by Classic, renamed Classic. Taken over by independent 13 June 1977, renamed Embassy. Closed 17 September 1977. Bingo club, Gala by July 2001.)

Monday 7 February: **The ODEON Theatre NORWICH,** Norfolk – Botolph Street. Architect: Harry Weedon (assistant: Basil Herring). £43,901. 2,054 seats: 1,246 stalls + 808 balcony. Closed 26 June 1971. (Sold 10 July 1971 to Sovereign Securities, demolished for cash payment plus shell of new Odeon on adjacent site.)

Monday 21 February: **The ODEON Theatre CHORLEY,** Lancashire – Market Street. Architect: Harry Weedon (assistant: P. J. Price). £35,571. 1,526 seats: 1,092 stalls + 434 balcony. Closed 6 February 1971. (Sold 9 August 1973 to Tudor Bingo for bingo club. Taken over by Gala, renamed Gala. Open in 2001.)

Saturday 26 February: **The ODEON Theatre ERITH,** Kent – High Street and Avenue Road. Architect: George Coles. £27,996. 1,246 seats: 826 stalls + 420 balcony. 1,226 seats in 1967. (Taken over 9 December 1967 by Classic, renamed Classic. Subdivided for stalls bingo plus new cinema in old balcony, opened 16 September 1973. Both taken over 1974 by Mecca, cinema renamed Mecca 3 January 1974. Cinema closed 25 September 1976. Balcony re-opened as part of bingo hall. Taken over 1995 by Jasmine, renamed Jasmine. Closed 4 February 1996. Disused.)

Monday 28 February: **The ODEON Theatre SPALDING,** Lincolnshire – London Road, corner of Haverhill Road. Architect: Harry Weedon (assistant: Basil Herring). £22,760. 1,208 seats, stadium plan: 886 front section + 322 raised rear section. 1,090 seats in 1967. (Taken over 9 December 1967 by Classic, renamed Classic. Twin from 7 May 1971, seating 768 & 248. Taken over 6 October 1974 by independent, renamed Regent 1 & 2. Renamed Gemini. Closed July 1983. Demolished October 1987. Retirement flats from July 2001: Georgian Court.)

Saturday 12 March: **The ODEON Theatre NEWPORT,** Monmouthshire – Clarence Place, at corner of East Usk Road, on site including former Palladium/Regal cinema. Architect:

Harry Weedon (assistant: Arthur J. Price). £34,381. 1,546 seats: 1,054 stalls + 492 balcony. Closed 30 May 1981. (Snooker hall circa 1986. Closed circa 1991. Capones American Bar nightclub. Listed building from 12 March 1999. Closed. Disused.)

Saturday 26 March: **AMBASSADOR KINGSWOOD**, Bristol, Gloucestershire – Regent Street. Opened by London & Southern as an Odeon subsidiary. Architect: F. C. Mitchell. 1,794 seats in 1939: 1,314 stalls + 480 balcony. Closed by war-time damage. Re-opened late March 1941. Renamed ODEON 6 November 1944. Closed 11 March 1961. (Reconstructed internally for Top Rank Bowl. Sold March 1969 to Safeway. Demolished. Safeways supermarket.)

Friday 8 April: leasing out of **ROYALTY BROADSTAIRS** (see 27 May 1935 for early history). (Taken over by independent, H. Godwin Longthorn. Subleased to Sax Cinemas in January 1939. Closed by bomb damage 1 November 1940.) Modernised and re-opened 3 August 1950 as ODEON. Closed 29 September 1956. (Disco. Demolished. Serene Court block of flats + one shop.)

Thursday 14 April: **The ODEON Theatre ELTHAM HILL**, London S.E.9 – Eltham Hill, at corner of Kingsground. Architect: Andrew Mather. £38,795. 1,711 seats, semi-stadium plan: 883 front + 828 stepped rear section. Renamed GAUMONT 28 November 1949. Closed 16 September 1967. (Top Rank Club for bingo. Renamed Mecca. Open in June 2001.)

Saturday 16 April: **The ODEON Theatre BALHAM**, London S.W.12 – Balham Hill at corner of Malwood Road. Architect: George Coles. £45,828. 1,822 seats: 1,216 stalls + 606 balcony. Closed 9 September 1972. (Re-opened 13 December 1974 as Asian cinema, renamed Liberty. Closed 1979. Auditorium gutted March-April 1983 for indoor market. Auditorium demolished circa May 1985. Foyers stripped for Majestic wine warehouse with frontage retained. Flats built on site of auditorium. Flats introduced above wine warehouse: Foyer Apartments.)

Monday 25 April: takeover (through London & Southern?) of **KENNING HALL CLAPTON, London E.5** – 229 Lower Clapton Road. (Opened pre-1915, former function room of adjacent White Hart public house.) 641 seats, one floor. New foyer and frontage added. (Taken over 2 March 1958 by independent. Closed June 1979. Nightclub from 1983: Dougies Dine and Dance in 2000.)

Wednesday 18 May: **The ODEON Theatre BRENTWOOD**, Essex – High Street. Architect: George Coles. £32,733. 1,350 seats: 920 stalls + 430 balcony. Closed 20 April 1974. (Taken over 1 May 1974 by Brentwood Council under compulsory purchase order. Demolished for part of Chapel High Shopping Centre which included Focus 1 & 2 cinemas.)

Monday 23 May: **The ODEON Theatre REDHILL**, Surrey – Station Road. Architect: Andrew Mather (assistant: Keith P. Roberts). £39,603. 1,474 seats: 1,000 stalls + 474 balcony. Closed 18 October 1975. (Nightclub, called British Embassy in 2000.)

Wednesday 1 June: **The ODEON Theatre PECKHAM**, London S.E.15 – 24/26 High Street, on site including former Queen's Theatre. Architect: Andrew Mather. £43,800. 2,110 seats: 1,442 stalls + 668 balcony. Columns on frontage removed in 1960s. Triple from 27 January 1974, seating 668 in former balcony + 118 & 118 in former rear stalls. (Taken over 1 November 1981 by independent, renamed Ace. Closed 1 December 1983. Demolished circa 1985. Flats.)

Sunday 5 June: **ALHAMBRA BARNSLEY**, Yorkshire – Doncaster Road. (Opened 1915 as live theatre.) 2,100 seats in 1939: 826 + 325 + 449. Closed 26 November 1960. (Top Rank Club for bingo. Sold, renamed Vale Bingo. Closed. Demolished 1982. Part of Alhambra Shopping Centre, at Sheffield Road rear entrance.)

June: **RIVIERA CHEETHAM HILL**, Manchester – Cheetham Hill Road. (Opened 14 May 1931. Architects: J. & H. Patterson. Decorative artist: A. Sherwood Edwards. 2,117 seats.) 2,117 seats in 1939: 1,625 stalls + 492 balcony. Renamed ODEON circa 1943. Closed 4 March 1961. (Reconstructed internally for Top Rank Bowl, opened 21 August 1961. Closed. Demolished. Between Comet Electric and Rayburn Trading retail warehouse units.)

Saturday 18 June: **The ODEON Theatre LLANELLY**, Carmarthenshire – Station Road, Lloyd Street and Minor Street. Architect: Harry Weedon (assistant: P. J. Price). £35,338. 1,450 seats: 900 stalls + 550 balcony. 1,364 seats in 1967. (Taken over 9 December 1967 by Classic, renamed Classic. Triple from 1 October 1971, seating 516 in former balcony extended forward + 273 & 122 in former rear stalls. Taken over 30 May 1976 by Borough Council, renamed Llanelli Entertainment Centre. Modernised: upstairs auditorium equipped for live shows plus films, renamed Theatr Elli in 1984, seating 500, with downstairs cinemas renamed Theatre Two and Three, seating 310 & 122. All open in June 2001.)

Monday 20 June: **The ODEON Theatre UXBRIDGE**, Middlesex – High Street. Architect: Andrew Mather (assistant: Keith P. Roberts). £30,400 including shops and offices. 1,837 seats: 1,215 stalls + 622 balcony. Triple from 25 April 1976, seating 630 in former balcony + 140 & 140 in former rear stalls. Closed 5 June 1982. (Demolished 1982. New two screen Odeon on part of enlarged redevelopment site. Closed 2001 in favour of multiplex elsewhere.)

Monday 27 June: **The ODEON Theatre HALIFAX**, Yorkshire – Broad Street, corner of Orange Street (also onto Great Albion Street). Architect: George Coles. £59,727. 2,058 seats: 1,344 stalls + 714 balcony. Closed 18 October 1975. (Top Rank Club for bingo. Renamed Mecca. Open in June 2001.) [Current Odeon is multiplex elsewhere.]

Saturday 16 July: **The ODEON Theatre BRISTOL**, Gloucestershire – Union Street and Broadmead. Architect: T. Cecil Howitt. £57,600. 1,945 seats: 1,051 stalls + 894 balcony. Closed 3 December 1940 by bomb damage. Re-opened 17 December 1940. Modernised in 1967. Triple from 27 May 1974, seating 844 in former balcony + 108 & 103 in former rear stalls. Closed 15 October 1983 for redevelopment of interior, architects Dowton & Hurst (Donald Armstrong). New Odeon opened 13

June 1985 above corner shop with new side entrance, seating 400 + 225 + 215. Open in June 2001, seating 399 + 244 + 215.)

Monday 18 July: **The Odeon Theatre EAST HAM,** London E.6 – 9 Barking Road, on site including former Boleyn cinema. Architect: Andrew Mather (assistant: Keith P. Roberts). £47,962. 2,212 seats: 1,418 stalls + 794 balcony. Modernised in 1960s. 1,840 seats. Closed 31 October 1981. (Taken over by independent, tripled and re-opened late 1995 as Asian cinema, named Boleyn Cinema, seating 794 former balcony + 270 & 270 former rear stalls. Open.)

Wednesday 27 July: **The Odeon Theatre HACKNEY ROAD,** London E.2 – 211 Hackney Road between Thurtle Road (now Dawson Street) and Scawfell Street. £44,926. 1,926 seats: 1,260 stalls + 666 balcony. Closed 20 May 1961. (Top Rank Club for bingo, opened 21 May 1961. Heavily altered. Renamed Mecca. Open in June 2001.)

Thursday 28 July: **The Odeon Theatre LEICESTER,** Leicestershire – Queen Street and Rutland Street. Architect: Harry Weedon (assistant: Robert Bullivant). £46,800. 2,182 seats: 1,307 stalls + 875 balcony. Modernised in 1960. Triple from 3 February 1974, seating 1,237 in former balcony and front stalls + 123 & 111 in rear stalls. Fourth cinema added circa 1988 in front stalls, seating 401, with new screen for upstairs cinema now seating 872. All closed 16 July 1997. Grade II listed building from 1998. Disused in 2001.) [Current Odeon is multiplex elsewhere.]

Saturday 30 July: **The ODEON Theatre AYR,** Ayrshire – Burns Statue Square. Architect: Andrew Mather. 1,732 seats: 1,303 stalls + 429 balcony. 1,468 seats in 1985. Triple from 10 July 1987, seating 433 in former balcony + 138 & 138 in former rear stalls. Fourth cinema added 1992 in front stalls with new screen in front of upstairs cinema and one rear stalls cinema reduced to 135 seats. Open in June 2001, seating 388 + 168 + 135 + 371.

Monday 3 October: **The ODEON Theatre DEPTFORD,** London S.E.8 – 23/27 Deptford Broadway at corner with Deptford Church Street, on site including former Palladium cinema. £45,000. 1,729 seats: 1,200 stalls + 529 balcony. Closed 16 June 1944 by bomb damage. Restored, architect: George Coles, and re-opened 17 December 1951. Closed 16 May 1970. (Sold 16 January 1973 to Marshamheath. Demolished 1988. Shops and flats on enlarged redevelopment site.)

Wednesday 12 October: **The ODEON Theatre LUTON,** Bedfordshire – Dunstable Road, Bury Park. Architect: Andrew Mather (assistant: Keith P. Roberts). £49,600. 1,958 seats: 1,332 balcony + 626 stalls. Triple from 24 November 1974, seating 800 in former balcony and front stalls + 115 & 110 in former rear stalls. Closed 4 June 1983. (Detripled, re-opened July 1983 as Top Rank Club for bingo. Renamed Mecca. Closed late January 1999. Grade II listed building from Spring 1999. Re-opened 9 February 2001 as Church of God in Christ.)

Monday 17 October: **The ODEON Theatre MILE END,** London E.3 – 401 Mile End Road, corner of Frederick Place. Architect: Andrew Mather (assistant: Keith P. Roberts). £49,654. 2,304 seats: 1,528 stalls + 776 balcony. Closed for modernisation, re-opened 27 December 1968. Closed 17 June 1972. Re-opened 8 September 1972 as Sundown for pop concerts and some films. Closed January 1973. (Leased by independent for Asian films, re-opened March 1975, renamed Liberty. Closed 1978. Demolished May 1984. Bosso House block of flats.)

Monday 7 November: **The ODEON Theatre SHANNON CORNER,** New Malden, Surrey – Kingston By-Pass and Burlington Road. Also known as ODEON NEW MALDEN and ODEON MERTON. Architect: George Coles. 1,611 seats: 961 stalls + 650 balcony. Closed 2 January 1960. (Offices for Decca Navigation. Closed circa 1979. Demolished February 1985. Car park.)

Monday 14 November: **The ODEON Theatre HAMILTON,** Lanarkshire – Townhead Street. Architect: Andrew Mather. £32,548. 1,819 seats: 1,353 stalls + 466 balcony. Closed 1 March 1980 for tripling. Re-opened 5 April 1980, seating 466 in former balcony with new screen + 224 & 310 in former stalls. Closed 26 August 1999. (Demolished 1999. Car park.)

Saturday 3 December: **The ODEON Theatre MOTHERWELL,** Lanarkshire – Brandon Street. £31,952. 1,752 seats: 1,242 stalls + 510 balcony. Closed 25 October 1975. (Taken over for County Bingo. Closed November 1995. Demolished 1996. Development site.)

Saturday 17 December: **The ODEON Theatre BRADFORD,** Yorkshire – Manchester Road, corner of Town Hall Square. Architect: Harry Weedon (assistant: Robert Bullivant). £65,000. 2,713 seats: 1,750 stalls + 963 balcony. Closed 31 August 1940 by bomb damage. Re-opened 11 November 1940. Closed 28 January 1961 for modernisation. Re-opened 27 February 1961, stalls seating reduced to 1,484. Closed 22 March 1969. (Sold to Bradford Corporation for redevelopment scheme. Demolished. West Yorkshire Police building.) [Odeon name passed to former Gaumont, then to new multiplex.]

Monday 19 December: **AMBASSADOR HAYES,** Middlesex – East Avenue. Opened by London & Southern, controlled by Odeon. Architect: F.C. Mitchell. 1,517 seats, semi-stadium: 989 stalls + 528 raised rear section. Closed 10 June 1961. (Demolished. GPO Centre telephone exchange, now British Telecommunications Centre.)

1939

Monday 6 February (through London & Southern subsidiary): **RIALTO SOUTHAMPTON,** Hampshire – 325 Shirley Road (auditorium along Janson Road). (Opened 9 January 1922. Booked circa 1932/33 by Cinema Service.) 945 seats: 737 stalls + 208 balcony. 928 seats. Closed 5 November

1960. (Top Rank Club for bingo. Closed June 1962. Blundell's furniture store. Disused in 1994. Town and Country Pine furniture store in 2001.)

Saturday 25 February: **The ODEON Theatre MIDDLES-BROUGH**, Yorkshire – Corporation Road. Architect: Harry Weedon (assistant: W. Calder Robson and/or Basil Herring). £41,350. 1,761 seats: 1,034 stalls + 727 balcony. Triple from 29 September 1974, seating 720 in former balcony + 110 & 110 in former rear stalls. Fourth cinema added late 1989 in front stalls area with new screen for upstairs cinema and minis enlarged: 611 seats upstairs + 129 & 148 in former rear stalls + 254 in former front stalls. Refurbished circa 1999. Closed 24 June 2001.

Monday 20 March: **The ODEON Theatre CAMBERWELL**, London S.E.5 – corner of Denmark Hill and Coldharbour Lane, partly on site of New Empire cinema. Architect: Andrew Mather (assistant: Keith P. Roberts). £59,853. 2,470 seats: 1,484 stalls + 986 balcony. Only balcony used in final years. Closed 5 July 1975. (Dickie Dirts jeans emporium from 24 October 1981. Demolished Spring 1993. Sold to London & Quadrant Housing Trust. Flats: The Foyer.)

Monday 1 May: **The ODEON Theatre DALSTON**, London N.1 – Stamford Road, off Kingsland Road. Architect: Andrew Mather. 2,064 seats: 1,319 stalls + 745 balcony. £45,000. Triple from 10 December 1972 seating 745 in former balcony + 120 & 120 in former rear stalls. Closed 31 March 1979. (Demolished 1984. Block of flats: De Beauvoir Place.)

Saturday 6 May: **The ODEON Theatre BLACKPOOL**, Lancashire – Dickson Road, between Lord Street and Springfield Road. Architects: Harry Weedon and W. Calder Robson. £82,500. 3,088 seats: 1,684 stalls + 1,404 balcony. Modernised from December 1964 to February 1965, closing for four days, seating reduced to 2,744. Triple from 16 October 1975, seating 1,404 in former balcony + 190 & 190 in former rear stalls. Grade II listed building from Spring 1994. Main cinema reduced to 1,375 seats. Closed 5 December 1998. [Current Odeon is multiplex elsewhere.]

Thursday 25 May: **The ODEON Theatre CANNING TOWN**, London E.16 – Barking Road, between Star Lane and Alexandra Street, backed by Edward Street. Architect: Andrew Mather (assistant: Keith P. Roberts). £51,175. 2,240 seats: 1,418 stalls + 822 balcony. Closed 2 October 1940 by bomb damage. Re-opened 3 March 1941. Closed 11 May 1941 by bomb damage. (Sold 15 December 1970 to East London Housing Association and site cleared for block of flats, named Odeon Court.)

Sunday 25 June: **BEDFORD CAMDEN TOWN**, London N.W.1 – 93/95 Camden High Street. (Former live theatre. Taken over 1933 by ABC. 1,259 seats.) 1,115 seats in 1939: 471 + 224 + 420 (gallery). Closed 11 December 1939. (Re-opened as variety theatre. Closed 1959. Demolished 1968. Curry's, Job Centre and other shops.)

And **EMPIRE BRISTOL**, Gloucestershire – Old Market Street. (Opened 13 April 1931, former variety theatre with some film use. Taken over circa October 1932 by ABC. 1,437 seats.) 1,452 seats in 1939: 1,132 stalls + 320 balcony. Closed 9 December 1939. (Re-opened 26 December 1939 as live theatre. Closed 1954. BBC Studios from mid-1950s to 1962. Demolished 1963. Pedestrian underpass.)

Saturday 26 August: **The ODEON Theatre ELMERS END**, Beckenham, Kent – 46 Croydon Road at Elmers End Green. Architect: Andrew Mather (assistant: Keith P. Roberts). £44,709. 1,518 seats: 1,028 stalls + 490 balcony. Closed 5 January 1957. (Demolished. Office tower, originally Muirhead's, now Maunsell House. Adjoining parade of shops and flats stands in June 2001.)

Monday 28 August: **The ODEON Theatre HENDON**, London N.W.4 – corner of Church Road and Parson Street. Architects: Harry Weedon and Robert Bullivant. £36,897. 1,362 seats: 868 stalls + 494 balcony. Closed 13 January 1979. (Demolished 1982. Ferrydale Lodge, block of flats.)

September: full amalgamation with COUNTY CINEMAS circuit which comprised:

PALACE ABERDEEN, Bridge Place. (Opened 8 April 1929 by Poole's circuit, former live theatre with some film use. 1,714 seats. Closed 7 March 1931 for internal reconstruction and extension, architect: C. T. Marshall of Marshall & Tweedy. Re-opened 28 November 1931, seating 2,000. Taken over June 1936 by County.) Closed 14 November 1959. (Altered and re-opened 24 March 1960 by Rank as The Palace dance hall. Renamed Fusion. Renamed Ritzy's Discotheque. Renamed Bonkers. Renamed The Palace, nightclub. Open in 2001.)

REGENT ABERDEEN, Justice Mill Lane. (Opened 27 February 1932 by Poole's circuit. Architect: T. Scott Sutherland. 1,430 seats. Taken over June 1936 by County.) Renamed ODEON 29 July 1940. (Triple from 8 April 1974 seating 793 in former balcony + 123 & 123 in former rear stalls. Front stalls converted to two further cinemas in 1991: 219 & 219 seats. Category C listed. Closed 13 June 2001. Sold for conversion to health & fitness centre.)

ALEXANDRA ALDERSHOT, Hampshire – Alexandra Road. (Taken over November 1927 by County. Rebuilt 1928, architect: Henry G. Baker, with balcony added and Italian atmospheric touches). 710 seats in 1939. Closed circa 1967. (Star bingo. Demolished 1986. Office block: Communications House.)

EMPIRE ALDERSHOT, Hampshire – High Street. (Opened 1 August 1930. Architect: Harold S. Scott. 1,599 seats. Taken over circa 1931 by County.) 1,458 seats in 1939. Renamed ODEON 18 January 1964. Closed 17 October 1981. (Christian centre: The King's Centre.)

MANOR PARK PAVILION ALDERSHOT, Hampshire – High Street. (Taken over January 1928 by County.) 836 seats in 1939. Closed 29 September 1956. (Demolished. Office block: Campbell House.)

COUNTY BLETCHLEY, Buckinghamshire – High Street. (Opened 1911, former Methodist chapel. Taken over circa January 1928 by County. Enlarged and renamed King George's Cinema. Renamed County in 1932. 460 seats.) 400 seats in 1939. Closed 29 June 1957. (Demolished circa 1972.)

EMPIRE BORDON, Hampshire – Bordon Camp. (Opened 29 October 1938 by W. J. May and County, reconstruction of existing premises, architect: David E. Nye.) 475 seats in 1939. (Taken over circa 1968 by independent. Closed August 1973.)

ARCADE CAMBERLEY, Surrey – London Road. (Opened 22 January 1923. Taken over circa 1936 by County.) 682 seats in 1939. Closed 29 September 1956.

REGAL CAMBERLEY, Surrey – 303 London Road. (Opened 27 August 1932 by County. Architect: Harold S. Scott.) 1,210 seats in 1939. Renamed ODEON circa 1947. 1,017 seats in 1967. (Taken over December 1967 by Classic, renamed Classic. Tripled with bingo from 1 October 1975, cinemas seating 444 + 155 + 129. Renamed Cannon 1985. Taken over 18 February 1994 by Robins, renamed Robins Cinemas. Taken over by independent. Open in June 2001, seating 420 + 114 + 94.)

RITZ CHELMSFORD, Essex – Baddow Road. (Opened 8 November 1935 by County, architect: Robert Cromie. Interior decoration: Mollo & Egan. 1,748 seats.) 1,750 seats in 1939. Renamed ODEON 1947. Closed 17 October 1981. (Demolished March/April 1990. Meadows multi-storey car park.) [Current Odeon is new cinema nearby.]

PLAZA CHICHESTER, Sussex – South Street. (Opened 18 December 1936 as total reconstruction of Picturedrome. Architect: Andrew Mather. 1,063 seats.) Renamed ODEON 13 May 1945. Closed 6 February 1960. (Fine Fare supermarket, opened 1961. Iceland store in 2000.)

HEADGATE COLCHESTER, Essex – St. John's Street. (Opened 31 November 1910, former Liberal Club and Assembly Rooms. Taken over 24 March 1935 by County. 320 seats on one floor.) (Leased to independent after 23 June 1952, renamed Cameo. 319 seats. Taken over 1972 by Star. Closed December 1976. Taken over by another independent. Closed. Interior demolished. Planet Ace.)

REGAL COLCHESTER, Essex – Crouch Street. (Opened 23 February 1931. Architect: Cecil Masey. 1,446 seats. Taken over 24 March 1935 by County.) 1,450 seats in 1939. Closed 1944 by fire for three months. Renamed ODEON September 1961. 1,200 seats. Triple from April 1974, seating 482 in former balcony + 110 & 110 in former rear stalls. Refurbished 1984. Small cinemas enlarged circa 1986, seating 150 & 150. Fourth cinema added 1987 in former front stalls. Two further cinemas opened in 1991. All six cinemas open in June 2001, seating 480 + 237 + 118 + 133 + 126 + 177.

HIPPODROME DERBY, Derbyshire – Green Lane. (Opened 15 September 1930, former live theatre. Taken over circa June 1936 by County. Modernised and re-opened 30 July 1938.) 1,901 seats in 1939. Transferred directly to Odeon March 1943. Closed 29 October 1950. (Live theatre. Closed 1959. Bingo club from 1962. Grade II listed building from 1996.)

HIPPODROME DEVONPORT, Plymouth, Devon – Prince's Street. (Opened December 1929, former live theatre gutted and enlarged, architects: Marshall & Tweedy.) 2,000 seats in 1939. Closed by bomb damage on 24 April 1941. Transferred directly to Odeon March 1943. (Site cleared. Salvation Army offices: Red Shield House.)

REX FARNBOROUGH, Hampshire – London Rough. (Opened 25 September 1937 by County. Architect: David E. Nye. 1,208 seats). 1,122 seats in 1967. (Taken over by 2 December 1967 by Classic, renamed Classic. Closed 16 June 1973, except for sex films briefly continued. Bingo club. Concert use. Demolished mid-1970s. Kingsmead House and Shopping Centre.)

SCALA FARNBOROUGH, Hampshire – Camp Road, North Camp. (Opened 14 November 1927. Architect: R. A. Briggs. 716 seats. Taken over circa 1936 by County.) 727 seats in 1939. Closed 27 October 1956. (Bingo club. Laser games centre. Church: Kingdom Hall of Jehovah's Witnesses.)

COUNTY FARNCOMBE, Godalming, Surrey – Meadow at corner of King's Road. (Opened 1921 as King George's. Taken over late July 1927 by County. Renamed County October 1936.) 583 seats in 1939. Renamed ODEON May 1945. Closed 28 January 1956. (Sausage pie factory. Deep freeze centre. Vickers supermarket. Demolished 2000. Flats: Surrey Cloisters.)

COUNTY FARNHAM, Surrey – 8 East Street. (Palace cinema taken over circa 1936 by County. Reconstructed, architect: Harold S. Scott, with balcony removed, and re-opened 26 December 1936 renamed County. 500 seats.) Closed 27 October 1956. (Auditorium demolished for shopping centre including J. Sainsbury supermarket. Frontage retained as Cambridge House.)

REGAL FARNHAM, Surrey – East Street. (Opened 31 March 1933 by County. Architect: Harold S. Scott.) 1,280 seats in 1939. Renamed ODEON 21 October 1962. (Taken over 23 August 1971 by Star, renamed Cinema. Split for bingo and twin cinemas named Studio 1 & 2 and re-opened 1971. Taken over by Classic. Closed 13 September 1985. Demolished 1987. Vacant site in 2001.)

COUNTY FLEET, Hampshire. (Opened 20 November 1937 by County as reconstruction of old County. Architect: David E. Nye.) 774 seats in 1939. Renamed ODEON circa 1945. Closed 12 October 1957. (Demolished. Shops, including Co-Operative Funeral Directors.)

ASTORIA FOLKESTONE, Kent – 24 Sandgate Road and Oxford Terrace. (Opened 20 April 1935. Architects: E. A. Stone & Ewen Barr. Interior decoration: Mollo & Egan. 1,650 seats. Taken over December 1935 by County.) Renamed ODEON 1 June 1940. Modernised April 1960. Closed 26 January 1974. (Demolished. Albion House offices with Boots store on ground floor in 2001.)

REGAL GODALMING, Surrey – Ockford Road. (Opened 2 August 1935 by County. Architect: Robert Cromie. Interior decoration: Mollo & Egan. 1,210 seats.) Renamed ODEON May 1945. 1,132 seats in 1967. Taken over 2 December 1967 by Classic, renamed Classic. Bingo club. Balcony opened as Classic cinema in 1971. Taken over by Mecca, cinema renamed Mecca. Closed 13 December 1975. Balcony re-opened as part of main auditorium for bingo. Closed. Demolished February/March 1996. Housing.)

REGAL GOLDERS GREEN, London N.W.11 – 765 Finchley Road. (Opened 19 September 1932 by County, conversion of ice rink, architect: Robert Cromie. 2,200 seats on one floor.) 2,218 seats in 1939. Closed 1 December 1956. (Top Rank Bowl, opened March 1960. Closed. Sold 25 October 1971 to Bruno Newton. Demolished February-March 1996. Offices: Smiths Ltd.)

PLAYHOUSE GUILDFORD, Surrey – High Street. (Opened circa 1922. Taken over 1929 by County.) 925 seats in 1939. Closed 12 June 1965. (Demolished. Tunsgate Square shopping arcade.)

PLAZA GUILDFORD, Surrey – Onslow Street. (Taken over 1930 as Central Hall by County. Renamed Plaza.) 511 seats in 1939. Closed 29 September 1956. (Bingo club. Nightclub: The Drink in 2001.)

REGAL HENLEY-ON-THAMES, Oxfordshire – Bell Street. (Opened 14 May 1937 by County, complete reconstruction of Picture House, architect: Arthur F. Hunt.) 941 seats in 1939. Renamed ODEON circa 1945. Closed 21 March 1959. (Re-opened 1960 by independent, renamed Regal. Closed 30 May 1986. Used in filming *Hope and Glory*, 1987. Demolished. Waitrose supermarket and access road.) (Present Regal is new cinema nearby.)

MAJESTIC HIGH WYCOMBE, Buckinghamshire – Castle Street. (Opened 27 January 1930. Architect: S. B. Pritlove. Interior decorator: W. E. Greenwood. 1,480 seats. Taken over circa 1932 by County.) Renamed ODEON August 1944. Closed 25 January 1969. (Demolished. Woolworth's.)

LIDO HOVE, Sussex – Denmark Villas. (Opened 6 May 1932 by County, conversion of ice rink, architect: Robert Cromie. 2,137 seats on one floor.) Renamed ODEON July 1944. Closed 18 February 1961. (Top Rank Bowl from 1961. Closed. Sold 30 April 1969 to Food Securities [Properties]. Demolished 1970. New Marina Car Sales.)

REGAL LICHFIELD, Staffordshire – Tamworth Street. (Opened 18 July 1932. Architect: Harold S. Scott. Operated for local owners by County from November 1932.) 1,235 seats in 1939. (Reverted to local owners' control circa 1941. Taken over by Mayfair circuit. Taken over 30 August 1943 by ABC. Taken over 1 July 1969 by Star. Part-week bingo. Closed 10 July 1974, bingo continuing. Bingo closed circa 1979. Supermarket, Kwiksave in 2001.)

REGAL MARGATE, Kent – Cecil Square. (Opened 21 December 1934 by County. Architect: Robert Cromie. 1,795 seats: 1,315 stalls + 480 balcony) Closed by bomb damage on night of 7 December 1941. (Entrance to magistrates' court + shopping centre.)

COUNTY MARLOW, Buckinghamshire – Spital Street. (Opened circa 1914 as Palace. Modernised 1926 and renamed King George's. Taken over July 1927 by County. Renamed County early 1937. Closed January 1938 on opening of new County – next entry.) Used as Odeon circuit offices during World War Two. Sold 1952. (Light industrial use.)

COUNTY MARLOW, Buckinghamshire – Station Road. (Opened 14 January 1938 by County. Architect: David E. Nye. 748 seats.) Renamed ODEON February 1941. (Taken over 22 March 1959 by independent, renamed Regal. 622 seats. Closed 24 March 1985. Demolished 1985. Offices.)

PLAZA NORTHAM, Southampton – 201 Northam Road. (Opened 11 October 1932. Architect: Robert Cromie. Interior decoration: Mollo & Egan. 2,015 seats. Taken over May 1934 by County.) 2,170 seats in 1939. Closed 30 November 1957. (Sold 6 January 1958 to Southern Television. Converted to television studios. Demolished. Office block.)

CARLTON NORWICH, Norfolk – All Saints Green. (Opened 1 February 1932 by Victor Harrison. Architect: J. Owen Bond. Taken over August 1936 by County.) 1,920 seats in 1939. Modernised and re-opened January 1960, renamed GAUMONT. (Closed 6 January 1973. Top Rank Club for bingo. Open as Mecca club in June 2001.)

RITZ NOTTINGHAM, Nottinghamshire – Angel Row. (Opened 4 December 1933 by County. Architects: Verity & Beverley with A. J. Thraves. 2,426 seats: 1,754 stalls + 672 balcony.) Renamed ODEON circa 1944. Twin from 12 July 1965, 1,450 seats in former stalls + 924 seats extending former balcony. Third cinema from 11 June 1970 in former restaurant area, 101 seats. Former stalls cinema tripled from 1 February 1976 seating 581 + 141 + 141 seats. Sixth cinema added 7 March 1988, 98 seats in former restaurant space. Seated 903 + 557 + 150 + 150 + 113 + 100 in 2000. Closed 28 January 2001.

REGENT PLYMOUTH, Devon – Frankfort Street/New George Street/ Cambridge Street. (Opened 21 November 1931. Architect: W. Watson of Chadwick, Watson. Taken over June 1936 by County. 3,254 seats in 1939. Taken over directly 17 June 1940, renamed ODEON. Closed 8 September 1962. (Demolished. Littlewood's store.)

PAVILION READING, Berkshire – 143/5 Oxford Road, corner of Russell Street. (Opened 21 September 1929. Architect: Harold S. Scott. 1,361 seats. Taken over 1930 by County.) 1,357 seats in 1939. Improved and renamed GAUMONT 19 January 1958. Closed 21 April 1979. (Bingo club. Snooker hall, using only stalls.)

VAUDEVILLE READING, Berkshire – 47 Broad Street, corner of Union Street. (Opened September 1921, enlarged reconstruction of earlier cinema, architects: Emden, Egan. 1,500 seats. Taken over September 1929 by County.) 1,457 seats in 1939. Renamed GAUMONT 23 February 1953. Closed 30 November 1957. (Largely demolished. Timothy White's store, later renamed Boots, open in 1995.)

BEACON SMETHWICK, Staffordshire – Brasshouse Lane. (Opened 30 September 1929. Architect: Harold S. Scott. Associated with County from November 1932.) 962 seats in 1939. (Taken over circa 1942 by Mayfair circuit. Taken over 30 August 1943 by ABC. Closed 15 February 1958. Asian cinema. Closed. Clothing factory.)

REGAL SOUTHAMPTON, Hampshire – Above Bar. (Opened 22 June 1934 by County, partly on site of Alexandra Picture House. Architects: Verity & Beverley. 1,756 seats: 1,078 stalls + 678 balcony.) 1,736 seats in 1939. Renamed ODEON April 1945. Closed 10 February 1962 for modernisation. Re-opened 7 May 1962. Closed 17 February 1979 for twinning. Re-opened 14 April 1979, seating 756 downstairs, and 26 May 1979 seating 478 seats upstairs. Third cinema added early 1988, 98 seats in former restaurant space. All closed 5 September 1993. (Demolished late 1993. Waterstone's bookshop, etc.) [Current Odeon is multiplex elsewhere.]

ASTORIA SOUTHEND-ON-SEA, Essex – 127 High Street. (Opened 15 July 1935. Architects: E. A. Stone & T. R. Somerford. Interior decoration: Mollo & Egan. 2,750 seats. Taken over June 1936 by County.) 2,745 seats in 1939. Renamed ODEON June 1940. Modernised 1960: 2,286 seats. Closed 7 January 1970 for subdivision into ground floor supermarket with two cinemas above with new entrance on Elmer Approach. New cinemas opened 4 November 1970 with 455 seats in former café/dance studio + 1,235 seats in former balcony extended. Closed 5 April 1997. (Disused.) [Current Odeon is multiplex elsewhere.]

RITZ SOUTHEND-ON-SEA, Essex – Church Road. (Opened 14 February 1935 by County. Architect: Robert Cromie. Interior decoration: Mollo & Egan. 2,250 seats.) Modernised 1956: 1,891 seats. Closed 29 July 1972. (Top Rank Club for bingo. Closed 1978. Demolished 1981. Part of Royals Shopping Centre.)

MAJESTIC STAINES, Middlesex – High Street. (Opened 11 December 1929. Architect: S. B. Pritlove. Interior decoration: W. E. Greenwood. 1,558 seats: 1,038 stalls + 520 balcony. Taken over circa 1932 by County.) 1,507 seats in 1939. Closed 27 May 1961. (Demolished. Shops and offices.)

ORPHEUM TEMPLE FORTUNE, Golders Green, London N.W.11 – Finchley Road. (Opened 1 October 1930. Architects: Yates, Cook & Darbyshire. 2,800 seats. Taken over circa 1932 by ABC. Taken over March 1934 by County.) Renamed ODEON circa 1945. Much live show use. Redecorated 1976. 2,343 seats. Closed 27 April 1974. (Demolished circa May 1982. Flats.)

CINEMA TYSELEY, Birmingham, Warwickshire – Warwick Road. (Opened circa 1921. Architect: Hurley Robinson. Balcony added in 1930. Associated with County from November 1932.) 960 seats in 1939. Closed December 1940 by Second World War bomb damage. Re-opened 1941 by independent. Taken over circa 1954 by Essoldo. Closed 1958. Shops.)

MAJESTIC WEMBLEY, Middlesex – 47 High Road. (Opened 11 January 1929. Architects: Field & Stewart. Interior decoration: W. E. Greenwood. Taken over circa 1935 by County.) 1,906 seats in 1939. Renamed ODEON 25 March 1956. Closed 27 May 1961. (Demolished. C&A store.) [Later Odeon was Wembley Hall Cinema renamed.]

COUNTY WEYBRIDGE, Surrey – Church Street. (Opened 24 June 1920 as Kinema. Taken over circa 1927 by County, renamed King George's. Renamed County late 1936.) Closed 29 September 1956. (Public hall: Weybridge Hall.)

REGAL WIMBLEDON, London S.W.19 – The Broadway. (Opened 20 November 1935 by County. Architect: Robert Cromie. Design: Mollo & Egan. 2,000 seats.) Renamed GAUMONT 28 November 1949. Renamed ODEON 9 September 1962. Triple from 5 November 1972, seating 705 seats in former balcony + 128 & 107 seats in former rear stalls. Mini-cinemas closed 6 January 1979 for enlargement. Re-opened 8 April 1979: 218 & 190 seats. New screen installed in front of old circle in 1985. Fourth & fifth cinemas opened 29 March 1991: 175 seats in former front stalls + 90 seats in former café. Open in June 2001, seating 662 + 90 + 190 + 175 + 226.

ROYAL WINCHESTER, Hampshire – Jewry Street. (Opened 1920, former Theatre Royal, live theatre. Taken over November 1934 by County. 514 seats.) 551 seats in 1939. (Taken over 1954 by independent. Taken over 1972 by Star. Closed 29 June 1974. Live theatre. Some cinema use from 24 August 1989. Closed circa 1996 for restoration. Scheduled to re-open for live use during 2001.)

By November 1939: takeover from ORR CIRCUIT of

ASTORIA EARLSDON, Coventry, Warwickshire – Albany Road. (Opened 3 November 1922 as Broadway. Taken over January 1934 by Charles Orr, renamed Astoria.) 791 seats in 1939: 547 stalls + 244 balcony. (Taken over 1 January 1955 by independent. Closed May 1959. Wades furniture warehouse. Factory for burglar alarms in 2001.)

GLOBE COVENTRY, Warwickshire – Primrose Hill. Returned to circuit - see 1925 entry.

REGAL COVENTRY, Warwickshire – Foleshill Road, Great Heath. (Opened 1911 as Grand. Taken over 1934 by Charles Orr.) 1,016 seats in 1939: 712 stalls + 304 balcony. Closed 26 November 1960. (Sketchley's dry cleaners by 1976. Front rebuilt.)

RIALTO COVENTRY, Warwickshire – Moseley Avenue. (Opened 1928 by Charles Orr.) 1,261 seats in 1939: 911 stalls + 350 balcony. Closed 1940 by blitz damage. Frontage demolished circa 1958.)

SCALA COVENTRY, Warwickshire – Far Gosford Street. (Opened 2 October 1935 by Charles Orr on site of old Scala. 1,559 seats.) 1,557 seats in 1939: 1,079 stalls + 478 balcony. Renamed ODEON 13 March 1950. Closed 2 February 1963. (Top Rank Club for bingo. Closed 1970 by fire. Demolished circa 1973. Car park.) [Odeon name passed to former Gaumont from 1967, then to new multiplex in 2000.]

27 November: part of PARAMOUNT CIRCUIT:

ASTORIA BRIXTON, London S.W.9 – 211 Stockwell Road. (Opened 19 August 1929. Architects: E.A. Stone & T.R. Somerford. Interior decoration: Marc Henri. 2,982 seats. Taken over December 1930 by Paramount.) Closed 29 July 1972. (Sundown discotheque. Closed. Grade II listed building from 16 January 1974. Listing upgraded 26 March 1990 to Grade II*. Academy live music venue.)

ASTORIA FINSBURY PARK, London N.4 – 232/6 Seven Sisters Road, corner of Ilsedon Street. (Opened 29 September 1930. Architect: E.A. Stone. Interior decoration: Marc Henri & Laverdet. 3,040 seats. Taken over December 1930 by Paramount.) 3,018 seats in 1939. Renamed ODEON 17 November 1970. Closed 25 September 1971. (Rainbow concert hall. Grade II* listed building from 16 January 1974. Taken over 1995 by Universal Church of the Kingdom of God. Auditorium restored 1999. Foyer restored 2001.)

PARAMOUNT LEEDS, Yorkshire – corner of The Headrow & Briggate. (Opened 22 February 1932 by Paramount. Architects: Frank T. Verity & Samuel Beverley. Exterior design: Sir Reginald Blomfield. 2,556 seats.) Renamed ODEON 15 April 1940. Closed September 1968 for twinning, architects: Gavin Patterson & Partners, interior design: Tony Sharp. Re-opened 15 May 1969, seating 978 in former balcony extended + 1,297 seats in former stalls. Third cinema opened 23 July 1978, seating 126 in former bar area. Downstairs cinema closed for triping. Re-opened 1 April 1988, seating 441 + 200 + 174. Grade II listed building (for exterior) from 15 October 1993. Open in June 2001, seating 982 + 441 + 200 + 174 + 126.

PARAMOUNT MANCHESTER – Oxford Street between George Street and St. James Street. (Opened 6 October 1930 by Paramount. Architects: Frank T. Verity and Samuel Beverley. 2,920 seats.) Renamed ODEON 8 April 1940. Closed 21 July 1973 for twinning. Re-opened 25 January 1974, seating 629 in former balcony + 1,030 in former stalls. Third cinema opened 10 June 1979 in former mezzanine, seating 211. Cinema 2 (former stalls) closed 1992 for tripling plus new cinemas on stage and in basement. Re-opened: 326 + 145 + 142 + 97 + 97 seats. Open in June 2001, seating: 629 + 326 + 145 + 97 + 203 + 142 + 97.

PARAMOUNT NEWCASTLE-ON-TYNE, Northumberland – Pilgrim Street. (Opened 7 September 1931 by Paramount. Architects: Verity & Beverley. 2,604 seats.) 2,602 seats in 1939. Renamed ODEON 22 April

1940. Closed 25 January 1975 for tripling. Re-opened 9 March 1975, seating 1,228 in former balcony extended forward + 158 & 250 in former rear stalls. Fourth cinema on former stage opened 1 February 1980, seating 361. Grade II listed building from October 2000. Open in June 2001, seating 1,228 + 159 + 250 + 361.

ASTORIA OLD KENT ROAD, London S.E.15 – 593/613 Old Kent Road, corner of Sandgate Street. (Opened 10 February 1930. Architect: Edward A. Stone. 2,899 seats. Taken over December 1930 by Paramount.) Closed 29 June 1968. (Mad Dog Bowl from May 1978. Astoria Sports Centre for skateboarding, squash, gyms, sauna. Demolished October 1984. DIY store.)

ASTORIA STREATHAM, London S.W.16 – 47/9 High Road. (Opened 30 June 1930. Architect: Edward A. Stone. Interior decoration: Marc Henri & Laverdet. 2,614 seats. Taken over December 1930 by Paramount.) 2,576 seats in 1939. Modernised and re-opened 18 September 1961, renamed ODEON. Triple from 16 December 1979, seating 1,095 in former balcony + 267 & 267 in former rear stalls. New screen installed in front of old circle circa 1990. Fourth cinema in front stalls & fifth cinema on former stage area opened 27 September 1991, seating 240 + 196, with one rear cinema reduced to 168 for entry passage. Refurbished from early to mid-2001 with two new cinemas in rear of former balcony plus front stalls cinema divided in two. Open in October 2001, seating 451 + 110 + 110 + 104 + 238 + 209 + 93 + 172.

1941

Circa February?: **HIPPODROME PUTNEY,** London S.W.15 – Felsham Road. (Opened circa May 1924, former live theatre. Taken over by United Picture Theatres from January 1928. Under Gaumont management from July 1930 as part of UPT circuit. Taken over July 1935 by ABC. Taken over circa 1938 by independent. 1,420 seats. Closed by war conditions.) Re-opened (by Odeon?) 17 February 1941. Odeon-operated by May 1941. Closed 14 January 1961. (Demolished. Flats.)

June 1941: **ST. JOHN'S WORCESTER** – Malvern Road. (Opened circa September 1914, 600 seats.) Taken over 29 September 1952 by independent. Closed August 1953. Bingo. Offices and meeting halls.)

Sunday 3 August 1941: **CAPITOL CARDIFF,** Glamorgan – 116/8 Queen Street. (Opened 24 December 1921. Architects: J. H. Phillips & Wride. 2,800 seats. Taken over circa 1931 by Paramount. Returned.) 2,453 seats in 1977: 1,445 stalls + 1,008 balcony. Closed 21 January 1978. (Demolished circa February 1983. Capitol shopping centre, including Odeon Capitol cinemas.)

BIBLIOGRAPHY

Books and booklets

All Pals Together – The Story Of Children's Cinema. By Terry Staples. (Edinburgh University Press, 1997.)

Cathedrals Of The Movies - A History Of British Cinemas And Their Audiences. By David Atwell. (The Architectural Press, London, 1980.)

Cinemas in Britain - One Hundred Years Of Cinema Architecture. By Richard Gray. (Lund Humphries/Cinema Theatre Association, London, 1996.)

Gaumont British Cinemas. By Allen Eyles. (Cinema Theatre Association/BFI Publishing, London, 1996. ISBN 0-85170-519-7 £19.99.) Companion volume to this Odeon history.

Golden Hill To Golden Square. By W. 'Bill' Cartlidge. (New Horizon, Bognor Regis, 1982.)

The Granada Theatres. By Allen Eyles. (Cinema Theatre Association/BFI Publishing, London, 1998. ISBN 0-85170-680-0 £19.99.) Companion volume to this Odeon history.

Memories Of Kent Cinemas. By Martin Tapsell. (Plateway Press, Croydon, 1987.)

Mr. Rank – A Study Of J. Arthur Rank And British Films. By Alan Wood. (Hodder and Stoughton, London, 1952.)

Odeon Cavalcade – An Illustrated Souvenir Review Of The Development And Progress Of The Odeon Theatres. Edited by Felix Brittain. Narrative by C. St. Brelade Seale. (E.T. Heron, London, 1939.) Officially authorised history of the company supported by much advertising from suppliers.

Seats In All Parts – Half A Lifetime At The Movies. By Leslie Halliwell. (Granada, London, 1985.)

United Artists – The Company Built By The Stars. By Tino Balio. (The University of Wisconsin Press, 1976.)

A Vision of the City – The Architecture of T. C. Howitt. By Ernie Scoffham. (Nottingham County Council Leisure Services Department, Nottingham, 1992.)

Articles

"Alight in the Dark: Pearce Signs – Pictures from the Company Archive." (*Picture House* no. 22, Summer 1997.) Includes many examples of Odeons lit up at night by floodlighting and neon.

"The Artist-Decorator." By Mrs. Oscar Deutsch. (*Kinematograph Weekly,* 18 June 1936, page 4.)

"County Cinemas." By Allen Eyles. (*Picture House* no. 9, Winter 1986, pages 21-27 and back cover.) Full history of the circuit.

"Double Feature. Two pioneers of the pictures." By Zoe Josephs. Magazine article on Oscar Deutsch and Sol Levy. (Seen as cutting, name of magazine unknown.)

"The Flying Ladies of Leicester Square." By Richard Gray. (*The Theatres Trust Newsletter* no. 50, December 1998. pages 6-9.) (Abridged as "The New-Look Odeon Leicester Square", *CTA Bulletin,* July/August 1998.) The design of the Odeon Leicester Square in the context of its 1998 refurbishment.

"Four Years of War in Heart of London's West End." By William H. Thornton, manager of the Odeon Leicester Square. (*Kinematograph Weekly,* 13 January 1944.) Reprinted under title "The Odeon At War" in *Picture House* no. 11, Winter 1987/8, page 29.

"Movies In Muswell Hill." By Daphne Hudson. (*World Film News,* May/June 1938, page 95.)

"The Odeon at 50." By Allen Eyles (*Picture House* no. 11, Winter 1987/8.) Includes list of every feature film shown. Plus note on the organ by Tony Moss.

"The Odeon Lewes." By John Fernee. (*Picture House* no. 2, Autumn 1982, pages 12-17.)

"Odeon Muswell Hill – The Case For Preservation." (*Picture House* no. 3, Spring 1983, pages 3-9, back cover.) With twenty-one photographs.

"Odeon Circuit, Showing British Spirit, Rebuilds Theatres As They're Bombed." Based on letter by Rita Cave. (*Motion Picture Herald,* 1 March 1941, page 51.)

"Oscar And The Odeons – 'A Romance Of Finance'." By Allen Eyles. (*Focus On Film* no. 22, Autumn 1975.) This was the original history of the circuit by the author of this book. It is totally superseded by the present volume. Readers' comments in the "For the Record" section of issues 23 and 24 and the "Feedback" section of issue 25 have also been re-used where appropriate.

INDEX OF ILLUSTRATIONS AND PRINCIPAL ODEON REFERENCES

The page numbers in italics refer to illustrations. The principal text references are confined to the main observations on new Odeons in the year of opening and to the factual information in the Chronology